Discrete Choice Analysis

MIT Press Series in Transportation Studies
Marvin L. Manheim, editor

1. *The Automobile and the Environment: An International Perspective*, edited by Ralph Gakenheimer, 1978

2. *The Urban Transportation System: Politics and Policy Innovation*, Alan Altshuler with James P. Womack and John R. Pucher, 1979

3. *Planning and Politics:* The Metro Toronto Transportation Review, Juri Pill, 1979

4. *Fundamentals of Transportation Systems Analysis. Volume I: Basic Concepts*, Marvin L. Manheim, 1979

5. *Traffic Flow on Transportation Networks*, Gordon F. Newell, 1980

6. *Miles to Go:* European and American Transportation Policies, James A. Dunn, Jr., 1981

7. *Air Quality Analysis for Urban Transportation Planning*, Joel L. Horowitz, 1982

8. *Port Economics*, Jan Owen Jansson and Dan Shneerson, 1982

9. *Discrete Choice Analysis: Theory and Application to Travel Demand*, Moshe Ben-Akiva and Steven R. Lerman, 1985

Discrete Choice Analysis:
Theory and Application to Travel Demand

Moshe Ben-Akiva
Steven R. Lerman

The MIT Press
Cambridge, Massachusetts
London, England

Second printing, 1987

This book was set in Times New Roman by Asco Trade Typesetting Ltd., Hong Kong, and printed and bound by Edwards Brothers, Inc. in the United States of America.

Library of Congress Cataloging-in-Publication Data

Ben-Akiva, Moshe E.
  Discrete choice analysis.

  (MIT Press series in transportation studies; 9)
  Bibliography: p.
  Includes index.
  1. Choice of transportation—Forecasting—Mathematical models. 2. Choice of transportation—Mathematical models. I. Lerman, Steven R. II. Title. III. Series.
  HE336.C5B46 1985   380.5′1   85-15164
  ISBN 0-262-02217-6

To our wives, Hagit and Lori,
and to our children, Ori, Lea, and Danna
and Deborah, Amy, and David

Contents

12   Models of Travel Demand: Future Directions

List of Tables

List of Figures

Series Foreword

Today the field of transportation is a well-established professional field, with numerous subspecialties and international journals, and with educational and research programs at many universities and other organizations around the world. It is a field in which the dominant philosophy is intermodal, multisectoral, and multidisciplinary. It is also a field in which researchers and practitioners can and do focus on specific facets, modes, sectors, disciplines, or methodologies, working in the context of this broad philosophy.

The approach of The MIT Press Series in Transportation Studies mirrors this philosophy. The series presents works across the broad spectrum of transportation concerns. Some volumes report significant new research, whereas others give analyses of specific policy, planning, management, or methodological issues. Still others show the close interaction between research and practical application in policy or management. Each individual work is intended to be an in-depth treatment from a particular viewpoint. Together the works in the series present a broad perspective on the field of transportation as a whole.

This book, the ninth in the series, presents the methods of discrete choice analysis and their applications in the modeling of transportation systems. These methods, developed over the last fifteen years, have proved particularly powerful in modeling demand and consumer behavior both in general and in transportation. This is the first text and reference work to cover this important field systematically. Students and professionals will find this book a major resource in understanding the significant results and techniques that have been developed in this important field.

Marvin L. Manheim

Preface

The methods of discrete choice analysis and their applications to travel demand modeling have been developed largely during the past fifteen years. The relatively new field has now evolved to the point where we believe a general text is appropriate. The literature is spread over many professional journal articles, and some are not easily accessible, especially to a newcomer to this field. The few existing books in this area are either research monographs or focus almost entirely on more advanced topics.

We have written this book to serve as both a graduate level text and a general professional reference. The book is oriented toward a reader who has had an introductory level course in probability and statistics, including some familarity with linear regression analysis. At MIT we have covered most of the subject matter in this book in a first-year graduate course on transportation demand forecasting. We have also used earlier versions of this text in a special short course on this topic that we offer at MIT during the summer for practicing professionals.

Although this book is methodological in nature, it is oriented toward applications. Throughout the book we have kept to a minimum the proofs of theoretical propositions and have provided references that point to where more technical detail can be found. Our emphasis has been on developing a sound understanding of theoretical results that are useful in many applications.

We have organized this book so that the first seven (or only the first five) chapters could serve as the text for a basic introduction to discrete choice analysis that covers the material needed to apply basic binary and multiple choice models. The topics treated in the later chapters are more advanced. They are useful for more complex discrete choice analyses. The more advanced part of the book culminates in the development of a complete travel demand model system presented in chapter 11 and an overview of the current research frontiers given in chapter 12.

A book of this scope cannot be completed without the assistance of many individuals. We have especially benefited from the contributions made by other colleagues with whom we have developed much of the material that serves as the basis for this book or whose ideas and work have been drawn upon in specific chapters. These individuals are listed here, and where appropriate, the specific chapter in which their work figures most prominently is noted: Terry Atherton (chapter 11), Andrew Daly, Bernard François (chapter 10), James Glock (chapter 7), Hugh Gunn (chapter 9),

Frank Koppelman (chapter 6), Marvin Manheim, Charles Manski, Daniel McFadden, Earl Ruiter (chapter 11), and Lionel Silman (chapter 9).

We are also indebted to Joel Horowitz, Hani Mahmassani, Victor Prins, Kenneth Small, and Robert Wolf for the detailed comments they provided on the early drafts of the chapters. The final product has been substantially improved by the technical and editorial assistance that we received from Joffre Swait in the final stages of preparing this manuscript.

Discrete Choice Analysis

1 Introduction

1.1 The Context of Transportation Demand Forecasting

Demand forecasting is an essential element in the analysis of transportation systems. It is concerned with the behavior of consumers of transportation services and facilities. Users include travelers and shippers of goods in urban, interurban, and international transport markets. In this book we focus on the use of econometric modeling to predict the behavior of these users. In particular, we analyze the response of users to changes brought about by new services, investments in infrastructure and to changes in operating and pricing policies.

Early studies of major investments in regional highway networks and rapid progress in computational technology have led to the development of procedures to forecast trips by origins and destinations and traffic volumes on the links of a network. These modeling procedures have been continually extended and improved and are being applied worldwide. They are well documented in the literature (e.g., Manheim 1979, Stopher and Meyburg 1975, Hutchinson 1974) and are supported by computer software systems such as the U.S. Department of Transportation's Urban Transportation Planning Systems (UTPS).

During the late 1960s and the 1970s there occurred in transportation systems analysis a shift from unimodal analysis of large capital decisions toward multimodal systems and considerations of pricing, operational policies, and the construction of new facilities. This has led to further developments and extensions of transportation forecasting and analytic approaches (e.g., Brand and Manheim 1973, and Weiner 1983) which have been synthesized by Wohl and Martin (1967) and Manheim (1979), among others. Other recent textbooks that we recommend for background reading are Morlok (1978), Meyer and Miller (1984), and Kanafani (1983).

A major innovation in the analysis of transportation demand was the development of *disaggregate travel demand models* based on discrete choice analysis methods. It is this set of developments on which we focus in this book. We are clearly concerned, however, with the forecasting of aggregate demands. The usual analytic approach is to subdivide the geographical area under study into zones. Then the origins and destinations of all travelers in a zone are represented by a single point within the zone, usually the geographical centroid. *Aggregate travel demand models* are directly estimated, with data on travel behavior at some level of aggregation within a geographical zone that serves as an observational unit for the statistical analysis.

Oi and Shuldiner (1962), Fleet and Robertson (1968), and McCarthy (1969) have analyzed the level of trip making by households in U.S. urban areas and have demonstrated the limitation of estimating models of trip generation rates with aggregated zonal data. It has been shown, for example, that for a standard linear regression model an aggregation of the data prior to estimation will result in a loss of precision of the estimated parameters if the aggregate groups are not homogeneous with respect to the values of the explanatory or independent variables (e.g., Kmenta 1971, sec. 9.2). Since most transportation studies collect microlevel data (typically surveys of individual households), analysts estimate models directly on this information without first aggregating it to a zonal level. Such models have come to be called *disaggregate*. A significant effect of the additional precision gained from this approach has been the ability to obtain reliable estimates for models with a much broader range of explanatory variables.

At the disaggregate, or microlevel, we observe that the behavior of an individual person, household, or firm can best be described with discrete variables. The classification of households, as an example, into car owners and noncar owners imply a binary—yes or no—dependent variable. The binary choice of travel mode between car and transit for a given trip appears to have been first applied in the discrete choice models by Warner (1962). Other aspects of travel demand require the use of dependent variables with more than two categories. The multiple categories may have a natural order, as in number of cars owned or number of trips, or may be qualitative and therefore with no natural order, as in choice of travel mode between three or more alternatives.

1.2   The Background of Discrete Choice Analysis

The basic problem confronted by discrete choice analysis is the modeling of choice from a set of mutually exclusive and collectively exhaustive alternatives. Our presentation of discrete choice analysis uses the principle of utility maximization. Briefly, a descision maker is modeled as selecting the alternative with the highest utility among those available at the time a choice is made. An operational model consists of parameterized utility functions in terms of observable independent variables and unknown parameters, and their values are estimated from a sample of observed choices made by decision makers when confronted with a choice situation.

It is impossible to specify and estimate a discrete choice model that will always succeed in predicting the chosen alternatives by all individuals. Therefore we adopt the concept of random utility, an idea that first appeared in psychology (Thurston 1927). The true utilities of the alternatives are considered random variables, so the probability that an alternative is chosen is defined as the probability that it has the greatest utility among the available alternatives.

Discrete choice problems have been of interest to researchers for many years in a variety of disciplines. As we said before, the origins of probabilistic choice models are in mathematical psychology (see Thurston 1927, Luce 1959, Marschak 1960, Luce and Suppes 1965, Bock and Jones 1968, Tversky 1972). But discrete or qualitative response models have also been used for many years in biometric applications (see Berkson 1944, Finney 1971, Cox 1970). A review of econometric applications of discrete choice models can be found in McFadden (1982), Manski (1981), and Amemiya (1981). For examples of applications in other fields and for treatment of some advanced topics that have been omitted from this book, the reader may consult the review papers mentioned and the recent books by Manski and McFadden (1981), Hensher and Johnson (1981), and Judge et al. (1980).

1.3   Transportation Applications of Discrete Choice Analysis

The early transportation applications of discrete choice models were made for the binary choice of travel mode (e.g., Warner 1962, Lisco 1967, Quarmby 1967, Lave 1969, Stopher 1969, Gronau 1970, de Donnea 1971, McGillivray 1972, Talvitie 1972, Wigner 1973, Watson 1974). Some of these studies focused on the estimation of a "value of time," the trade-off between travel time and travel cost implied by a travel demand model. This value has been used to assign a monetary value to the travel time savings in the evaluation of alternative transportation projects (e.g., see Bruzelius 1979). Other researchers emphasized the development of policy-sensitive models for predictions of the market shares of alternative modes (e.g., see Stopher and Lisco 1970).

Further progress in transportation applications following these early studies was accompanied by improved discrete choice modeling methods.

The research during the early 1970s was oriented toward mode choice models with more than two alternatives, and applications to other travel-related choices such as trip destination, trip frequency, car ownership, residential location, and housing (Rassan et al. 1971, CRA 1972, Ben-Akiva 1973, 1974, Brand and Manheim 1973, McFadden 1974, Domencich and McFadden 1975, Richards and Ben-Akiva 1975, Lerman and Ben-Akiva 1975, Lerman 1976).

The choice of mode for travel to work has been investigated extensively by many researchers (e.g., Atherton and Ben-Akiva 1975, Ben-Akiva and Richards 1975, Parody 1976, Train 1976, Daly and Zachary 1979). These studies have used different types of data from widely differing urban areas, developed more comprehensive model specifications with socioeconomic variables, and tested the forecasting accuracy of the models with data from before and after changes in transportation systems. Most of the examples that we used in the first part of this book are therefore mode choice models for work trips with two or more alternative modes.

The modeling of other dimensions of travel demand using discrete choice models often presents methodological and data problems, some of which are addressed in the more advanced chapters of this book. The most significant issues are the treatment of interdependencies among related choices and the practical and theoretical problems posed by a choice from the large number of alternatives. These problems arise in the choice of trip destination or type of vehicle.

There are many other important issues involved in the modeling of travel demand besides the theory and practice of disaggregate choice models covered in this book. A large collection of recent papers on disaggregate models and other topics can be found in the proceedings of a series of conferences on travel behavior modeling that include Transportation Research Board (1974), Stopher and Meyburg (1976), Hensher and Stopher (1970), and Brog et al. (1980).

1.4 Outline of the Book

The following chapters of this book develop the basic concepts and methods of discrete choice analysis and describe the applications of the methodology to travel demand modeling. The coverage includes choice theories, alternative model formulations, properties of choice models, estimation methods and their properties, tests used in the process of model development, and procedures to use these models in applications for aggregate forecasting. Chapter 2 provides a review of statistical methods which are required to comprehend the material on model estimation and testing in later chapters. Chapter 3 presents the various conceptual approaches of choice theories that are the foundations of the operational probabilistic choice models developed in the subsequent chapters. With this background we then present, in chapters 4 and 5, the derivations and estimation methods of binomial and multinomial choice models of different forms with an emphasis on the logistic and the multinomial logit models. These are by far the most widely applied discrete choice models. The properties of the models and of the procedures for estimating their parameters are described in detail.

Chapter 6 addresses the issue of aggregate forecasting with disaggregate models. In principle, this problem is straightforward, but in practice, it requires an application of numerical procedures some of which require different assumptions in order to be of use.

Chapter 7 returns to the informal and formal tests that have proved to be most useful during the process of estimating a discrete choice model. The various tests are demonstrated with examples of travel choice models that have been used in transportation analyses in urbanized areas in the United States and Brazil.

The remaining chapters of the book cover more advanced methodological topics that have important applications in transportation demand analysis. The estimation procedures described in the earlier chapters did not address a variety of the so-called choice-based survey designs that are available to almost all urban transportation studies from public transport on-board surveys. Chapter 8 provides a brief overview of the basic concepts of survey design as well as implications of different designs on model estimation.

Chapter 9 deals with methods to reduce the number of alternatives in models with large choice sets for estimation and forecasting. The applications of these methods are illustrated with destination choice models for nonwork trips.

Chapter 10 is concerned with the properties and the applications of the nested logit model, a generalization of multinomial logit. This model is particularly useful for mulitdimensional choice situations which are encountered in systems of travel demand models that are not limited to the choice of mode but may also include the choice of travel frequency for different purposes, choices of destinations, and so on.

The application of these more advanced methods to model systems and a discussion of the steps involved in the process of model system development are presented in chapter 11.

Finally, chapter 12 briefly considers more advanced topics and the results of recent research. The purpose of this chapter is to provide an overview with references for further study of more complex applications of discrete choice methods.

2 Review of the Statistics of Model Estimation

Travel demand analysis relies heavily on the statistical theory of model estimation and testing. In presenting various models, we have assumed that readers have at least a basic knowledge of probability theory and statistics at the level of an advanced undergraduate or introductory graduate course. Moreover we have assumed that readers have at least a rudimentary understanding of linear regression analysis, at least up to simple regression.

In this chapter we review the aspects of the statistics of model estimation on which we draw most heavily. We also present in somewhat greater detail topics not often covered in introductory statistics courses but necessary for understanding material in subsequent chapters.

We should make it clear at the outset that the review in this chapter is in no way exhaustive. It is instead intentionally selective. No proofs of various propositions are included, and we have intentionally restricted our presentation to those statistical methods of direct relevance to discrete choice analysis. In many instances we present results intuitively and omit many of the technical qualifiers that usually go along with various theorems. Readers who are interested in a broader or more theoretical presentation should refer to any of the standard econometrics texts generally available; examples include Theil (1971), Johnston (1972), Rao (1973), and Judge et al. (1980).

2.1 The Estimation Problem

We begin by characterizing the general problem of model estimation. This will give an intuitive basis for various methods to be discussed later and provide an opportunity to develop some basic notation.

In subsequent chapters we will derive a great number of travel demand models. These models will be based on some specific assumptions about how travelers choose whether to travel, where to travel, and so on. In all of these models our a priori knowledge about the travel demand process will be limited; inevitably there will be parameters in the models whose values we will not know. To operationalize a model, we will have to rely on empirical observations to enable us to make statistical inferences about the unknown parameters.

The classical linear regression model provides an example of this distinction between what we are willing to specify a priori and what we infer statistically. Consider a simple regression model:

$$\frac{\text{household}}{\text{trips/day}} = \beta_1 + \beta_2 \left(\frac{\text{household}}{\text{income}} \right) + \xi. \tag{2.1}$$

In more general notation we will write such models as

$$y = \beta_1 + \beta_2 x + \xi, \tag{2.2}$$

where

y = the dependent variable,

β_1, β_2 = unknown parameters,

x = the independent variable,

ξ = the disturbance term.

Having specified a simple model such as equation 2.2, we assume that the functional form of the equation is known to us a priori. However, we usually do not know parameters β_1 and β_2; the goal of model estimation is to make inferences about their values. In more general cases, as we will explore in subsequent chapters, models will often not be linear, and the number of unknown parameters will be considerably greater than two.

Most of the classical statistical theories for estimating the parameters of models deal with situations such as the simple example given here, where the form of the model is assumed to be known with certainty and the parameters values are totally unknown. Although we will focus primarily on this case, the reader should be aware that it represents a theoretical idealization rather than a practical reality. We are seldom absolutely certain about the functional form of travel demand models, and we are rarely in total ignorance about at least the signs and magnitudes of different parameters. Although there are nonclassical estimation methods designed to deal with these situations, they are theoretically and computationally difficult and are rarely used (e.g., Raiffa and Schlaifer 1961). Instead, most analysts reflect their uncertainty about the functional form of the models they estimate by exploring alternative model specifications. Similarly they use their prior expectations about the model's parameters to make judgments about whether model results "make sense." These informal procedures are often difficult to justify completely on theoretical grounds, but they are nevertheless universally applied. Indeed, the line between the "science" of model estimation (as reflected in formal statistical theory) and the "art" (as reflected in the application of professional judgment as part of the model-building process) is rarely well defined.

With the foregoing as prologue, we now can set forth a general statement of the model estimation problem. We will adopt the convention of denoting an arbitrary vector of parameters by θ and use the notation β to apply only to the coefficients of linear functions, as in equation 2.2.

Model Estimation

Let y be a random variable, and let $\mathbf{x}$ be a vector of known variables that influence the distribution y. Denote this dependence as $y \sim f(\mathbf{x}, \theta)$, where f is the distribution of y, and θ is a vector of parameters, at least some of which are unknown a priori. Using a sample of observations from the process being modeled, drawn in some known way from the whole population, a function of the observations is constructed to estimate the unknown parameters. Such a function is called an *estimator*.

This definition has embodied some terminology that demands more precise definition. First, for example, note that although y is often a scalar quantity, it can be a vector, representing a system of equations. In this case some of the entries in $\mathbf{x}$ are often themselves some of the entries in $\mathbf{y}$ and are consequently random variables whose distributions are determined by some other variables and parameters in the model. In most of our applications in this book we will deal with situations where the model is only a single equation.

Second, note that y is by definition a random variable. The randomness of y is significant, because it will generally imply that our estimators for θ will themselves be random variables.

Third, there is an important distinction in this definition between the *population* and any *sample* drawn from it. In most travel demand analyses it is customary to assume that the population is infinite, although any sample consists of a finite number of observations. As will be discussed in detail later in this chapter, we will often be interested in the properties of estimators as the sample gets increasingly larger.

Fourth, note that the statement of the model estimation problem includes the requirements that the sample be taken "in some known way." In most situations we will assume that observations are drawn at random from the entire population. However, in later chapters we will also explore the problem of model estimation when more complicated sampling strategies are employed.

Any method of estimation will rely on the information inherent in the sample. We will denote the sample as $\{(x_1, y_1), (x_2, y_2), \ldots, (x_N, y_N)\}$, where N is the number of observations in the sample. Any "solution" to the estimation problem will be in general a function of these data. We will use $\hat{\theta}_N$ to denote an estimator of θ and write

$$\hat{\theta}_N = g[(x_1, y_1), (x_2, y_2), \ldots, (x_N, y_N)]. \tag{2.3}$$

It is important to stress the distinction between θ and $\hat{\theta}_N$. The former is a *deterministic quantity* that is unknown to the analyst. The value $\hat{\theta}_N$ is (before the sample is drawn) a *random variable*; one can logically think of it as having a mean, a variance, and a distribution. Of course after the sample is taken and the function g is evaluated, $\hat{\theta}_N$ is simply some number or vector of numbers. To distinguish between the random variable $\hat{\theta}_N$ and its realization for any particular sample, we term the random variable an estimator and any given realization of it an estimate.

Let us consider a very simple example to illustrate these definitions. Suppose we have some variable z that is normally distributed with unknown mean μ and variance σ^2, both of which we want to estimate. In the previous notation, $\theta = [\mu, \sigma^2]$, x is null, and the model can be written as

$$z = \mu + \xi,$$

where ξ is a random variable that is normally distributed with mean zero and variance σ^2.

Given a sample from this distribution, denoted by $\{z_1, z_2, \ldots, z_N\}$, we can now explore various possible estimators of the mean μ. For example, consider the following estimators:

$$\hat{\mu}_N^1 = g_1(z_1, z_2, \ldots, z_N) = \frac{1}{N} \sum_{n=1}^{N} z_n, \tag{2.4}$$

$$\hat{\mu}_N^2 = g_2(z_1, z_2, \ldots, z_N) = \frac{\max(z_n) + \min(z_n)}{2}, \tag{2.5}$$

$$\hat{\mu}_N^3 = g_3(z_1, z_2, \ldots, z_N) = \text{median}(z_1, z_2, \ldots, z_N), \tag{2.6}$$

$$\hat{\mu}_N^4 = g_4(z_1, z_2, \ldots, z_N) = \frac{1}{N-1} \sum_{n-1}^{N} z_n. \tag{2.7}$$

We define the median as the value of z_n in the sample with exactly $(N-1)/2$ observations both greater and less than it if N is odd, or the average of the two observations with $(N - 2)/2$ less than and $(N - 2)/2$ greater than them if N is even.

Each of these four estimators represents a different rule for inferring μ. They will in general produce numerically different estimates when evaluated for any sample.

2.2   Criteria for Evaluating Estimators

The obvious question raised by the preceding simple example is how we should decide which of the estimators to use. In order to choose among alternative estimators, we must first define useful criteria against which they can be evaluated. These criteria reflect properties that we believe an ideal estimator should have.

There are two major classes of properties: small sample and asymptotic (or large sample) properties. In general, these are distinguished by the fact that so-called small sample properties hold exactly for any size sample (i.e., for any value of N), whereas large sample properties hold only in the limit as $N \to \infty$. Most introductory courses in statistics or econometrics place heavy emphasis on small sample properties, reflecting the relative success theoreticians have had in proving that certain estimators have such properties for a limited class of models. Unfortunately, for most of the more complicated models we will explore in this book, it has been impossible to find estimators with desirable small sample properties. Instead, only asymptotic properties are demonstrated.

Before proceeding further, we illustrate the distinction between small sample and asymptotic properties with a brief example. Consider again the problem of estimating the mean μ of some distribution. One of the most intuitive properties we would like an estimator to have is *unbiasedness*, defined as

$$\mathscr{E}[\hat{\mu}_N] = \mu \qquad \text{for all } N, \tag{2.8}$$

where $\mathscr{E}$ denotes the expected value operator. Intuitively, this property implies that for any fixed sample size, the random variable $\hat{\mu}_N$ has mean μ. This is a small sample property because it is defined as holding for all values of the sample size. The asymptotic counterpart to unbiasedness is termed *asymptotic unbiasedness*, defined as

$$\lim_{N \to \infty} \mathscr{E}[\hat{\mu}_N] = \mu. \tag{2.9}$$

It should be evident that all unbiased estimators are asymptotically unbiased; the converse, however, is not true.

Suppose we now compare $\hat{\mu}_N^1$ and $\hat{\mu}_N^4$, defined earlier, with respect to the criterion of small sample and asymptotic unbiasedness:

$$\mathscr{E}[\hat{\mu}_N^1] = \mathscr{E}\left[\frac{1}{N}\sum_{n=1}^{N} z_n\right] = \frac{1}{N}\sum_{n=1}^{N}\mathscr{E}[z_n] = \frac{1}{N}\cdot N\mu = \mu, \tag{2.10}$$

$$\mathscr{E}[\hat{\mu}_N^4] = \mathscr{E}\left[\frac{1}{N-1}\sum_{n=1}^{N} z_n\right] = \frac{1}{N-1}\sum_{n=1}^{N}\mathscr{E}[z_n] = \frac{1}{N-1}\cdot N\cdot\mu = \left(\frac{N}{N-1}\right)\mu. \tag{2.11}$$

Thus $\hat{\mu}_N^1$ is unbiased, but $\hat{\mu}_N^4$ is biased. However, if we compare their properties as N gets larger, both are asymptotically unibiased because

$$\lim_{N\to\infty}\left(\frac{N}{N-1}\right)\mu = \mu. \tag{2.12}$$

Although the fact that $\hat{\mu}_N^1$ is unbiased was intuitively evident in this example, it will generally not be simple to prove an estimator is unbiased in more complicated situations.

2.3   Small Sample Properties

Distribution of Estimators

The most direct means of presenting small sample properties is to begin with the concept of the distribution of an estimator. As emphasized earlier, any estimator $\hat{\theta}_N = g[(x_1,y_1),(x_2,y_2),\ldots,(x_N,y_N)]$ is a function of random variables and is therefore itself a random variable. As such it has a distribution that depends on x, the distribution of y given x, and the function g. *Small sample properties are simply statements about the distribution of $\hat{\theta}_N$.* Thus in our previous example the property of unbiasedness was just a statement that the distribution of $\hat{\theta}_N$ was such that $\mathscr{E}[\hat{\theta}_N] = \theta$ for all N. If we denote the distribution of any estimator $\hat{\theta}_N$ as $f(\hat{\theta}_N)$, then this property can be expressed as

$$\int_{\hat{\theta}_N = -\infty}^{\infty} \hat{\theta}_N f(\hat{\theta}_N)\, d\hat{\theta}_N = \theta. \tag{2.13}$$

An example of an estimator whose distribution is characterized by this property is given in figure 2.1.

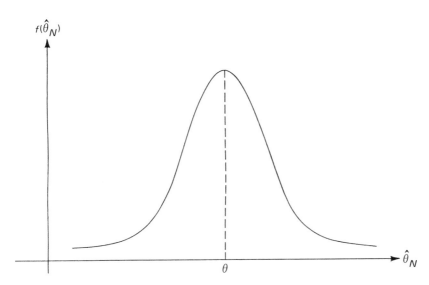

Figure 2.1
The distribution of an unbiased estimator

Efficiency

Unbiasedness is only one of many desirable small sample properties. Consider the case illustrated in figure 2.2 where we have two different estimators, $\hat{\theta}_N^1$ and $\hat{\theta}_N^2$, each of which we know is unbiased. We would like to have a property that reflects our intuition that $\hat{\theta}_N^2$ is in some sense better than $\hat{\theta}_N^1$, since it is distributed more "tightly" around the true value θ. One such property is *efficiency*, which is based on the variance of the distribution of the estimator. In the case of the two estimators in figure 2.2, we say that $\hat{\theta}_N^2$ is more efficient than $\hat{\theta}_N^1$ because $\mathrm{var}(\hat{\theta}_N^2) < \mathrm{var}(\hat{\theta}_N^1)$.

In addition to being useful in comparing two or more estimators, we often use the concept of efficiency as applied to unbiased estimators in an absolute sense. An estimator $\hat{\theta}_N$ is defined as *efficient* if it meets both of the following two criteria:

1. It is unbiased.
2. No other unbiased estimator has smaller variance.

Cramér-Rao Bound: Scalar Case

The definition of efficiency for unbiased estimators is useful only if we can identify estimators for which it holds. This may not be easy because the

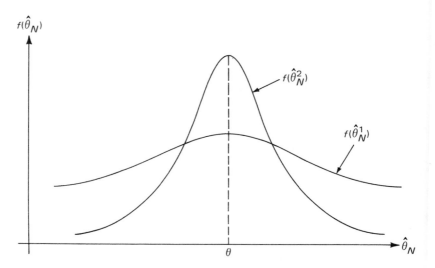

Figure 2.2
Comparison of two unbiased estimators

number of possible unbiased estimators is limitless. Proving that any particular unbiased estimator has lower variance than all others may be difficult. Fortunately the Cramér-Rao theorem often makes it easy to prove the absolute efficiency of an estimator.

The simplest case of the Cramér-Rao theorem is when θ is a scalar quantity. A simple version of the theorem is as follows:

CRAMÉR-RAO THEOREM (for unbiased estimators, θ scalar): Let $\hat{\theta}_N = g[(\mathbf{x}_1, y_1), (\mathbf{x}_2, y_2), \ldots, (\mathbf{x}_N, y_N)]$ be any unbiased estimator of a scalar θ. Let $f(y_1, y_2, \ldots, y_N)$ be the joint distribution of $(y_1, y_2, \ldots, y_N)$ conditioned on the observed values $(\mathbf{x}_1, \mathbf{x}_2, \ldots, \mathbf{x}_N)$. Assume the $\mathbf{x}_n$'s are non-stochastic. In the usual case where the y_n's are drawn independently and at random from the population, $f(y_1, y_2, \ldots, y_N) = f(y_1|\mathbf{x}_1)f(y_2|\mathbf{x}_2) \ldots f(y_N|\mathbf{x}_N)$, where $f(y_n|\mathbf{x}_n)$ is the distribution of y_n conditioned on the observed value $\mathbf{x}_n$. Define $\mathscr{L} = \log f(y_1, y_2, \ldots, y_N)$ to be the log likelihood function of the sample. (The interpretation and evaluation of likelihood functions are explored further in section 2.5.) Then

$$\mathrm{var}(\hat{\theta}_N) \geq \frac{1}{-\mathscr{E}[\partial^2 \mathscr{L}/\partial\theta^2]}. \tag{2.14}$$

We call equation 2.14 the Cramér-Rao bound.

The consequence of this theorem is that if we can find some unbiased estimator $\hat{\theta}_N$ that meets this bound exactly, then we are guaranteed that no other unbiased estimator can have smaller variance. Thus the estimator is efficient. However, the theorem does not ensure the existence of an unbiased estimator that exactly attains the bound.

The key to the Cramér-Rao bound is the term

$$-\mathscr{E}\left[\frac{\partial^2 \mathscr{L}}{\partial \theta^2}\right],$$

which is referred to as the *information* in the sample. Recall that $\mathscr{L}$ (the log likelihood) is a function of the distribution of the sample and is consequently a random variable. One can therefore logically think of its derivatives with respect to θ as random variables and hence define their expectation.

Consider again the example of estimating the mean of a normal distribution, and suppose we know $\sigma^2 = 1$, so there is only one unknown parameter. In this case

$$f(z_n) = \frac{1}{\sqrt{2\pi}} e^{-(z_n - \mu)^2/2} \tag{2.15}$$

and

$$\mathscr{L} = \log f(z_1, z_2, \ldots, z_N) \tag{2.16}$$
$$= -\sum_{n=1}^{N} \log \sqrt{2\pi} - \frac{1}{2} \sum_{n=1}^{N} (z_n - \mu)^2.$$

Thus

$$\frac{\partial^2 \mathscr{L}}{\partial \mu^2} = -N \tag{2.17}$$

and

$$\text{var}(\hat{\theta}_N) \geq \frac{1}{-(-N)} = \frac{1}{N}. \tag{2.18}$$

Now consider the estimator

$$\hat{\mu}_N^1 = \frac{1}{N} \sum_{n=1}^{N} z_n. \tag{2.19}$$

We showed earlier that $\hat{\mu}_N^1$ is unbiased. If we can also show that its variance meets the bound in equation 2.14, then we will have shown it is efficient. To do this, we note that

$$\text{var}(\hat{\mu}_N^1) = \text{var}\left(\frac{1}{N}\sum_{n=1}^{N} z_n\right) = \frac{1}{N^2}\sum_{n=1}^{N}\text{var}(z_n) = \frac{N}{N^2} = \frac{1}{N} \tag{2.20}$$

since $\text{var}(z_n) = 1$. Thus $\hat{\mu}_N^1$ is efficient.

Cramér-Rao Bound: Vector Case

The Cramér-Rao theorem extends to the case where θ is a vector. In this case we interpret $\text{var}(\hat{\theta}_N)$ to denote a matrix, and our inequality will be defined in a matrix sense. In words, the theorem states that the variance-covariance matrix of any unbiased estimator must be greater than or equal to some matrix which we will define shortly. This means that if θ is a vector with K entries,

$$\text{var}(\hat{\theta}_N) \geq \mathbf{A}, \tag{2.21}$$

where $\mathbf{A}$ is a $K \times K$ matrix. Here the inequality means that there exists no unbiased estimator with variance-covariance matrix $\bar{\mathbf{A}}$ such that $\mathbf{A} - \bar{\mathbf{A}}$ (in the matrix sense of subtraction term by term) is positive definite. A positive definite matrix is one in which the determinants of all the cofactors are positive. The theorem is as follows:

CRAMÉR-RAO THEOREM   (for unbiased estimators, θ a vector):   Define $\hat{\theta}_N$ and $\mathscr{L}$ as in the scalar version of the theorem. Then

$$\text{var}(\hat{\theta}_N) \geq \mathbf{B}^{-1} \tag{2.22}$$

where

$$\mathbf{B} = \begin{bmatrix} -\mathscr{E}\left[\dfrac{\partial^2 \mathscr{L}}{\partial\theta_1^2}\right] & -\mathscr{E}\left[\dfrac{\partial^2 \mathscr{L}}{\partial\theta_1\partial\theta_2}\right] & \cdots & -\mathscr{E}\left[\dfrac{\partial^2 \mathscr{L}}{\partial\theta_1\partial\theta_K}\right] \\[2ex] -\mathscr{E}\left[\dfrac{\partial^2 \mathscr{L}}{\partial\theta_2\partial\theta_1}\right] & -\mathscr{E}\left[\dfrac{\partial^2 \mathscr{L}}{\partial\theta_2^2}\right] & \cdots & -\mathscr{E}\left[\dfrac{\partial^2 \mathscr{L}}{\partial\theta_2\partial\theta_K}\right] \\[2ex] \vdots & & & \\[1ex] -\mathscr{E}\left[\dfrac{\partial^2 \mathscr{L}}{\partial\theta_K\partial\theta_1}\right] & -\mathscr{E}\left[\dfrac{\partial^2 \mathscr{L}}{\partial\theta_K\partial\theta_2}\right] & \cdots & -\mathscr{E}\left[\dfrac{\partial^2 \mathscr{L}}{\partial\theta_K^2}\right] \end{bmatrix}. \tag{2.23}$$

The matrix $\mathbf{B}$ is termed the information matrix. Rather than writing it out in matrix form, we will often use the notation $\mathbf{B} = -\mathscr{E}[\nabla^2\mathscr{L}]$, where ∇^2 is an operator generating the $K \times K$ matrix of partial second derivatives. ($\nabla^2 \mathscr{L}$ is also termed the Hessian of $\mathscr{L}$ with respect to $\boldsymbol{\theta}$.)

To illustrate the application of this theorem, we use the example of estimating the parameters of a normal distribution but now consider the case when both the mean μ and the variance σ^2 are unknown. In this case

$$\mathscr{L} = \log \left[\prod_{n=1}^{N} \frac{1}{\sqrt{2\pi}\sigma} e^{-[(z_n - \mu)/\sigma]^2/2} \right]$$

$$= -N \log \sqrt{2\pi} - \frac{N}{2} \log \sigma^2 - \frac{1}{2} \sum_{n=1}^{N} \left(\frac{z_n - \mu}{\sigma} \right)^2 . \tag{2.24}$$

The matrix $\mathbf{B}$ is as follows:

$$\mathbf{B} = \begin{bmatrix} -\mathscr{E}\left[\dfrac{N}{\sigma^2} \right] & 0 \\ 0 & -\mathscr{E}\left[\dfrac{-N}{2\sigma^4} \right] \end{bmatrix} = \begin{bmatrix} \dfrac{N}{\sigma^2} & 0 \\ 0 & \dfrac{N}{2\sigma^4} \end{bmatrix} . \tag{2.25}$$

Thus

$$\operatorname{var} \begin{pmatrix} \hat{\mu}_N \\ \hat{\sigma}_N^2 \end{pmatrix} \geq B^{-1} = \begin{bmatrix} \dfrac{\sigma^2}{N} & 0 \\ 0 & \dfrac{2\sigma^4}{N} \end{bmatrix} . \tag{2.26}$$

It is important to stress that the simplicity of this result is a particular property of the normal density function. For example, the off-diagonal terms in $\mathbf{B}$ generally will be nonzero, and the value of $-\mathscr{E}[\partial^2 \mathscr{L}/\partial\theta_k \partial\theta_l]$ will be difficult, if not impossible, to evaluate analytically. The value $-\mathscr{E}[\partial^2 \mathscr{L}/\partial\theta_k \partial\theta_l]$ may also include terms that are functions of the unknown parameters, $\boldsymbol{\theta}$. For example, σ^2 appears in equation 2.26. In this case we often estimate the elements of $\mathbf{B}$ by substituting $\hat{\boldsymbol{\theta}}_N$ for $\boldsymbol{\theta}$.

2.4　Asymptotic Properties

Since it may be difficult to derive the distribution of an estimator for any value of N, we must often resort to a variety of approximations to prove whether or not an estimator has useful properties. The most common such approximation is to show that whatever the distribution of $\hat{\boldsymbol{\theta}}_N$, it converges in some well-defined way to something reasonably simple and tractable as the sample gets larger.

Consistency

The asymptotic property that is most widely applicable is *consistency*. Intuitively an estimator that is consistent has a distribution that "collapses" on the true parameter value as the sample gets larger. More precisely, $\hat{\theta}_N$ is a consistent estimator for θ if

$$\lim_{N \to \infty} [Pr(\theta - \mathbf{q} \le \hat{\theta}_N \le \theta + \mathbf{q})] = 1 \tag{2.27}$$

where $Pr(\ )$ denotes the probability of the event in parentheses and $\mathbf{q}$ is a vector of arbitrarily small positive numbers defined to be of the same dimension as θ. If $\hat{\theta}_N$ is a consistent estimator of θ, we generally write this as

$$\operatorname*{plim}_{N \to \infty} \hat{\theta}_N = \theta \tag{2.28}$$

where plim is defined in equation 2.27 and called the probability *limit* of the random variable.

Consistency is unfortunately a relatively weak property; a large number of consistent estimators will often be available, some of which may be very biased or inefficient. For example, consider two estimators for the mean of a distribution:

$$\hat{\mu}_N^1 = \frac{1}{N} \sum_{n=1}^{N} z_n, \tag{2.29}$$

or

$$\hat{\mu}_N^5 = \begin{cases} \dfrac{1}{N/2} \sum_{n=1}^{N/2} z_n & \text{if } N \text{ is even,} \\[2ex] \dfrac{1}{(N-1)/2} \sum_{n=1}^{(N-1)/2} z_n & \text{if } N \text{ is odd.} \end{cases} \tag{2.30}$$

It is possible to verify that both of these are consistent estimators of μ, yet it should be obvious that $\hat{\mu}_N^1$ is more efficient than $\hat{\mu}_N^5$.

Conversely, it is difficult to imagine how, based purely on statistical theory, one could justify the use of an estimator that was not consistent. On occasion an analyst will use an inconsistent estimator because no tractable alternative is available. It should be stressed that this is only considered when there is ample evidence from simulation studies or other sources that the inconsistency is small in some well-defined sense.

The Slutsky Theorem

A useful result in proving consistency is the Slutsky theorem. Stated briefly, this theorem is as follows:

SLUTSKY THEOREM: If plim $\hat{\theta}_N = \theta$ and $h(\hat{\theta}_N)$ is a continuous function of $\hat{\theta}_N$, then plim $h(\hat{\theta}_N) = h(\theta)$.

In words, this implies that continuous functions of consistent estimators are consistent estimators for the functions. As an example of the usefulness of this result, suppose we had an estimator $\hat{\theta}_{N1}$ for θ_1 and $\hat{\theta}_{N2}$ for θ_2. The Slutsky theorem guarantees that if $\hat{\theta}_{N1}$ and $\hat{\theta}_{N2}$ are consistent, then $\hat{\theta}_{N1}/\hat{\theta}_{N2}$ is a consistent estimator for θ_1/θ_2.

Asymptotic Distributions and Variance

The remaining asymptotic properties we will use are based on the occasionally confusing concept of the asymptotic distribution of an estimator. If we think of an estimator $\hat{\theta}_N$ as having some distribution (which may be unknown), we are often able to show that whatever that distribution is, it can be approximated better and better by some known distribution as the sample gets larger.

The sense in which the approximation becomes "better and better" is important. If $f_N(\hat{\theta})$ is the true distribution of $\hat{\theta}_N$, it converges to $f_0(\hat{\theta})$ when

$$\lim_{N \to \infty} f_N(\hat{\theta}) = f_0(\hat{\theta}) \tag{2.31}$$

for all values of $\hat{\theta}$. In most cases the distribution of the estimators we will use will converge to the normal multivariate distribution. More precisely, the vector $\sqrt{N}(\hat{\theta}_N - \theta)$ is normally distributed as $N \to \infty$. Such estimators are termed *asymptotically normal*.

We will often be interested in knowing the variance of the asymptotic distribution, called simply the *asymptotic variance*. This should not be confused with the limit (as $N \to \infty$) of the var($\hat{\theta}_N$), which for consistent estimators is in fact zero. Instead, it represents the variance of the distribution that (in the asymptotic sense) approximates the true distribution of $\hat{\theta}_N$.

Consider as an example a random variable Y that is Bernoulli distributed with parameter p. Thus

$$f(y) = \begin{cases} p & \text{if } y = 1, \\ (1 - p) & \text{if } y = 0, \\ 0 & \text{otherwise.} \end{cases} \qquad (2.32)$$

Suppose we estimate p by observing the sample $\{y_1, y_2, \ldots, y_N\}$ and taking

$$\hat{p} = \frac{\sum_{n=1}^{N} y_n}{N}. \qquad (2.33)$$

Since y_n is Bernoulli distributed, $\sum_{n=1}^{N} y_n = N\hat{p} = \theta$ is binomially distributed with mean Np and variance $Np(1 - p)$. Thus $\hat{p}$ has expected value p and variance $p(1 - p)/N$. One can show that the distribution of $\hat{p}$ converges, as $N \to \infty$, to a normal distribution with mean p and variance $p(1 - p)/N$. For any given N, we would term $p(1 - p)/N$ the asymptotic variance of $\hat{p}$. This is quite different from

$$\lim_{N \to \infty} \text{var}(\hat{p}) = 0. \qquad (2.34)$$

2.5   Methods of Estimation

There are a number of general approaches to finding estimators that have some or all of the preceding properties. The two methods that we will use most often are *maximum likelihood* and *least squares*. Each of these is described in this section.

Maximum Likelihood

Maximum likelihood estimation is probably the most general and straightforward procedure for finding estimators. Stated simply, *a maximum likelihood estimator is the value of the parameters for which the observed sample is most likely to have occurred.*

Assuming that the observations in the sample are drawn independently and at random from the population and that the x_n's are nonstochastic, we can write the likelihood of the sample straightforwardly as a function of the parameters. The likelihood of the sample conditioned on the parameters θ is simply

$$\mathscr{L}^* = \prod_{n=1}^{N} f(y_n | x_n, \theta). \qquad (2.35)$$

We then solve for the estimate $\hat{\theta}_N$ which maximizes $\mathscr{L}^*$.

The most widely used approach is to maximize the logarithm of $\mathscr{L}^*$ rather than $\mathscr{L}^*$ itself. This does not change the values of the parameter estimates because the logarithmic function is strictly monotonically increasing. Thus we solve

$$\max_{\boldsymbol{\theta}_N} \log \mathscr{L}^* = \max_{\boldsymbol{\theta}_N} \mathscr{L} = \max_{\boldsymbol{\theta}_N} \sum_{n=1}^{N} \log f(y_n | \mathbf{x}_n, \hat{\boldsymbol{\theta}}_N). \tag{2.36}$$

In most cases of interest $\mathscr{L}$ will be continuous in $\boldsymbol{\theta}_N$, so if a solution to equation 2.36 exists, it must satisfy the usual first-order conditions.

$$\frac{\partial \mathscr{L}}{\partial \hat{\theta}_{Nk}} = 0 \qquad \text{for } k = 1, \ldots, K, \tag{2.37}$$

where $\hat{\theta}_{Nk}$ is the kth element in $\hat{\boldsymbol{\theta}}_N$.

Since the preceding equations are necessary but not sufficient for a maximum of $\mathscr{L}$, we must also check the second-order conditions. For any $\hat{\boldsymbol{\theta}}_N$ satisfying equation 2.37 to be a local maximum, the Hessian matrix, $\nabla^2 \mathscr{L}$, must be negative semidefinite when evaluated at $\hat{\boldsymbol{\theta}}_N$. Among the solutions that satisfy this, we select the one for which $\mathscr{L}$, the log likelihood function, is greatest.

This procedure appears straightforward. However, in practice all the solutions to equation 2.37 may be very difficult to find. We will discuss some of the practical techniques for solving such systems for estimating the parameters of specific models in chapter 4.

Let us consider our simple example of estimating the mean and variance of the normal distribution. (Recall that we have already derived the log likelihood function for a particular sample $\{z_1, z_2, \ldots, z_N\}$, in this case equation 2.24.) The log likelihood function is

$$\mathscr{L} = -N \log \sqrt{2\pi} - \frac{N}{2} \log \sigma^2 - \frac{1}{2\sigma^2} \sum_{n=1}^{N} (z_n - \mu)^2. \tag{2.38}$$

Using the first-order conditions, we find

$$\frac{\partial \mathscr{L}}{\partial \hat{\mu}_N} = \frac{1}{\hat{\sigma}_N^2} \sum_{n=1}^{N} (z_n - \hat{\mu}_N) = 0, \tag{2.39}$$

$$\frac{\partial \mathscr{L}}{\partial \hat{\sigma}_N^2} = \frac{-N}{2\hat{\sigma}_N^2} + \frac{1}{2\hat{\sigma}_N^4} \sum_{n=1}^{N} (z_n - \hat{\mu}_N)^2 = 0. \tag{2.40}$$

Solving for $\hat{\mu}_N$ and $\hat{\sigma}_N^2$, we obtain

$$\hat{\mu}_N = \frac{1}{N} \sum_{n=1}^{N} z_n, \tag{2.41}$$

$$\hat{\sigma}_N^2 = \frac{1}{N} \sum_{n=1}^{N} (z_n - \hat{\mu}_N)^2. \tag{2.42}$$

Thus the sample average is in fact the maximum likelihood estimator for the mean of a normal process. In addition the average sum of squared deviations about the estimator of the mean is the maximum likelihood estimator for σ^2. (The reader can verify that $\hat{\mu}_N$ and $\hat{\sigma}_N^2$ as defined in equations 2.41 and 2.42 are in fact a maximum of equation 2.38.)

Although the details are not included here, maximum likelihood estimators have the following properties under fairly general assumptions about the process under study:

1. They are consistent.
2. They are asymptotically normal.
3. They are asymptotically efficient, and hence their asymptotic variance is given by the Cramér-Rao bound.

Note that these are all large sample properties. *Maximum likelihood estimators are not in general unbiased or efficient.* In the example given $\hat{\mu}_N$ happens to be unbiased, but one can show that $\hat{\sigma}_N^2$ is in fact downward biased. To be specific $\mathscr{E}[\hat{\sigma}_N^2] = [(N-1)/N]\sigma^2$.

Least Squares

Least squares estimation has been most widely studied in the case of linear regression, that is, where

$$y = \beta_1 x_1 + \beta_2 x_2 + \cdots + \beta_K x_K + \xi. \tag{2.43}$$

The technique, however, is potentially more general.

In the general context, least square estimators are those values of $\hat{\theta}_N$ that minimize the sum of squared differences between the observed and expected values of the observations. Stated analytically, $\hat{\theta}_N$ is a least squares estimator for θ if it is the solution to

$$\min_{\hat{\theta}_N} Q = \min_{\hat{\theta}_N} \sum_{n=1}^{N} (y_n - \mathscr{E}[y_n | \hat{\theta}_N, \mathbf{x}_n])^2, \tag{2.44}$$

where $\mathscr{E}[y_n | \hat{\theta}, \mathbf{x}_n]$ is the expected value of y_n conditional on $\hat{\theta}_N$ and $\mathbf{x}_n$. As with maximum likelihood estimation we typically solve for $\hat{\theta}_N$ by setting the first derivative of Q with respect to the elements in $\hat{\boldsymbol{\theta}}_N$ equal to zero:

$$\frac{\partial Q}{\partial \hat{\theta}_{Nk}} = -2 \sum_{n=1}^{N} (y_n - \mathscr{E}[y_n | \hat{\boldsymbol{\theta}}_N, \mathbf{x}_n])$$

$$\cdot \frac{\partial \mathscr{E}[y_n | \hat{\boldsymbol{\theta}}_N, \mathbf{x}_n]}{\partial \hat{\theta}_{Nk}} = 0 \qquad \text{for } k = 1, \ldots, K.$$

(2.45)

The general properties of least square estimators, *when applied to the linear model*, are covered in detail in any standard econometrics text. Basically, least squares estimators for equation 2.43 are consistent and unbiased under very general assumptions about the distribution of the disturbances. The basic properties of the ordinary least squares (OLS) estimator for the standard linear model are established in the Gauss-Markov theorem. Under the assumptions of that theorem the OLS estimator is best (i.e., has smallest variance) of all linear and unbiased estimators. Under still more restrictive conditions one can show that they are efficient as well. However, these results hold for linear models only; the properties of least squares estimators for other models must be established on a case by case basis.

There are some instances in which the least squares estimator is identical to the maximum likelihood estimator. For example, this is true for the estimator of the mean of the normal process we have used so often in this chapter. Such a case is of interest because it immediately implies that the asymptotic properties of least squares estimators are known.

2.6 Key Statistical Tests

In this book we will often use statistical tests to make inferences about various parameters. Most of these tests are covered in standard introductory courses in statistics. However, some draw on asymptotic distribution theory and may be new to many readers. We assume readers have a basic understanding of hypothesis testing, so we review here only the specific application of relevance.

The Normal, t, and Quasi-t Tests

In many cases we will know that some estimator $\hat{\boldsymbol{\theta}}_N$ is normally distributed, and we will have an estimate of its variance (or more typically, its asymptotic variance). In such instances we will often want to test if any particular element k of $\hat{\mathbf{\theta}}_N$ differs significantly from zero or some other known value θ_k^*. (Recall that $\hat{\mathbf{\theta}}_N$ is a vector of K parameter estimates.)

The simplest form of this test is where $\hat{\theta}_{Nk}$ has a known variance. If it is normally distributed with variance σ_k^2, then under the null hypothesis that $\theta_k = \theta_k^*$, the test statistic

$$Z = \frac{\hat{\theta}_{Nk} - \theta_k^*}{\sigma_k} \tag{2.46}$$

is normally distributed with mean 0, variance 1. This result can be used to test hypotheses such as

$$H_0: \theta_k = \theta_k^*,$$
$$H_1: \theta_k \neq \theta_k^*, \tag{2.47}$$

where H_0 denotes the null hypothesis and H_1 denotes the alternate hypothesis.   For example, if $\sigma_k^2 = 4$ and we wish to test if some normally distributed estimator differs significantly from $\theta_k^* = 0$ at the 5% level of significance, we proceed by finding the region $(L_{0.025}, L_{0.975})$, such that under the null hypothesis

$$Pr(\hat{\theta}_{Nk} \leq L_{0.025}) + Pr(\hat{\theta}_{Nk} \geq L_{0.975}) = 0.05, \tag{2.48}$$

or equivalently

$$Pr(L_{0.025} \leq \hat{\theta}_{Nk} \leq L_{0.975}) = 0.95. \tag{2.49}$$

Since

$$\frac{\hat{\theta}_{Nk} - \theta_k^*}{\sigma_k} = \frac{\hat{\theta}_{Nk}}{2} \tag{2.50}$$

is normally distributed with mean 0, variance 1, we know (from a standard table of the cumulative normal distribution) that under the null hypothesis

$$Pr(-1.96 \leq \frac{\hat{\theta}_{Nk}}{2} \leq 1.96) = 0.95. \tag{2.51}$$

Hence

$$L_{0.025} = -3.92,$$
$$L_{0.975} = 3.92, \tag{2.52}$$

implying that we reject the null hypothesis if $|\hat{\theta}_{Nk}| \geq 3.92$.

Typically we will not know the actual variance of $\hat{\theta}_{Nk}$. Instead, we will have only an estimate of it. In the simple case where we are estimating the mean and variance of a normal population, we often use the estimators

$$\hat{\mu}_N = \frac{1}{N} \sum_{n=1}^{N} z_n \tag{2.53}$$

$$\hat{\sigma}_N^2 = s_N^2 = \frac{1}{N-1} \sum_{n=1}^{N} (z_n - \hat{\mu}_N)^2, \tag{2.54}$$

where s_N^2 is an unbiased estimator of σ^2. A well-known result is that under the hypothesis that the mean of the distribution is μ^*, the statistic

$$t^* = \frac{\hat{\mu}_N - \mu^*}{s_N/\sqrt{N}} \tag{2.55}$$

is t-distributed with $N - 1$ degrees of freedom. This statistic is usually used to solve for the critical region (i.e., the values of $\hat{\mu}_N$ for which H_0 will be rejected) for a given significance level α by constructing the statement

$$Pr\left[t_{N-1,\alpha/2} \leq \frac{\hat{\mu}_N - \mu^*}{s_N/\sqrt{N}} \leq t_{N-1,1-\alpha/2} \right] = 1 - \alpha, \tag{2.56}$$

where $t_{N-1,\alpha/2}$ and $t_{N-1,1-\alpha/2}$, respectively, denote the $\alpha/2$ and $1 - \alpha/2$ cumulants of the t distribution with $N - 1$ degrees of freedom. This yields a critical region of

$$|\hat{\mu}_N - \mu^*| \geq t_{N-1,1-\alpha/2}\left(\frac{s_N}{\sqrt{N}}\right). \tag{2.57}$$

As you may have noted, the critical region for this test is symmetric around the value μ^*. For this reason the test is said to be "two tailed."

When we wish to test hypotheses of the type,

$$H_0: \hat{\mu}_N \geq \mu^*,$$
$$H_1: \hat{\mu}_N < \mu^*, \tag{2.58}$$

we utilize test statistic 2.55, but we must now define a "one-tailed" critical region at the α significance level as follows:

$$\hat{\mu}_N - \mu^* \geq t_{N-1,1-\alpha}\left(\frac{s_N}{\sqrt{N}}\right). \tag{2.59}$$

As an example, suppose $N = 16$ and $s_N = 9$, and we wish to test at the $\alpha = 0.10$ level the following hypothesis:

$$H_0: \mu^* = 1,$$
$$H_1: \mu^* \neq 1. \tag{2.60}$$

The critical region is

$$|\hat{\mu}_{16} - 1| \geq 1.753(\tfrac{3}{4}) = 1.315. \tag{2.61}$$

Thus, if $\hat{\mu}_N$ is greater than 2.315 or less than 0.315, we would reject H_0.

If $\hat{\boldsymbol{\theta}}_N$ is a normally distributed vector, then the statistic $\hat{\theta}_{Nk}/\hat{\sigma}_{Nk}$ is generally t distributed with $N - K$ degrees of freedom. This result is most often used in standard regression analysis, where if we are willing to accept the assumption that the disturbances are normally distributed (along with other assumptions about their structure), then one can show that the least square estimators are also normally distributed with variance-covariance matrix given by the Cramér-Rao bound.

The case of principal interest to us is the one where $\hat{\boldsymbol{\theta}}_N$ is asymptotically normally distributed, and we use the Cramér-Rao bound to estimate its variance. Here we will use what we shall term a "*quasi-t test.*" Basically we use the t test with $N - K$ degrees of freedom and ignore the fact that all our estimators are only asymptotically normal rather than normal in small samples. When $N - K$ is large (e.g., greater than 30), we are for all practical purposes using a normal test because the t distribution converges quite rapidly to the normal. We will use this test quite often in this book to determine whether particular parameters in our model differ from some constant (usually 0).

F Test for Linear Models

When we are using the standard linear model in equation 2.43 and we estimate its parameters by least squares, we will often be interested in testing whether any particular model is significantly better than a more restricted form. When we can express the restrictions as *linear constraints* on the coefficients $\beta_1, \beta_2, \ldots, \beta_K$ and are willing to assume that the disturbances are normally distributed, we can apply the generalized F test (e.g., Kmenta 1971, pp. 366–374).

This test is best illustrated by example. In perhaps the simplest case we have a model

$$y = \beta_1 x_1 + \beta_2 x_2 + \cdots + \beta_K x_K + \xi, \tag{2.62}$$

and we wish to test whether we can reject the null hypothesis $\beta_1 = \beta_2$ and $\beta_{K-1} = \beta_K$. To be concrete, suppose y is the number of trips made by a household, x_1 and x_2 are two indicator variables for specific population groups (e.g., income groups), x_{K-1} is the number of automobiles owned, and x_K is the number of motorcycles owned. The hypothesis $\beta_1 = \beta_2$ implies that, all else being equal, the average trip rates of the two groups are equal. The hypothesis that $\beta_{K-1} = \beta_K$ is equivalent to stating that automobiles and motorcycles have the same marginal effect on trip generation. To construct this test, we first estimate the coefficient of the *unrestricted model* by least squares. (We have assumed that the disturbance terms satisfy the assumptions of the Gauss-Markov theorem.) Defining the estimates as $\hat{\boldsymbol{\beta}}^u$, we compute

$$Q^u = \sum_{n=1}^{N} (\hat{y}_n^u - y_n)^2, \tag{2.63}$$

where $\hat{y}_n^u = \hat{\beta}_1^u x_{1n} + \hat{\beta}_2^u x_{2n} + \cdots + \hat{\beta}_{K-1}^u x_{K-1,n} + \hat{\beta}_K^u x_{Kn}$ is the estimated expected value of y_n.

We then construct a *restricted model* that embodies the restrictions $\beta_1 = \beta_2$ and $\beta_{K-1} = \beta_K$. We can write the model as

$$y = \beta''(x_1 + x_2) + \cdots + \beta^*(x_{K-1} + x_K) + \xi^R, \tag{2.64}$$

which reflects the restrictions $\beta'' = \beta_1 = \beta_2$ and $\beta^* = \beta_{K-1} = \beta_K$. We estimate $(\beta'', \ldots, \beta_{K-2}, \beta^*)$ by least squares and use these estimates (defined as $\hat{\boldsymbol{\beta}}^R$) to compute

$$Q^R = \sum_{n=1}^{N} (\hat{y}_n^R - y_n)^2, \tag{2.65}$$

where $\hat{y}_n^R = \beta''^R(x_1 + x_2) + \cdots + \beta^{*R}(x_{K-1,n} + x_{Kn})$. Since $\hat{y}^R$ embodies restrictions that are not in $\hat{y}^u$, it is straightforward to show that $Q^R \geq Q^u$.

We then construct the test statistic

$$F^* = \frac{(Q^R - Q^u)/r}{Q^u/(N - K)}, \tag{2.66}$$

where r is the number of restrictions imposed. (In our example $r = 2$.) This statistic is F distributed under the null hypothesis with $(r, N - K)$ degrees of freedom. Thus we reject H_0 if the computed value of the statistic exceeds the critical value of the F distribution for $(r, N - K)$ degrees of freedom. Note that for the case of $r = 1$, $F^* = t^{*2}$, so one can use either the F or t tests.

The F test is quite general and can embody a wide range of null hypotheses about the coefficients in the model. Two examples of common uses are as follows:

1. To test the null hypothesis that all the coefficients except the constant term are zero. If $x_{1n} = 1$ for all n, so β_1 is a constant term in the linear model, this corresponds to the null hypothesis that

$$\beta_2 = \beta_3 = \cdots = \beta_{K-1} = \beta_K = 0. \tag{2.67}$$

Hence $r = K - 1$ and $Q^R = \sum_{n=1}^{N} (y_n - \bar{y})^2$, where $\bar{y}$ is the sample mean.
2. To test if the two or more groups within the population share all the same underlying coefficients. To construct this test, we estimate the parameters of the same model on the complete sample and on the subsamples corresponding to the different groups separately. The value of Q^R is the sum of squared errors in the pooled model, and Q^u is the total (taken over all the separate models) of the sums of squares. In this test $r = (G - 1) \cdot K$, where G is the number of groups defined.

The Likelihood Ratio Test

The likelihood ratio test serves the same function for maximum likelihood estimation that the F test serves for least squares. In this case, however, we compare the log likelihood functions for the unrestricted and restricted models of interest. We will let $\mathscr{L}^u$ and $\mathscr{L}^R$ denote the values of the log likelihood function at its maximum for the unrestricted and restricted models, respectively. Again let r denote the number of independent restrictions imposed on the parameters in computing $\mathscr{L}^R$. One can show that $\mathscr{L}^u \geq \mathscr{L}^R$.

The test statistic for the null hypothesis that the restrictions are true is

$$-2(\mathscr{L}^R - \mathscr{L}^u), \tag{2.68}$$

which is *asymptotically* distributed as χ^2 (chi squared) with r degrees of freedom. (See Theil 1971, p. 396, for a derivation of this statistic.) Thus, if $-2(\mathscr{L}^R - \mathscr{L}^u)$ is "large" in the statistical sense, we reject the null hypothesis that the restrictions are true. We will illustrate the uses of this test in chapter 4.

2.7 Summary

This chapter highlights the aspects of the theory of model estimation that will be used most extensively in later chapters. The general problem of estimating model parameters has been defined. Two groups of properties of estimators, small sample and asymptotic, were defined as follows:

Small Sample Properties

1. Unbiasedness. $\mathscr{E}[\hat{\boldsymbol{\theta}}_N] = \boldsymbol{\theta}$.
2. Efficiency.   For $\hat{\boldsymbol{\theta}}_N$ unbiased, $\text{var}(\hat{\boldsymbol{\theta}}_N)$ is less than or equal to the variance of any other unbiased estimator.

Asymptotic Properties

1. Asymptotic unbiasedness. $\lim_{N \to \infty} \mathscr{E}[\hat{\boldsymbol{\theta}}_N] = \boldsymbol{\theta}$.
2. Consistency. $\lim_{N \to \infty} Pr(\boldsymbol{\theta} - \mathbf{q} \leq \hat{\boldsymbol{\theta}}_N \leq \boldsymbol{\theta} + \mathbf{q}) = 1$ for any arbitrarily small, positive value of $\mathbf{q}$.
3. Asymptotic normality.   The distribution of $\hat{\boldsymbol{\theta}}_N$ approaches the normal distribution as $N \to \infty$.
4. Asymptotic efficiency.   If $\hat{\boldsymbol{\theta}}_N$ is consistent, then the variance of its asymptotic distribution is less than or equal to that of any other consistent estimator.

The *Cramér-Rao bound* for unbiased estimators of both scalars and vectors was stated. This bound provides a limiting value for the variance (or asymptotic variance) of any unbiased (or consistent) estimator and thus is a standard against which such estimators can be evaluated. There is no guarantee that an estimator meeting this bound will necessarily exist; however, if one is found, we know immediately that it is the minimum variance estimator.

We also presented the statistical tests most frequently used in travel demand analysis. Briefly summarized, these tests and their most common uses are as follows:

1. Normal test.   Test if the mean of a normal distribution equals some given value when variance is known.
2. t Test.   Test if mean of normal distribution equals some given value when variance is estimated (used principally in linear regression analysis to test single coefficients).

3. Quasi-*t* test.   Application of *t* test when estimator is asymptotically normally distributed.

4. *F* test.   Used to test a set of linear restrictions on the parameters of models estimated by least squares.

5. Likelihood ratio test.   Used to test a set of restrictions on the parameters of models estimated by maximum likelihood.

3 Theories of Individual Choice Behavior

3.1 Introduction

In general, we are interested in the behavior of a large number of individuals or organizations expressed in terms of aggregate quantities such as the market demand for a commodity or a service. However, this aggregate behavior is the result of individual decisions. Thus the modeling of individual behavior is either explicitly or implicitly at the core of all predictive models of aggregate behavior. The purpose of this chapter is to describe some principles of individual choice theories that are useful in the formulation of empirical discrete choice models.

We are concerned here with a theory of behavior that is (1) *descriptive*, in the sense that it postulates how human beings behave and does not prescribe how they ought to behave, (2) *abstract*, in the sense that it can be formalized in terms which are not specific to particular circumstances, and (3) *operational*, in the sense that it results in models with parameters and variables that can be measured or estimated.

Unfortunately there does not exist a single, universally accepted choice theory that satisfies these requirements. Alternative theories differ primarily in the level of detail in which they idealize the thought processes that produce observed behavior. The level of description in this book is coarse relative to recent developments in psychological research because of our interest in a wide range of applications and our emphasis on making operational predictions for a large number of individuals.

Therefore we begin with a presentation of a general framework for choice theories. We describe some common assumptions used for these theories and then focus on classical economic consumer and discrete choice theories, which suppose the existence of a single objective function called utility. With this theoretical background we then proceed to present in detail the theories and properties of probabilistic choice models which are the basis for the empirical discrete choice models developed in the following chapters.

3.2 A Framework for Choice Theories

A choice can be viewed as an outcome of a sequential decision-making process that includes the following steps:

1. definition of the choice problem,
2. generation of alternatives,

Table 3.1
A mode choice example

Alternatives	Attributes		
	Travel time (t)	Travel cost (c)	Comfort (o)
Car	t_1	c_1	o_1
Bus	t_2	c_2	o_2
Walk	t_3	c_3	o_3

3. evaluation of attributes of the alternatives,
4. choice,
5. implementation.

An example of a choice problem would be that of a commuter deciding on a mode of travel to work. His or her environment and the supply of transportation services determine the alternative modes available for the trip, although he or she may not be aware of all the possibilities. Suppose that the commuter's alternatives are car, bus, and walking. In the next step of the decision process the commuter evaluates or collects information about the attributes of every available alternative. Assume that there are three relevant attributes: travel time, travel cost, and comfort. Table 3.1 schematically shows the information available to the commuter. This information is then processed to arrive at a choice of travel mode. To do this, the commuter applies a decision rule—a specific sequence of calculations such as select the fastest mode that costs less than one dollar, irrespective of comfort. The final step in this decision-making process is obviously the trip to work itself, using the chosen mode.

Thus a specific theory of choice is a collection of procedures that defines the following elements:

1. decision maker,
2. alternatives,
3. attributes of alternatives,
4. decision rule.

These elements will be described in more detail shortly. It is worth noting that not all observed choice behavior is an outcome of such an explicit decision-making process. An individual can, for example, follow a habit, assume some form of conventional behavior, follow intuition, or imitate someone else who is considered to be an expert or a leader. However, these forms of behavior can be represented as a choice process in which the decision maker generates only one alternative.

The Decision Maker

The unit of decision making can be an individual person or a group of persons, such as a family or a household. It can also be an organization such as a firm or a government agency. By considering a group of persons or an organization as a single decision maker, it is possible to abstract partially the complex interactions within, say, a household or a firm. Thus, though we will refer to the decision maker as an individual, it is taken to represent an "actor" in a more general sense.

Individuals face different choice situations and have widely different tastes. Therefore, though we are ultimately interested in predicting aggregate demand, we must explicitly treat the differences in decision-making processes among individuals. To illustrate this, consider the car travel cost variable in the mode choice example. It will depend on the type of car used and the local price of gasoline. Moreover the extent to which the commuter is willing to pay the higher travel cost of a car may depend on this individual's income.

Further differences may arise among group decision processes because of the variations of within-group interactions that affect the outcomes. For example, in selecting an automobile, some household decisions may be the result of the preferences of a single, dominant household member, whereas other household choices may result from complex intrahousehold bargaining processes.

The Alternatives

Any choice is, by definition, made from a nonempty set of alternatives. The environment of the decision maker determines what we shall call the *universal set* of alternatives. Any single decision maker considers a subset of this universal set, termed a *choice set*.

This latter set includes the alternatives that are both feasible to the decision maker and known during the decision process. The feasibility of an alternative is defined by a variety of constraints such as physical availability (e.g., the availability of a bus service between the commuter's home and place of work), monetary resources (e.g., a taxi fare may be unafford-

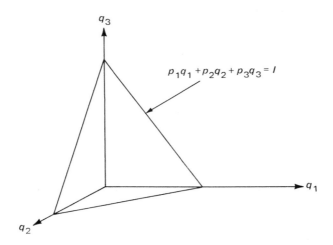

Figure 3.1
A continuous choice set

able to a low-income worker), time availability (e.g., the walk mode may be infeasible for a long-distance commuter), informational constraints (e.g., lack of knowledge about the bus service), and so on. Swait (1984) has further discussion of the role of environmental and personal constraints on the composition of the choice set.

It will prove useful to distinguish between two general types of choice sets. In the first type the choice set is continuous. This is most natural in the case of "commodity bundles" that form the basis for much of neoclassical microeconomic demand analysis. For example, the choice set might be defined as the set of all economically feasible amounts of milk (q_1), bread (q_2), and butter (q_3) purchased by a household. In this case it is natural to think of the choice set as depicted in figure 3.1, where p_1, p_2, and p_3 represent the prices of milk, bread, and butter, respectively, and I is the household's available income.

The second type of choice set—and the one we shall focus on in this book—is where the alternatives are naturally discontinuous. As an example suppose we are interested in a household's choice of one of a set of three televisions, denoted A, B, and C. In this case, assuming the household can afford any of the three models, the choice set is simply the set of "points" defined as $\{A, B, C\}$.

The distinction between these two types of choice sets will be expanded on in section 3.6.

Alternative Attributes

The attractiveness of an alternative is evaluated in terms of a vector of attribute values. The attribute values are measured on a scale of attractiveness that can be ordinal (e.g., car is the fastest mode) or cardinal (e.g., the travel cost of 50 cents). When the alternatives are homogeneous (e.g., milk or butter) and an alternative is just a vector of quantities of such commodities, then this vector of "attributes" simply reduces to the quantities. However, the case of interest in this book is the one where alternatives are heterogeneous and where decision makers may have different choice sets, evaluate different attributes, and assign diverse values for the same attribute of the same alternative. In these cases it will be much more natural to work directly with a general characterization of each alternative by its attributes rather than just the quantities associated with it.

We do not distinguish here between certain and uncertain outcomes. For example, travel time by automobile in congested urban areas may be an uncertain attribute for modal choice because of its great variability from day to day. This aspect of auto travel would be represented as an attribute of the alternative. We could consider, for example, the variance of travel time as an additional attribute. Another example is a consumer who, before buying a new television set, evaluates the expected maintenance costs of alternative brands. The purchase price of a specific new television set may be known with certainty, but its performance over time can only be evaluate in terms of expectations or ranges of possible values.

The Decision Rule

A choice from a choice set containing two or more alternatives requires a decision rule. It describes the internal mechanisms used by the decision maker to process the information available and arrive at a unique choice. There exists a wide variety of decision rules that have been proposed in the literature (e.g., see the lists given by Slovic et al. 1977 and Svenson 1979). These rules can be classified into the following four categories:

1. Dominance.   An alternative is dominant with respect to another if it is better for at least one attribute and no worse for all other attributes. This is the least controversial principle of decision-making theories. However, in most situations it does not lead to a unique choice. At best this rule can be used to eliminate inferior alternatives from a choice set. In the commuter choice example consider the availability of an additional public transport mode, say a subway line. It can be eliminated from an individual's choice set if, for example, it has equal fare and level of comfort but longer travel time. This assumes that comfort, cost, and travel time are the only attributes of relevance to the individual. It is highly unlikely there will be a mode of travel that is the fastest, cheapest and most comfortable. In most real-world decisions there are many attributes of relevance to each decision maker, and it is very rare to find an alternative that is dominant over all attributes.

Additional complexity may be introduced by an assumption (of a range of indifference or a threshold level) for each attribute. In other words, for one alternative to be better than another, the difference in the attribute values must exceed a threshold. Thus a travel time difference of five minutes or less, for example, may be considered by a decision maker too small to make a difference in his or her preference ranking of alternative modes.

2. Satisfaction.   For every attribute assume a level that serves as a satisfaction criterion. This may be defined as a "level of aspiration" based on the decision maker's expectations of the attainable, derived from his or her current information and previous experiences. Thus an alternative can be eliminated if it does not meet the criterion of at least one attribute. Again this rule by itself will not necessarily lead to a choice. In combination with other rules, such as dominance, it can be more decisive. Such an example would be a choice of an alternative that meets the criterion for at least one attribute and is no worse than the other alternatives for all the other attributes.

The commuter may, for example, set upper limits on the travel time and travel cost to be met by car and bus, and car is then chosen because of a higher level of comfort.

3. Lexicographic rules.   Suppose that the attributes are rank ordered by their level of "importance." The decision maker chooses the alternative that is the most attractive for the most important attribute. When attributes are qualitative (i.e., they reflect an intrinsic, discrete quality of an alternative rather than a numerical value), all alternatives possessing this quality would be kept. In the case where the use of the most important attribute fails to eliminate all but one alternative, the decision maker goes on with the second most important attribute and continues until the process reaches a unique choice.

Alternatively, the process can, at each stage, eliminate the most inferior alternative. Suppose, for example, that the commuter first considers travel time and eliminates the walk mode as the slowest alternative. If cost is considered second and the bus fare is smaller than the car travel cost, then the bus will be selected.

The combination of lexicographic and satisfaction rules is also known as "elimination by aspects." The process begins with the most important attribute and eliminates the alternatives that do not meet its criterion level. If two or more alternatives are left, it continues with the second most important attribute, and so forth (Tversky 1972).

4. Utility.   This class of decision rules assumes commensurability of attributes. This means that the attractiveness of an alternative expressed by a vector of attributes values is reducible to a scalar. This defines a single objective function expressing the attraction of an alternative in terms of its attributes. In the following we will refer to this index of attractiveness as *utility*, a measure that the decision maker attempts to maximize through his or her choice. Depending on the area of application, this objective function can be defined more specifically, such as cost to be minimized or profit to be maximized.

The supposition of a single index is based on the notion of trade-offs, or compensatory offsets, that a decision maker is using explicitly or implicitly in comparing different attributes. (The three previous decision rules are noncompensatory.)

For the commuter mode choice example this implies that the information in table 3.1 is reduced to three utility values, U_1, U_2, and U_3. The commuter will select the mode with the highest utility—that is, the mode with the best combination of travel time, travel cost, and comfort. Thus the more costly mode may be chosen if it compensates sufficiently by offering better service.

A utility function can be constructed in many different ways. The most important distinction is between ordinal and cardinal utilities. Ordinal utility is just a mathematical expression of a preference ranking of alternatives. An ordinal utility is unique only up to an order-preserving transformation. The comparisons of the numerical assignments to the utilities of alternatives have no meaning except for the relationships of greater than, less than, or equal to. A cardinal utility, on the other hand, implies some uniqueness of its numerical assignment and is therefore more restrictive than an ordinal utility. The latter is used most often in theories of decision making under uncertainty in which decision makers are assumed to maximize a measure of expected utility. Taking expectation involves multiplication and addition that, to be meaningful, require the use of cardinal utility. In the following developments based on the concept of a utility function, we will assume an ordinal utility unless it is otherwise stated.

The emphasis placed here on the hypothesis of utility maximization is due to its extensive use in the development of predictive models of human behavior. It results in formulations of choice processes that are amenable to mathematical analysis and statistical applications.

3.3   Rational Behavior

The common use of the term "rational behavior" is based on the beliefs of an observer about what the outcome of a decision should be. Obviously different observers may have varying beliefs and may assume different objective functions. Thus, as colloquially used, the notion of rationality is not a useful concept in describing individual behavior.

In the scientific literature the concept is used to describe the decision process itself. In general, it means a consistent and calculated decision process in which the individual follows his or her own objectives, whatever they may be. It stands in contrast to impulsiveness, in which individuals respond to choice situations in different ways depending on their variable psychological state at the time a decision is made.

Simon (1957) developed the distinction between "perfect" and "bounded" rationality. The classical concept of perfect rationality assumes an omniscient individual who can gather and store large quantities of information, perform very complex computations, and make consistent decisions based on those computations. Bounded rationality recognizes the constraints on the decision process that arise from limitations of human beings as problem solvers with limited information-processing capabilities.

Thus it is clear that even in its scientific use the concept of rationality can be ambiguous unless defined by a specific set of rules. In this book we will use it to describe a decision maker with *consistent and transitive preferences*. For example, it implies that a commuter, under identical circumstances, will repeat the same choice of mode, and if mode one is preferred to mode two and mode two is preferred to mode three, then mode one is also preferred to mode three.

3.4 Economic Consumer Theory

The basic approach to the mathematical theories of individual preferences is that of microeconomic consumer theory. The objective of the theory is to provide the means for the transformation of assumptions about desires into a demand function expressing the action of a consumer under given circumstances. This section provides a brief outline of the key concepts of this theory that are useful for the subsequent sections. For detailed expositions the reader is referred to many available microeconomic textbooks at different levels of presentation; see, for example, Layard and Walters (1978) and Varian (1978).

An individual consumer is choosing a consumption bundle

$$\mathbf{Q} = \{q_1, \ldots, q_L\}, \tag{3.1}$$

where $q_1, \ldots, q_L$ are the quantities of each of the commodities and services, $l = 1, 2, \ldots, L$. In consumer theory these quantities are generally assumed to be nonnegative continuous variables. The mathematical analysis employed by this theory to produce its most important results are dependent on this assumption. In the following section on discrete choice theory we will not make this assumption. We will therefore employ different mathematical approaches.

The consumer is faced with a budget that defines the consumption possibilities, or the choice set. For a fixed income, I, and fixed prices, p_1, $p_2, \ldots, p_L$, the budget constraint is

$$\sum_{l=1}^{L} p_l q_l \leq I. \tag{3.2}$$

In the classical approach to consumer theory there is no explicit treatment of attributes in addition to the quantities $q_1, \ldots, q_L$ that define an alternative.

The consumer is assumed to have preferences over alternative consumption bundles, for instance,

$$\mathbf{Q}^i \succcurlyeq \mathbf{Q}^j \tag{3.3}$$

means that consumption bundle $\mathbf{Q}^i$ is at least as good as $\mathbf{Q}^j$. Rational behavior is defined in the sense of a transitive preference ordering of alternatives; therefore, if

$$\mathbf{Q}^i \succcurlyeq \mathbf{Q}^j$$

and

$$\mathbf{Q}^j \gtrsim \mathbf{Q}^s,$$

then

$$\mathbf{Q}^i \gtrsim \mathbf{Q}^s.$$

It is also assumed that the consumer has the ability to compare all possible alternatives. Under these assumptions there exists an ordinal utility function

$$U = U(q_1, \ldots, q_L) \tag{3.4}$$

that expresses mathematically the consumer's preferences and is unique up to an order-preserving transformation. Thus

$$U(\mathbf{Q}^i) \geq U(\mathbf{Q}^j) \tag{3.5}$$

is equivalent to equation 3.3.

The consumer selection of the most preferred bundle that satisfies the budget constraint 3.2 can therefore be formulated mathematically as the maximization of 3.4 subject to 3.2 with respect to $q_1, \ldots, q_L$.

To demonstrate this technique, consider a simple example with two commodities and the following utility function:

$$U(q_1, q_2) = \beta_0 q_1^{\beta_1} q_2^{\beta_2} \tag{3.6}$$

where β_0, β_1, and β_2 are the positive parameters for the tastes of a consumer. For this problem the consumer can always increase his or her utility with increasing income. Therefore we need to solve the following optimization problem:

$$\max_{q_1, q_2} U = \beta_0 q_1^{\beta_1} q_2^{\beta_2} \tag{3.7}$$

subject to $p_1 q_1 + p_2 q_2 = I.$

Form the Lagrangian function for this problem to obtain

$$\max_{q_1, q_2, \lambda} \left[\beta_0 q_1^{\beta_1} q_2^{\beta_2} - \lambda(p_1 q_1 + p_2 q_2 - I) \right], \tag{3.8}$$

where λ is the Lagrange multiplier. Differentiate to obtain the first-order conditons:

$$\beta_0 \beta_1 q_1^{\beta_1 - 1} q_2^{\beta_2} - \lambda p_1 = 0,$$
$$\beta_0 \beta_2 q_1^{\beta_1} q_2^{\beta_2 - 1} - \lambda p_2 = 0, \tag{3.9}$$
$$p_1 q_1 + p_2 q_2 - I = 0.$$

These conditions can be solved for the *demand functions*, expressing the choice of the consumer for given prices and income:

$$q_1 = \frac{\beta_1}{\beta_1 + \beta_2} \cdot \frac{I}{p_1} \tag{3.10}$$

and

$$q_2 = \frac{\beta_2}{\beta_1 + \beta_2} \cdot \frac{I}{p_2}. \tag{3.11}$$

The demand functions provide an expression for the "optimal" consumption bundle that can now be substituted in the utility function to obtain the maximum utility that is achievable under the given prices and income which is called the *indirect utility function*. Thus for this example the indirect utility is

$$U(p_1, p_2, I) = \beta_0 \left(\frac{I}{\beta_1 + \beta_2} \right)^{\beta_1 + \beta_2} \left(\frac{\beta_1}{p_1} \right)^{\beta_1} \left(\frac{\beta_2}{p_2} \right)^{\beta_2}. \tag{3.12}$$

The foregoing theory deals with a single consumer whose tastes are implicitly contained in the form and the parameter values of the utility function. In empirical applications, when observations of different consumers are used to estimate unknown parameters of demand functions, it is necessary to specify how tastes, and consequently utility functions, vary among consumers. This is the reason why socioeconomic characteristics of the consumers are introduced into empirical demand functions and why sometimes the estimation is performed separately for different socioeconomic groups.

However, we would always expect to find a difference between the observed choice and the one predicted by an empirical demand function. This difference is treated as a random error and is attributed to consumer optimization errors and measurement errors in the available data.

3.5   Extensions of Consumer Theory

Economic consumer theory is developed without any assumptions about the nature of the alternatives. As a result without further restrictions the demand functions that are derived have very limited empirical usefulness because they require information on the prices of all commodities. Moreover with a large number of commodities the consumer is assumed to solve an unreasonably complex optimization problem. Therefore empirical demand functions include only the prices of "related" commodities.

In principle, all commodities and services to which the consumer devotes some fraction of his or her budget are related because of the budget constraint. However, it is possible to impose some plausible structure on the utility function that restricts this dependence. Strotz (1957, 1959) proposed the concept of a "utility tree." The commodities are arranged into groups or branches, and the total utility function is composed from separable branch utilities as follows:

$$U = U[U^1(q_1^1, \ldots, q_{L_1}^1), U^2(q_1^2, \ldots, q_{L_2}^2), \ldots, U^B(q_1^B, \ldots, q_{L_B}^B)], \tag{3.13}$$

where

$U^b(q_1^b, \ldots, q_{L_b}^b) = $ the utility of the commodities in branch $b = 1, \ldots, B$,

$$L = L_1 + L_2 + \cdots + L_B,$$

$B = $ the number of branches.

The function $U[\ ]$ determines the level of separability between branches. Strong separability implies an additive function. The branches correspond to "natural" groups of commodities such as housing, food, clothing, vacation, and transportation. Behaviorally, a utility tree can be interpreted as a representation of a sequential decision process. The consumer follows a two-stage procedure. The first stage consists of the decision on the allocation of the available resources, namely income to the different branches. The consumer can be assumed to base this allocation on some composite prices, such as an average cost of food or an index of vacation-related prices. In the second stage the consumer decides on the within-branch allocations. Given that income is allocated to a branch, this is a classical consumer theory problem applied to a subset of commodities.

Another interpretation of a separable utility function was proposed by

Muth (1966). It views the commodities and services purchased by the consumer as inputs into a home production process, the output of which is a bundle of "nonmarket" goods. The utility function is thus defined over these final goods which can be interpreted in the same manner as the branches of a utility tree. For each final good the consumer possesses a production function expressing the quantity of the final good as a function of the input market commodities.

Another and probably more fundamental interpretation was suggested by Lancaster (1966). He defined utility in terms of the attributes of the commodities. The production process in Muth's interpretation is replaced by technical relationships between commodities and attributes. The consumer derives utility from the attributes; the preferences for commodities are indirect in the sense that they arise because the commodities are needed to "produce" attributes.

Becker (1965) extended the traditional consumer theory formulation by adding a time constraint. The utility function is defined in terms of human activities. Performing an activity requires the purchase of market commodities and services and the spending of time. This again defines a partial utility function (or a technological relationship expressing the utility or quantity) of an activity as a function of commodities and time. This function can also include other attributes of an activity such as comfort or safety.

3.6   Discrete Choice Theory

Now we will present the same concepts applied in consumer theory but with a discrete representation of the set of alternatives. A continuous space of alternatives assumed in consumer theory allows the use of calculus to derive demand functions, as demonstrated in section 3.4. However, if the consumption of one or more commodities can be zero, the maximization problem may have a "corner" solution, a point where the usual first-order conditions for an optimum do not hold.

Consider again the commuter mode choice problem depicted in table 3.1, with the following utility function:

$$U = U(q_1, q_2, q_3), \tag{3.14}$$

where we impose the restrictions that

$$q_1 = \begin{cases} 1 & \text{if mode 1 is chosen,} \\ 0 & \text{otherwise;} \end{cases}$$

$$q_2 = \begin{cases} 1 & \text{if mode 2 is chosen,} \\ 0 & \text{otherwise;} \end{cases}$$

$$q_3 = \begin{cases} 1 & \text{if mode 3 is chosen,} \\ 0 & \text{otherwise;} \end{cases}$$

and that only one alternative is chosen:

$$q_1 q_2 = q_1 q_3 = q_2 q_3 = 0. \tag{3.15}$$

Under these restrictions the utility function can attain only three possible values corresponding to the three "corners" of figure 3.1,

$$U(1,0,0), \quad U(0,1,0), \quad \text{and} \quad U(0,0,1),$$

and is therefore not differentiable with respect to the quantities q_1, q_2, and q_3.

Because this example deals with a set of discrete choices, it is impossible to use the maximization techniques of calculus to derive demand functions. Thus a discrete representation of alternatives necessitates a different analytical approach. Note, however, that we will retain the concept of the rational consumer; the only difference between choice theory and consumer theory will be that instead of deriving demand functions, we will work directly with the utility functions.

For the commuter choice problem with three alternative modes we define a utility function expressed in terms of the attributes of the alternatives as follows:

$$U_1 = U(t_1, c_1, o_1),$$

$$U_2 = U(t_2, c_2, o_2), \tag{3.16}$$

$$U_3 = U(t_3, c_3, o_3).$$

The function $U(\ )$, which maps the attributes values to a utility scale, is an ordinal utility function. Alternative 1, for example, will be chosen if and only if

$$U_1 > U_2 \tag{3.17}$$

and

$$U_1 > U_3. \tag{3.18}$$

Indifference between two alternatives occurs when there is a tie or the difference between two utilities is smaller than some perceptual threshold level. If, for example,

$$U_1 = U_2 \tag{3.19}$$

and

$$U_1 > U_3, \tag{3.20}$$

the commuter is indifferent between bus and auto, and the choice is therefore indeterminate. (We will later resolve this potential problem by assuming that there is no possibility of a tie.) When ties are ignored, alternative 1 is chosen if and only if

$$U_1 \geq U_2 \tag{3.21}$$

and

$$U_1 \geq U_3. \tag{3.22}$$

The most difficult assumption to make involves the form of the utility function. An additive utility function is most often assumed for convenience as follows:

$$U_1 = -\beta_1 t_1 - \beta_2 c_1 + \beta_3 o_1,$$
$$U_2 = -\beta_1 t_2 - \beta_2 c_2 + \beta_3 o_2, \tag{3.23}$$
$$U_3 = -\beta_1 t_3 - \beta_2 c_3 + \beta_3 o_3,$$

when $\beta_1, \beta_2, \beta_3 > 0$ are parameters that express the tastes of the commuter.

Application of this theory to predict how the commuter will respond to changes requires that we assign numerical values to the parameters. The approach taken to this estimation problem is called "revealed preferences." In this approach we use information about utilities that can be inferred from observations of choice behavior. Consider, for example, repeated observations of a commuter's mode choice decisions with different values of the attributes. One simple approach to inferring $\beta_1, \beta_2,$ and β_3 is to find the values of the parameters such that the chosen mode always has the highest utility. Since the utilities are ordinal, the dimensions of this search can be reduced by redefining the utilities:

$$U_1 = -\beta_1 t_1 - c_1 + \beta_3 o_1,$$

$$U_2 = -\beta_1 t_2 - c_2 + \beta_3 o_2, \tag{3.24}$$

$$U_3 = -\beta_1 t_3 - c_3 + \beta_3 o_3.$$

A division by a positive constant (β_2) does not alter the ranking. Assume, for simplicity, that $\beta_3 = 0$. Thus a choice of mode 1 over mode 2 implies that

$$\beta_1 (t_1 - t_2) \le c_2 - c_1. \tag{3.25}$$

If

$$t_1 - t_2 > 0 \quad \text{and also} \quad c_2 - c_1 > 0 \tag{3.26}$$

(otherwise we have a simple case of dominance), we obtain the following upper bound:

$$\beta_1 \le \frac{c_2 - c_1}{t_1 - t_2}. \tag{3.27}$$

In the next observation suppose, for example, that we include mode 3 with improved travel times and costs and the commuter selects mode 3 over mode 1. Thus

$$\beta_1 (t_3 - t_1) \le c_1 - c_3. \tag{3.28}$$

If

$$t_3 - t_1 < 0 \quad \text{and} \quad c_1 - c_3 < 0, \tag{3.29}$$

we obtain the following lower bound:

$$\beta_1 \ge \frac{c_3 - c_1}{t_1 - t_3}. \tag{3.30}$$

More observations produce other inequalities that will further narrow down the range of possible values of β_1.

Note that if under the same circumstances (i.e., the same values of travel times and costs) the commuter is once observed to select mode 1 and a second time to select mode 2, we can assume an indifference relationship between the two alternatives. Thus

$$U_1 = U_2, \tag{3.31}$$

and in this simple example we can derive a unique estimate

$$\beta_1 = \frac{c_2 - c_1}{t_1 - t_2}, \tag{3.32}$$

provided that

$$t_1 \neq t_2. \tag{3.33}$$

Cases of dominance such as

$$t_1 \leq t_2 \tag{3.34}$$

and

$$c_1 \leq c_2 \tag{3.35}$$

do not contain useful information for the estimation of β_1 in this problem. Inconsistent inequalities mean that the assumption of preference transitivity is violated. We will consider this possibility in detail in the next section.

This process of determination of the parameters can also be demonstrated graphically for a simple binary example. Figure 3.2 shows a number of revealed preferences for alternatives 1 and 2, plotted in the space of $(t_1 - t_2)$ and $(c_2 - c_1)$; the dots represent choice of alternative 1, and the crosses, choice of alternative 2. For utility functions similar to 3.24, the parameter β_1 is determined by pivoting the line through the origin until all the dotes are below and all the crosses are above it. If such a β_1 can be found, it is an indication that preference transitivity holds. If, however, the final value of β_1 does not clearly distinguish between the choice of the two alternatives, the transitivity assumption is violated.

In more general terms we consider a universal set of alternatives, denoted C. The constraints faced by an individual decision maker n determine his or her choice set $C_n \subseteq C$. As in consumer theory the individual is assumed to have consistent and transitive preferences over the alternatives that determine a unique preference ranking. Thus a real-valued utility index associated with every alternative can be defined,

$$U_{in}, i \in C_n \tag{3.36}$$

such that alternative $i \in C_n$ is chosen if and only if

$$U_{in} > U_{jn}, \quad \text{all } j \neq i, j \in C_n. \tag{3.37}$$

Using Lancaster's approach, or the concept of an indirect utility, define the utility function in terms of attributes

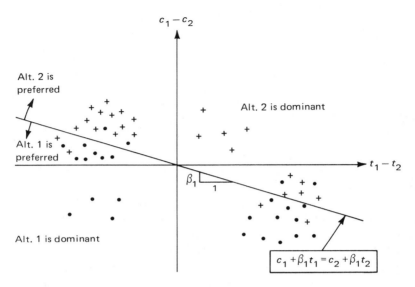

Figure 3.2
Graphic example of parameter determination

$$U_{in} = U(z_{in}), \tag{3.38}$$

where z_{in} is a vector of the attribute values for alternative i as viewed by decision maker n. Income and time budgets and other external restrictions determine the choice set C_n. The indirect utility interpretation means that these budgets can also be included in the utility function. Generally, in empirical applications we will introduce into the utilities a vector of socioeconomic characteristics that explains the variability of tastes across the portion of the population to which our model of choice behavior applies. Thus we write

$$U_{in} = U(z_{in}, S_n), \tag{3.39}$$

where S_n is a vector of characteristics of the decision maker n such as income, age, and education.

3.7 Probabilistic Choice Theory

The first developments of probabilistic choice theories were in the field of psychology. A comprehensive review of these early developments is given in Luce and Suppes (1965). The development of these theories arose from the need to explain experimental observations of inconsistent and nontransitive preferences. In choice experiments individuals have been observed not to select the same alternative in repetitions of the same choice situations. Moreover, by changing choice sets, violations of the transitive preferences assumption are also observed.

A probabilistic choice mechanism was introduced to explain these behavioral inconsistencies. One can argue that human behavior is inherently probabilistic. It can also be argued, however, that behavior which is probabilistic amounts to an analyst's admission of a lack of more precise knowledge about individuals' decision processes. If it were possible to specify the causes of these inconsistencies, the deterministic choice theory of section 3.6 could be used. These causes, however, are usually unknown, or known but not measurable.

Another type of inconsistency arises in empirical applications when we observe the choices made by a sample of individuals. In this case we may observe two or more individuals with identical choice sets, attributes, and socioeconomic characteristics, selecting different alternatives. An example would be the case of two identical commuters who select different modes for what appear to be identical trips to work. The probabilistic mechanism can be used to capture the effects of unobserved variations among decision makers and unobserved attributes of the alternatives. It can also take into account pure random behavior as well as errors due to incorrect perceptions of attributes and choices of suboptimal alternatives. Thus probabilistic choice theories can be used to overcome one of the weaknesses of consumer theory discussed earlier.

There is clearly an unresolvable dichotomy between the assertion of a fundamentally probabilistic behavior and what may only appear to us to be probabilistic because of our inability to understand fully and to measure all the relevant factors that affect human behavior. Referring to this dichotomy, Luce and Suppes (1965) distinguish between two approaches to the introduction of the probabilistic choice mechanism: constant utility and random utility.

Constant Utility

In the *constant utility* approach the utilities of the alternatives are fixed. Instead of selecting the alternative with the highest utility the decision maker is assumed to behave with choice probabilities defined by a probability distribution function over the alternatives that includes the utilities as parameters.

The selection of a probability distribution function in the constant utility approach can only be based on specific assumptions with respect to properties of choice probabilities.

Denote the probability of decision maker n choosing alternatives i as

$P_n(i)$,

or as

$P(i|C_n)$

when an explicit notation for the choice set is also useful. Obviously we require that

$$0 \leq P(i|C_n) \leq 1, \qquad \text{all } i \in C_n, \tag{3.40}$$

where the equality signs hold in the limiting case of a deterministic choice, and that

$$\sum_{i \in C_n} P(i|C_n) = 1. \tag{3.41}$$

The usual theorems of probability theory are assumed to hold. In particular, since one and only one alternative is chosen, the following must hold:

$$P(i \text{ and } j|C_n) = 0, \qquad i \neq j \in C_n, \tag{3.42}$$

and

$$P(i \text{ or } j|C_n) = P(i|C_n) + P(j|C_n), \qquad i \neq j \in C_n. \tag{3.43}$$

Generally, for any subset of the choice set $\tilde{C}_n \subseteq C_n$, we can write

$$P(\tilde{C}_n|C_n) = \sum_{i \in \tilde{C}_n} P(i|C_n), \tag{3.44}$$

expressing the probability that the choice lies in the subset $\tilde{C}_n$.

It is also possible to calculate the following conditional probability:

$$P(i|\tilde{C}_n \subseteq C_n) = \frac{P(i|C_n)}{P(\tilde{C}_n|C_n)} \tag{3.45}$$

for any alternative $i \in \tilde{C}_n \subseteq C_n$, provided that

$P(j|C_n) > 0$

for at least one alternative $j \in \tilde{C}_n$. For the commuter mode choice example this means that we can calculate the conditional probability of mode 1 being chosen given that the choice is alternative 1 or alternative 2 and that for at least one of these two modes the choice probability is positive.

The simplest constant utility model was derived by Luce (1959) as a result of the following assumption, referred to as the "*choice axiom*":

A set of choice probabilities defined for all the subsets of a finite set C_n satisfy the choice axiom provided that for all i, $\tilde{C}_n$ and C_n such that $i \in \tilde{C}_n \subseteq C_n$,

$$P(i|\tilde{C}_n \subseteq C_n) = P(i|\tilde{C}_n) \tag{3.46}$$

whenever the conditional probability exists.

In other words, if some alternatives are removed from a choice set, the relative choice probabilities from the reduced choice set are unchanged. The choice probabilities from a subset of alternatives is dependent only on the alternatives included in this subset and is independent of any other alternatives that may exist. We substitute assumption 3.46 in the definition of the conditional choice probability 3.45 to obtain

$$P(i|C_n) = P(i|\tilde{C}_n)P(\tilde{C}_n|C_n), \qquad i \in \tilde{C}_n \subseteq C_n, \tag{3.47}$$

which in words states that the choice probability of i from C_n is the product of the choice probability of i from the subset $\tilde{C}_n$ and the probability that the choice lies in $\tilde{C}_n$. Note that this product is independent of the definition of $\tilde{C}_n$. Thus the property of the *independence from irrelevant alternatives* (IIA) is obtained as follows:

$$\frac{P(i|\tilde{C}_n)}{P(j|\tilde{C}_n)} = \frac{P(i|C_n)}{P(j|C_n)}, \qquad i,j \in \tilde{C}_n \subseteq C_n. \tag{3.48}$$

Luce (1959) argues that the IIA property can be viewed as a probabilistic version of the concept of transitivity. However, it can be shown that the validity of the choice axiom depends on the structure of the choice set. Suppose that for the commuter mode choice example the choice probabilities are

$$P_n(\text{car}) = \tfrac{1}{2},$$

$$P_n(\text{bus}) = \tfrac{1}{2}, \tag{3.49}$$

$$P_n(\text{walk}) = 0.$$

Now suppose that another bus service is introduced that is equal in all attributes to the existing bus service except that its buses are painted differently. We now have red and blue buses as two of the available alternatives. Under the choice axiom the ratio of choice probabilities is constant, and therefore the new choice probabilities will be

$$P_n(\text{car}) = \tfrac{1}{3},$$

$$P_n(\text{red bus}) = \tfrac{1}{3}, \tag{3.50}$$

$$P_n(\text{blue bus}) = \tfrac{1}{3}.$$

This is unrealistic because the commuter will in reality be most likely to treat the two bus modes as a single alternative and behave with the following choice probabilities:

$$P_n(\text{car}) = \tfrac{1}{2},$$

$$P_n(\text{red bus}) = \tfrac{1}{4}, \tag{3.51}$$

$$P_n(\text{blue bus}) = \tfrac{1}{4}.$$

Thus the validity of the choice axiom is restricted to choice sets with distinct alternatives. The foregoing example reflects an extreme case where two alternatives in a choice set are for all practical purposes identical and should really be considered a single alternative.

Luce (1959) proves that if the choice axiom holds and a utility measure is directly proportional to the choice probability, then there exists a "strict utility" model as follows:

$$P(i|C_n) = \frac{U_{in}}{\sum_{j \in C_n} U_{jn}}, \tag{3.52}$$

where the utilities are now restricted to be positive and must be defined on a ratio scale which is unique up to multiplication by a positive constant. Note that this equation also applies to any subset $\tilde{C}_n \subseteq C_n$.

Tversky (1972) showed that Luce's choice axiom is a special case of the *simple scalability* property. It holds whenever the choice probabilities can be expressed as follows:

$$P(i|C_n) = h_{J_n-1}(U_{in} - U_{1n}, \ldots, U_{in} - U_{i-1,n}, U_{in} - U_{i+1,n}, \ldots,$$
$$U_{in} - U_{J_n,n}), \tag{3.53}$$

where J_n is the number of alternatives in the choice set and h_{J_n-1} is monotonically increasing in all its $J_n - 1$ arguments. This property also implies the existence of *order independence*; namely, if

$$P(i|C_n) \geq P(j|C_n), \tag{3.54}$$

then

$$P(i|\tilde{C}_n) \geq P(j|\tilde{C}_n), \tag{3.55}$$

for any $\tilde{C}_n$ and $i, j \in \tilde{C}_n \subseteq C_n$. The IIA property is a special case of order independence, as it entails a constant ratio

$$\frac{P(i|C_n)}{P(j|C_n)} = \frac{P(i|\tilde{C}_n)}{P(j|\tilde{C}_n)} \tag{3.56}$$

for any $\tilde{C}_n$ and $i, j \in \tilde{C}_n \subseteq C_n$.

To illustrate these concepts, consider a choice problem in which a commuter has the following choice probabilities for modes of travel:

$$P(\text{car}) = 0.4,$$

$$P(\text{bus}) = 0.6. \tag{3.57}$$

Now suppose that a subway line is constructed and the commuter is indifferent to the choice between this new service and the old bus service. Consider the following choice probabilities under the new situation:

$$P(\text{car}) = 0.36,$$

$$P(\text{bus}) = 0.32, \tag{3.58}$$

$$P(\text{subway}) = 0.32.$$

This is a reasonable behavior pattern in which the new public transit mode has increased the overall attractiveness of public transport, thereby reducing the car choice probability from 0.4 to 0.36. If the bus and the subway were perceived as indentical modes, we would have the same case as the blue bus/red bus example, so the new probabilities will be

$$P(\text{car}) = 0.4,$$

$$P(\text{bus}) = 0.3, \tag{3.59}$$

$$P(\text{subway}) = 0.3.$$

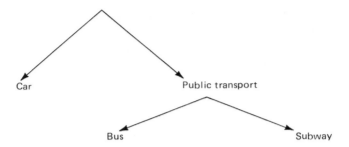

Figure 3.3
An example of a choice hierarchy

Note, however, that both of these sets of new choice probabilities violate the order-independence property. With the first choice set of bus and auto we have

$$P(\text{bus}) > P(\text{car}), \tag{3.60}$$

but in the second choice set (which also includes subway) we have

$$P(\text{bus}) < P(\text{car}), \tag{3.61}$$

which means that a simple scalable model does not hold in this case. Also note that an IIA model is consistent with the following new choice probabilities:

$$P(\text{car}) = 0.25,$$

$$P(\text{bus}) = 0.375, \tag{3.62}$$

$$P(\text{subway}) = 0.375,$$

such that the ratio

$$\frac{P(\text{car})}{P(\text{bus})} = \frac{2}{3} \tag{3.63}$$

is maintained. Thus the validity of a simple scalable model is questionable whenever alternatives are perceived to be similar. For these examples it is possible to introduce an assumption of a *choice hierarchy*, such as depicted in figure 3.3. In the case of identical alternatives it is simple to redefine the alternatives before we apply a simple scalable model. However, for non-identical alternatives it is possible to assume a choice hierarchy with different choice mechanisms applying to the different stages of the hierarchy. For example, we can assume that the choice axiom applies at each level of the hierarchy but is not valid for the full set of alternatives. In other words, the choice axiom may be valid for a choice within a subset (e.g., bus vs. subway), for a choice between subsets (e.g., bus and subway vs. car), but it does not apply for the choice from the whole set of alternatives (e.g., car vs. bus vs. subway).

The problem for the analyst is to know whether a decision maker does indeed decompose a certain decision into a hierarchical choice process and, if so, what is the specific structure that he or she uses. In some cases it may appear as if there are "natural" partitions of the alternatives, as shown in the example in the figure. However, for more complex decisions there are many possible choice hierarchies, and different structures can yield different choice probabilities. This means that in applications the general theories presented in this chapter should be adapted to the special character of the alternatives. Reasonable choice hierarchies may be postulated and empirically tested against each other.

Random Utility

The random utility approach, formalized by Manski (1977), is more in line with consumer theory. The observed inconsistencies in choice behavior are taken to be a result of observational deficiencies on the part of the analyst. The individual is always assumed to select the alternative with the highest utility. However, the utilities are not known to the analyst with certainty and are therefore treated by the analyst as random variables. From this perspective the choice probability of alternative i is equal to the probability that the utility of alternative i, U_{in}, is greater than or equal to the utilities of all other alternatives in the choice set. This can be written as follows:

$$P(i|C_n) = Pr[U_{in} \geq U_{jn}, \text{ all } j \in C_n]. \tag{3.65}$$

Note that we assume that no ties occur.

In this approach we derive choice probabilities by assuming a joint probability distribution for the set of random utilities

$$\{U_{in}, i \in C_n\}.$$

The basis for this distributional assumption is a logical argument about the underlying sources of the randomness of the utilities. Manski (1973) identified four distinct sources of randomness:

1. unobserved attributes,
2. unobserved taste variations,
3. measurement errors and imperfect information,
4. instrumental (or proxy) variables.

The effect of each of these on the distribution of the utilities is considered next.

Unobserved Attributes   The vector of attributes affecting the decision is incomplete. Therefore the utility function

$$U_{in} = U(\mathbf{z}_{in}, \mathbf{S}_n, z_{in}^U) \tag{3.66}$$

includes an element z_{in}^U which is observationally a random variable, and consequently the utility is in itself random.

Unobserved Taste Variations   The utility function

$$U_{in} = U(\mathbf{z}_{in}, \mathbf{S}_n, S_n^U) \tag{3.67}$$

may have an unobserved argument S_n^U which varies among individuals. Since the variation of S_n^U is unknown, U_{in} is observationally a random variable.

Measurement Errors   The true utility function is

$$U_{in} = U(\tilde{\mathbf{z}}_{in}, \mathbf{S}_n) \tag{3.68}$$

and the attributes $\tilde{\mathbf{z}}_{in}$ are not observable. We observe $\mathbf{z}_{in}$ which is an imperfect measurement of $\tilde{\mathbf{z}}_{in}$. We substitute

$$\tilde{\mathbf{z}}_{in} = \mathbf{z}_{in} + \tilde{\varepsilon}_{in}, \tag{3.69}$$

where $\tilde{\varepsilon}_{in}$ is the unknown measurement error, into the utility function in 3.68 to get a utility

$$U_{in} = U(\mathbf{z}_{in} + \tilde{\varepsilon}_{in}, \mathbf{S}_n), \tag{3.70}$$

which contains a random element.

Instrumental Variables   The true utility function is

$$U_{in} = U(\tilde{\tilde{\mathbf{z}}}_{in}, \mathbf{S}_n), \tag{3.71}$$

but some elements of $\tilde{\tilde{\mathbf{z}}}_{in}$ are not observable. Therefore $\tilde{\tilde{\mathbf{z}}}_{in}$ is replaced with $\mathbf{z}_{in}$ which includes instrumental variables (i.e., variables related to actual attributes). We substitute

$$\tilde{\mathbf{z}}_{in} = g(\mathbf{z}_{in}) + \tilde{\tilde{\varepsilon}}_{in}, \tag{3.72}$$

where g denotes the imperfect relationship between instruments and attributes and $\tilde{\tilde{\varepsilon}}_{in}$ is again a random error, into the utility function 3.71 to obtain the utility

$$U_{in} = U[g(\mathbf{z}_{in}) + \tilde{\tilde{\varepsilon}}_{in}, \mathbf{S}_n], \tag{3.73}$$

which contains a random element.

In general, we can express the random utility of an alternative as a sum of observable (or systematic) and unobservable components of the total utilities as follows:

$$U_{in} = V(\mathbf{z}_{in}, \mathbf{S}_n) + \varepsilon(\mathbf{z}_{in}, \mathbf{S}_n) = V_{in} + \varepsilon_{in}, \tag{3.74}$$

and expression 3.65 can be rewritten as

$$P(i|C_n) = Pr[V_{in} + \varepsilon_{in} \geq V_{jn} + \varepsilon_{jn}, \text{ all } j \in C_n]. \tag{3.75}$$

To derive a specific random utility model, we require an assumption about the joint probability distribution of the full set of disturbances,

$$\{\varepsilon_{jn}, j \in C_n\}.$$

Alternative distributional assumptions and the resulting probabilistic choice models are considered in great detail in the following chapters. It is useful, however, to note here that assuming *independently and identically distributed* (IID) random utilities results in a simple scalable model. This occurs because the choice probability of alternative i is only a function of the differences

$$V_{in} - V_{jn}, \quad j \neq i, j \in C_n,$$

as arguments in equation 3.53.

3.8   Summary

This chapter has presented some of the basic elements of a decision problem. In it we characterized a choice as the outcome of five steps:

1. definition of the choice problem,
2. generation of alternatives,

3. evaluation of attributes of alternatives,

4. choice, and

5. implementation.

The decision maker for any choice problem can be treated as a single individual, or more abstractly as a family group, a firm, or a public agency. Different decision rules, including dominance, satisfaction, lexicographic rules, and the optimization of a scalar objective function were considered. Although all of these are potentially useful, the remainder of this book will focus on the last of these decision rules, which will generally be referred to as utility maximization.

Neoclassical economic consumer theory was briefly considered. This view of demand is appropriate to situations where the feasible choices are continuous variables such as the quantities of various homogeneous consumption commodities. However, the types of problems considered in subsequent chapters are better described as a selection of one of a finite set of discrete bundles of attributes. For such problems discrete choice theory is a more appropriate basis for demand analysis. In particular, probabilistic choice theory that specifies the probability with which an individual will select any feasible alternative provides a potentially powerful framework for analyzing discrete choice situations.

Two distinct interpretations of probabilistic choice theory were reviewed. The *constant utility approach*, rooted primarily in mathematical psychology, hypothesizes that the utilities of alternatives are constant and that the choice probabilities for an individual are functions parameterized by those utilities. The alternate perspective, the *random utility approach*, is more consistent with consumer theory. In this view utilities are treated by the analyst as random due to observational deficiencies resulting from (1) unobserved attributes, (2) unobserved taste variations, (3) measurement errors, and (4) use of instrumental (or proxy) variables. Decision makers are assumed always to choose the utility-maxmizing alternatives; the choice probabilities are interpreted as the analyst's statement of the probability that for any decision maker, the utility of an alternative will exceed the utilities of all other feasible alternatives.

The subsequent chapters will build on the basic concept of random utilities. In particular, we will begin with this relatively abstract concept and make plausible further assumptions to derive a rich class of operational models of individual choice.

4 Binary Choice Models

In the preceding chapter we developed the concept of the individual decision maker who, faced with a set of feasible discrete alternatives, selects the one that yields greatest utility. We noted that for a variety of reasons the utility of any alternative is, from the perspective of the analyst, best viewed as a random variable. This leads directly to the notion of random utility models in which the probability of any alternative i being selected by person n from choice set C_n is given by the following:

$$P(i|C_n) = Pr(U_{in} \geq U_{jn}, \forall j \in C_n). \tag{4.1}$$

We ignore the probability that $U_{in} = U_{jn}$ for any i and j in the choice set. Formally, if the distributions of U_{in} and U_{jn} can be characterized by a probability density function, $Pr(U_{in} = U_{jn}) = 0$.

In this chapter we pursue this basic idea further by considering the special case where C_n contains exactly two alternatives. Such situations lead to what are termed *binary choice models*. For convenience we will denote the choice set C_n as $\{i,j\}$, where, for example, alternative i might be the option of driving to work and alternative j would be using transit. The probability of person n choosing i is

$$P_n(i) = Pr(U_{in} \geq U_{jn}), \tag{4.2}$$

and the probability of choosing alternative j is

$$P_n(j) = 1 - P_n(i).$$

Our goal in this chapter is to develop the basic theory of random utility models into a class of operational binary choice models.

A detailed discussion of binary models will serve a number of purposes. First, the simplicity of binary choice situations makes it possible to develop a range of practical models which is greater than feasible in more complicated choice situations. Second, there are many basic conceptual problems that are easiest to illustrate in the context of binary choice. Many of the solutions we will present in this chapter can be directly applied to more complicated situations.

In section 4.1 we first consider how the general theory developed in chapter 3 can be made operational. Then in section 4.2 we derive the most widely used binary choice model forms. Section 4.3 presents two examples of actual binary mode choice models.

In Section 4.4. we consider the problem of estimating the parameters of a binary choice model by maximum likelihood (briefly discussed in section

2.5). This is followed by a simple example and then a more extended example of maximum likelihood estimation in section 4.5.

Section 4.6 describes other estimation methods, and section 4.7 summarizes the key results for the entire chapter.

4.1 Making Random Utility Theory Operational

We begin by partitioning the development of any binary choice model into three basic steps:

1. The separation of total utility into deterministic and random components of the utility function.
2. The specification of the deterministic component.
3. The specification of the random component.

Each of these is considered in turn in this section.

Deterministic and Random Utility Components

Recalling that U_{in} and U_{jn} are random variables, we begin by dividing each of the utilities into two additive parts as follows:

$$U_{in} = V_{in} + \varepsilon_{in},$$
$$U_{jn} = V_{jn} + \varepsilon_{jn}.$$

(4.3)

V_{in} and V_{jn} are called the *systematic (or representative)* components of the utility of i and j; ε_{in} and ε_{jn} are the random parts and are called the *disturbances* (or random components).

It is important to stress that V_{in} and V_{jn} are functions and are assumed here to be deterministic (i.e., nonrandom). The terms ε_{in} ε_{jn} may also be functions, but they are random from the observational perspective of the analyst.

Loosely speaking, V_{in} and V_{jn} can be thought of as the means of U_{in} and U_{jn}, respectively. This interpretation, though intuitive, can be misleading since the utility is ordinal, not cardinal (see section 3.2); we can shift the scale of measurement by simply transforming both U_{in} and U_{jn} by any strictly monotonically increasing function. For example, suppose that we have a very simple case where i and j are driving and using transit to work, respectively, and the only observed attribute that affects choice is travel time, t. Let us assume that

$$U_{An} = -0.25 - 0.05t_{An} + \varepsilon_{An},$$
$$U_{Tn} = -0.05t_{Tn} + \varepsilon_{Tn},$$
(4.4)

where the subscripts A and T now denote the auto and transit modes, respectively.

In this case we can rewrite the probability of the individual taking transit as

$$P_n(T) = Pr(U_{Tn} \geq U_{An})$$
$$= Pr(-0.05t_{Tn} + \varepsilon_{Tn} \geq -0.25 - 0.05t_{An} + \varepsilon_{An}).$$
(4.5)

Thus, if the travel time on transit and auto for person n were 30 and 15 minutes, respectively, one might state that person n's mean transit utility was $-0.05(30) = -1.5$, and that the average auto utility was $-0.25 - 0.05(15) = -1$. However, the reason this interpretation is somewhat loose is that if we were to rewrite the utilities as

$$U_{An} = 100 - 0.25 - 0.05t_{An} + \varepsilon_{An}$$

and

$$U_{Tn} = 100 - 0.05t_{Tn} + \varepsilon_{Tn},$$
(4.6)

we would find that the probability of transit was unchanged:

$$P_n(T) = Pr(100 - 0.05t_{Tn} + \varepsilon_{Tn}$$
$$\geq 100 - 0.25 - 0.05t_{An} + \varepsilon_{An})$$
(4.7)
$$= Pr(-0.05t_{Tn} + \varepsilon_{Tn} \geq -0.25 - 0.05t_{An} + \varepsilon_{An}).$$

Thus adding a constant (in this case, 100) to both utilities does not affect the choice probabilities even though it shifts the functions V_{in} and V_{jn}. Another equivalent interpretation is that since utility is an arbitrarily defined scale, to speak of it as having a mean without first providing some referent against which the utility is measured simply does not make sense.

There is a third way to think about this relative nature of the utilities. Let us rewrite the probability that n chooses alternative i as

$$P_n(i) = Pr(U_{in} \geq U_{jn})$$
$$= Pr(V_{in} + \varepsilon_{in} \geq V_{jn} + \varepsilon_{jn})$$
(4.8)
$$= Pr(\varepsilon_{jn} - \varepsilon_{in} \leq V_{in} - V_{jn}).$$

In this version of equation 4.2 we can see that for a binary choice situation, the absolute levels of V and ε do not matter; all that matters is whether the difference in the V's is less than the difference of the ε's.

Specification of the Systematic Component

We have already noted that the specification of the absolute levels of ordinal utilities is irrelevant; only their difference matters. We could therefore develop binary choice models by specifying only the differences, ignoring the individual components. However, to maintain consistency with later chapters in which we analyze choice situations with more than two alternatives, we will write each utility function separately, keeping in mind that only their difference matters in terms of the choice probabilities.

The first issue in specifying V_{in} and V_{jn} is to ask, What types of variables can enter these functions? As discussed in chapter 3, for any individual n any alternative i can be characterized by a vector of attributes z_{in}. In our example of mode choice, z_{in} might include travel time, cost, comfort, convenience, and safety. It is also useful to characterize the decision maker n by another vector of attributes, which we shall denote by S_n. These are often variables such as income, auto ownership, household size, age, occupation, and sex. The problem of specifying the functions V_{in} and V_{jn} consists of defining combinations of z_{in}, z_{jn}, and S_n which reflect reasonable hypotheses about the effects of such variables.

It will generally be convenient to define a new vector of attributes x which includes both z_{in} and S_n. Notationally we write the vectors $x_{in} = h(z_{in}, S_n)$ and $x_{jn} = h(z_{jn}, S_n)$, where h is a vector-valued function. Now we can write the systematic components of the utilities of i and j as

$$V_{in} = V(x_{in})$$

and   (4.9)

$$V_{jn} = V(x_{jn}).$$

The second question is then, What is a reasonable functional form for V? Here we will generally be concerned with two, sometimes contradictory criteria for selecting a functional form. First, we would like the function to reflect any theory we have about how the various elements in x influence utility; second, we would like to use functions that have convenient computational properties that make it easy to estimate their unknown parameters. In most cases of interest researchers faced with these conflicting criteria have chosen to use functions that are *linear in the parameters*. If we denote $\boldsymbol{\beta} = [\beta_1, \beta_2, \ldots, \beta_K]'$ as the vector of K unknown parameters,

$$V_{in} = \beta_1 x_{in1} + \beta_2 x_{in2} + \beta_3 x_{in3} + \cdots + \beta_K x_{inK},$$

$$V_{jn} = \beta_1 x_{jn1} + \beta_2 x_{jn2} + \beta_3 x_{jn3} + \cdots + \beta_K x_{jnK}. \tag{4.10}$$

The reader should note that we have adopted the convention that both utilities have the same vector of parameters. It is important to stress that this is only a notational convention because, by appropriately defining the various elements in $\mathbf{x}$, we can effectively give each systematic utility function different coefficients. Consider the case where

$$V_{An} = -0.25 - 0.05 t_{An},$$

$$V_{Tn} = -0.05 t_{Tn}. \tag{4.11}$$

In this case it appears as though the auto utility has an additional term equal to -0.25. We can "convert" this model into the form of equation 4.10 by defining our x's as follows:

$$x_{An1} = 1,$$

$$x_{Tn1} = 0,$$

$$x_{An2} = t_{An}, \tag{4.12}$$

$$x_{Tn2} = t_{Tn},$$

with $K = 2$, $\beta_1 = -0.25$, and $\beta_2 = -0.05$.

Thus

$$V_{An} = \boldsymbol{\beta}' \mathbf{x}_{An} = \beta_1 x_{An1} + \beta_2 x_{An2} = -0.25 - 0.05 t_{An},$$

$$V_{Tn} = \boldsymbol{\beta}' \mathbf{x}_{Tn} = \beta_1 x_{Tn1} + \beta_2 x_{Tn2} = -0.05 t_{Tn}. \tag{4.13}$$

We should also stress that just as in regression analysis, linearity in the parameters is not as restrictive an assumption as one might first think. *Linearity in parameters is not equivalent to linearity in the attributes $\mathbf{z}$ and $\mathbf{S}$.* We allow for any function $\mathbf{h}$ of the attributes so that polynomial, piecewise linear, logarithmic, exponential, and other real transformations of the attributes are valid for inclusion as elements of $\mathbf{x}$. Some of the range of such functions will be explored as part of examples described later in this chapter and in subsequent chapters. We will also consider some problems that introduce nonlinearities in the parameters in chapters 7 and 9.

Finally, we note that we have implicitly assumed that the parameters $\beta_1, \beta_2, \ldots, \beta_K$ are the same for all members of the population. Again this is not as restrictive as it may seem at first glance. If different socioeconomic groups are believed to have entirely different parameters $\boldsymbol{\beta}$, then it is possible to develop an entirely distinct model for each subgroup. This is termed *market segmentation* (see section 7.5). In the extreme case a market segment corresponds to a single individual, and a vector of parameters will be specific to an individual. In addition, if the preferences or tastes of different members of the population vary systematically with some known socioeconomic attribute, we can define some of the elements in $\mathbf{x}$ to reflect this. For example, it is not unusual to define as an attribute cost divided by income, reflecting the a priori belief that the importance of cost declines as the inverse of a traveler's income. As an advanced topic in chapter 5, we also consider the case where $\beta_1, \beta_2, \ldots, \beta_K$ are treated as random variables distributed across the population.

Specification of the Disturbances

Our last remaining component of an operational binary choice model is the disturbance terms. As with the systematic components V_{in} and V_{jn}, we can discuss the specification of binary choice models by considering only the difference $\varepsilon_{jn} - \varepsilon_{in}$ rather than each element ε_{in} and ε_{jn} separately. Whereas in section 4.1 we chose to keep the V's separate, here we shall be somewhat more eclectic. We will choose the interpretation that is most convenient and insightful for the purposes of exposition.

We begin first by considering the problem of the mean of the disturbances. As discussed in section 4.1, the choice probabilities are unaffected by the addition of a constant to both utilities; we can add or subtract any number from each, and their relative value (as measured by their difference) is unaffected. Another aspect of the mean of the disturbances is that there is no real distinction between shifting the mean of the disturbance of one alternative's utility and shifting the systematic component by the same amount. Thus, if the mean of alternative i's disturbance is some amount greater than that of alternative j's disturbance, we can fully represent the difference by adding that amount to V_{in}. *This implies that as long as one can add a constant to the systematic component, the means of disturbances can be defined as equal to any constant without loss of generality.* Usually the most convenient assumption is that all the disturbances have zero means. We will maintain the convention of assuming any nonzero means of the disturbances are "absorbed" into the systematic component of the utility function, unless noted otherwise.

In addition to the mean of the disturbances we must ensure that their scale is consistent with that of the V's. Again any strictly monotonic transformation of the utilities U_{in} and U_{jn} will not affect the choice probabilities. To see this, suppose the total utility of alternatives i and j are as given in equation 4.3. Note that

$$P_n(i) = Pr(U_{in} \geq U_{jn}) = Pr(V_{in} + \varepsilon_{in} \geq V_{jn} + \varepsilon_{jn})$$
$$= Pr(\alpha V_{in} + \alpha \varepsilon_{in} \geq \alpha V_{jn} + \alpha \varepsilon_{jn}), \qquad \text{for any } \alpha > 0. \tag{4.14}$$

Thus, just as adding a constant to each utility did not affect the choice probabilities, multiplying both by a positive constant does not. Hence, to make our V's unique, we must "fix their scale." This is typically done by placing some restrictions on the disturbances. For example, if we assume that $\varepsilon_{jn} - \varepsilon_{in}$ is distributed with variance equal to 1, we in effect define their scale as follows:

$$\text{var}[\alpha(\varepsilon_{jn} - \varepsilon_{in})] = \alpha^2 \text{var}(\varepsilon_{jn} - \varepsilon_{in}) = 1,$$

which implies that

$$\alpha = \frac{1}{\text{var}(\varepsilon_{jn} - \varepsilon_{in})^{1/2}}.$$

Obviously any other assumed value for the variance would work as well. The choice is entirely arbitrary, and we usually use a scale that is analytically or computationally convenient.

Given an appropriate scaling of the disturbances, we can now ask, What is an appropriate functional form for the distribution of ε_{in} and ε_{jn}, or for $\varepsilon_{jn} - \varepsilon_{in}$? Basically varying the assumptions about the distributions of ε_{in} and ε_{jn} (or equivalently, assumptions about their difference) leads to different choice models. However, it makes little sense to think of the specification of the distribution of the ε's independently from the specification of the V's. In particular, since the ε's reflect the various sources of observational error discussed in chapter 3, different specifications of V will lead to different appropriate distributions for ε.

To illustrate this, we return to our example of auto and transit mode choice. Suppose we have an admittedly unrealistic situation where individuals evaluate *only* time and cost in selecting between the two modes and there are no other factors influencing their choices. Also suppose the total utilities of the two alternatives are

$$U_{An} = \beta_1 t_{An} + \beta_2 c_{An},$$
$$U_{Tn} = \beta_1 t_{Tn} + \beta_2 c_{Tn},$$

(4.15)

where c_{An} and c_{Tn} denote the cost of using auto and transit, respectively. Note that because by assumption there are no other choice-relevant attributes, the disturbance terms, which are always zero, can be omitted. Now let us consider the case where the analyst has information only about travel costs, rather than both cost and time. The disturbances of the utilities now become the effect of the time, the unobserved attribute. Moreover the distribution of the disturbances across the population arises from the distribution of $\beta_2 t_{An}$ and $\beta_2 t_{Tn}$ across the population of travelers.

In actual applications the disturbances will be a composite of a great number of unobserved effects, each of which contributes in some way to the disturbances' distribution. Although it will often be difficult to make strong statements about the overall distribution of the disturbances, we will occasionally be able to obtain insights into how to improve models by thinking more carefully about what "goes into" the ε's. This will become increasingly relevant when we discuss multinomial choice models in chapter 5.

With the foregoing as background we now explore specific binary choice models. Our presentation is divided into two parts. First, in section 4.2 we derive the most common binary choice models and give some examples in section 4.3. Then in sections 4.4, 4.5, and 4.6 we discuss the methods that can be used to estimate the models's parameters, giving further examples of actual applications of the procedures we derive.

4.2   Common Binary Choice Models

The derivation of any binary choice model is conceptually straightforward. In each subsection we begin by making some assumption about the distribution of the two disturbances or about the difference between them. Given one of these assumptions, we then solve for the probability that alternative i is chosen. (The probability that j is chosen is trivially equal to $1 - P_n(i)$.) As a final step we explore some of the properties of each model.

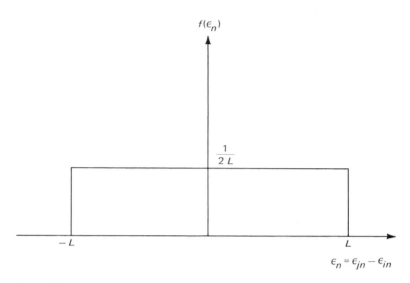

Figure 4.1
Uniform distribution

The Linear Probability Model

Perhaps the easiest model to develop is the case where the *difference* in disturbances, $\varepsilon_{jn} - \varepsilon_{in}$, is uniformly distributed between two fixed values $-L$ and L, with $L > 0$. We define $\varepsilon_{jn} - \varepsilon_{in} = \varepsilon_n$ and its density function as $f(\varepsilon_n)$. This density function, sketched in figure 4.1, gives rise to the *linear probability model*. Solving for $P_n(i)$, we find

$$P_n(i) = Pr(V_{in} + \varepsilon_{in} \geq V_{jn} + \varepsilon_{jn})$$

$$= Pr(\varepsilon_{jn} - \varepsilon_{in} \leq V_{in} - V_{jn}) = Pr(\varepsilon_n \leq V_{in} - V_{jn}).$$

Thus the choice probability of alternative i is given by the cumulative distribution function of ε_n, which for the preceding uniform distribution is

$$P_n(i) = \begin{cases} 0 & \text{if } V_{in} - V_{jn} < -L, \\ \displaystyle\int_{-L}^{V_{in}-V_{jn}} f(\varepsilon_n)\, d\varepsilon_n = \dfrac{V_{in} - V_{jn} + L}{2L} & \text{for } -L \leq V_{in} - V_{jn} \leq L, \\ 1 & \text{if } V_{in} - V_{jn} > L. \end{cases}$$

$$(4.16)$$

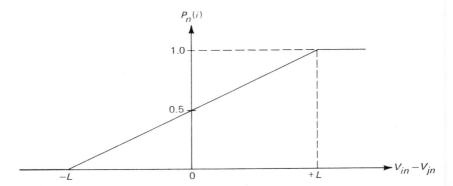

Figure 4.2
The linear probability model

When V is linear in its parameters, $V_{in} - V_{jn} = \boldsymbol{\beta}'\mathbf{x}_{in} - \boldsymbol{\beta}'\mathbf{x}_{jn} = \boldsymbol{\beta}'(\mathbf{x}_{in} - \mathbf{x}_{jn})$. This function is graphed in figure 4.2. It has the obvious property of being linear in the interval $[-L, L]$. However, it is "kinked" at the points L and $-L$. These two points at which the derivative is discontinuous present some theoretical difficulties. In addition one inevitably finds that after the model is estimated, some members of the population choose alternative i despite the fact that the model predicts that there is zero probability of them doing so. This problem arises because we have assumed that the density of $\varepsilon_{jn} - \varepsilon_{in}$ drops off to zero at the points $-L$ and L.

Note also that the choice of value for the parameter L determines the scale of the utility and is therefore arbitrary. It is often convenient to select $L = \frac{1}{2}$, but any value will do. To see this, consider the linear-in-parameters case.

Here

$$P_n(i) = Pr(\varepsilon_{jn} - \varepsilon_{in} \leq V_{in} - V_{jn})$$

$$= Pr[\varepsilon_{jn} - \varepsilon_{in} \leq \boldsymbol{\beta}'(\mathbf{x}_{in} - \mathbf{x}_{jn})] \qquad (4.17)$$

$$= Pr[\alpha(\varepsilon_{jn} - \varepsilon_{in}) \leq \alpha\boldsymbol{\beta}'(\mathbf{x}_{in} - \mathbf{x}_{jn})],$$

for any $\alpha > 0$. *Thus, rescaling the distribution of $\varepsilon_{jn} - \varepsilon_{in}$ to be uniform between $-\alpha L$ and αL, and rescaling the vector of coefficients $\boldsymbol{\beta}$ by a factor α, yields exactly the same choice probabilities.* The choice of α is therefore arbitrary, and $L = \frac{1}{2}$ means that α was arbitrarily set to $2L$.

Binary Probit

Because of behaviorally unrealistic "kinks" in the linear probability model and because of its forecasts of unrealistic, extreme probabilities in some circumstances, researchers have looked for more appropriate specifications of the distribution of the disturbances. One logical assumption is to view the disturbances as the sum of a large number of unobserved but independent components. By the central limit theorem the distribution of the disturbances would tend to be normal.

To be more specific, suppose that ε_{in} and ε_{jn} are both normal with zero means and variances σ_i^2 and σ_j^2, respectively. Suppose further that they have covariance σ_{ij}. Under these assumptions the term $\varepsilon_{jn} - \varepsilon_{in}$ is also normally distributed with mean zero but with variance $\sigma_i^2 + \sigma_j^2 - 2\sigma_{ij} = \sigma^2$.

We can use this result to solve for the choice probabilities as follows:

$$P_n(i) = Pr(\varepsilon_{jn} - \varepsilon_{in} \le V_{in} - V_{jn})$$

$$= \int_{\varepsilon = -\infty}^{V_{in} - V_{jn}} \frac{1}{\sqrt{2\pi}\,\sigma} \exp\left[\frac{-1}{2}\left(\frac{\varepsilon}{\sigma}\right)^2 \right] d\varepsilon, \ \sigma > 0,$$

$$= \frac{1}{\sqrt{2\pi}} \int_{-\infty}^{(V_{in} - V_{jn})/\sigma} \exp\left[-\frac{1}{2}u^2 \right] du = \Phi\left(\frac{V_{in} - V_{jn}}{\sigma} \right), \tag{4.18}$$

where $\Phi(\ )$ denotes the standardized cumulative normal distribution. This model is called *binary probit*. In the case where $V_{in} = \boldsymbol{\beta}' \mathbf{x}_{in}$ and $V_{jn} = \boldsymbol{\beta}' \mathbf{x}_{jn}$,

$$P_n(i) = \Phi\left(\frac{\boldsymbol{\beta}'(\mathbf{x}_{in} - \mathbf{x}_{jn})}{\sigma} \right). \tag{4.19}$$

Again note that in this case $1/\sigma$ is the scale of the utility function which can be set to an arbitrary positive value, usually $\sigma = 1$. The binary probit function is sketched in figure 4.3 for $\sigma = 1$. Note that the choice function has a characteristic sigmoidal shape and that the choice probabilities are never zero or one. They approach zero and one as the systematic components of the utilities become more and more different.

The binary probit choice probabilities depend only on σ, not on σ_i^2, σ_j^2, and σ_{ij}. Thus the variances and covariance of the two disturbances are irrelevant to the choice probabilities. Moreover even the choice of σ is arbitrary since, by rescaling σ and $\boldsymbol{\beta}$ by any positive constant α, we do not affect the choice probabilities at all. It is customary to choose $\sigma = 1$ as the scale, though any other value would serve as well.

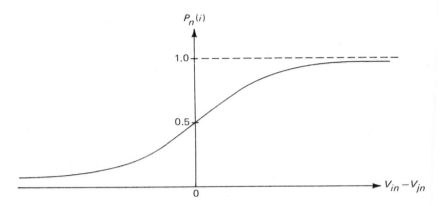

Figure 4.3
The binary probit model

Binary probit has been widely used in diverse fields. Its origins are in toxicology, where $V_{in} - V_{jn}$ represents the dosage of some toxic substance to which a population is exposed and $P_n(i)$ is interpreted as the probability that a member of the population falls ill or dies (see Finney 1971). One of the first transport applications of this model is due to Lisco (1967) who analyzed the mode choice of commuters in Chicago. We use some of his results in section 4.3 as an example of how binary choice models can be specified.

To compare the scale of a linear probability model with $L = \frac{1}{2}$ with that of a binary probit model with $\sigma = 1$, we note that the variance of the assumed uniform distribution is $L^2/3$, which implies that the standard deviation of the linear probability model is fixed at $1/(2\sqrt{3})$, whereas it is 1 for the binary probit model. This normalization implies that the scaled probit coefficients will be $2\sqrt{3}$ times greater than the scaled linear probability model coefficients.

Binary Logit

Although binary probit is both intuitively reasonable and there is at least some theoretical grounds for its assumptions about the distribution of ε_{in} and ε_{jn}, it has the unfortunate property of not having a closed form. Instead, we must express the choice probability as an integral. This aspect of binary probit provides the motivation for searching for a choice model that is "probitlike" but also more convenient analytically. One such model is *binary logit*.

The binary logit model arises from the assumption that $\varepsilon_n = \varepsilon_{jn} - \varepsilon_{in}$ is logistically distributed, namely

$$F(\varepsilon_n) = \frac{1}{1 + e^{-\mu\varepsilon_n}}, \qquad \mu > 0, \; -\infty < \varepsilon_n < \infty, \tag{4.20}$$

$$f(\varepsilon_n) = \frac{\mu e^{-\mu\varepsilon_n}}{(1 + e^{-\mu\varepsilon_n})^2}, \tag{4.21}$$

where μ is a positive scale parameter. Besides approximating the normal distribution quite well, the logistic distribution is analytically convenient. Although the approximation is good, it should be noted that the logistic distribution has "fatter" tails than the normal. To provide continuity with the development of the multinomial choice models in chapter 5, the assumption that ε_n is logistically distributed is equivalent to assuming that ε_{in} and ε_{jn} are independent and identically Gumbel (or type I extreme value) distributed (see section 5.2 for more details).

Under the assumption that ε_n is logistically distributed, the choice probability for alternative i is given by

$$P_n(i) = Pr(U_{in} \geq U_{jn})$$

$$= \frac{1}{1 + e^{-\mu(V_{in} - V_{jn})}} \tag{4.22}$$

$$= \frac{e^{\mu V_{in}}}{e^{\mu V_{in}} + e^{\mu V_{jn}}}.$$

This is the binary logit model. Note that if V_{in} and V_{jn} are linear in their parameters,

$$P_n(i) = \frac{e^{\mu\boldsymbol{\beta}'\mathbf{x}_{in}}}{e^{\mu\boldsymbol{\beta}'\mathbf{x}_{in}} + e^{\mu\boldsymbol{\beta}'\mathbf{x}_{jn}}}$$

$$\tag{4.23}$$

$$= \frac{1}{1 + e^{-\mu\boldsymbol{\beta}'(\mathbf{x}_{in} - \mathbf{x}_{jn})}}.$$

In the case of linear-in-parameters utilities, the parameter μ cannot be distinguished from the overall scale of the $\boldsymbol{\beta}$'s. For convenience we generally make an arbitrary assumption that $\mu = 1$. This corresponds to assuming the variances of ε_{in} and ε_{jn} are both $\pi^2/6$, implying that $\text{var}(\varepsilon_{jn} - \varepsilon_{in}) = \pi^2/3$. Note that this differs from the standard scaling of binary probit models, where we set $\text{var}(\varepsilon_{jn} - \varepsilon_{in}) = 1$, and it implies that the scaled probit

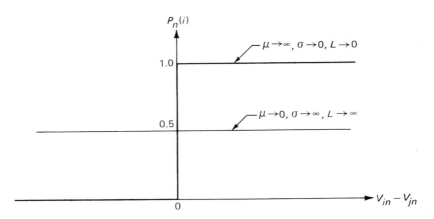

Figure 4.4
Limiting cases of linear, probit, and logit binary models

coefficients are $\pi/\sqrt{3}$ times larger than the scaled probit coefficients. The reader should be careful to rescale either the logit or probit utilities when comparing coefficients from the two models.

Limiting Cases of the Linear, Probit, and Logit Models

There are two limiting cases of a choice model of special interest, both involving extreme values of the scale parameter. For the logit model the first case is for $\mu \to \infty$, for which the choice probability of i becomes

$$P_n(i) = \begin{cases} 1 & \text{if } V_{in} - V_{jn} > 0, \\ 0 & \text{if } V_{in} - V_{jn} < 0; \end{cases}$$

that is, as $\mu \to \infty$, the choice model is deterministic. On the other hand, when $\mu \to 0$, the choice probability of i becomes $\frac{1}{2}$. Intuitively the model predicts equal probability of choice for each alternative.

These two limiting cases are portrayed graphically in figure 4.4. We also show there that the deterministic limit exists for both the probit ($\sigma \to 0$) and linear ($L \to 0$) models; the equal probability limits for these models are equivalent to the conditions $\sigma \to \infty$ and $L \to \infty$, respectively.

Other Binary Choice Models

Although the linear probability, probit, and logit models have dominated other possible models in actual applications, the range of possible binary choice models is essentially limitless. Any well-defined assumption about

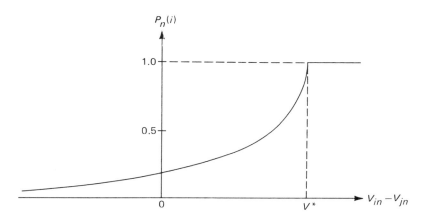

Figure 4.5
Right-truncated exponential

the distribution of $\varepsilon_{jn} - \varepsilon_{in}$ will lead to a choice model. It will of course not always be possible to derive this assumed distribution from reasonable assumptions about the separate distributions of ε_{in} and ε_{jn}. Indeed, it can be shown that the uniform distribution that resulted in the linear probability model cannot be generated as the difference between two independent and identically distributed random variables.

Three other binary choice models are at least worth noting, though we will not use them further in this book:

1. *Arctan probability model*

$$P_n(i) = \frac{1}{2} + \frac{1}{\pi} \tan^{-1}(V_{in} - V_{jn}); \qquad (4.24)$$

the inverse tangent function is defined in radians.

2. *Right-truncated exponential*

$$P_n(i) = \begin{cases} e^{-(V^* - V_{in} + V_{jn})} & \text{if } V_{in} - V_{jn} < V^*, \\ 1 & \text{if } V_{in} - V_{jn} \geq V^*. \end{cases} \qquad (4.25)$$

3. *Left-truncated exponential*

$$P_n(i) = \begin{cases} 1 - e^{-(V_{in} - V_{jn} - V^*)} & \text{if } V_{in} - V_{jn} > V^*, \\ 0 & \text{if } V_{in} - V_{jn} \leq V^*. \end{cases} \qquad (4.26)$$

The last two of these three choice models are graphed in figures 4.5 and 4.6.

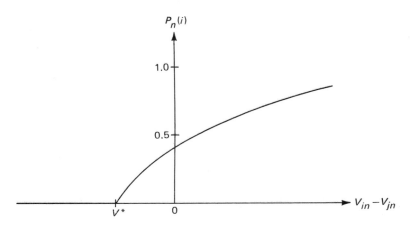

Figure 4.6
Left-truncated exponential

The arctan model is not sketched, for it closely resembles both logit and probit. It can be derived by assuming that ε_{in} and ε_{jn} are independent and identically Cauchy distributed. The two exponential models are qualitatively distinct from the other functional forms and do not arise from any explicit assumptions on the separate disturbances.

4.3 Examples of Binary Choice Models

To clarify some of the aspects of specifying binary choice models, we will consider two actual examples. At this stage we consider only the structure of the particular models and not how their coefficients are estimated. In section 4.5 we will return to one of these examples for a further discussion of statistical issues.

The two models include one of the earliest binary probit models applied to a transportation problem, by Lisco (1967), and a more recent binary logit model reported in Cambridge Systematics (1976). Both models assume a systematic utility function that is linear in its parameters.

Lisco's Binary Probit Model

In a study of Chicago commuters Lisco (1967) collected data on workers who chose between automobile and commuter railroad from a Chicago suburb. Following our earlier notational convention, we will denote these modes as A and T, respectively. The systematic component of the utility included eight parameters (i.e., $K = 8$).

The specification of the model is given in tabular form in table 4.1. The two rows correspond to the auto and transit utilities, and the columns correspond to the eight coefficients labeled β_1 through β_8. The entries in the table define the variables that enter into the model. Entries in the last row are the coefficient estimates found by Lisco.

This example provides a concrete basis for some notes about the specification of binary choice models. Consider the first column (under the heading β_1). The variable, defined as 1 in the auto alternative and 0 in the transit alternative, is termed an *alternative-specific constant*. The alternative-specific constant reflects the mean of $\varepsilon_{jn} - \varepsilon_{in}$, that is, the difference in the utility of alternative i from that of j when "all else is equal." It should be noted that it would make no sense to have *two* alternative-specific constants (one for auto and one for transit) because all that matters is their difference. In the model depicted in table 4.1, the estimate for β_1 is negative, reflecting a relative preference for the transit mode.

The second and third coefficients correspond to the attributes of travel time and travel cost. Here time is measured in minutes and cost in cents. Note that the coefficients of time and cost are the same in the two utilities. We term such variables *generic*. This represents an assumption that a minute (or a cent) has the same marginal (dis)utility whether it is incurred on the auto or transit mode. The estimate of β_2 and β_3 is negative since, all else being equal, travelers prefer lower time and cost alternatives in commuting.

The next two variables (under the columns headed β_4 and β_5) are called *alternative-specific socioeconomic* variables. Basically these variables reflect the differences in preferences for auto and transit as functions of income and age. One can view such variables much in the same way as the alternative-specific constant, except that instead of using a 0 or 1, each individual has a *different* value of the variables. For any given individual the variable is in effect a constant. As with the alternative-specific constants it would make no sense to define these variables in both alternatives because all that matters is the effect of income and age on the *relative* utility.

The choice of including income and age as alternative specific to the auto alternative or redefining them so they have nonzero values in the transit alternative is wholly arbitrary. Reversing the definition simply reverses the sign of the corresponding coefficient, leaving the differences in the utilities (and consequently the choice probabilities) unaltered.

Table 4.1

Lisco's binary probit model: $P_n(A) = (1/\sqrt{2\pi}) \int_{u=-\infty}^{V_{An}-V_{Tn}} e^{-u^2/2}\, du$

	β_1	β_2	β_3	β_4	β_5	β_6	β_7	β_8
Auto utility, V_{An}	1	Time on auto (min)	Cost on auto (¢)	Household income	Age	1 if commuter is unmarried or spouse cannot drive or drives to work with spouse; 0 otherwise	1 if commuter married and has working spouse who drives to work independently; 0 otherwise	1 if female; 0 if male
Transit utility, V_{Tn}	0	Time on transit (min)	Cost on transit (¢)	0	0	0	0	0
Estimated coefficients	−1.379	−0.084	−0.012	1.999	0.068	−0.234	1.262	0.648

The final three variables are also alternative-specific socioeconomic variables. These are essentially identical to the income and age variables, except that they are dummy variables (i.e., they take values of 0 or 1 only). The interpretation of the coefficients β_6, β_7, and β_8 is that being a single person household or having a nondriving spouse (or one who works but shares the work trip with the commuter) inclines the traveler toward transit (as compared to not being in that group), whereas being female or in a household with a working spouse who commutes independently to work inclines one toward auto use (as compared to being male or in a different type of household). Note that when we interpret these results, we are making statements about how one group's preference differs from another's. The dummy variable divides the population into two subgroups, and its coefficients measures some difference betwen the subgroups. It would make no sense to add a ninth variable in the model, defined as

$$x_{An9} = \begin{cases} 1 & \text{if male,} \\ 0 & \text{if otherwise,} \end{cases}$$

$$x_{Tn9} = 0,$$

(4.27)

because it would reflect exactly the same effect as the eighth variable. In technical terms we would say that the coefficients of these two variables cannot be *identified* because it is impossible to tell the effect of one from the other. (We will discuss identifiability further in later chapters.)

Binary Logit Example

Our second example is a binary logit model using data from a 1968 survey in the Metropolitan Washington area (Cambridge Systematics 1976). (This large data base will be used for a subsequent example in this book—a multiple-choice model.) As in Lisco's model the two travel alternatives are auto and transit. In this case, however, transit is the bus mode rather than rail rapid transit.

The specification of the model is summarized in table 4.2. Note that here there are seven coefficients labeled $\beta_1, \ldots, \beta_7$. Rather than discuss each variable in detail, we consider only the relevant differences between the utilities defined in tables 4.1 and 4.2.

1. Travel time has been divided into two components, in-vehicle and out-of-vehicle time. This division reflects the observation that travelers would generally prefer to spend a minute traveling in a vehicle than a minute

Table 4.2
Binary logit model: $P_n(A) = e^{V_{An}}/(e^{V_{An}} + e^{V_{Tn}})$

	β_1	β_2	β_3	β_4	β_5	β_6	β_7
Auto utility, V_{An}	1	Auto in-vehicle time (min)	Auto out-of-vehicle time (min)	Auto out-of-pocket cost (¢)	0	Household auto ownership	1 if workplace is in downtown Washington; 0 otherwise
Transit utility, V_{Tn}	0	Transit in-vehicle time (min)	Transit out-of-vehicle time (min)	0	Transit fare (¢)	0	0
Estimated coefficients	1.454	−0.00897	−0.0308	−0.0115	−0.00708	0.770	−0.561

waiting for or walking to one. In the case of the transit mode, out-of-vehicle time includes walking to a bus stop, waiting for the vehicle, any transfer time, and walking from a bus stop to the final destination. Auto out-of-vehicle time includes time spent going to and from the vehicle.

The coefficients of both time variables are negative, as expected, and the coefficient of out-of-vehicle time is about two and a half times that of in-vehicle time. This ratio is typical for work mode choice models.

2. The two time-related variables are treated as generic; however, the cost variable is treated as *alternative specific*. Basically it is assumed that a minute has the same marginal effect on each alternative's utility, whereas a cent in fare and out-of-pocket cost have *different* marginal effects. This may be attributable to differences in how people perceive auto costs and transit fares, since the former are not usually incurred directly out of pocket with each trip made.

3. The alternative-specific socioeconomic variables used are entirely different from those used by Lisco. Here household automobile ownership and a dummy variable for whether the traveler works downtown are used. The auto ownership variable obviously reflects the important effect of having a large number of autos available in choosing to use the auto mode. The dummy variable for whether or not the traveler works downtown reflects the fact that auto use to downtown areas has associated with it a high degree of travel time unreliability. Even though the mean time may be identical for a suburban- and urban-destined worker, the variance of the urban traveler's time will generally be much greater. The uncertainty about arrival time may induce downtown workers to leave from home somewhat earlier than their suburban counterparts in order to avoid being late for work too frequently. This extra time may be viewed as a source of disutility to the urban traveler (see Abkowitz 1980).

4.4 Maximum Likelihood Estimation of Binary Choice Models

We turn now to the problem of econometrically inferring the parameters $\beta_1, \ldots, \beta_K$ from a sample of observations. We will restrict our discussion in this section to the most typical case where our data consists of individuals drawn at random from the population. (Extensions to other types of sampling procedures are developed in chapter 8.)

Each observation consists of the following:

1. An indicator variable defined as

$$y_{in} = \begin{cases} 1 & \text{if person } n \text{ chose alternative } i, \\ 0 & \text{if person } n \text{ chose alternative } j. \end{cases}$$

(Note that y_{jn} is defined trivially by the identity $y_{in} + y_{jn} \equiv 1$.)
2. Two vectors of attributes x_{in} and x_{jn}, each containing K values of the relevant variables.

In practice it may be necessary to construct x_{in} and x_{jn} from various sources. For example, the travel times and costs used in the examples of section 4.3 were derived from engineering estimates of operating speeds, wait and walk time, auto operating, and parking costs. In addition care must be exercised to ensure that the sample consists of individuals for whom both alternatives are feasible. Referring again to the preceeding examples, travelers who worked or lived in places where no transit service was provided were eliminated from the sample.

Given a sample of N observations, our problem then becomes one of finding estimates $\hat{\beta}_1, \hat{\beta}_2, \ldots, \hat{\beta}_K$ that have some or all of the desirable properties of statistical estimators reviewed in chapter 2. We will consider in detail the most widely used estimation procedure—maximum likelihood. Least squares and other less widely used approaches are briefly discussed in section 4.6.

General Formulation for Maximum Likelihood Estimation of Binary Choice Models

Although in some instances the maximum likelihood estimation procedure can become computationally burdensome, it is conceptually quite straightforward. We will proceed by first analyzing the application of maximum likelihood to any general binary choice model and then explore the specifics of estimating the parameters of the linear probability, probit, and logit models.

Consider the likelihood of any sample of N observations. Since they are by assumption drawn at random from the whole population, the likelihood of the entire sample is the product of the likelihoods of the individual observations. If we define $\mathscr{L}^*$ as the likelihood function, we obtain

$$\mathscr{L}^*(\beta_1, \beta_2, \ldots, \beta_K) = \prod_{n=1}^{N} P_n(i)^{y_{in}} P_n(j)^{y_{jn}}, \tag{4.28}$$

where $P_n(i)$ is of course a function of $\beta_1, \ldots, \beta_K$. We will in general find it more convenient to analyze the logarithm of $\mathscr{L}^*$, denoted as $\mathscr{L}$ and written as follows:

$$\mathscr{L}(\beta_1, \ldots, \beta_K) = \sum_{n=1}^{N} [y_{in} \log P_n(i) + y_{jn} \log P_n(j)], \tag{4.29}$$

or, noting that $y_{jn} = 1 - y_{in}$ and $P_n(j) = 1 - P_n(i)$,

$$\mathscr{L}(\beta_1, \ldots, \beta_K) = \sum_{n=1}^{N} \{y_{in} \log P_n(i) + (1 - y_{in}) \log [1 - P_n(i)]\}. \tag{4.30}$$

We will then solve for the maximum of $\mathscr{L}$ by differentiating it with respect to each of the β's and setting the partial derivatives equal to zero. Thus we seek estimates $\hat{\beta}_1, \hat{\beta}_2, \ldots, \hat{\beta}_K$ that solve

$$\max \mathscr{L}(\hat{\beta}_1, \hat{\beta}_2, \ldots, \hat{\beta}_K), \tag{4.31}$$

which, if they exist, must satisfy the necessary conditions that

$$\frac{\partial \mathscr{L}}{\partial \hat{\beta}_k} = \sum_{n=1}^{N} \left\{ y_{in} \frac{\partial P_n(i)/\partial \hat{\beta}_k}{P_n(i)} + y_{jn} \frac{\partial P_n(j)/\partial \hat{\beta}_k}{P_n(j)} \right\} = 0, \quad \text{for } k = 1, \ldots, K. \tag{4.32}$$

In many cases of practical interest we can show that the likelihood function is globally concave, so that if a solution to the first-order conditions exists, it is unique. However, readers should be warned that usually it is quite possible that there will be multiple solutions to the first-order conditions, only one of which constitutes the maximum likelihood estimate.

As stated in section 2.5, the maximum likelihood estimates are, under relatively general conditions, consistent, asymptotically efficient, and asymptotically normal. Thus the asymptotic variance-covariance matrix of the estimates is given by

$$-\mathscr{E}[\nabla^2 \mathscr{L}]^{-1}, \tag{4.33}$$

where $\nabla^2 \mathscr{L}$ is the matrix of the second derivatives of the log likelihood function with respect to the parameters evaluated at the true parameters. Thus the entry in the kth row and the lth column is

$$[\nabla^2 \mathscr{L}]_{kl} = \frac{\partial^2 \mathscr{L}}{\partial \beta_k \partial \beta_l}. \tag{4.34}$$

Since we do not know the actual values of the parameters at which to evaluate the second derivatives, or the distribution of x_{in} and x_{jn} over which to take their expected value, we generally use an estimated variance-covariance matrix evaluated at the estimated parameters $\hat{\beta}$ and the sample distribution of x_{in} and x_{jn} to estimate their true distribution. Thus we use

$$\mathscr{E}\left[\frac{\partial^2 \mathscr{L}}{\partial \beta_k \partial \beta_l}\right] \cong \sum_{n=1}^{N} \left[\frac{\partial^2 [y_{in} \log P_n(i) + y_{jn} \log P_n(j)]}{\partial \beta_k \partial \beta_l}\right]_{\beta = \hat{\beta}} \qquad (4.35)$$

as a consistent estimator of the true value.

Computational Aspects of Maximum Likelihood

The solution of the first-order conditions in equation 4.32 can prove to be a significant computational problem. These equations are typically non-linear, and even simple two-variable problems are awkward to solve without the aid of a programmable calculator or computer. Two somewhat similar procedures have proved to be most useful in solving such equations.

In cases where the second derivatives can be computed without great difficulty and the likelihood function is globally concave, the Newton-Raphson method is often simple to implement and computationally efficient. As with virtually all numerical optimization procedures, the algorithm proceeds in iterations, each of which attempts to find a point that is closer to the maximum in the sense of having greater likelihood.

In terms of formal steps the Newton-Raphson algorithm operates as follows:

STEP 0:   Choose $\hat{\beta}_0 = [\beta_{01}, \beta_{02}, \ldots, \beta_{0K}]'$ as an initial guess for the parameters. ($\hat{\beta}_0 = 0$ is often convenient unless some better guess is available.) Set the iteration counter $\omega = 0$. Set e_1 and e_2 to be small positive numbers. (Typical values for e_1 and e_2 are 10^{-4} and 10^{-2}, respectively.)

STEP 1:   Linearize the function $\nabla \mathscr{L}(\beta)$ around $\hat{\beta}_\omega$. The approximate first-order conditions are given by

$$\nabla \mathscr{L}(\hat{\beta}_\omega) + \nabla^2 \mathscr{L}(\hat{\beta}_\omega)(\hat{\beta} - \hat{\beta}_\omega) = 0.$$

STEP 2:   Solve the linearized form for $\hat{\beta}_{\omega+1} = \hat{\beta}_\omega - [\nabla^2 \mathscr{L}(\hat{\beta}_\omega)]^{-1} \nabla \mathscr{L}(\hat{\beta}_\omega)$.

STEP 3:   Check if $\hat{\beta}_{\omega+1} - \hat{\beta}_\omega$ is "small." Typical criteria are

$$\left[\frac{1}{K} \sum_{k=1}^{K} (\hat{\beta}_{\omega+1,k} - \beta_{\omega k})^2\right]^{1/2} < e_1$$

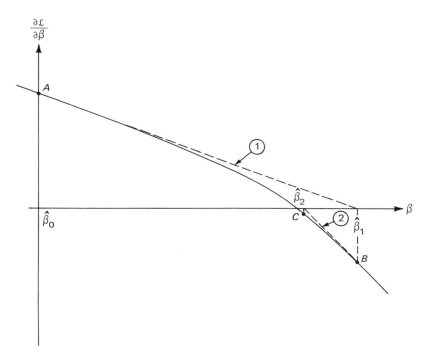

Figure 4.7
Illustration of Newton-Raphson algorithm

and/or

$$\left| \frac{\hat{\beta}_{\omega+1,k} - \hat{\beta}_{\omega k}}{\hat{\beta}_{\omega k}} \right| < e_2 \qquad \text{for all } k = 1, \ldots, K.$$

If these conditions are satisfied, terminate with $\hat{\boldsymbol{\beta}}_{\omega+1}$ as the solution. Otherwise, set $\omega = \omega + 1$, and go to step 1.

This algorithm is easiest to illustrate in one dimension (i.e., for the case where $K = 1$). Figure 4.7 depicts the iteration process. The curved solid line represents the function $\nabla \mathscr{L}(\boldsymbol{\beta})$, and we are attempting to solve for the value of $\hat{\boldsymbol{\beta}}$ that satisfies

$$\frac{\partial \mathscr{L}(\hat{\boldsymbol{\beta}})}{\partial \hat{\boldsymbol{\beta}}} = 0. \qquad (4.36)$$

In this diagram the horizontal axis represents $\boldsymbol{\beta}$, and the vertical axis is $\partial \mathscr{L}(\boldsymbol{\beta})/\partial \boldsymbol{\beta}$. The initial value of $\hat{\boldsymbol{\beta}}_0$ is zero, so point A represents the first trial value for $\partial \mathscr{L}(\hat{\beta})/\partial \hat{\beta}$. Line 1 is a linear approximation to $\partial \mathscr{L}(\hat{\beta})/\partial \hat{\beta}$ at A, and $\hat{\beta}_1$ is the next trial solution. Since $|\hat{\beta}_0 - \hat{\beta}_1|$ is large, the function $\partial \mathscr{L}(\hat{\beta})/\partial \hat{\beta}$ is now linearized around the point $(\hat{\beta}_1, \partial \mathscr{L}(\hat{\beta}_1)/\partial \hat{\beta}_1)$, yielding line 2 which passes through B. The root of the linear approximation is then solved for. This yields the point $\hat{\beta}_2$, with corresponding value of $\partial \mathscr{L}/\partial \beta$ at point C. The process would continue until the change in $\hat{\beta}$ is "small."

Almost all the other procedures used to solve for the maximum likelihood estimates can be summarized by changing steps 1 and 2 of the Newton-Raphson method. Basically these procedures find a direction where the log likelihood function is increasing and then search along that direction for the best possible estimate. Each method uses a somewhat different way of finding a search direction and searching along it. Widely used approaches include the gradient method, the Davidon-Fletcher-Powell (DFP) method (see Himmelblau 1972) and the Berndt-Hall-Hall-Hausman (BHHH) method (Berndt et al. 1974). All of these techniques have the advantage of not requiring an explicit evaluation of the matrix of second derivatives. Readers are referred to a readable text on nonlinear programming by Himmelblau (1972) or a more specific discussion of the application of these various methods to maximizing likelihood functions in Daganzo (1979). Those interested in the algorithmic aspects of the estimation problem are also urged to consult Dennis and Schnabel (1983).

Application to Specific Binary Models

For reasons discussed later, maximum likelihood is generally not used to estimate the linear probability model. First, we shall focus primarily on the application of maximum likelihood estimation to binary logit. The extension to binary probit is straightforward.

Logit   In the case of binary logit the log likelihood function becomes

$$\mathscr{L} = \sum_{n=1}^{N} \left\{ y_{in} \log \left(\frac{e^{\beta' x_{in}}}{e^{\beta' x_{in}} + e^{\beta' x_{jn}}} \right) + y_{jn} \log \left(\frac{e^{\beta' x_{jn}}}{e^{\beta' x_{jn}} + e^{\beta' x_{in}}} \right) \right\}. \tag{4.37}$$

Note that the scale parameter μ is assumed equal to 1 for convenience.

For the sake of notational simplicity we define

$$x_n = x_{in} - x_{jn} \tag{4.38}$$

so that each element of x_n is defined as $x_{nk} = x_{ink} - x_{jnk}$ for $k = 1, \ldots, K$. In this notation

$$P_n(i) = \frac{1}{1 + e^{-\boldsymbol{\beta}'\mathbf{x}_n}} \quad \text{and} \quad P_n(j) = \frac{e^{-\boldsymbol{\beta}'\mathbf{x}_n}}{1 + e^{-\boldsymbol{\beta}'\mathbf{x}_n}}.$$

We also note that

$$\frac{\partial \log P_n(i)}{\partial (\boldsymbol{\beta}'\mathbf{x}_n)} = \frac{e^{-\boldsymbol{\beta}'\mathbf{x}_n}}{(1 + e^{-\boldsymbol{\beta}'\mathbf{x}_n})^2} \cdot (1 + e^{-\boldsymbol{\beta}'\mathbf{x}_n}) = P_n(j) \tag{4.39}$$

and

$$\frac{\partial \log P_n(j)}{\partial (\boldsymbol{\beta}'\mathbf{x}_n)} = -P_n(i). \tag{4.40}$$

So

$$\frac{\partial \mathscr{L}(\boldsymbol{\beta})}{\partial \beta_k} = \sum_{n=1}^{N} [y_{in} P_n(j) x_{nk} - y_{jn} P_n(i) x_{nk}]$$

$$= \sum_{n=1}^{N} [y_{in}(1 - P_n(i)) - (1 - y_{in}) P_n(i)] x_{nk} \tag{4.41}$$

$$= \sum_{n=1}^{N} [y_{in} - P_n(i)] x_{nk}, \qquad k = 1, \dots, K.$$

Thus, to find the maximum likelihood estimate, we have to solve a system of K nonlinear equations in K unknowns $\hat{\beta}_1, \hat{\beta}_2, \dots, \hat{\beta}_K$ of the form

$$\sum_{n=1}^{N} [y_{in} - P_n(i)] x_{nk} = 0, \qquad k = 1, \dots, K. \tag{4.42}$$

The second derivatives can also be solved for as follows:

$$\frac{\partial^2 \mathscr{L}}{\partial \beta_k \partial \beta_l} = -\sum_{n=1}^{N} P_n(i)(1 - P_n(i)) x_{nk} x_{nl}. \tag{4.43}$$

Under certain regularity conditions, if there is a solution to the first-order conditions of equation 4.42, it is the only solution. To show this, we need only to prove that the log likelihood is globally concave. A sufficient condition for this is that the matrix of second derivatives is negative semidefinite for all values of $\boldsymbol{\beta}$. If we denote $\mathbf{A}$ as an $N \times K$ matrix of real values with entries

$$a_{nk} = [P_n(i)(1 - P_n(i))]^{1/2} x_{nk},$$

then the matrix

$\mathbf{A'A} = \nabla^2 \mathscr{L}.$

Since all the entries in $\mathbf{A}$ are real, $\mathbf{A'A}$ is positive semidefinite, and $-\mathbf{A'A}$ is therefore negative semidefinite.

A few aspects of the maximum likelihood estimates for logit are worth noting. First, suppose x_{nk} is an alternative-specific constant so that x_{nk} always equals 1. In this instance the kth first-order condition simplifies to

$$\sum_{n=1}^{N} [y_{in} - P_n(i)] = 0, \tag{4.44}$$

implying that

$$\sum_{n=1}^{N} y_{in} = \sum_{n=1}^{N} P_n(i). \tag{4.45}$$

In words, this means that the total number of individuals in the sample who are observed choosing alternative i will equal the sum (taken over the entire sample) of the choice probabilities when evaluated at the maximum likelihood estimates. (Since $y_{jn} = 1 - y_{in}$ and $P_n(j) = 1 - P_n(i)$, this will hold for alternative j as well.) This property holds regardless of the specification of the other variables. Viewed another way, the maximum likelihood estimators have the desirable property that the predicted share choosing i (of the sample on which the model was estimated) equals the observed share.

This property extends to the case of alternative-specific dummy variables. Suppose a variable is defined as

$$x_{ink} = \begin{cases} 1 & \text{for some subset of the sample,} \\ 0 & \text{for the remainder of the sample,} \end{cases}$$

$x_{jnk} = 0.$

In this case $x_{nk} = x_{ink} - x_{jnk}$ is 1 for the relevant subset of the sample, and 0 otherwise. Now let us order the observations so that the first N' falls into the group for which $x_{nk} = 1$. The kth first-order condition then reduces to

$$\sum_{n=1}^{N'} [y_{in} - P_n(i)] = 0, \tag{4.46}$$

or

$$\sum_{n=1}^{N'} y_{in} = \sum_{n=1}^{N'} P_n(i). \tag{4.47}$$

In words, this implies that *within the subset* of the sample defined by the alternative-specific dummy variable, the sum of the predicted choice probabilities for alternative i will equal the number of people actually choosing it.

We can also use the first-order conditions to obtain a slightly different perspective on why it is meaningless to have two alternative-specific constants, one in each alternative. Basically one can show that having two constants will produce a situation where there are multiple solutions to the first-order conditions. If the constants are the first two variables in $\mathbf{x}_n$, and if $[\hat{\beta}_1, \hat{\beta}_2, \ldots, \hat{\beta}_K]$ is a solution to equation 4.42, then $[\hat{\beta}_1 + \alpha, \hat{\beta}_2 + \alpha, \hat{\beta}_3, \ldots, \hat{\beta}_K]$ will also be a solution for any constant α. In a geometric sense the log likelihood function will have a "ridge" of points, all of which are maxima.

Probit Solution for the maximum likelihood estimates for binary probit exactly parallels the solution for logit. Using the same notational convention,

$$\mathscr{L} = \sum_{n=1}^{N} \{ y_{in} \log \Phi(\boldsymbol{\beta}'\mathbf{x}_n) + (1 - y_{in}) \log [1 - \Phi(\boldsymbol{\beta}'\mathbf{x}_n)] \}. \tag{4.48}$$

The first derivatives are

$$\frac{\partial \mathscr{L}}{\partial \beta_k} = \sum_{n=1}^{N} \left[\frac{y_{in}\phi(\boldsymbol{\beta}'\mathbf{x}_n)}{\Phi(\boldsymbol{\beta}'\mathbf{x}_n)} - \frac{(1 - y_{in})\phi(\boldsymbol{\beta}'\mathbf{x}_n)}{1 - \Phi(\boldsymbol{\beta}'\mathbf{x}_n)} \right] x_{nk} \quad \text{for } k = 1, \ldots, K, \tag{4.49}$$

where ϕ is the standardized normal density function.

We again set these derivatives equal to zero and solve for $\hat{\beta}_1, \hat{\beta}_2, \ldots, \hat{\beta}_K$. As in the case of binary logit, under certain regularity conditions this solution can be shown to be unique (see Daganzo 1980).

4.5 Examples of Maximum Likelihood Estimation

Simple Example Revisited

To illustrate the application of maximum likelihood to binary logit estimation, we return to the simple two-variable problem described in equation 4.11. In this model the two alternatives again are labeled auto A and transit T, and we assume that the specification of the model is as displayed in table 4.3. The two variables correspond to an alternative specific constant and a single generic variable, labeled for convenience as travel time.

Table 4.3
Simple binary example

	β_1		β_2
Auto utility, V_{An}	1		Auto travel time (min)
Transit utility, V_{Tn}	0		Transit travel time (min)

Table 4.4
Data for simple binary example

Observation number	Auto time	Transit time	Chosen alternative
1	52.9	4.4	Transit
2	4.1	28.5	Transit
3	4.1	86.9	Auto
4	56.2	31.6	Transit
5	51.8	20.2	Transit
6	0.2	91.2	Auto
7	27.6	79.7	Auto
8	89.9	2.2	Transit
9	41.5	24.5	Transit
10	95.0	43.5	Transit
11	99.1	8.4	Transit
12	18.5	84.0	Auto
13	82.0	38.0	Auto
14	8.6	1.6	Transit
15	22.5	74.1	Auto
16	51.4	83.8	Auto
17	81.0	19.2	Transit
18	51.0	85.0	Auto
19	62.2	90.1	Auto
20	95.1	22.2	Transit
21	41.6	91.5	Auto

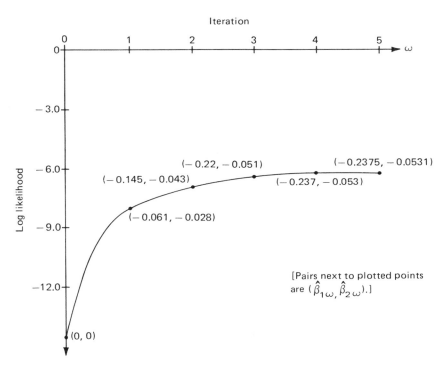

Figure 4.8
Log likelihood values in estimation of simple binary logit example

A sample of 21 observations has been generated and is shown in table 4.4. The actual data were created using Monte Carlo simulation, assuming the true coefficients in equation 4.11 (i.e., $\beta_1 = -0.25$ and $\beta_2 = -0.05$). The Newton-Raphson method was then used on the sample to solve for the logit maximum likelihood estimates. Figure 4.8 plots the values of the log likelihood function over the five iterations. The pattern of convergence, where the first few iterations come quite close to the maximum of the log likelihood function, is quite typical. At convergence the greatest percentage change in either of the coefficients estimates between consecutive iterations was about 0.2%, and the root mean square of the changes was less than 0.0005.

Table 4.5 is a summary table of the final coefficient estimates in a typical format for reporting choice model estimation results. Each row corresponds to a variable, and the columns list the coefficient number, a

Table 4.5
Estimation results for simple binary logit example

Variable number	Variable name	Coefficient estimate	Asymptotic standard error	t statistic
1	Auto constant	-0.2375	0.7505	-0.32
2	Travel time (min)	-0.0531	0.0206	-2.57

Summary statistics
Number of observations = 21
Number of cases = 21
$\mathscr{L}(\mathbf{0}) = -14.556$
$\mathscr{L}(\mathbf{c}) = -14.532$
$\mathscr{L}(\hat{\boldsymbol{\beta}}) = -6.166$
$-2[\mathscr{L}(\mathbf{0}) - \mathscr{L}(\hat{\boldsymbol{\beta}})] = 16.780$
$-2[\mathscr{L}(\mathbf{c}) - \mathscr{L}(\hat{\boldsymbol{\beta}})] = 16.732$
$\rho^2 = 0.576$
$\bar{\rho}^2 = 0.439$

mnemonic description of the variable, the coefficient estimate, its estimated asymptotic standard error, and its asymptotic t statistic (see chapter 2 for a description of how these are computed).

Below these figures is a group of summary statistics for the entire estimation run. These are as follows (the reader may wish to refer back to chapter 2 for a description of some of these statistics):

1. The number of observations.
2. The number of cases, which is defined as the sum of the number of alternatives available to each observation minus the number of observations. (For binary models this value always equals the number of observations. When we consider multiple-choice situations, the number of cases will exceed the number of observations.)
3. $\mathscr{L}(\mathbf{0})$, which is the value of the log likelihood function when all the parameters are zero. In binary choice models it is the log likelihood of the most naive possible model, that is, one in which the choice probabilities are $\frac{1}{2}$ for each of the two alternatives.
4. $\mathscr{L}(\mathbf{c})$, which is the value of the log likelihood function when only an alternative-specific constant is included. This corresponds to the log likelihood for another naive model in which the choice probability for each

alternative simply equals the fraction of the sample choosing the alternative. In this simple case 10 of the 21 observed chose auto, and 11 chose transit, so for the naive model $P_n(\text{auto}) = 0.476$ and $P_n(\text{transit}) = 0.524$. $\mathscr{L}(\mathbf{c})$ will be greater than or equal to $\mathscr{L}(\mathbf{0})$.

5. $\mathscr{L}(\hat{\boldsymbol{\beta}})$, which is the value of the log likelihood function at its maximum.

6. $-2(\mathscr{L}(\mathbf{0}) - \mathscr{L}(\hat{\boldsymbol{\beta}}))$, which is a statistic used to test the null hypothesis that all the parameters are zero. It is asymptotically distributed as χ^2 with K degrees of freedom (see section 2.6). Here $K = 2$, and the value of the statistic is 16.780, which indicates that we can reject the null hypothesis that all the parameters are zero at the 0.01 level of significance.

7. $-2(\mathscr{L}(\mathbf{c}) - \mathscr{L}(\hat{\boldsymbol{\beta}}))$, which is another test statistic. This is used to test the null hypothesis that all the parameters other than the alternative-specific constant are all zero. It is asymptotically distributed as χ^2 with $K - 1$ degrees of freedom in binary choice models. Here $K - 1 = 1$, and the value of the statistic is 16.732, indicating that the null hypothesis can be rejected at the 0.01 level of significance.

In addition the table reports two measures of goodness of fit, ρ^2 and $\bar{\rho}^2$.

8. ρ^2, an informal goodness-of-fit index that measures the fraction of an initial log likelihood value explained by the model. It is defined as $1 - (\mathscr{L}(\hat{\boldsymbol{\beta}})/\mathscr{L}(\mathbf{0}))$. For a binary choice model with an alternative specific constant, ρ^2 must lie between 0 and 1. ρ^2 is analogous to R^2 used in regression, but it should be used with somewhat more caution. Values of ρ^2 will depend on the type of model being estimated. The measure is most useful in comparing two specifications developed on the exact same data. Here $\rho^2 = 0.576$ (ρ^2 is occasionally defined as $1 - \mathscr{L}(\hat{\boldsymbol{\beta}})/\mathscr{L}(\mathbf{c})$). Although ρ^2 is most often used informally, it can be shown that $\rho^2/(1 - \rho^2)$ is asymptotically distributed as F with (K, K) degrees of freedom. When the alternative definition $\rho^2 = 1 - \mathscr{L}(\hat{\boldsymbol{\beta}})/\mathscr{L}(\mathbf{c})$ is used, then $[K/(K - 1)](\rho^2/1 - \rho^2)$ is approximately F distributed with $(K - 1, K)$ degrees of freedom under the null hypothesis that $\boldsymbol{\beta} = \mathbf{c}$.

9. $\bar{\rho}^2$, another informal goodness-of-fit measure which is similar to ρ^2 but corrected for the number of parameters estimated. As shown in chapter 7, this measure is defined as $\bar{\rho}^2 = 1 - (\mathscr{L}(\hat{\boldsymbol{\beta}}) - K)/\mathscr{L}(\mathbf{0})$.

The literature on discrete choice modeling of transport demand will often make reference to a third measure of goodness of fit known as "% right." This statistic is defined as $(100/N) \cdot \sum_n \hat{y}_n$, where $\hat{y}_n$ is 1 if the highest predicted probability corresponds to the chosen alternative, and 0 otherwise. We do not recommend the use of this statistic for evaluating model performance because it can mask poor goodness of fit. For example, suppose we have a sample of 100 observations, 90 of which chose alternative 1 and 10 of which chose alternative 2. Now suppose we adopt the model $P_n(1) = 0.9 \, \forall n$. The "% right" statistic will be 90% for this model, despite the fact that it completely misclassifies every observation choosing alternative 2!

A different approach to calculate the "% right" is to use the calculated choice probabilities as follows:

$$\frac{100}{N} \sum_n \sum_i P_n(i)^{y_{in}}.$$

For the simple model assumed before this measure is equal to

$$90 \times 0.9 + 10 \times 0.1 = 82\%,$$

which is smaller than the 90% right obtained with the first method. However, in this later method of prediction we maintain the desirable property of replicating the shares of the alternatives as follows:

$$\frac{1}{N} \sum_n P_n(i) = \frac{1}{N} \sum_n y_{in}.$$

This last measure of "% right" is better represented by the value of the log likelihood function which is the objective function being maximized and is more sensitive to low values of predicted probabilities for the chosen alternative.

Thus the preferred procedure for evaluating a model is to use the log likelihood value or transforms of it, such as ρ^2 and $\bar{\rho}^2$. The insensitivity of the "% right" statistic, in addition to its potential for completely misleading indications, argue against its use.

Washington, D.C., Logit Model Revisited

To show how actual empirical results from maximum likelihood estimation may be presented, we return to the binary logit example given in section 4.3 (see table 4.2 for a summary of the specification). Table 4.6 summarizes the estimates using the same format for presenting model estimation results as in table 4.5. Here our sample consisted of 1,476 work trips made in

Table 4.6
Washington, D.C., binary logit model

Variable number	Variable name	Coefficient estimate	Asymptotic standard error	t statistic
1	Auto constant	1.45	0.393	3.70
2	In-vehicle time (min)	−0.00897	0.00630	−1.42
3	Out-of-vehicle time (min)	−0.0308	0.0106	−2.90
4	Auto out-of-pocket cost (¢)	−0.0115	0.00262	−4.39
5	Transit fare	−0.00708	0.00378	−1.87
6	Auto ownership (specific to auto mode)	0.770	0.213	3.16
7	Downtown workplace Dummy (specific to auto mode)	−0.561	0.306	−1.84

Summary statistics
Number of observations = 1476
Number of cases = 1476
$\mathscr{L}(0) = -1023$
$\mathscr{L}(\hat{\beta}) = -347.4$
$-2[\mathscr{L}(0) - \mathscr{L}(\hat{\beta})] = 1371.7$
$\rho^2 = 0.660$
$\bar{\rho}^2 = 0.654$

Washington, D.C., in 1968. (This model was estimated in 1973 using a version of the estimation program that did not provide all the summary statistics listed in table 4.5.)

Note that for all the coefficients, except the one for in-vehicle time, we can reject the null hypothesis that the true value is zero at the 0.10 significance level, though some others are not statistically different from zero at the 0.05 significance level. (For a two-tailed test the critical values of the quasi-t statistic are ± 1.65 and ±1.96 for the 0.10 and 0.05 significance levels, respectively.) In addition we can reject the null hypothesis that all the parameters are jointly zero at the 99% level.

We will return to the problem of interpreting estimation results is subsequent chapters. At this point the reader should gain familiarity with reading tables 4.5 and 4.6 and understand the mechanics of the various statistical tests we have discussed. If necessary, review the appropriate sections of chapter 2 before proceeding. Further formal and informal means of evaluating model specifications will be developed in chapter 7.

4.6   Other Estimation Methods for Binary Choice Models

Linear Probability Models

An alternative estimation procedure to maximum likelihood is *least squares*. This approach applies most naturally to the linear probability model. In its simplest form one can regress y_{in}, the observed choice indicator, on $\mathbf{x}_n = \mathbf{x}_{in} - \mathbf{x}_{jn}$, the vector of attribute differences.

This procedure has the advantage of computational simplicity and can be done with any of the widely available computer statistical analysis packages. Although these estimates are consistent and unbiased, they can be shown to be less than fully efficient because the disturbances are heteroskedastic. To see this, note that if we write

$$y_{in} = \boldsymbol{\beta}'\mathbf{x}_n + \xi_n, \tag{4.50}$$

the disturbance ξ_n can take only two values: $P_n(i)$ and $1 - P_n(i)$. These two values occur with probabilities $[1 - P_n(i)]$ and $P_n(i)$, respectively. Thus $\text{var}(\xi_n) = P_n(i)[1 - P_n(i)]$, which is obviously not constant for all n. One possible solution is to use ordinary least squares to obtain initial estimates for $\boldsymbol{\beta}$, use those estimated values to compute an estimated $P_n(i)$, and apply weighted least squares. However, simulation experiments reported by Domencich and McFadden (1975) indicate that this approach tends to weight extreme observations too heavily.

A more fundamental problem with estimating the linear probability model was discussed earlier; some observations will be inconsistent with the estimated model in that they will choose an alternative with a predicted probability of zero. This will occur because of sampling error even when the model is correctly specified. One approach to resolving this is constrained least squares, in which we restrict the least squares estimates to the parameters that make all observations consistent. This of course increases the cost of estimation and requires a special computer program. Moreover it will not guarantee that predictions made on another sample of data will not have inconsistencies. Finally, although the constrained least squares estimates are consistent, they are no longer unbiased and are more sensitive to specification errors.

These issues are explored in greater detail by Domencich and McFadden (1975) who conclude that the simple ordinary least squares estimates are probably to be preferred.

Nonlinear Models: Least Squares and Berkson's Method

Least squares procedures can also be applied to probit, logit, or other choice models. In general, the estimates will be the parameters $\hat{\beta}$ that solve

$$\min_{\beta} Q = \sum_{n=1}^{N} [y_{in} - P_n(i)]^2. \tag{4.51}$$

The necessary conditions for a solution to equation 4.51 are

$$\frac{\partial Q}{\partial \hat{\beta}_k} = -2 \sum_{n=1}^{N} [y_{in} - P_n(i)] \frac{\partial P_n(i)}{\partial \hat{\beta}_k} = 0, \qquad \text{for all } k, \tag{4.52}$$

or more simply

$$\sum_{n=1}^{N} [y_{in} - P_n(i)] \frac{\partial P_n(i)}{\partial \hat{\beta}_k} = 0, \qquad k = 1, \ldots, K. \tag{4.53}$$

This approach yields consistent estimates (see White 1980). However, it can be computationally difficult and has no theoretical advantage over maximum likelihood. It has therefore not been used in actual practice.

An alternative least squares procedure developed by Berkson (1953) does offer some significant advantages over maximum likelihood in certain instances. Berkson's procedure is based on the observation that linear-in-parameters binary choice models can be easily transformed to put them in a form amenable to standard regression analysis. Any such model can be written as

$$P_n(i) = F(\beta' x_n), \tag{4.54}$$

where x_n is defined again as $x_{in} - x_{jn}$. Thus as long as F, a proper cumulative distribution function, is strictly monotonically increasing, we can write

$$F^{-1}(P_n(i)) = \beta' x_n, \tag{4.55}$$

in which the right-hand side is a simple linear function. To be more specific, consider binary logit and probit. Here we have the following:

$$\log \left[\frac{P_n(i)}{P_n(j)} \right] = \beta' x_n \qquad \text{for the binary logit model} \tag{4.55}$$

and

$$\Phi^{-1}[P_n(i)] = \beta' x_n \qquad \text{for binary probit.} \tag{4.56}$$

The natural problem with applying this result is that $P_n(i)$ is of course not observed; all we observe is y_{in}, a $(0, 1)$ indicator of whether the person chose alternative i or j. Berkson's procedure divides the sample into homogeneous subgroups and uses the *share of each group* choosing each alternative as estimates of the choice probabilities. These shares, appropriately transformed, become the left-hand side variables in the regression.

More formally, Berkson's procedure assumes that the sample of N decision makers can be divided into $G(< N)$ subgroups of size $N_1, N_2, N_3,$ $\ldots, N_G$, where

$$\sum_{g=1}^{G} N_g = N.$$

Each subgroup is assumed to be homogeneous in terms of $x_n = x_{in} - x_{jn}$. We denote x_g, $g = 1, \ldots, G$ as the value of x_n for the gth group. We also define R_{ig} and R_{jg} as the share of the gth group choosing alternatives i and j, respectively. We use R_{ig} and R_{jg} as estimates of $P_n(i)$ and $P_n(j)$, respectively, for group g. For logit this implies that we estimate the parameters via the regression

$$\log\left(\frac{R_{ig}}{R_{jg}}\right) = \beta' x_g + \xi_g.$$

Cox (1970) notes that the disturbance term ξ_g is heteroscedastic and suggests a two-stage estimator to gain efficiency. The heteroscedasticity arises because $R_{ig} \cdot N_g$ is binomially distributed (Domencich and McFadden 1975, p. 109). For probit we use

$$\Phi^{-1}(R_{ig}) = \beta' x_g + \xi_g.$$

ξ_g is a disturbance term in the regression attributable to the fact that R_{ig} is only an estimate of $P_n(i)$. In both cases we have G grouped observations.

The main advantage of Berkson's method is that it allows use of standard regression packages and reduces the number of data points from the original N to a smaller number G. It can be shown that this procedure yields consistent estimates of β, where consistency is defined here as $N_g \to \infty$ for all g. Despite its obvious appeal Berkson's method is not widely used in travel demand analysis for a number of significant reasons. First, it requires division of the sample into homogeneous groups. As Domencich and McFadden (1975) note, even if each of the K variables in the model can take only 2 values, this still implies 2^K homogeneous groups. For typical values of K this implies a very large value of G. (For $K = 10$ there would be 1,024 different groups.) Second, travel demand data are quite expensive to gather, so the total sample may be small, and the number of observations per group will be small if G is large. As a consequence the variance of R_{ig} and R_{jg} will be large.

A third, related problem is that when N_g is small for many groups, it will not be at all unusual in some groups for one of the observed shares choosing i or j to be zero. This will make $F^{-1}(R_{ig})$ undefined for logit or probit models, requiring that these cells not be used or that more aggregated groups be formed.

Fourth, since many of the attributes used in travel demand analysis are continuous, forming groups requires an arbitrary categorization along some attributes and the use of the within-group mean as "representative" attributes for the group. This will tend to introduce an error-in-variables problem into the model. Some simple simulation results reported by Domencich and McFadden (1975) indicate that this may not be of great practical importance.

Despite these difficulties Berkson's method should be considered when appropriate and will generally be most useful under the following conditions:

1. The available sample is extremely large, as is occasionally the case with air traffic data or in some freight demand problems, where large samples of waybills may be available.
2. The data are only available in aggregated form, as is often the case with the U.S. Census data (aggregation in this case is to preserve the anonymity of respondents).
3. The model structure uses only a small number of categorized variables so that the number of cells is reasonably small.
4. Each respondent to a survey is observed making a large number of repeated decisions so that each individual's choices form a natural basis for grouping.

Other Estimation Methods

Although both maximum likelihood and least squares estimations have been used in almost all actual applications of binary choice models, they by no means exhaust the full spectrum of possible estimation methods. There are other approaches for estimating choice models that differ fundamentally from these two procedures.

One interesting class of approaches includes methods that are similar to maximum likelihood but optimize a somewhat different function. An example of such a procedure is given in chapter 8, where we show that even though the likelihood function is extremely complicated, there exists another simpler function that yields consistent (though not necessarily as efficient) parameter estimates.

A second class of procedures are what might be termed *nonparametric* estimation methods. By this we mean that they do not make a specific distributional assumption on the ε's but rather hypothesize that the distribution of the disturbances belongs to a class that has some very general properties. One relatively intuitive procedure was proposed by Manski (1975). This approach, termed *maximum score estimation*, selects parameters so that the fraction of the sample who chose the alternative with greatest systematic component of the utility is maximized. (This is equivalent to maximizing the % right statistic discussed in section 4.5.) Manski shows that the maximum score estimates are not in general unique because more than one value of the parameter estimate $\hat{\beta}$ may yield the same % right value. As the sample gets larger, the problem of nonuniqueness typically becomes less significant.

Maximum score estimates are consistent under some very general conditions. The most relevant of these conditions is that for each individual in the population the choice probability must be monotonically increasing with its systematic component of utility—that is, the greater V_{in} is, the greater $P_n(i)$. We do not even require that each individual's disturbances come from the same distribution as long as all the disturbances have this property.

Another procedure proposed recently by Cosslett (1983) is slightly more restrictive than Manski's approach in that it requires all individual's disturbances to come from the same unknown distribution. Cosslett then derives estimates of the choice probabilities as a function of $V_{in} - V_{jn}$ along with $\hat{\beta}$. Though quite general, the procedure is somewhat difficult computationally and is still being studied. Actually Cosslett's method is a maximum likelihood estimator where both the choice model and the coefficients β are unknown. We include it in this section because it is so different from the usual maximum likelihood approaches.

4.7 Summary

This chapter has taken the abstract theory developed in chapter 3 and shown how it can be translated into an operational method for analyzing binary choice situations. We have shown that it is useful to partition the utility of an alternative into two parts, a systematic component (V) and a random disturbance (ε). Different assumptions about the distributions of the disturbances lead to different binary choice models.

The most useful situations are where the systematic component of the utility is a linear function of the parameters. We expressed this as

$$V_{in} = \boldsymbol{\beta}'\mathbf{x}_{in} \quad \text{and} \quad V_{jn} = \boldsymbol{\beta}'\mathbf{x}_{jn},$$

where $\mathbf{x}_{in}$ and $\mathbf{x}_{jn}$ are variables that are functions of the attributes of i and j, respectively, as well as those of decision maker n.

Three practical models were derived using different assumptions about the disturbance terms. These were as follows:

$\varepsilon_{jn} - \varepsilon_{in}$ uniform $\rightarrow$ linear probability model

ε_{in} and ε_{jn} normal $\rightarrow$ binary probit model

$\varepsilon_{jn} - \varepsilon_{in}$ logistic $\rightarrow$ binary logit model

The latter two models are numerically quite similar, though logit is analytically the more tractable.

Maximum likelihood and least square estimators for the unknown parameters were derived. Some of the computational aspects of maximum likelihood estimation were presented along with some examples of hypothetical and actual binary choice models.

In the next chapter we extend much of our analysis to the more general case of interest, *multinomial choice models*. We will focus primarily on extensions of binary logit, exploiting the ease with which it can be generalized beyond binary situations.

5 Multinomial Choice

We now turn to the development of models for the more general case where the choice set, C_n, can consist of more than two alternatives. (Recall that the choice set is subscripted by the person's index, to indicate that choice sets may vary across individuals.) In such instances the derivation of useful choice models and appropriate estimation methods becomes considerably more complex than for binary choice analysis. In particular, it is not sufficient simply to specify the univariate distribution of the differences in disturbances, $\varepsilon_{jn} - \varepsilon_{in}$. Instead, we will have to characterize the complete joint distribution of all the disturbances.

Our presentation proceeds as follows. In section 5.1 we analyze the general problem of multinomial choice for random utility models. Then, due to the ease with which it extends to multinomial choice analysis, we will focus most of our attention on *multinomial logit* (MNL). The derivation, properties, estimation, and an example of this model will be covered in the next five sections. Section 5.7 then briefly describes some models that differ from multinomial logit by allowing for less restrictive assumptions about the distribution of disturbance terms. A summary of the chapter is given in section 5.8.

5.1 Theory of Multinomial Choice

We begin by assuming that for the problem being studied, the analyst can define some set C that includes all potential choices for some population. We call C the universal, or master, choice set, and define J to be the number of elements in it. Each member of the population has some subset of C as his or her choice set. For example, in a mode choice model, C may consist of eight elements:

1. driving alone,
2. sharing a ride,
3. taxi,
4. motorcycle,
5. bicycle,
6. walking,
7. transit bus,
8. rail rapid transit.

However, for any particular traveler the actual choice set, C_n, may be considerably smaller. A worker may live or work beyond the reasonable limits of transit service, thus eliminating options 7 and 8. Some workers may not own an automobile, making driving alone infeasible. For others the work trip may be too long for walking to be viewed as a viable option.

Obviously what constitutes a feasible alternative for any particular individual may be difficult for the analyst to determine. How far is "too far to walk"? Is bicycling really feasible in certain climates? Do some people know about the existence of transit services that they might use? These types of questions require the analyst to make informed judgments about what Manski (1977) terms the *choice set generation process*. At this stage we will assume that each individual's choice set can be specified by the analyst using some reasonable, deterministic rules.

We must realize, however, that this imputation of the choice set by the analyst is in effect a potentially crude model of a complex interaction between an individual decision maker and his or her environment. It is possible to formulate choice models that explicitly account for choice set generation, albeit at a great cost in terms of complexity. The reader is directed to Swait and Ben-Akiva (1984a, b) for a review of the relevant literature and the estimation of several models of probabilistic choice set generation. Specific model formulations are discussed in Ben-Akiva and Swait (1984a).

Given that each individual has a feasible choice set denoted by C_n, we define $J_n \leq J$ to be the number of feasible choices. Following the development of random utility theory of chapter 3, the probability that any element i in C_n is chosen by decision maker n is given by

$$P_n(i) = Pr(U_{in} \geq U_{jn}, \forall j \in C_n). \tag{5.1}$$

As in chapter 4 we divide the utility of each alternative into a deterministic and random component:

$$P_n(i) = Pr(U_{in} \geq U_{jn}, \forall j \in C_n, j \neq i)$$

$$= Pr(V_{in} + \varepsilon_{in} \geq V_{jn} + \varepsilon_{jn}, \forall j \in C_n, j \neq i) \tag{5.2}$$

$$= Pr(\varepsilon_{jn} \leq V_{in} - V_{jn} + \varepsilon_{in}, \forall j \in C_n, j \neq i).$$

Any particular multinomial choice model can be derived using equation 5.2 given specific assumptions on the joint distribution of the disturbances. Let $f(\varepsilon_{1n}, \varepsilon_{2n}, \ldots, \varepsilon_{J_n n})$ denote the joint density function of the disturbance terms.

Without loss of generality consider alternative i to be the first alternative in C_n. Then

$$P_n(1) = \int_{\varepsilon_{1n}=-\infty}^{\infty} \int_{\varepsilon_{2n}=-\infty}^{V_{1n}-V_{2n}+\varepsilon_{1n}} \cdots$$

$$\int_{\varepsilon_{J_nn}=-\infty}^{V_{1n}-V_{J_nn}+\varepsilon_{1n}} f(\varepsilon_{1n}, \varepsilon_{2n}, \ldots, \varepsilon_{J_nn})\, d\varepsilon_{J_nn}\, d\varepsilon_{J_n-1,n} \cdots d\varepsilon_{1n}$$

(5.3)

Obviously, if we are interested in cases other than $i = 1$, we can simply reorder the choices in C_n appropriately to use equation 5.3. Note that the integration is carried over a subspace of the disturbances where

$$U_{in} = \max\{U_{1n}, U_{2n}, \ldots, U_{J_nn}\}.$$

Although equation 5.3 is the most direct way of expressing the choice probability in the abstract, it is often not the most convenient way to derive $P_n(i)$ for a particular situation. Two other forms for the choice probability can also be used. In the first we denote $F_i(\varepsilon_{1n}, \varepsilon_{2n}, \ldots, \varepsilon_{J_nn})$ as the partial derivate of F (the cumulative distribution function of the disturbances) with respect to ε_{in}. Using this notation (and again assuming for convenience that the alternatives are ordered so that $i = 1$), we can express $P_n(1)$:

$$P_n(1) = \int_{\varepsilon_{1n}=-\infty}^{\infty} F_1(\varepsilon_{1n}, V_{1n} - V_{2n} + \varepsilon_{1n}, V_{1n} - V_{3n}$$

$$+ \varepsilon_{1n}, \ldots, V_{1n} - V_{J_nn} + \varepsilon_{1n})\, d\varepsilon_{1n}.$$

(5.4)

In words, equation 5.4 can be interpreted as follows. Set the disturbance ε_{1n} at some given value. The integrand is then the probability that ε_{1n} equals that value *and* all the other disturbances satisfy the condition $V_{1n} + \varepsilon_{1n} \geq V_{jn} + \varepsilon_{jn}$, $\forall j \in C_n$. By integrating over all possible values of ε_{1n}, we obtain the total probability that alternative 1 is chosen.

The third, and perhaps the most insightful way to express $P_n(i)$, is to reduce the multinomial choice problem to a binary one. To do this, we note that the condition

$$U_{in} \geq U_{jn}, \qquad \forall j \in C_n, j \neq i,$$

(5.5)

is in fact equivalent to

$$U_{in} \geq \max_{\substack{j \in C_n \\ j \neq i}} U_{jn}.$$

(5.6)

Thus we can create what is in effect a "composite" alternative out of all the elements in C_n other than i, and we use the utility of the best alternative in the composite to represent the entire composite. If U_{in} exceeds the utility of the composite alternative, then i is chosen; otherwise, it is not. Thus

$$P_n(i) = Pr\left[V_{in} + \varepsilon_{in} \geq \max_{\substack{j \in C_n \\ j \neq i}} (V_{jn} + \varepsilon_{jn}) \right]. \tag{5.7}$$

Of course, since U_{jn} is a random variable, $\max_{\substack{j \in C_n \\ j \neq i}} U_{jn}$ will also be random. Thus, to utilize equation 5.7, we will have to derive the distribution of the utility of the composite alternative from the underlying distribution of the disturbances, F. In most instances this is a formidable task. However, in the multinomial logit case it is feasible. This facet of the multinomial logit model leads to some of its most valuable properties and has made it the most widely used method for discrete choice analysis.

5.2   The Multinomial Logit Model

Definition of Multinomial Logit

The multinomial logit (MNL) model is expressed as

$$P_n(i) = \frac{e^{V_{in}}}{\sum_{j \in C_n} e^{V_{jn}}}. \tag{5.8}$$

The reader can verify straightforwardly that this reduces to binary logit when $J_n = 2$ and that equation 5.8 defines a proper probability mass function since

$$0 \leq P_n(i) \leq 1, \qquad \text{for all } i \in C_n, \tag{5.9}$$

and

$$\sum_{i \in C_n} P_n(i) = 1. \tag{5.10}$$

This model (or equivalent variants of it) can be derived in a great number of ways. Its original formulation is due to Luce (1959), a mathematical psychologist. He derived a form of equation 5.8 by making assumptions about the choice probabilities rather than the disturbances. To be consistent with the rest of this book, we derive equation 5.8 by restating a result attributed to Marschak (1960). The particular line of proof uses equation 5.7, though other forms, such as equations 5.3 or 5.4, could serve equally well.

If we assume that $U_{in} = V_{in} + \varepsilon_{in}$, for all $i \in C_n$, and that all the disturbances ε_{in} are (1) independently distributed, (2) identically distributed, and (3) Gumbel-distributed with a location parameter η, and a scale parameter $\mu > 0$, then

$$P_n(i) = \frac{e^{\mu V_{in}}}{\sum_{j \in C_n} e^{\mu V_{jn}}}. \tag{5.11}$$

As in the case of binary logit the assumption of a constant η for all alternatives, or $\eta = 0$, is not in any sense restrictive as long as each systematic utility has a constant term. Similarly the assumption that the disturbances are Gumbel distributed can be defended as an approximation to the normal density. It is used only for reasons of analytic convenience.

However, the assumption that the disturbances are independent and identically distributed (IID) represents an important restriction. First, it constrains all the disturbances to have the same scale parameter μ. Although the choice of μ is arbitrary since it simply sets the scale of the utilities (see section 4.2), the fact that each disturbance has the *same* value of μ implies that the variances of the random components of the utilities are equal. Furthermore, as we will discuss extensively in section 5.3, the assumption of independence of the disturbances may, in some situations, be difficult to defend.

Rather than derive equation 5.11 directly, we will first digress by stating some properties of the Gumbel distribution. These properties will be used in subsequent chapters, and the reader may wish to refer to them later. Relevant proofs can be found in Johnson and Kotz (1970) and Domencich and McFadden (1975).

The Gumbel Distribution: Basic Properties

Say ε is Gumbel distributed. Then

$$F(\varepsilon) = \exp[-e^{-\mu(\varepsilon - \eta)}], \qquad \mu > 0, \tag{5.12}$$

and

$$f(\varepsilon) = \mu e^{-\mu(\varepsilon - \eta)} \exp[-e^{-\mu(\varepsilon - \eta)}], \tag{5.13}$$

where η is a location parameter and μ is a positive scale parameter.

This distribution has the following properties:

1. The mode is η.
2. The mean is $\eta + \gamma/\mu$, where γ is Euler constant (~ 0.577).

3. The variance is $\pi^2/6\mu^2$.

4. If ε is Gumbel distributed with parameters (η, μ) and V, and $\alpha > 0$ are any scalar constants, then $\alpha\varepsilon + V$ is Gumbel distributed with parameters $(\alpha\eta + V, \mu/\alpha)$.

5. If ε_1 and ε_2 are independent Gumbel-distributed variates with parameters (η_1, μ) and (η_2, μ), respectively, then $\varepsilon^* = \varepsilon_1 - \varepsilon_2$ is logistically distributed:

$$F(\varepsilon^*) = \frac{1}{1 + e^{\mu(\eta_2 - \eta_1 - \varepsilon^*)}}. \tag{5.14}$$

6. If ε_1 and ε_2 are independent Gumbel distributed with parameters (η_1, μ) and (η_2, μ), respectively, then

$$\max(\varepsilon_1, \varepsilon_2)$$

is Gumbel distributed with parameters

$$\left(\frac{1}{\mu}\ln(e^{\mu\eta_1} + e^{\mu\eta_2}), \mu\right).$$

7. As a corollary to proposition 6, if $(\varepsilon_1, \varepsilon_2, \ldots, \varepsilon_J)$ are J independent Gumbel-distributed random variables with parameters (η_1, μ), (η_2, μ), $\ldots, (\eta_J, \mu)$, respectively, then $\max(\varepsilon_1, \varepsilon_2, \ldots, \varepsilon_J)$

is Gumbel distributed with parameters

$$\left(\frac{1}{\mu}\ln \sum_{j=1}^{J} e^{\mu\eta_j}, \mu\right).$$

The first three of these properties are self-explanatory; they describe the mode, mean, and variance of a Gumbel-distributed variable. Property 4 states simply that the Gumbel distribution is preserved over linear transformations. Property 5 describes the distribution of the difference between two independent Gumbel variates *that have the same scale parameter μ*. This property, along with property 4, provides a straightforward means of deriving the binary logit model.

Properties 6 and 7 state that the maximum of independent Gumbel variates that have a common scale parameter is itself Gumbel distributed. The location parameter of the maximum

$$\frac{1}{\mu}\ln \sum_{j=1}^{J} e^{\mu\eta_j}$$

is equal to the expected value of the maximum minus a constant (γ/μ). It will play an important role in much of our later analysis.

Derivation of Multinomial Logit

Given the preceding properties, the multinomial logit model can be straightforwardly derived. Our proof is a variant of one by Domencich and McFadden (1975); for convenience we will assume $\eta = 0$ for all the disturbances. If we, as before, order the alternatives so that $i = 1$, then

$$P_n(1) = Pr\left[V_{1n} + \varepsilon_{1n} \geq \max_{j=2,\ldots,J_n}(V_{jn} + \varepsilon_{jn})\right]. \tag{5.15}$$

Define

$$U_n^* = \max_{j=2,\ldots,J_n}(V_{jn} + \varepsilon_{jn}). \tag{5.16}$$

From property 7, U_n^* is Gumbel distributed with parameters

$$\left(\frac{1}{\mu}ln\sum_{j=2}^{J_n}e^{\mu V_{jn}}, \mu\right).$$

Using property 4, we can write $U_n^* = V_n^* + \varepsilon_n^*$, where

$$V_n^* = \frac{1}{\mu}ln\sum_{j=2}^{J_n}e^{\mu V_{jn}}$$

and ε_n^* is Gumbel distributed with parameters $(0, \mu)$.

Since

$$P_n(1) = Pr(V_{1n} + \varepsilon_{1n} \geq V_n^* + \varepsilon_n^*)$$

$$= Pr[(V_n^* + \varepsilon_n^*) - (V_{1n} + \varepsilon_{1n}) \leq 0], \tag{5.17}$$

by property 5 we have that

$$P_n(1) = \frac{1}{1 + e^{\mu(V_n^* - V_{1n})}}$$

$$= \frac{e^{\mu V_{1n}}}{e^{\mu V_{1n}} + e^{\mu V_n^*}} \tag{5.18}$$

$$= \frac{e^{\mu V_{1n}}}{e^{\mu V_{1n}} + \exp(ln\sum_{j=2}^{J_n}e^{\mu V_{jn}})} = \frac{e^{\mu V_{1n}}}{\sum_{j=1}^{J_n}e^{\mu V_{jn}}}$$

Note the presence of the scale parameter μ in each of the terms of (5.18). This parameter is not identifiable, just as it was not in the binary case (see section 4.2), so the usual procedure is to set it arbitrarily to a convenient value, such as 1. Although this is operationally necessary, we must not let it obscure our understanding of the role of μ in the model. Through it we reflect the assumption of homoscedastic disturbances; if this assumption is inappropriate for the population in question, it is necessary to take suitable measures (see section 7.5) to model correctly the choice utilities.

Limiting Cases of the Multinomial Logit Model

As in the binary case (see section 4.2), there are two limiting cases of the MNL that result from extreme values of μ:

CASE **1**

$$\lim_{\mu \to 0} P_n(i) = \frac{1}{J_n}, \qquad \forall i \in C_n.$$

As $\mu \to 0$, the variance of the disturbances approaches infinity. The choice model then provides no information, so the alternatives are equally likely.

CASE **2**

$$\lim_{\mu \to \infty} P_n(i) = \lim_{\mu \to \infty} \frac{1}{1 + \sum_{\substack{j \in C_n \\ j \neq i}} e^{\mu(V_{jn} - V_{in})}}$$

$$= \begin{cases} 1 & \text{if } V_{in} > \max_{\substack{j \in C_n \\ j \neq i}} V_{jn}, \\ 0 & \text{if } V_{in} < \max_{\substack{j \in C_n \\ j \neq i}} V_{jn}. \end{cases}$$

In the event of a tie among the utilities for some of the alternatives,

$$V_{in} = \max_{\substack{j \in C_n \\ j \neq i}} V_{jn},$$

the limit is $1/J_n^*$ for the J_n^* alternatives for which

$$V_{in} = \max_{j \in C_n} V_{jn}, \qquad i = 1, \ldots, J_n^*,$$

and is zero for the remaining $J_n - J_n^*$ alternatives. Note that as $\mu \to \infty$, the variance of the utility disturbances approaches zero and a deterministic choice model is obtained because all the information about individual preferences is included in the systematic utilities.

Linear-in-Paramaters Logit Model

Up to this point in our discussion we have not imposed any functional form on V_{in}, the systematic component of the utility function. As in the case of binary choice it is generally computationally convenient to restrict V_{in} to the class of linear-in-parameters functions. Following our convention of defining a single vector of coefficients β that applies to all the utility functions, we can write this restricted version of multinomial logit as

$$P_n(i) = \frac{e^{\beta' x_{in}}}{\sum_{j \in C_n} e^{\beta' x_{jn}}}, \tag{5.19}$$

where x_{in} and x_{jn} are vectors describing the attributes of alternatives i and j.

5.3   Properties of Logit

Independence from Irrelevant Alternatives Property (IIA)

One of the most widely discussed aspects of the multinomial logit model is the independence from irrelevant alternatives property, or IIA, discussed in section 3.7. Although much of the published literature on IIA has been extremely insightful, some authors have inappropriately interpreted it, creating substantial confusion for practitioners.

Stated succinctly, the IIA property holds that for a specific individual the ratio of the choice probabilities of any two alternatives is entirely unaffected by the systematic utilities of any other alternatives. This can be easily shown to hold in the case of MNL as follows:

$$\frac{P_n(i)}{P_n(l)} = \frac{e^{V_{in}}/\sum_{j \in C_n} e^{V_{jn}}}{e^{V_{ln}}/\sum_{j \in C_n} e^{V_{jn}}} = \frac{e^{V_{in}}}{e^{V_{ln}}}$$

$$= e^{V_{in} - V_{ln}}. \tag{5.20}$$

This seemingly simple property has some important ramifications. In some instances it can give rise to somewhat odd and erroneous predictions. One of the most widely cited anomalies is the *red bus/blue bus paradox* described in section 3.7.

To understand fully the IIA property and its implications, one must go back to the original assumptions from which the multinomial logit model is derived. Although all of the assumptions listed in section 5.2 are needed to produce the specific form of the IIA property, the core of the problem is the assumption that the disturbances are mutually independent. This assumption requires that the sources of errors contributing to the disturbances must do so in a way such that the total disturbances are independent. In the case of red buses and blue buses this is wholly implausible since both these alternatives share all the unobserved characteristics of buses. In fact, rather than being independent, the disturbances of the red and blue bus modes are more reasonably assumed to be perfectly correlated. *Although models other than multinomial logit might produce different numerical results, any model based on the assumption that all the disturbances are independent would necessarily yield counterintuitive forecasts for the red bus/blue bus problem.*

Another way to see why multinomial logit yields incorrect forecasts for this situation is to trace through the steps in its derivation. Let us define alternatives 1, 2, and 3 as auto, red bus, and blue bus, respectively. By the construction of the original paradox, $V_{1n} = V_{2n} = V_{3n}$, so we let V_n be the systematic component of the utility for any of the three alternatives. If we follow the line of proof in section 5.2, we note that we relied on the fact that

$$U_n^* = \max(U_{2n}, U_{3n}) = V_n^* + \varepsilon_n^*, \tag{5.21}$$

where $V_n^* = \ln(e^{V_n} + e^{V_n}) = \ln 2 + V_n$ and ε_n^* is Gumbel distributed with parameters $(0, 1)$. This step assumed that the disturbances for alternatives 2 and 3 were independent. However, if they are perfectly correlated, then the maximum of U_{2n} and U_{3n} is, for the case of the two bus modes with equal systematic utility, simply $V_n + \varepsilon_n$. In a sense the assumption of independence makes V_n^* too high by an amount equal to $\ln 2$. Moreover, if we correct this overestimate, then

$$P_n(\text{auto}) = Pr(V_n + \varepsilon_{1n} \geq V_n + \varepsilon^*) = \frac{1}{1 + e^{V_n - V_n}} = \frac{1}{2}, \tag{5.22}$$

which is the intuitively correct answer. Thus it would be possible to use a logit model for the choice among the three alternatives in this example only if we define the systematic utilities for the two bus alternatives as $V_n - \ln 2$.

A common misinterpretation of the IIA property is that it applies to the population as a whole. Thus it is often interpreted as implying that the ratio of the *shares of the population* choosing any two alternatives is unaffected by the utilities of other alternatives. Except in one extreme (and wholly

Table 5.1
Data for a heterogeneous population without the IIA property

	P_n (downtown)	P_n (suburb 1)	P_n (suburb 2)
Before new center			
Group 1	0.95	0.05	
Group 2	0.05	0.95	
Population share	0.50	0.50	
After new center			
Group 1	0.9048	0.0476	0.0476
Group 2	0.0256	0.4872	0.4872
Population share	0.4652	0.2674	0.2674

unrealistic) case, this is simply not true. We demonstrate this by the following simple counterexample.

Suppose that the destinations of shopping trips in a small city are equally divided between a suburban shopping center and the downtown area. If a new suburban center with observed attributes that are identical to the first one is built, would the logit model predict that it would draw one-third of the population, taken equally from the trips to the downtown area and the original suburban center? The answer is, in general, no.

To see this, suppose that the entire population of trips is composed of only two, equal-sized groups that are internally homogeneous in their observed attributes. The first group has predicted choice probabilities of 0.95 and 0.05 for the downtown and the original suburban center, respectively; for the second group, the probabilities are reversed. Table 5.1 summarizes the predicted probabilities before and after the second suburban center is introduced. Note that though the IIA property does apply to each homogeneous group, *it does not apply to the population as a whole*. In this example, rather than forecasting a shift of the downtown share of shopping destinations from $\frac{1}{2}$ to $\frac{1}{3}$ (as in the red bus/blue bus case), the share decreases only to 0.4652.

The key here is that the choice probabilities before the new shopping center is added are not the same across the population. Rather, there are two distinct market segments in the population with very different systematic preferences.

The idea that IIA may be more or less believable depending on whether heterogeneities in the population are accounted for in the model is a significant one. It implies that whether or not logit is an appropriate model for a particular choice situation is not something that can be judged in the abstract. Rather, one must examine the particular specification of the systematic component of the utility function and ask if it reasonably accounts for population heterogeneities. As a practical consequence logit models that include many socioeconomic attributes in an appropriate way stand a far better chance of yielding reasonable forecasts than those that omit such variables.

We will return to the problem of identifying when the IIA property is violated in chapter 7 where we discuss statistical tests for specification errors.

Elasticities of Logit

One useful property of demand models is the concept of an elasticity. (Readers are assumed to have a basic understanding of direct and cross elasticities as well as the distinction between a point and arc elasticity. Readers interested in a review of these concepts and their application to travel demand analysis are referred to Manheim 1979. All the examples discussed here are point elasticities.) In defining elasticities for discrete choice models, we must distinguish between disaggregate and aggregate elasticities.

A disaggregate elasticity represents the responsiveness of an individual's choice probability to a change in the value of some attribute. The simplest case is the elasticity of the probability of an individual choosing alternative i with respect to a change in some attribute that is an independent variable in the model, namely one of the x_{ink}'s. In this case the *direct elasticity* of logit is given by

$$E_{x_{ink}}^{P_n(i)} = \frac{\partial P_n(i)}{\partial x_{ink}} \cdot \frac{x_{ink}}{P_n(i)} = \frac{\partial \ln P_n(i)}{\partial \ln x_{ink}}$$

$$= [1 - P_n(i)]x_{ink}\beta_k. \tag{5.23}$$

Similarly the *disaggregate cross elasticity* of the probability alternative i that is selected with respect to an attribute of alternative j is

$$E_{x_{jnk}}^{P_n(i)} = \frac{\partial \ln P_n(i)}{\partial \ln x_{jnk}} = -P_n(j)x_{jnk}\beta_k, \qquad \text{for } j \neq i. \tag{5.24}$$

One property of logit is that it has *uniform cross elasticities*—that is, the cross elasticities of all alternatives with respect to a change in an attribute affecting only the utility of alternative j are equal for all alternatives $i \neq j$. This aspect of the multinomial logit model is another manifestation of the IIA property, discussed in the previous section.

There are many cases where the formulas defined in equations 5.23 and 5.24 are not appropriate. One relatively simple instance is where the independent variable is a function of some attribute of interest, z_{ink}, such as $x_{ink} = h^k(\mathbf{z}_{ink})$. In this case

$$E_{z_{ink}}^{P_n(i)} = [1 - P_n(i)]\beta_k \cdot \frac{\partial h^k}{\partial z_{ink}} z_{ink}. \tag{5.25}$$

If, for example, $x_{ink} = \ln(\text{travel time}_{in})$, then

$$E_{time_{in}}^{P_n(i)} = [1 - P_n(i)] \cdot \beta_k. \tag{5.26}$$

Similarly the cross elasticity for an attribute that enters into the utility of an alternative in transformed form is

$$E_{z_{jnk}}^{P_n(i)} = -P_n(j) \cdot \beta_k \cdot \frac{\partial h^k}{\partial z_{jnk}} \cdot z_{jnk}, \qquad \text{for } j \neq i.$$

A more complicated case occurs when one of the attributes in the model is an alternative-specific socioeconomic variable that enters into more than one utility function. In this case the effect of an incremental change in the socioeconomic variable will not only shift one utility, it will shift all of the utilities in which that variable appears. Similarly, if some variable such as travel time appears in more than one independent variable (e.g., time and time squared), then an incremental change in travel time will influence more than one independent variable.

One must be extremely careful when applying elasticity formulas to account fully for such complications. Although the functional form of the elasticity for any particular situation is problem specific, it is always possible to apply the definition of a point elasticity directly, taking care to ensure that the derivatives of the choice probabilities with respect to the variable of interest appropriately account for how that variable enters all the utility functions.

Aggregate elasticities summarize the responsiveness of some group of decision makers rather than that of any individual. For example, suppose that we wish to know the effect of an incremental change in a variable on the *expected share* of the group choosing alternative i. To solve for this, we define $\bar{P}(i)$ as the expected share of the group choosing alternative i, and note that

$$\bar{P}(i) = \frac{\sum_{n=1}^{N} P_n(i)}{N}, \tag{5.28}$$

where N is the number of decision makers in the group. Suppose we now alter the value of some variable x_{jnk} for each individual by some increment so that

$$\frac{\partial x_{jnk}}{x_{jnk}} = \frac{\partial x_{jn'k}}{x_{jn'k}} = \frac{\partial x_{jk}}{x_{jk}}, \qquad \text{for all } n, n' = 1, 2, \ldots, N, \tag{5.29}$$

where

$$x_{jk} = \frac{1}{N} \sum_{n=1}^{N} x_{jnk}.$$

(This corresponds to a uniform percentage change in x_{jnk} across all members of the group.) For this type of change the aggregate elasticity is as follows:

$$E_{x_{jk}}^{\bar{P}(i)} = \frac{\sum_{n=1}^{N} P_n(i) E_{x_{jnk}}^{P_n(i)}}{\sum_{n=1}^{N} P_n(i)}, \tag{5.30}$$

which is simply a weighted average of the individual level elasticities using the choice probabilities as weights.

The disaggregate elasticities of equations 5.23 and 5.24 can be written as

$$E_{x_{jnk}}^{P_n(i)} = [\delta_{ij} - P_n(j)] x_{jnk} \beta_k,$$

where δ_{ij} is the Kronecker delta function, which equals 1 for $i = j$ and 0 for $i \neq j$. Substituting this expression in 5.30, we obtain

$$E_{x_{jnk}}^{\bar{P}(i)} = \frac{\beta_k}{N \cdot \bar{P}(i)} \cdot \sum_{n=1}^{N} P_n(i) [\delta_{in} - P_n(j)] x_{jnk}.$$

Note that for a cross elasticity we set $\delta_{ij} = 0$ and obtain an expression that depends on both i and j. This demonstrates once again that the uniform disaggregate cross elasticities that result from the IIA property need not hold at the aggregate level.

We will explore the problem of aggregate prediction in considerably greater detail in chapter 6.

The Incremental MNL Model

Using elasticities is one way to predict changes due to modifications in the independent variables. For the linear-in-parameters multinomial logit model there is a convenient form known as the *incremental logit* which can be used to predict changes in behavior on the basis of the *existing choice probabilities of the alternatives* and *changes in variables* that obviates the need to use the full set of independent variables to calculate the new choice probabilities.

Derivation of the incremental form of the logit model is relatively straightforward. The linear-in-parameters logit model predicts the probability that individual n will choose alternative i from the set of alternatives C_n, as given by equation 5.19. The revised choice probability resulting from a change in utilities is given by

$$P_n'(i) = \frac{e^{V_{in}+\Delta V_{in}}}{\sum_{j \in C_n} e^{V_{jn}+\Delta V_{jn}}}$$

where

ΔV_{in} = the change in utility for alternative i

$$= \sum_{k=1}^{K} \beta_k \Delta x_{ink},$$

Δx_{ink} = the change in the kth independent variable for alternative i and individual n.

Divide both the numerator and the denominator by $\sum_{j \in C_n} e^{V_{jn}}$ to obtain the incremental logit model:

$$P_n'(i) = \frac{P_n(i)e^{\Delta V_{in}}}{\sum_{j \in C_n} P_n(j)e^{\Delta V_{jn}}}.$$

Thus to predict changes with a linear-in-parameters MNL choice model, we need to know the choice probabilities in the base case and the changes in utilities due only to the affected variables. It is not necessary to recalculate the full utilities.

5.4 Specification of a Multinomial Logit Model

The specification of a multinomial logit model consists of a number of distinct steps. First, we must define the universal choice set C for the problem under study. This step may require some judgments about which alternatives can be ignored. For example, in most U.S. cities we do not model motorcycles as a separate mode, and we restrict the set of destinations to some previously defined study area. Also many standard surveys do not include walk trips, and we must therefore omit walking as an element of C.

The next step is to define the choice set for each individual. As discussed before, this is generally done by applying reasonable judgments about what constitutes the feasibility of an alternative in any particular situation.

Finally, the particular variables entering into the utility functions must be defined. More will be said about these steps in subsequent chapters. Our goal in this section is to illustrate at least some of the issues involved in developing a choice model through an example based on a study by Ben-Akiva et al. (1976, 1977). We will describe the specification of this model in this section, reserving a discussion of the estimation results for section 5.6.

The universal choice in this example consists of three modes to work:

1. driving alone,
2. sharing a ride,
3. transit bus.

The study was performed using data from Washington, D.C. All the information used is from 1968, and all monetary measures are in 1968 dollars.

The definition of the modes requires some comment. Ride sharing is defined as the use of an automobile by more than one traveler. This definition spans a variety of ride-sharing arrangements, including daily paid carpools, intrahousehold ride sharing, and informal carpools for a single trip. This type of "aggregation of alternatives" is quite common in demand analysis. Here it reflects the problems of distinguishing these various forms of ride sharing in the available data. We return to the theoretical and practical problems involved in aggregating alternatives in chapter 9.

The rules used for determining which subset of the three potential alternatives is feasible for each individual were entirely judgmental. Three rules were used, defined as follows:

1. Any worker without a driver's license cannot drive alone.
2. Any worker in a household without an automobile cannot drive alone.

3. Any worker living or working in an area where there is no transit stop within a half mile walk was assumed not to have transit service.

Note that these rules always leave ride sharing as an option.

The specification of the systematic utilities is given in table 5.2. This table is identical in format to those used to describe binary choice models in chapter 4. The only difference is that here there are three rather than two rows, one for each potential mode. As in the case of binary choice models, the variables include alternative-specific constants, attributes of the transportation modes (termed level-of-service attributes), and alternative-specific socioeconomic characteristics.

Most of the issues raised in discussing the specification of binary models extend directly to multinomial choice. For example, in binary choice models it made sense to have only one constant. Its coefficient reflected the relative utility (all else equal) of the alternative in which the constant was included as compared to the one from which it was omitted. In a multinomial choice example we must again have an alternative that acts as a referent, so we can logically include two constants in the present example. We have included these constants in the driving alone and ride-sharing alternatives.

In the general case we can include as many as $J - 1$ constants. As in binary choice the selection of the referent alternative has no effect on the model other than to shift the values of the estimated constants, preserving their differences.

Similarly we can use any particular socioeconomic variable as alternative specific in as many as $J - 1$ alternatives. In our example the socioeconomic attributes "autos per licensed driver" and the dummy variable for downtown workplaces appear in the drive-alone and shared-ride alternatives; transit again acts as an arbitrarily selected referent.

Not all the socioeconomic variables are included in this way. For example, the "disposable income" measure (defined to approximate the amount of income remaining after expenditures for basic family needs) has the same coefficient in both the shared-ride and drive-alone utilities. This was done after tests on earlier forms of the model indicated no behaviorally important or statistically significant differences between the two separate coefficients. The inclusion of this form of the variable implies that disposable income does not affect the relative utilities of ride sharing and driving alone but rather each one's utility as compared to transit.

Table 5.2
Example of multinomial choice model

	β_1	β_2	β_3	β_4	β_5	β_6	β_7	β_8
Drive-alone utility	1	0	Round-trip, auto in-vehicle time (min)[a]	Round-trip, auto out-of-vehicle time/distance (min/mi)	Round-trip, auto out-of-pocket cost/disposable income[b]	Autos per licensed driver[e]	0	1 if workplace is downtown; 0 otherwise
Shared-ride utility	0	1	Round-trip, shared-ride in-vehicle time (min)[a]	Round-trip, shared-ride out-of-vehicle time/distance (min/mile)[a]	Round-trip, shared-ride out-of-pocket cost[c]/disposable income[b]	0	Autos per licensed driver[e]	0
Transit utility	0	0	Round-trip transit in-vehicle time (min)	Round-trip transit out-of-vehicle time/distance (min/mi)	Round-trip transit fare/disposable income[b]	0	0	0

	β_9	β_{10}	β_{11}	β_{12}	β_{13}	β_{14}
Drive-alone utility	0	Disposable income[b]	1 if traveler is primary worker[d]	0	0	0
Shared-ride utility	1 if workplace is downtown; 0 otherwise	Disposable income[b]	0	1 if government worker; 0 otherwise	Number of workers	(Employment density at workplace) × (one-way trip distance) (employees/mi)
Transit utility	0	0	0	0	0	0

a. In-vehicle and out-of-vehicle times for ride sharing assumed to be five minutes greater than direct driving each way.
b. Disposable income defined as household annual income minus $800 per household member.
c. Out-of-pocket cost for ride sharing estimated assuming 2.5 travelers per auto.
d. Primary worker in a household was defined on basis of skill level of worker.
e. Ratio set to zero if there are no licensed drivers in household.

5.5 Estimation of Multinomial Logit

There is little additional material to be discussed regarding the estimation
of multinomial choice models beyond what is said in chapter 4 for binary
models. All of the general procedures extend straightforwardly, though
their computational burden grows as the number of alternatives increases.
Rather than simply repeat much of section 4.4 in more general form, we
consider only the estimation of the multinomial logit model. As we will
show, logit has some special properties that under certain circumstances
greatly simplify estimation of its parameters. Most of this theory is attributable to McFadden (1974).

Maximum Likelihood

As in chapter 4, let N denote the sample size and define

$$y_{in} = \begin{cases} 1 & \text{if observation } n \text{ chose alternative } i, \\ 0 & \text{otherwise.} \end{cases}$$

The likelihood function for a general multinomial choice model is

$$\mathcal{L}^* = \prod_{n=1}^{N} \prod_{i \in C_n} P_n(i)^{y_{in}}, \tag{5.31}$$

where for a linear-in-parameters logit

$$P_n(i) = \frac{e^{\boldsymbol{\beta}'\mathbf{x}_{in}}}{\sum_{j \in C_n} e^{\boldsymbol{\beta}'\mathbf{x}_{jn}}}. \tag{5.32}$$

Taking the logarithm of equation 5.31, we seek a maximum to

$$\mathcal{L} = \sum_{n=1}^{N} \sum_{i \in C_n} y_{in} \left(\boldsymbol{\beta}'\mathbf{x}_{in} - \ln \sum_{j \in C_n} e^{\boldsymbol{\beta}'\mathbf{x}_{jn}} \right). \tag{5.33}$$

Setting the first derivatives of $\mathcal{L}$ with respect to the coefficients equal to
zero, we obtain the necessary first-order conditions:

$$\frac{\partial \mathcal{L}}{\partial \beta_k} = \sum_{n=1}^{N} \sum_{i \in C_n} y_{in} \left(x_{ink} - \frac{\sum_{j \in C_n} e^{\boldsymbol{\beta}'\mathbf{x}_{jn}} x_{jnk}}{\sum_{j \in C_n} e^{\boldsymbol{\beta}'\mathbf{x}_{jn}}} \right) = 0, \quad \text{for } k = 1, \ldots, K. \tag{5.34}$$

Or, in more compact form

$$\sum_{n=1}^{N} \sum_{i \in C_n} [y_{in} - P_n(i)] x_{ink} = 0, \quad \text{for } k = 1, \ldots, K. \tag{5.35}$$

The reader can verify that the second derivatives of $\mathscr{L}$ are given by

$$\frac{\partial^2 \mathscr{L}}{\partial \beta_k \partial \beta_l} = -\sum_{n=1}^{N} \sum_{i \in C_n} P_n(i) \left[x_{ink} - \sum_{j \in C_n} x_{jnk} P_n(j) \right]$$
$$\cdot \left[x_{inl} - \sum_{j \in C_n} x_{jnl} P_n(j) \right].$$

(5.36)

All of the properties of the maximum likelihood estimation of binary logit extend to the multinomial case. Under relatively weak conditions McFadden (1974) shows that $\mathscr{L}$ in equation 5.33 is globally concave, so if a solution to the equation 5.35 exists, it is unique. The maximum likelihood estimator of β is consistent, asymptotically normal, and asymptotically efficient.

The first-order conditions (equation 5.35) can be rewritten as

$$\frac{1}{N} \sum_{n=1}^{N} \sum_{i \in C_n} y_{in} x_{ink} = \frac{1}{N} \sum_{n=1}^{N} \sum_{i \in C_n} P_n(i) x_{ink}, \qquad k = 1, \ldots, K.$$

This means that the average value of an attribute for the chosen alternatives is equal to the average value predicted by the estimated choice probabilities. In particular, if an alternative-specific constant is defined for an alternative i, then at the maximum likelihood estimates,

$$\sum_{n=1}^{N} y_{in} = \sum_{n=1}^{N} P_n(i),$$

(5.37)

implying that the sum of the choice probabilities for alternative i (taken over the sample) equals the number in the sample that chose i. Similarly, when an alternative-specific dummy variable defines some segment of the population, then equation 5.37 will apply, the sums being taken only over the relevant group.

The computational methods used for solving the system of K equations in 5.35 are identical to those used in the binary case.

Maximum Likelihood for Repeated Observations

There are some instances where each individual is observed repeatedly while the attributes of the alternatives remain constant. For example, rather than observing travelers' mode choices for a single day, we might observe all their daily choices over an entire month. We could solve for the maximum likelihood estimates simply by treating each day for each individual as a separate observation. However, this would be computationally inefficient because it would not exploit the fact that the attributes of the alternatives were the same for groups of observations defined by each individual's trips. A more efficient (in the computational sense) approach is to rewrite the likelihood function. To do this, we define D_{in} = number of times individual n chose alternative i, and $D_n = \sum_{i \in C_n} D_{in}$.

The likelihood of the sample is then

$$\mathcal{L}^* = \prod_{n=1}^{N} \frac{D_n!}{\prod_{j \in C_n} D_{jn}!} \prod_{i \in C_n} P_n(i)^{D_{in}}. \tag{5.38}$$

Thus the log likelihood function is given by

$$\mathcal{L} = \sum_{n=1}^{N} \left\{ \ln D_n! - \sum_{j \in C_n} \ln D_{jn}! + \sum_{i \in C_n} D_{in} \ln P_n(i) \right\}. \tag{5.39}$$

We can then proceed as before by taking first derivatives and solving for the estimate $\hat{\boldsymbol{\beta}}$ for which they are equal to zero.

The procedures of treating each individual's trips as separate and independent observations and using equation 5.39 yield exactly the same results in all respects but one. This exception is that the values of the log likelihood functions will differ by a constant that depends on the D_{in}'s and will correspond to the first two terms in brackets in equation 5.39:

$$\sum_{n=1}^{N} \left(\ln D_n! - \sum_{j \in C_n} \ln D_{jn}! \right). \tag{5.40}$$

The difference is usually of no real importance because most statistical tests that use the value of the log likelihood function involve *differences* in log likelihoods evaluated on the exact same data; hence the term in equation 5.40 would cancel. It will, however, affect values of ρ^2 and $\bar{\rho}^2$. In comparing results of different analyses of repeated choices, the reader should be careful to check whether the reported value of the log likelihood does or does not include the term in equation 5.40.

Least Squares

As discussed in chapter 4, least squares estimation is rarely used on disaggregate data. However, Berkson's method, extended by Theil (1969), can be applied to estimate the parameters of the multinomial logit model. To show this, we note that

$$\ln\left(\frac{P_n(i)}{P_n(J_n)}\right) = V_{in} - V_{J_n n} = \boldsymbol{\beta}'(\mathbf{x}_{in} - \mathbf{x}_{J_n n}). \tag{5.41}$$

(See equation 5.20 to prove this.) Thus we can group observations that share common values of $(\mathbf{x}_{in} - \mathbf{x}_{J_n n})$ and use the share of the group choosing alternatives i and J_n as estimates of $P_n(i)$ and $P_n(J_n)$, respectively. If N_{ig} denotes the number of members of group g choosing i, and J_g is the number of alternatives available to members of group g, then we would use the regression

$$\ln\left(\frac{N_{ig}}{N_{J_g g}}\right) = \boldsymbol{\beta}'(\mathbf{x}_{ig} - \mathbf{x}_{J_g g}) + \xi_{ig} \tag{5.42}$$

to obtain an estimate of $\boldsymbol{\beta}$. Each group would correspond to $(J_g - 1)$ observations in the regression. We have implicitly assumed here that each group consists of individuals with the same choice set. This is not essential, but it corresponds to the case where grouping is most likely to be feasible.

All of our comments on Berkson's method stated in chapter 4 apply to its multinomial extension. However, the problems of finding homogeneous groups in the multinomial case are compounded by the fact that choice sets can vary across the population (making grouping more difficult), and the number of alternatives is greater. These factors tend to make the number of disaggregate observations needed to form groups considerably larger. Application of the Berkson-Theil method for multinomial logit is therefore extremely difficult except when the data base is large or when repeated observations on individuals' choices are available.

Other Estimators

Most other estimators become computationally intractable when applied to large choice sets. To our knowledge, none of the estimators discussed in section 4.6 have been actually used in practice for multinomial choice.

5.6 Example of Estimation Results

Estimation results for multinomial choice models are summarized in essentially the same way as for binary choice. Table 5.3 is such a summary for maximum likelihood estimation of the model described in section 5.4. In terms of explaining this summary table, only a few comments beyond those in chapter 4 are relevant.

Table 5.3
Estimation results for multinomial logit choice model

Variable number	Variable name	Coefficient estimate	Asymptotic standard error	t statistic
1	Drive-alone constant	−3.24	0.472	−6.9
2	Shared-ride constant	−2.24	0.400	−5.6
3	In-vehicle time (min)	−0.0154	0.00577	−2.7
4	Out-of-vehicle time/dist (min/mi)	−0.160	0.0392	−4.1
5	Cost (¢)/annual income ($/yr)	−28.8	12.7	−2.3
6	Autos/driver (specific to drive alone)	3.99	0.396	10.1
7	Autos/driver (specific to shared ride)	1.62	0.305	5.3
8	Downtown workplace dummy (specific to drive alone)	−0.854	0.311	−2.8
9	Downtown workplace dummy (specific to shared ride)	−0.404	0.297	−1.4
10	Disposable income ($/yr) (specific to drive alone and shared ride)	0.00007	0.0000202	3.5
11	Primary worker dummy (specific to drive alone)	0.890	0.186	4.8
12	Government worker dummy (specific to shared ride)	0.287	0.161	1.8
13	Number of workers (specific to shared ride)	0.0983	0.0954	1.0
14	(Employment density) × (distance) (specific to shared ride)	0.00063	0.000470	1.3

Summary statistics
Number of observations = 1,114
Number of cases = 2,924
$\mathscr{L}(\mathbf{0}) = -1,054.0$
$\mathscr{L}(\hat{\boldsymbol{\beta}}) = -727.4$
$-2[\mathscr{L}(\mathbf{0}) - \mathscr{L}(\hat{\boldsymbol{\beta}})] = 653.2$
$\rho^2 = 0.3099$
$\bar{\rho}^2 = 0.2966$

First, the number of cases is no longer equal to the number of observations. However, it does not equal $N \cdot (J - 1)$, since each individual can have a different choice set. Rather, the number of cases is given by $\sum_{n=1}^{N} (J_n - 1)$.

In a similar vein $\mathscr{L}(\mathbf{0})$, the value of the log likelihood function when all parameters are zero (i.e., when the alternatives are assumed to have equal probability of being chosen) is no longer simply $-N \ln 2$. Rather it is $-\sum_{n=1}^{N} \ln J_n$.

A few specific aspects of the particular model summarized in table 5.3 are also worth noting. The coefficients of the two alternative specific variables for autos per licensed driver both have positive coefficients that are significantly different from zero at the 0.01 level. The positive sign reflects the fact that travelers from households with high auto ownership (relative to the number of drivers) will tend, all else equal, to prefer driving alone and ride sharing over transit. However, the coefficient for the variable in the utility of the drive alone alternative is greater than the one for sharing a ride. This reflects the fact that when driving alone and sharing a ride are compared, increasing auto ownership is associated with an increased preference for driving alone.

This same type of ordering occurs with the coefficients of the alternative-specific dummy variables for downtown destinations. For this variable, however, the two coefficients are negative, indicating that downtown workers are less inclined to drive alone or share a ride to work than their suburban-employed counterparts. Also, in comparing driving alone with ride sharing, downtown workers have greater preference for ride sharing than suburban workers.

All the coefficient estimates have the expected sign. However, not all the coefficient estimates are significantly different from zero at the usual 5% or 10% levels of significance. Although some researchers use this type of criterion as the sole basis for omitting a variable in later specifications, we do not believe this is good practice. Many of the reasons for this are discussed in subsequent chapters. It suffices here to note that the inability to reject the hypothesis that some coefficient is zero at a particular significance level does not imply that the hypothesis must be accepted.

5.7   Other Multinomial Choice Models

Multinomial logit is by far the most widely used multinomial choice model to date, but there are other models that have been developed and applied.

(Material in this section is more advanced and may be skipped without loss of continuity except in chapters 9 and 10.) These models fall into two distinct classes. The first might be termed logit extensions, in that they are generalizations of multinomial logit. The second class is nonlogit-based models. Only one member of this class, multinomial probit, has actually been used. In this section we briefly described models in these two classes. In later chapters we will explore some particular special cases in greater detail.

Random Coefficients Logit

In analyzing the demand for different types of automobiles in the United States, the Electric Power Research Institute (EPRI) implemented a form of the multinomial logit model that allows for the parameters, $\boldsymbol{\beta}$, to be distributed across the population (EPRI 1977). Thus each individual's coefficients, $\boldsymbol{\beta}_n$, differ from the population mean, $\boldsymbol{\beta}$, by some unobserved amount. This difference, termed taste variation, constitutes an additional source of randomness. In this work it is assumed that the absolute value of coefficients are independent and lognormally distributed, imposing the restriction that the coefficients for all members of the population have the same sign.

If each individual's coefficients were observable, the model could be expressed as follows:

$$P_n(i) = \frac{e^{\boldsymbol{\beta}_n' x_{in}}}{\sum_{j \in C_n} e^{\boldsymbol{\beta}_n' x_{jn}}}, \tag{5.43}$$

where $\boldsymbol{\beta}_n = [\beta_{1n}, \beta_{2n}, \ldots, \beta_{Kn}]'$. However, we usually do not observe replications of each individual's choices, so $\boldsymbol{\beta}_n$ is not estimable. Instead, we use the assumption that each β_{nk} is independent and lognormally distributed with parameters (β_k, σ_k^2), and estimate both β_k and σ_k^2 for all k.

Since $\boldsymbol{\beta}_n$ is unknown, the left-hand side of equation 5.43 cannot be evaluated. Instead, its expected value, taken across the population, is used. Thus the choice probability is given by

$$P_n(i) = \int_{\beta_{1n}} \cdots \int_{\beta_{Kn}} \frac{e^{\boldsymbol{\beta}_n' x_{in}}}{\sum_{j \in C_n} e^{\boldsymbol{\beta}_n' x_{jn}}} f(\beta_{Kn}) \ldots f(\beta_{1n}) \, d\beta_{Kn} \ldots d\beta_{1n}, \tag{5.44}$$

where $f(\beta_{kn})$ is the lognormal density function.

The estimation of this model is quite complex because no closed form solution to the integral in equation 5.44 exists. Moreover the model now has $2K$ rather than K unknown parameters because each element in $\boldsymbol{\beta}$ is described by a two-parameter distribution. The EPRI estimated the parameters of the model via maximum likelihood, using Monte Carlo integration to approximate the value of $P_n(i)$.

Ordered Logistic

Amemiya (1975) describes a model that applies to ordered discrete alternatives, such as the number of trips taken or the number of automobiles owned by a household. This model represents the choice as the outcome of a sequence of binary decisions, each one consisting of the decision of whether to accept the current value or "take one more." Thus it is not based on the assumption of global utility maximization. The decision maker stops when the first local optimum is reached. We denote U_{in}^c as the utility of proceeding to the next alternative given that the ith alternative has been reached, U_{in}^s as the utility of stopping at the ith value given that the ith alternative was reached.

The probability individual n accepts the ith alternative is

$$P_n(i) = Pr(U_{1n}^c \geq U_{1n}^s \cap U_{2n}^c \geq U_{2n}^s \cap \ldots \cap U_{i-1,n}^c \geq U_{i-1,n}^s \cap U_{in}^s \geq U_{in}^c).$$

Assuming that the disturbances of the utility differences $U_{in}^c - U_{in}^s$ are independently logistic distributed, this joint event can be written as the product of binary logits:

$$P_n(i) = \left(\frac{e^{V_{1n}^c}}{e^{V_{1n}^c} + e^{V_{1n}^s}}\right)\left(\frac{e^{V_{2n}^c}}{e^{V_{2n}^c} + e^{V_{2n}^s}}\right)\cdots\left(\frac{e^{V_{i-1,n}^c}}{e^{V_{i-1,n}^c} + e^{V_{i-1,n}^s}}\right)\left(\frac{e^{V_{in}^s}}{e^{V_{in}^s} + e^{V_{in}^c}}\right)$$

$$= \left(1 - \frac{1}{1 + e^{-(V_{in}^c - V_{in}^s)}}\right)\prod_{j=1}^{i-1}\frac{1}{1 + e^{-(V_{jn}^c - V_{jn}^s)}}.$$

(5.45)

One of the useful features of this structure is that it can be estimated via maximum likelihood using existing logit estimation computer programs. Each binary element in the product in equation 5.45 is simply treated as a separate observation, ignoring the fact that groups of observations come from the same individual's choices. *This is only possible because the disturbances are assumed to be independent at each stage of the decision sequence.*

Hendrickson and Sheffi (1978) (also Sheffi 1979) and Hall (1980) have applied this model to represent a household's trip generation and search for a residence, respectively. Daly and van Zwam (1981) have applied this model to predict the frequency of "tours" rather than one-way trips. Lerman and Mahmassani (1984) have explored numerous extensions to account for correlation across disturbances and various sources of observational error. Small (1981) discusses other properties of this and other "ordered response" models.

The Generalized Extreme Value (GEV) Model

In a significant generalization of multinomial logit McFadden (1978) has derived the generalized extreme value (GEV) model. This is actually a large class of models which includes multinomial logit. Although the number of possible models within this class is limitless, only a few particular forms have as yet been explored. Here we simply define the GEV model and give a single example to illustrate how various special cases are derived. The model is defined as follows:

THE GEV MODEL: Let $G(y_1, y_2, \ldots, y_{J_n})$, for y_1, y_2, ..., $y_{J_n} \geq 0$, be a function with the following properties:

1. G is non-negative.
2. G is homogeneous of degree $\mu > 0$; that is $G(\alpha y_1, \alpha y_2, \ldots, \alpha y_{J_n}) = \alpha^\mu G(y_1, y_2, \ldots, y_{J_n})$.
3. $\lim_{y_i \to \infty} G(y_1, y_2, \ldots, y_{J_n}) = \infty$, for $i = 1, 2, \ldots, J_n$.
4. The lth partial derivative of G with respect to any combination of l distinct y_i's, $i = 1, \ldots, J_n$, is non-negative if l is odd, and nonpositive if l is even.

In his work McFadden assumed that G is homogeneous of degree one; subsequently Ben-Akiva and François (1983) demonstrated that G can be μ homogeneous, as defined in property 2.

If G satisfies these conditions and $G_i(y_1, y_2, \ldots, y_{J_n})$ denotes $\partial G / \partial y_i$, $i = 1, 2, \ldots, J_n$, then

$$P_n(i) = \frac{e^{V_{in}} G_i(e^{V_{1n}}, e^{V_{2n}}, \ldots, e^{V_{J_n n}})}{\mu G(e^{V_{1n}}, e^{V_{2n}}, \ldots, e^{V_{J_n n}})} \tag{5.46}$$

defines the GEV model. Note that due to the μ homogeneity of $G(\cdot)$, $G_i(\cdot)$ is $\mu - 1$ homogeneous.

McFadden (1978) shows that the choice model defined by equation 5.46 is consistent with random utility maximization.

One case of the GEV model, the nested logit, will be discussed extensively in chapter 10. Here we show how this theorem can be used by demonstrating that the multinomial logit model belongs to the family of GEV models.

Suppose $G = \sum_{j=1}^{J_n} y_j^\mu$. This satisfies the four properties for a GEV model because

1. $G \geq 0$ if $y_1, y_2, \ldots, y_{J_n} \geq 0$.
2. $G(\alpha y_1, \alpha y_2, \ldots, \alpha y_{J_n}) = \sum_{j=1}^{J_n} (\alpha y_j)^\mu = \alpha^\mu \sum_{j=1}^{J_n} y_j^\mu = \alpha^\mu G(y_1, y_2, \ldots, y_{J_n})$.
3. $\lim_{y_i \to \infty} G = \infty$ for all $i = 1, 2, \ldots, J_n$.
4. $\partial G / \partial y_i = \mu y_i^{\mu-1}$, which is non-negative. All higher-order derivatives for two or more distinct arguments are zero and are therefore both non-negative and nonpositive.

Given G, the corresponding choice probability is

$$P_n(i) = \frac{\mu \cdot e^{V_{in}(\mu-1)} \cdot e^{V_{in}}}{\mu \sum_{j=1}^{J_n} e^{\mu V_{jn}}}$$

$$= \frac{e^{\mu V_{in}}}{\sum_{j=1}^{J_n} e^{\mu V_{jn}}},$$

which is the multinomial logit model.

Due to the μ homogeneity of G, we can use Euler's theorem (e.g., see Layard and Walters 1978) to write

$$\mu G(\ldots) = \sum_{j=1}^{J_n} y_j G_j(\ldots).$$

Hence the GEV model of equation 5.46 can be rewritten as

$$P_n(i) = \frac{e^{V_{in} + \ln G_i(\ldots)}}{\sum_{j=1}^{J_n} e^{V_{jn} + \ln G_j(\ldots)}}. \tag{5.47}$$

In equation 5.47 we have rewritten the GEV model as a multinomial logit model but with an extra twist: the utilities of the alternatives are functions not only of their own attributes (through the V's) but also of the attributes of competing alternatives (through the partial derivatives of the $G(\ )$ function). It has been suggested in the literature (e.g., Ben-Akiva 1974) that the IIA property of the MNL model can be circumvented by the addition of some linear-in-parameters function $h(V_1, \ldots, V_{J_n})$ to the V's; Ben-Akiva has shown that this approach can result in counterintuitive elasticities. Through equation 5.47, however, we see how such a correction for IIA can be formulated so that the resulting model is consistent with utility maximization. Note, however, that the resulting choice model is not linear in parameters and so requires a special estimation procedure.

Expression 5.47 makes intuitive the derivation of the MNL model. For the MNL,

$$\ln G_i(\ldots) = \ln \mu + (\mu - 1)\ln e^{V_{in}} = \ln \mu + (\mu - 1)V_{in}.$$

Therefore

$$P_n(i) = \frac{e^{V_{in} + \ln \mu + (\mu - 1)V_{in}}}{\sum_{j=1}^{J_n} e^{V_{jn} + \ln \mu + (\mu - 1)V_{jn}}}$$

$$= \frac{e^{\mu V_{in}}}{\sum_{j=1}^{J_n} e^{\mu V_{jn}}}.$$

Having a definition for a class of models and actually formulating realizations from that class are two different things. To date we know of only three GEV models: the MNL, the nested logit (to be covered in chapter 10), and the ordered generalized extreme value (not to be confused with the ordered logistic of the previous section) of Small (1981). As the state of the art progresses, however, we are sure to see further development of this flexible class of discrete choice models.

Multinomial Probit

We can extend binary probit straightforwardly by assuming that the vector of disturbances $\varepsilon_n = [\varepsilon_{1n}, \varepsilon_{2n}, \ldots, \varepsilon_{Jn}]'$ is multivariate normal distributed with a vector of means $\mathbf{0}$ and a $J \times J$ variance-covariance matrix Σ_ε. This model, however, requires a solution of a $J_n - 1$ dimensional integral to evaluate the choice probabilities. Hausman and Wise (1978) use a transformation to reduce the dimensionality of the integral to $J_n - 2$.

The concept of multinomial probit appeared in mathematical psychology in writings by Thurstone (1927), but its computational difficulty made it unusable until quite recently. Recent works by Dutt (1976), Hausman and Wise (1978), Daganzo, Bouthelier, and Sheffi (1977) and Albright, Lerman, and Manski (1977) have resolved some of the computational problems. However, only a few, very limited applications have appeared in the travel demand literature, and there is still no evidence to suggest in which situations the greater generality of multinomial probit is worth the additional computational problems resulting from its use.

One useful aspect of multinomial probit is the ease with which random taste variation can be incorporated into the model when the systematic component of the utility function is linear in the parameters. To show this, we define the individual's parameters, β_n, as follows:

$$\beta_n = \beta + \psi_n. \tag{5.48}$$

Then we write

$$U_{in} = \beta_n' x_{in} + \varepsilon_{in} = \beta' x_{in} + (\psi_n' x_{in} + \varepsilon_{in}). \tag{5.49}$$

Here ψ_n is a vector of deviations defining the difference between individual n's parameters and the average for the population. By construction, ψ_n is a vector with K entries and mean zero. We define Σ_ψ as the $K \times K$ variance-covariance matrix of ψ_n.

Note that if we assume that ε_n and ψ_n are both normally distributed, then the composite disturbance for each utility is a linear combination of normal variates and is consequently normal. To be more specific, if

$$\varepsilon_{in}^* = \varepsilon_{in} + \psi_n' x_{in}, \tag{5.50}$$

then the vector $\varepsilon_n^* = [\varepsilon_{1n}^*, \varepsilon_{2n}^*, \ldots, \varepsilon_{Jn}^*]'$ is multivariate normal with mean 0. If X_n is the $K \times J_n$ matrix with columns $x_{1n}, x_{2n}, \ldots, x_{Jn}$, then the variance-covariance matrix of ε_n^* is given by $\Sigma_\varepsilon + X_n' \Sigma_\psi X_n$. Thus the multinomial probit model with linear-in-parameters systematic utilities allows for normally distributed taste variations. A more complete treatment of the theory of multinomial probit is given in Daganzo (1980).

5.8 Summary

This chapter discussed the analysis of multinomial choice problems. The general formulation of multinomial choice probabilities was described, and a particular form, *multinomial logit*, was derived. The multinomial logit model is based on the following assumptions about the disturbance terms of the utilities:

1. they are independent,
2. identically distributed, and
3. Gumbel (or type I extreme value) distributed.

One useful form of the multinomial logit model has linear-in-parameters systematic utilities.

The *independence from irrelevant alternative* (*IIA*) property of logit was described. This property holds that for any two alternatives, the ratio of their choice probabilities is independent of the systematic utility of any other alternatives in the choice set. The potential problems that can arise when two alternatives have correlated disturbances were discussed. It was shown that use of the multinomial logit model does not imply that IIA will hold at the aggregate level.

The elasticities of logit were also derived. Logit has *uniform cross elasticities*—that is, the cross elasticity of the choice probability of alternative i with respect to an attribute of alternative j is the same for all alternatives $i \neq j$.

Maximum likelihood estimation of the logit model's parameters was discussed for the cases of a single observation per decision maker and replicated observations. The Berkson-Theil method for least squares estimation was also developed. An example of a logit model was given for mode choice to work.

Finally, some multinomial choice models other than logit were briefly summarized. The models discussed here are the random coefficients logit, the ordered logistic, the generalized extreme value (GEV) model, and the multinomial probit.

6 Aggregate Forecasting Techniques

Up to this point we have focused almost exclusively on the problem of predicting *individual* behavior. The choice models derived in chapters 4 and 5 predict the probabilities with which any particular individual will take various actions. However, predictions for a specific individual are generally of little use in helping make investment or planning decisions. Instead, most real-world decisions are based (at least in part) on the forecast of some *aggregate demand*, such as the number of trips of various types made in total by some population or the amount of freight shipped between different city pairs. Some linkage between the disaggregate level models described previously and the aggregate level forecasts of interest to planners and decision makers is obviously needed.

This chapter presents the various methods for making aggregate forecast with disaggregate models. We begin in section 6.1 by defining the problem of aggregating decisions across a relevant population and then discussing why simple approaches may not be adequate. Section 6.2 presents a typology of the various methods that have been used to make aggregate forecasts. In section 6.3 the five major categories of solutions are presented. Section 6.4 compares the various approaches, assessing both the theoretical and empirical evidence for the accuracy of each approach. Finally, section 6.5 summarizes the chapter.

6.1 The Problem of Aggregation across Individuals

The first issue to resolve in considering the problem of making an aggregate forecast is to define the relevant aggregate population. In some cases this may be quite simple. For example, we may be interested in total transit ridership within an urban area, and the relevant population will therefore be all residents of the city. For other planning purposes there may be many relevant subpopulations. We might, for example, want separate aggregate forecasts for different portions of a city or for different income groups depending on the type of information needed in reaching the decision at hand.

Assume that the populations for which aggregate forecasts are needed have been defined. Consider any one of these populations and denote it as T. The next relevant issue is measuring the number of decision makers in T. Generally, this is done by drawing on existing data sources such as census counts, utility records, or telephone directories. In some cases, it may be

Table 6.1
x_n for example model (see table 5.2)

Auto in-vehicle time
Shared-ride in-vehicle time
Transit in-vehicle time
Auto out-of-vehicle time/distance
Transit out-of-vehicle time/distance
Shared-ride out-of-vehicle time/distance
Auto cost/disposable income
Shared ride cost/disposable income
Transit fare/disposable income
Autos per licensed driver
Downtown workplace dummy variable
Disposable income
Primary worker dummy variable
Government worker dummy variable
Number of workers
Employment density at workplace/distance

---

necessary to estimate the population's size by conducting a supplementary survey or by combining information from a variety of sources.

Assuming that the size of T is known, we now turn to the core of the problem of aggregating across individuals—predicting the share of the population choosing each alternative. Let us denote the number of decision makers as N_T. We will write the probability an individual n in T chooses an alternative i as $P(i|x_n)$, where x_n is defined as all the attributes affecting the choice that appear in some way in the model, regardless of which utility function they appear in. For example, in the logit model described in section 5.4, x_n would have all the entries listed in table 6.1. *If we knew the value of x_n for every member of the population T*, then making an aggregate prediction would be at least conceptually straightforward. The total expected number of individuals in T choosing any alternative i, denoted by $N_T(i)$, would simply be

$$N_T(i) = \sum_{n=1}^{N_T} P(i|x_n). \tag{6.1}$$

It should be noted that $N_T(i)$ is the *expected value* of the aggregate number of individuals in the population choosing i. It is both a consistent and unbiased estimate of the actual number of people choosing i. Since the choices of individuals are probabilistic, the actual aggregate number choosing i is a random variable. In most real-world forecasting situations, T is large enough so that the distinction between the actual share of the population using i and its expected value is negligible. In what follows we will assume that the population is large and ignore this distinction. Since for any alternative i each individual's choice can be viewed as a Bernoulli event with probabilities $P(i|\mathbf{x}_n)$ and $1 - P(i|\mathbf{x}_n)$, respectively, the actual share of the population using it is the average of N_T Bernoulli variables. If the choice probabilities are known with certainty, we can show that the variance of the aggregate usage of i must be less than or equal to $1/4N_T$.

A slightly more convenient form of equation 6.1 is based on a prediction of the *share* of the population choosing i. If we let $W(i)$ denote the fraction of population T choosing alternative i, then

$$W(i) = \frac{1}{N_T} \sum_{n=1}^{N_T} P(i|\mathbf{x}_n) = \mathscr{E}[P(i|\mathbf{x})]. \tag{6.2}$$

The use of equation 6.1 or 6.2 imposes a hopelessly unrealistic data requirement; we will virtually never know each individual's complete vector of choice-relevant attributes. Even if we did, the use of either equation 6.1 or 6.2 for a population of any reasonable size would be computationally infeasible. If the distribution of the attributes $\mathbf{x}_n$ in the population T is continuous and represented by the density function $p(\mathbf{x})$, then equation 6.2 can be expressed as

$$W(i) = \int_{\mathbf{x}} P(i|\mathbf{x})p(\mathbf{x})\,\mathbf{dx} = \mathscr{E}[P(i|\mathbf{x})]. \tag{6.3}$$

However, $p(\mathbf{x})$ is generally unknown, and even if it were known, the computational burden of evaluating this integral may be prohibitive.

Stated briefly, *the problem of aggregating across individuals is to develop methods for reducing the required data and computation needed to predict aggregate usage of various alternatives.*

Finally, the reader should recognize that in actual applications the analyst never knows $P(i|\mathbf{x}_n)$. Only an estimate of it is available because the underlying parameters are unknown. This problem is discussed further in section 6.4.

6.2   Typology of Aggregation Methods

The available methods for aggregating across individuals approximate equation 6.1 or 6.2 in some way, thereby reducing the needed data and computation at the expense of the accuracy of the forecast. From the analyst's point of view the goal is to find a method that provides the best combination of accuracy and cost for a specific forecasting situation.

Our typology of aggregation procedures draws on terminology proposed by Koppelman (1975) in the most comprehensive study of this subject. He defines five general types of aggregation procedures, though some can be viewed as special cases of the others. Each procedure reduces the problem of aggregating forecasts across individuals by making some simplifying assumptions about the choice model, the population, or both. The five procedures and brief comments on their respective assumptions are as follows:

1. Average individual.   Constructs an "average individual" for the population and uses the choice probability for that average individual as an approximation for $W(i)$.

2. Classification.   Divides the population into G nearly homogeneous subgroups with sizes $N_1, N_2, \ldots, N_G$ and uses the choice probability of the average individual within each subgroup. $N_T(i)$ is estimated as the weighted sum of the G average individual forecasts, where the weights are the values of $N_g, g = 1, \ldots, G$.

3. Statistical differentials.   Approximates the distribution of attributes in the population by its moments and uses those moments in an approximation for $W(i)$. Typically only the first and second central moments of the distribution are considered.

4. Explicit integration.   Represents the distribution of the attributes in the population with an analytically convenient continuous distribution. This changes equation 6.3 as follows:

$$W(i) \cong \int_{\mathbf{x}} P(i|\mathbf{x})\tilde{p}(\mathbf{x})\,\mathbf{dx},$$

where $\tilde{p}(\mathbf{x})$ is the approximate distribution of $\mathbf{x}$ across the population. Since $\mathbf{x}$ will in most applications include both continuous and discrete elements, this integration should be thought of in the generalized sense, taking sums or integrals as appropriate. For some combinations of $P(i|\mathbf{x})$ and $\tilde{p}(\mathbf{x})$, a closed-form solution to the integral can be found.

5. Sample enumeration.   Uses a sample to represent the entire population. Equation 6.2 is then applied to the sample, and the resulting value of $W(i)$ is used as an estimate of the population's value.

In the following section we will develop the theory of using each of these methods in greater detail and comment on some of their properties.

6.3   Description of Aggregation Procedures

Average Individual Procedure

To apply the average individual aggregation procedure, we create a "representative individual," using his or her characteristics to represent the entire population. More formally, define $\bar{\mathbf{x}}$ as the mean of $p(\mathbf{x})$. Then, in using this procedure, we approximate $W(i)$ as $P(i|\bar{\mathbf{x}})$.

A simple graphical example serves to illustrate the error that the approximation produces. Suppose the population consists of exactly two individuals with characteristics x_1 and x_2, respectively, and suppose further that x is a scalar. Let $P(i|x)$ be as illustrated in figure 6.1. Here $P(i|\bar{x})$ is marked as the forecast, and $W(i)$ denotes the actual value, where

$$W(i) = \frac{P(i|x_1) + P(i|x_2)}{2}. \tag{6.4}$$

The difference, denoted by Δ, is what we will term the aggregation error. Consider, for example, a simple binary logit model $P(1|x_n) = 1/(1 + e^{-x_n})$, and the following numerical values:

$x_1 = 2.0,$

$x_2 = 0.5,$

$\bar{x} = 1.25.$

The correct share of alternative 1 is found to be $P(1|x_1) = 0.88$, $P(1|x_2) = 0.62$, so that $W(1) = 0.75$. The average individual forecast is $P(1|\bar{x}) = 0.78$; hence the aggregation error is 0.03. Note that because both x_1 and x_2 are positive, the aggregation is performed over a concave region of $P(1|x_n)$, and therefore we have in this example $P(1|\bar{x}) > W(1)$.

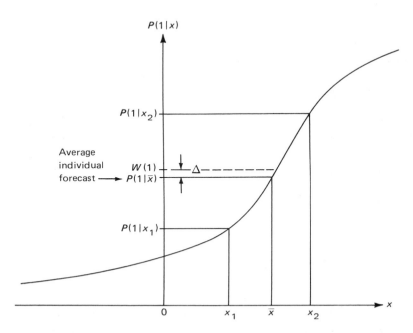

Figure 6.1
Error due to average individual aggregation

The average individual procedure has the following properties:

1. If the choice model is linear over the range of $\mathbf{x}$ in the population, Δ will be zero. This is because for any *linear* function h,

$$\mathscr{E}[h(\mathbf{x})] = h(\mathscr{E}[\mathbf{x}]).$$

Generally, $|\Delta|$ is small when $h(\mathbf{x})$ is nearly linear (in a loosely defined sense).
2. The value of Δ can be positive or negative depending both on the form of $P(i|\mathbf{x})$ and $p(\mathbf{x})$. If $P(i|\mathbf{x})$ is concave over the range of $\mathbf{x}$ in the population, $\mathscr{E}[P(i|\mathbf{x})] \leq P(i|\bar{\mathbf{x}})$, and the average individual choice probability may overestimate $W(i)$. Conversely, if $P(i|\mathbf{x})$ is convex over the range of $\mathbf{x}$, then $P(i|\bar{\mathbf{x}})$ may underestimate $W(i)$.
3, Koppelman (1975) analyzes the value of Δ under some simplified conditions. Let

$$\bar{V}_i = \int_{\mathbf{x}_i} V(\mathbf{x}_i) p(\mathbf{x}_i)\, \mathbf{dx}_i, \qquad (6.5)$$

Table 6.2
$|\Delta|$ for average individual aggregation as function of mean and variance of utilities

σ_V^2 (variance of $V_{in} - V_{jn}$)	$|\bar{V}|$ (mean of $V_{in} - V_{jn}$)						
	0.0	0.5	1.0	1.5	2.0	2.5	3.0
1	0	0.05	0.08	0.07	0.06	0.03	0.02
2	0	0.08	0.12	0.12	0.10	0.06	0.04
3	0	0.09	0.15	0.16	0.14	0.10	0.07
∞	0	0.19	0.34	0.43	0.48	0.49	0.499

Source: Koppelman (1975).

Table 6.3
$|\Delta|$ as a percentage of $W(i)$ for average individual aggregation procedure

σ_V^2 (variance of $V_{in} - V_{jn}$)	$|\bar{V}|$ (mean of $V_{in} - V_{jn}$)						
	0	0.5	1.0	1.5	2.0	2.5	3.0
1	0	7.8	10.5	8.1	6.5	3.1	2.0
2	0	13.1	16.7	14.8	11.4	6.5	4.2
3	0	15.0	21.7	20.8	16.7	11.2	7.5
∞	0	38.0	68.0	86.0	96.0	98.0	100.0

Source: Adapted from Koppelman (1975).

where $\mathbf{x}_i$ is the subvector of $\mathbf{x}$ affecting the systematic utility of alternative i and $p(\mathbf{x}_i)$ is its distribution. For example, if V is linear in its parameters, then $\bar{V}_i = \boldsymbol{\beta}'\bar{\mathbf{x}}_i$. Koppelman shows that under certain conditions there will be only one value of $\bar{V}$ for which $\Delta = 0$. Also the skewness of the distribution of the V's will affect Δ.

4. In simple numerical examples the value of $|\Delta|$ can be shown to increase as the variance of the distribution $p(\mathbf{x})$ grows. The errors for even reasonable situations can be quite substantial. Consider, for example, a simple binary choice situation in which the probit model is used:

$$P_n(i) = \Phi(V_{in} - V_{jn}), \qquad (6.6)$$

and $V_{in} - V_{jn}$ is normally distributed across the population with mean $\bar{V}$, variance σ_V^2. In this case $|\Delta|$ is given by table 6.2 as a function of $|\bar{V}|$ and σ_V^2. Table 6.3 expresses $|\Delta|$ as a percentage of the true value of $W(i)$. Note that the true value of $W(i)$ exceeds 0.5 for all the cases evaluated. The percentage errors when $-|\bar{V}|$ is used can be much greater because $W(i)$ will be small.

Classification

Classification is simply a logical extension of the average individual aggregation method. It is based on the observation that average individual aggregation is in general most inaccurate when the distribution of **x** has high variance. Given this, in the classification forecasting method we partition the population into relatively homogeneous subgroups and simply apply average individual aggregation to each subgroup.

Stated more formally, the classification method proceeds in the following steps:

1. Partition the population T into G mutually exclusive, collectively exhaustive subgroups, each corresponding to the portion of the population with a range of the attribute vector equal to set $\{\mathbf{X}_g\}$, $g = 1, \ldots, G$.
2. Estimate the number of decision makers in each group, denoted by N_g, $g = 1, \ldots, G$.
3. For each group choose some representative value $\tilde{\mathbf{x}}_g$.
4. Approximate $W(i)$ as

$$W(i) \cong \sum_{g=1}^{G} \frac{N_g}{N_T} P(i|\tilde{\mathbf{x}}_g). \tag{6.7}$$

It should be obvious that classification is identical to the average individual procedure when $G = 1$ and $\tilde{\mathbf{x}}_1 = \bar{\mathbf{x}}$. Equation 6.7 is also equivalent to the approximation of the integral in equation 6.3 by the trapezoidal rule.

The key to classification lies in the partitioning of the entire space of possible attributes into subsets. Usually as the number of groups rises, the accuracy of the approximation in equation 6.7 will increase, but so will the data requirements and computational difficulties associated with making a forecast. Establishing a trade-off between the number of groups and the accuracy of the forecast represents an area of judgment for the analyst. Some useful insights into how different classifications affect the errors due to aggregation can be given.

1. It is important to stress that the attributes in $\mathbf{x}_n$ are combined in the model to form the systematic utility. The goal of a good classification system is therefore not to establish groups in which the within-group variation in **x** is small. *Rather, we want groups with small within-group variation in the V's.* Reid (1978) suggests classifying directly on the values of the systematic utilities rather than the underlying variables in **x**. This is a reasonable approach but requires knowledge of the fraction of the population in each utility class, which can only be derived by integrating $p(\mathbf{x})$ over various subsets. Inasmuch as the only practical way of doing this is often via classification of **x**, there may be little gained from utility-based classification.

2. It is generally infeasible to classify by every dimension in **x**. For example, in table 6.1 there are 16 different variables that constitute **x**. Even if we divided each variable into only two categories, there would be $2^{16} = 65{,}536$ different groups!

3. As a consequence of points 1 and 2, it generally makes sense to select a small number of independent variables on which to classify the population. In a loose sense the variables chosen should be "important" to the choice process in that they have a large effect on the systematic utility of at least one alternative and have a wide distribution across the population. For example, in the three-mode logit model described in chapter 5, a variable such as autos per licensed driver might be a good candidate for defining classes.

4. Each of the G classes contributes to the forecast $W(i)$ in proportion to its share of the population, N_g/N_T. All else equal, it therefore makes sense to avoid classes that are disproportionately small because the computational effort associated with forecasting for any single class is independent of the size of the class.

5. Classes defined for portions of the population for which $P(i|\mathbf{x})$ is nearly linear do not need to be finely subdivided. This is because average individual aggregation works quite well for subpopulations with nearly linear choice probabilities.

6. Some classes will often have open sets $\{\mathbf{X}_g\}$, making it difficult to define $\tilde{\mathbf{x}}_g$. For example, if income were used as a basis for classification, one class might be all travelers from households with income over \$30,000 per year. It may be useful to obtain detailed information on the conditional distribution of income, given it exceeds \$30,000, and solve for the conditional expected value of income. One might also define the upper income range to include a small fraction of the population, thereby reducing the influence of the chosen $\tilde{\mathbf{x}}_g$ on the total forecast $W(i)$. (This is only an apparent contradiction to guideline 4. The important aspect of point 4 was the phrase "all else equal." In this case the estimated value of $\tilde{\mathbf{x}}_g$ for an open set $\{\mathbf{X}_g\}$ may have much greater error than for the other groups.)

7. The different classes can vary in their available choices as well as their values of $\tilde{\mathbf{x}}_g$. Again referring to the three-mode model described in chapter 5, the class of households for which autos per licensed driver is zero would not have the option of driving alone in their choice set, whereas other classes would. As we will discuss further in section 6.4, this turns out to be a significant aspect of a good classification scheme.

8. Some variables that are components of $\mathbf{x}$ are often classified automatically as part of a demand analysis. For example, we generally divide a study area into geographical zones and predict travel volumes between zones as a function of interzonal times, costs, and so forth. The zones serve as a "natural" classification for the level-of-service variables that enter into the choice model.

9. To make forecasts using equation 6.7, it will be necessary to predict the values of class sizes N_g, $g = 1, \ldots, G$. This may be more difficult for some classification schemes than for others. For example, auto ownership is often predicted as part of a typical urban travel demand analysis, and it often is simple to use or adapt those forecasts for the purposes of using classification.

Statistical Differentials

The method of statistical differentials is a technique for approximating the expected value of a function of random variables from information about the moments of their joint distribution. It was first suggested as an approach for aggregation across alternatives by Talvitie (1973).

The method is best illustrated by beginning with equation 6.3,

$$W(i) = \int_{\mathbf{x}} P(i|\mathbf{x})p(\mathbf{x})\,d\mathbf{x}.$$

The function $P(i|\mathbf{x})$ is now expanded as a second-order Taylor's series around $\bar{\mathbf{x}}$, so ignoring high-order terms, we have

$$P(i|\mathbf{x}) \cong P(i|\bar{\mathbf{x}}) + \sum_{r=1}^{R} \frac{\partial}{\partial x_r} P(i|\mathbf{x})\bigg|_{\bar{\mathbf{x}}} (x_r - \bar{x}_r)$$

$$+ \frac{1}{2}\sum_{r=1}^{R}\sum_{r'=1}^{R} \frac{\partial^2}{\partial x_r \partial x_{r'}} P(i|\mathbf{x})\bigg|_{\bar{\mathbf{x}}} (x_r - \bar{x}_r)(x_{r'} - \bar{x}_{r'}), \tag{6.8}$$

where R = the number of elements in $\mathbf{x}$,

$\quad x_r$ = the rth element in $\mathbf{x}$,

$\quad \bar{x}_r$ = the rth element in $\bar{\mathbf{x}}$.

Substituting equation 6.8 into 6.3, we obtain

$$W(i) \cong \int P(i|\bar{\mathbf{x}}) p(\mathbf{x})\, d\mathbf{x} + \sum_{r=1}^{R} \int \frac{\partial}{\partial x_r} P(i|\mathbf{x})\bigg|_{\bar{\mathbf{x}}} (x_r - \bar{x}_r) p(\mathbf{x})\, d\mathbf{x}$$

$$+ \frac{1}{2} \sum_{r=1}^{R} \sum_{r'=1}^{R} \int \frac{\partial^2}{\partial x_r \partial x_{r'}} P(i|\mathbf{x})\bigg|_{\bar{\mathbf{x}}} (x_r - \bar{x}_r)(x_{r'} - \bar{x}_{r'}) p(\mathbf{x})\, d\mathbf{x}. \tag{6.9}$$

Noting that the $P(i|\bar{\mathbf{x}})$ and its derivatives evaluated at $\bar{\mathbf{x}}$ are not functions of $\mathbf{x}$, we obtain

$$W(i) \cong P(i|\bar{\mathbf{x}}) \int p(\mathbf{x})\, d\mathbf{x} + \sum_{r=1}^{R} \frac{\partial P(i|\mathbf{x})}{\partial x_r}\bigg|_{\bar{\mathbf{x}}} \int (x_r - \bar{x}_r) p(\mathbf{x})\, d\mathbf{x}$$

$$+ \frac{1}{2} \sum_{r=1}^{R} \sum_{r'=1}^{R} \frac{\partial^2 P(i|\mathbf{x})}{\partial x_r \partial x_{r'}}\bigg|_{\bar{\mathbf{x}}} \int (x_r - \bar{x}_r)(x_{r'} - \bar{x}_{r'}) p(\mathbf{x})\, d\mathbf{x} \tag{6.10}$$

$$= P(i|\bar{\mathbf{x}}) + \frac{1}{2} \sum_{r=1}^{R} \sum_{r'=1}^{R} \frac{\partial^2 P(i|\mathbf{x})}{\partial x_r \partial x_{r'}}\bigg|_{\bar{\mathbf{x}}} \operatorname{cov}(x_r, x_{r'}).$$

The last line of equation 6.10 results from the definition of $p(\mathbf{x})$ as a density function (therefore integrating to one) and the definitions of $\bar{x}_r$ and $\operatorname{cov}(x_r, x_{r'})$.

As an example of how the method of statistical differential works, consider a simple binary logit model for the case where $\mathbf{x}_n$ has only two scalar entries, x_{in} and x_{jn}, corresponding to attributes of alternatives i and j, respectively. Thus

$$P(i|x) = \frac{e^{\beta x_{in}}}{e^{\beta x_{in}} + e^{\beta x_{jn}}} = \frac{1}{1 + e^{-\beta x_n}}, \tag{6.11}$$

where $x_n = x_{in} - x_{jn}$. Suppose that x_{in} and x_{jn} are jointly distributed with mean $\bar{x}_i$ and $\bar{x}_j$, respectively, and that $\operatorname{var}(x_{in}) = \sigma_i^2$, $\operatorname{var}(x_{jn}) = \sigma_j^2$, and $\operatorname{cov}(x_{in}, x_{jn}) = \sigma_{ij}$.

In this case $x_n = x_{in} - x_{jn}$ has mean $\bar{x} = \bar{x}_i - \bar{x}_j$ and variance $\sigma^2 = \sigma_i^2 + \sigma_j^2 - 2\sigma_{ij}$. To apply equation 6.10, we note that

$$\frac{\partial^2 P(i|x_n)}{\partial x_n^2} = -\beta^2 P(i|x_n)[1 - P(i|x_n)][2P(i|x_n) - 1]. \tag{6.12}$$

Using equation 6.10, we find that

$$W(i) \cong \frac{1}{1 + e^{-\beta \bar{x}}}$$

$$- \frac{\beta^2}{2} \left(\frac{1}{1 + e^{-\beta \bar{x}}} \right) \left(\frac{e^{-\beta \bar{x}}}{1 + e^{-\beta \bar{x}}} \right) \left(\frac{2}{1 + e^{-\beta \bar{x}}} - 1 \right) \sigma^2. \tag{6.13}$$

Some relevant points about the statistical differentials procedure are as follows:

1. A useful interpretation of equation 6.10 is that the second term on the right-hand side of equation 6.10 represents a "correction" to the average individual forecast, $P(i|\bar{x})$.
2. There is no guarantee that the correction term makes the statistical differentials procedure more accurate than the average individual method. In particular, even though $P(i|x_n)$ was approximated by a Taylor's series, the statistical differentials approximation does *not* have all the properties of a Taylor's series, primarily because the terms in the equation 6.10 represent integrals of the Taylor series terms taken over $p(x)$. Thus, even though the statistical differential series converges to the true value of $W(i)$ as we increase the number of higher-order terms (and if $p(x)$ meets certain regularity conditions), there is no guarantee that the convergence will be "fast" in any particular sense.
3. In theory the approximation for $W(i)$ could always be improved by using a large enough number of higher-order terms in the series expansion for $P(i|x_n)$. In practice these terms would be functions of the central moments of $p(x)$ which, beyond the second order, are extraordinarily difficult to forecast. In fact even the covariance terms in equation 6.10 may be difficult to predict, and it may be necessary to ignore some and judgmentally estimate others.

Explicit Integration

The fourth aggregation procedure we consider exploits the fact that the integral expression in equation 6.3 is solvable for particular combinations of $p(x)$ and $P(i|x)$. Thus, by approximating $p(x)$ by some known distribution, we can obtain $W(i)$ via direct integration.

There are two ways of deriving the results relevant to explicit integration. The most direct approach is actually to solve the integral expression for $W(i)$. A somewhat more subtle approach, however, is both easier analytically and considerably more insightful. *The key to this latter approach is to treat the difference between any alternative's attributes, $\mathbf{x}_{in}$, and the population mean, $\bar{\mathbf{x}}_i$, as a source of random observational error resulting from the aggregation process.* Thus we define

$$\tilde{\boldsymbol{\varepsilon}}_{in} = \mathbf{x}_{in} - \bar{\mathbf{x}}_i, \tag{6.14}$$

where $\tilde{\boldsymbol{\varepsilon}}_{in}$ is a vector of deviations, not a scalar. We also assume that the population is defined so that all individuals in it have the same choice set C. If this is not the case, the population must be further divided, and separate aggregate forecasts must be made for each subgroup. Assuming that the systematic component of utility is linear in parameters, the definition of $\tilde{\boldsymbol{\varepsilon}}_{in}$ enables us to express the total utility of an alternative i as

$$U_{in} = \boldsymbol{\beta}' \mathbf{x}_{in} + \varepsilon_{in} = \boldsymbol{\beta}' \bar{\mathbf{x}}_i + (\boldsymbol{\beta}' \tilde{\boldsymbol{\varepsilon}}_{in} + \varepsilon_{in}). \tag{6.15}$$

We can now treat $\tilde{\boldsymbol{\varepsilon}}_{in}$ as a random variable distributed across the population and define an "aggregate systematic utility" for the population, denoted by $\bar{V}_i$ as $\boldsymbol{\beta}' \bar{\mathbf{x}}_i$, and express the utility as follows:

$$U_{in} = \bar{V}_i + \varepsilon_{in}^*, \tag{6.16}$$

where $\varepsilon_{in}^* = \boldsymbol{\beta}' \tilde{\boldsymbol{\varepsilon}}_{in} + \varepsilon_{in}$.

The probability of any randomly drawn individual in the population choosing alternative i is simply $W(i)$, and this is given by

$$W(i) = Pr(\bar{V}_i + \varepsilon_{in}^* \geq \bar{V}_j + \varepsilon_{jn}^*, \forall j \in C), \tag{6.17}$$

which can be evaluated using the joint distribution of $\{\varepsilon_{in}^*, \ldots, \varepsilon_{Jn}^*\}$. Thus the solution to equation 6.17 is equivalent to explicit integration of $P(i|\mathbf{x})$ over $p(\mathbf{x})$.

With this result we can now ask, What combinations of the distributions of ε_{in} and $\tilde{\boldsymbol{\varepsilon}}_{in}$ yield a distribution for ε_{in}^* for which equation 6.17 is tractable? Only two combinations have to date yielded useful results. We consider both of these.

CASE 1 (PROBIT AND NORMALLY DISTRIBUTED ATTRIBUTES): If the original disturbances in the utilities are normally distributed and $p(\mathbf{x})$ is normal (implying that the $\tilde{\boldsymbol{\varepsilon}}_{in}$ are normal), then $\boldsymbol{\beta}' \tilde{\boldsymbol{\varepsilon}}_{in} + \varepsilon_{in}$ is a linear combination of normal variates and is consequently normal. We can therefore express $W(i)$ as what might be termed an *aggregate probit model*.

This result was first noted by McFadden and Reid (1975) for the binary case and was extended by Bouthelier (1978) for multinomial probit. Here we reproduce only the binary version. Let $\tilde{\sigma}_i^2$ denote the variance of $\boldsymbol{\beta}'\tilde{\boldsymbol{\varepsilon}}_{in}$, $\tilde{\sigma}_j^2$ denote the variance $\boldsymbol{\beta}'\tilde{\boldsymbol{\varepsilon}}_{jn}$, and $\tilde{\sigma}_{ij}$ be the covariance between $\boldsymbol{\beta}'\tilde{\boldsymbol{\varepsilon}}_{in}$ and $\boldsymbol{\beta}'\tilde{\boldsymbol{\varepsilon}}_{jn}$. Let $\sigma^2 = \tilde{\sigma}_i^2 + \tilde{\sigma}_j^2 - 2\tilde{\sigma}_{ij}$ be the variance of $(\boldsymbol{\beta}'\tilde{\boldsymbol{\varepsilon}}_{in} - \boldsymbol{\beta}'\tilde{\boldsymbol{\varepsilon}}_{jn})$. (The value of σ^2 can be derived by defining the vector $\mathbf{x}_n = \mathbf{x}_{in} - \mathbf{x}_{jn}$ and letting $\boldsymbol{\Sigma}_x$ denote the variance-covariance matrix of $\mathbf{x}$. Then $\sigma^2 = \boldsymbol{\beta}'\boldsymbol{\Sigma}_x\boldsymbol{\beta}$.) Given this notation, equation 6.17 becomes

$$Pr(U_{in} \geq U_{jn}) = Pr[\boldsymbol{\beta}'\overline{\mathbf{x}}_i + \boldsymbol{\beta}'\tilde{\boldsymbol{\varepsilon}}_{in} + \varepsilon_{in} \geq \boldsymbol{\beta}'\overline{\mathbf{x}}_j + \boldsymbol{\beta}'\tilde{\boldsymbol{\varepsilon}}_{in} + \varepsilon_{jn}]$$
$$= Pr(\boldsymbol{\beta}'(\tilde{\boldsymbol{\varepsilon}}_{jn} - \tilde{\boldsymbol{\varepsilon}}_{in}) + (\varepsilon_{jn} - \varepsilon_{in}) \leq \boldsymbol{\beta}'(\overline{\mathbf{x}}_i - \overline{\mathbf{x}}_j)]. \tag{6.18}$$

Making the usual assumption in binary probit that the variance of $\varepsilon_{jn} - \varepsilon_{in}$ is normalized to one, equation 6.18 implies that

$$W(i) = \Phi\left(\frac{\boldsymbol{\beta}'(\overline{\mathbf{x}}_i - \overline{\mathbf{x}}_j)}{\sqrt{1 + \sigma^2}}\right). \tag{6.19}$$

We implicitly assume that the $\tilde{\boldsymbol{\varepsilon}}$'s are independent of the ε's. This is reasonable because they arise from totally distinct observational processes.

Summarized briefly, when the distribution of attributes of the population is normal and the underlying choice model is probit, the aggregate share is the same as the average individual forecast, except that the variance of the disturbance is increased from 1 to $1 + \sigma^2$, and as a result the scale of the aggregate model is smaller than the scale of the individual model.

Figure 6.2 depicts $W(i)$ as a function of $\boldsymbol{\beta}'(\overline{\mathbf{x}}_i - \overline{\mathbf{x}}_j)$ for various levels of σ^2. The average individual forecast corresponds to the case $\sigma^2 = 0$ in this figure. Note that the values in table 6.2 were calculated by using this result:

$$|\Delta| = \Phi(\overline{V}) - \Phi\left(\frac{\overline{V}}{\sqrt{1 + \sigma_V^2}}\right).$$

The extension of this result to multinomial probit proceeds in exactly the same fashion, except that we must maintain the joint distribution of all the disturbance terms and $\boldsymbol{\beta}'\tilde{\boldsymbol{\varepsilon}}_{in}$'s. The resulting algebra is, however, somewhat cumbersome. Interested readers are referred to Bouthelier (1978) or Daganzo (1979).

CASE 2 (LOGIT AND NORMALLY DISTRIBUTED ATTRIBUTES): When the disturbance terms of the utilities are independent and identically Gumbel distributed, Westin (1974) has shown that the term

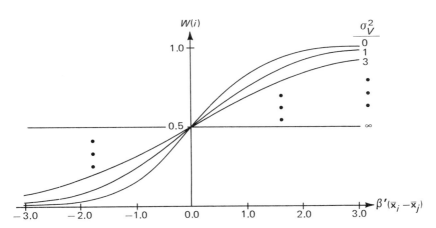

Figure 6.2
Population shares for binary probit and normal $p(\mathbf{x})$

$$\boldsymbol{\beta}'(\tilde{\varepsilon}_{jn} - \tilde{\varepsilon}_{in}) + (\varepsilon_{jn} - \varepsilon_{in}) \tag{6.20}$$

is in fact S_B distributed. (This rarely used distribution is described in Johnson and Kotz 1972, vol. 2, pp. 23–27.) Thus for the binary case

$$W(i) = F_B[\boldsymbol{\beta}'(\bar{\mathbf{x}}_i - \bar{\mathbf{x}}_j)], \tag{6.21}$$

where F_B denotes the cumulative S_B distribution. No closed form solution for equation 6.21 exists, but tables for the S_B distribution function are available.

This result can be generalized to multivariate cases, resulting in the value of $W(i)$ being a cumulant of the *multivariate S_B distribution*. However, evaluation of this cumulative function has not been explored beyond the three-alternative case.

Some specific comments on explicit integration are as follows:

1. The assumption of normality of the attributes in the population may be violated, particularly for qualitative or integer attributes such as dummy variables or auto ownership. In these cases it may be useful first to classify the population by the important discrete attributes and then to use explicit integration on each class.

2. Koppelman (1975) has shown in numerical experiments that if the distribution of $\boldsymbol{\beta}'(\tilde{\varepsilon}_{jn} - \tilde{\varepsilon}_{in})$ is skewed rather than symmetric, the error due to using explicit integration assuming normality is quite small (less than 3%) over the entire range of reasonable conditions.

3. For some combinations of skewness in the actual distribution of the attributes and differences in attribute means, the explicit integration method produces errors that are greater than the average individual method. However, these ranges are very narrow.

4. The results for explicit integration do not hold when the parameters are assumed to be distributed randomly across the population (see section 5.7). This is due to the fact that if both β and $\tilde{\varepsilon}_{in}$ are random, then $\beta'\tilde{\varepsilon}_{in}$ is the sum of products of random variables, which is not normally distributed even if both β and $\tilde{\varepsilon}_{in}$ are normal.

Sample Enumeration

The last of the procedures we will discuss is sample enumeration. In its simplest form, sample enumeration uses a random sample of the population as "representative" of the entire population. The predicted share of the sample choosing alternative i is used as an estimate for $W(i)$:

$$\hat{W}(i) = \frac{1}{N_s} \sum_{n=1}^{N_s} P(i|\mathbf{x}_n), \tag{6.22}$$

where N_s is the number of individuals in the sample.

Sample enumeration can also be used when the sample is drawn nonrandomly from the population. For example, suppose the sample is (endogenously or exogenously) stratified so that different groups within the population are sampled at different rates. In this case it is straightforward first to classify the population into the groups used for stratification of the sample, apply the sample enumeration method to each group, and then compute an estimate of $W(i)$ as the weighted sum of the within-class forecasts. Mathematically this corresponds to equation 6.23:

$$\hat{W}(i) = \sum_{g=1}^{G} \left(\frac{N_g}{N_T}\right) \frac{1}{N_{sg}} \sum_{n=1}^{N_{sg}} P(i|\mathbf{x}_n), \tag{6.23}$$

where N_{sg} is the size of the sample for the gth group, and N_g and N_T are as before.

Sample enumeration can be adapted to deal with a particularly troublesome forecasting problem. In some instances the complete choice set is very large because either the number of original alternatives is inherently great (as often occurs in destination choice models) or, when forecasts are made for successive time intervals, the choice in any period can depend on some or all prior choices (as might be the case for residential location decisions). In the case of time-dependent choices, if there are J choices and τ time intervals, there are J^τ possible choice "paths" over time.

In both these situations we can often adopt some form of Monte Carlo simulation to reduce the computational burden of producing a forecast. Two common applications are as follows:

1. Random sampling from the choice set. This approach applies only when we use logit. Because of the IIA property, if we first randomly sample a subset of each individual's possible choices and then use sample enumeration to estimate $W(i)$, the resulting estimator is consistent. (As we will discuss further in section 9.3, this procedure and numerous variants can also be used in estimating the parameters of a logit model.)
2. Simulation of outcomes. When an individual faces a sequence of τ decisions, we are often not particularly interested in forecasting the fraction of the population selecting each of the possible J^τ choice paths. Rather, we are more concerned with estimating the fraction of the population making each choice at each time, resulting in $J\tau$ forecasts. One way of exploiting this result is actually to simulate the choice process for each individual in the sample.

This latter procedure can be illustrated by means of a binary choice example. Consider an individual n at time 1. Let $P_n(i)$ and $P_n(j)$ denote the predicted probability that n chooses alternatives i and j, respectively. We then draw a random variable u_1 uniformly distributed between 0 and 1 and "assign" the individual to alternative i at time 1 if $P_n^1(i) \leq u_1$, or to alternative j otherwise. At time period 2 we forecast $P_n^2(i)$ and $P_n^2(j)$ *conditional on the assigned choice for time period 1*. We again draw a uniformly distributed random variable and assign the individual to i or j, as appropriate. This procedure continues through all τ time periods. In doing this for all N_s individuals, we keep a count of $N^t(i)$, the number in the sample "assigned" to i at time t. We then use

$$\hat{W}^t(i) = \frac{N^t(i)}{N_s} \tag{6.24}$$

as an estimate of the share of the population choosing i at time t.

The following aspects of sample enumeration are worth noting:

1. The predicted aggregate shares are estimates and are consequently subject to sampling error. When the choice probabilities or the sample are small, the sampling error may be a large fraction of $W(i)$.

2. The sample enumeration estimator of $W(i)$ is consistent as long as the parameter estimates used are consistent. (This can be shown straightforwardly from the Slutsky theorem stated in section 2.4. The variance of the sample enumeration forecast will vary inversely with N_s, the sample size.)

3. Sample enumeration makes it easy to produce forecasts for different socioeconomic groups. All one need do is keep separate tabulations of the choice probabilities for each of the socioeconomic groups of interest. If, however, the groups are only a small fraction of the original N_s individuals in the sample, the variance of the subpopulation forecasts may be quite high.

4. Although using Monte Carlo simulation in a sample enumeration forecasting procedure retains the property of consistently estimating $W(i)$, it generally increases the variance of the forecast.

5. Sample enumeration is well suited for forecasting the effects of policies that differentially impact various population groups. To forecast the changes in aggregate shares under some policy, one simply changes the values of the appropriate independent variables for each affected individual in the sample. For example, suppose we wanted to test the effects of rebating the transit fares of low-income travelers using different sliding scales, each based on gross household income. For each formula we would appropriately change the transit fare for each traveler and perform a sample enumeration forecast. This type of procedure is straightforward to program on a computer because it essentially involves execution of the same steps for each observation in the sample.

6.4   A Comparison of Methods for Aggregate Forecasting

Each of the five procedures described in section 6.3 has some relative strengths and weaknesses. In this section we explore both the theoretical and empirical evidence about the procedures in order to suggest some guidelines for choosing the procedures most appropriate to any particular situation.

In comparing the various procedures, Koppelman (1975) and Koppelman and Ben-Akiva (1977) found that classification works extremely well even when a relatively small number of classes is used. However, they also

Table 6.4
Root mean square errors due to classification (in %)

	Demographic classification		
	3 groups a. No drive-alone alternative b. Autos available < 1. c. Autos available ≥ 1.	*3 groups* a. Autos available ≤ 0.25. b. Autos available between 0.25 and 1 c. Autos available ≥ 1.	*2 groups* a. No drive-alone alternative b. Drive alone available
Level of geographic aggregation			
45 districts	3.3	9.9	5.2
10 groups	2.9	8.4	5.2
4 rings	2.8	7.9	5.3

Source: Koppelman (1975).

concluded that it is crucial that the classes not include *segments with very different choice sets*. In applying a three-mode logit choice model similar to the one described in chapter 5, Koppelman experimented with different levels of geographic and socioeconomic aggregation, applying classification to make forecasts of work trip modal shares for downtown workers. Comparing forecasts of trips made using classification with the trips forecast using sample enumeration on a large survey, he obtained the weighted root mean square errors due to classification. Some of his results are summarized as percentage errors in table 6.4. The root mean square (rms) error was weighted to account for the fact that the number of observations in the survey varied across classes. If $O_g(i)$ is the sample enumeration forecast of the share of travelers in group g using i, then the error measure is

$$\text{rms} = \left\{ \sum_{g=1}^{G} \frac{N_g}{N_T} \sum_{i \in C_g} O_g(i) \left[\frac{W_g(i) - O_g(i)}{W_g(i)} \right]^2 \right\}^{1/2},$$

where C_g is the choice set for group g. Because the original home interview surveys were large and only origin-destination pairs with over 30 trips were used, the aggregation error in the sample enumeration forecast was assumed small enough to ignore. The demographic groups were defined on the basis of whether or not driving alone was in the choice set and the number of autos available to the household. The most notable feature of the table is that the use of only two demographic groups results in an aggregation error of only 5.2 to 5.3% when the grouping is based only on the choice set. Conversely, the aggregation error for three groups is almost twice as great when the demographic classification fails to include the choice set definition.

This result also extends to the statistical differential procedure. Aggregation errors can be quite large unless the groups within the population with different choice sets are treated separately. In some numerical examples Koppelman (1975) also shows that when the variance of the utility distribution is high, the errors in the statistical differentials procedure exceed those of even the average individual approach, suggesting that the statistical differential procedure is inappropriate when applied to a very heterogeneous population.

In addition to the error introduced by aggregation there is a forecast error due to the fact that the coefficients used to compute the choice probabilities are estimates and are consequently subject to sampling errors. If the systematic utilities are linear in their parameters, the asymptotic variance of the systematic utilities is given by

$$\text{var}\,[\hat{\beta}'\mathbf{x}_{in}] = \mathbf{x}_{in}'\Sigma_{\beta}\mathbf{x}_{in}, \tag{6.25}$$

where Σ_{β} is the asymptotic variance-covariance matrix of the coefficient estimates. Similarly

$$\text{cov}\,(\hat{\beta}'\mathbf{x}_{in}, \hat{\beta}'\mathbf{x}_{jn}) = \mathbf{x}_{in}'\Sigma_{\beta}\mathbf{x}_{jn}. \tag{6.26}$$

Given this, as a first-order approximation (Cramér 1957),

$$\text{var}\,[\hat{P}_n(i)] = \sum_{j \in C_n} \sum_{i \in C_n} \frac{\partial P_n(i)}{\partial(\beta'\mathbf{x}_{in})} \frac{\partial P_n(j)}{\partial(\beta'\mathbf{x}_{jn})} \cdot \text{cov}\,(\hat{\beta}'\mathbf{x}_{in}, \hat{\beta}'\mathbf{x}_{jn}). \tag{6.27}$$

Using equations 6.26 and 6.27, Koppelman (1975) finds that for a "typical" traveler in his sample the standard error of the estimate of the choice probability is about 11% of the estimate itself. (This mode choice model was estimated on a sample of 874 travelers taken from the 1968 Washington, D.C., Home Interview Survey. This is a different subsample from the same data base used in the example discussed in chapter 5.) This result, along with those in table 6.4, suggests that at least in this particular case study the errors due to the randomness in the parameter estimates exceed those due to the aggregation procedure even when relatively simple aggregation methods are adopted.

Bouthelier (1978) has suggested a *hybrid procedure*, first using classification for discrete variables and then applying explicit integration for the subpopulations defined by the discrete variables. In numerical experiments with a probit model he shows that the assumption of normally distributed independent variables is a good approximation once the key discrete variables are controlled for. This type of hybrid procedure can also be used to combine the classification and statistical differentials methods, using classification to reduce the within-group variance sufficiently so that the statistical differentials approximation is reasonably accurate.

A key difference between a disaggregate choice model with $U_{in} = V_{in} + \varepsilon_{in}$ and an aggregate model with $U_{in} = \bar{V}_i + \varepsilon_{in}^*$ is that $\mathrm{var}\,(\varepsilon_{in}) \leq \mathrm{var}\,(\varepsilon_{in}^*)$. Since the scale of the choice model is inversely proportional to the standard deviation of the random utilities, we conclude that an aggregate choice model with $\bar{V}_i$ replacing V_{in} will not have a larger scale than a disaggregate model. This observation suggests the following hybrid aggregation procedure for a MNL model:

1. Estimate a disaggregate MNL model

$$P_n(i) = \frac{e^{\beta x_{in}}}{\sum_{j \in C_n} e^{\beta' x_{jn}}}.$$

2. Group the data into relatively homogeneous market segments with identical choice sets. Calculate $\bar{x}_{ig}$, the average of x_{in} for group $g = 1, \ldots, G$.

3. For every observation in the estimation sample, replace the values of x_{in} with $\bar{x}_{ig}$ from the group to which it belongs.

4. Estimate a new scale parameter $\tilde{\mu}$ for the following model:

$$P_n(i) = \frac{e^{\tilde{\mu}(\beta' \bar{x}_{ig})}}{\sum_{j \in C_g} e^{\tilde{\mu}(\beta' \bar{x}_{jg})}},$$

where the vector $\hat{\beta}$ is the estimate obtained in step 1. This model includes only one unknown parameter, $\tilde{\mu}$, which corrects for the substitution of $\bar{x}_{ig}$ for x_{in}. It should satisfy the restriction $0 < \tilde{\mu} \leq 1$. This estimation is easy to execute with a standard logit estimation procedure because the specification is particularly simple: there is just one generic variable whose coefficient is $\tilde{\mu}$. The data of course are just the disaggregate data used to calculate $\hat{\beta}$ in step 1. Note that this is equivalent to the use of repeated observations for each market segment (see section 5.5).

5. Forecast using the classification procedure, and apply the logit model to the subpopulations averages using the scaled-down vector of coefficients $\tilde{\mu} \cdot \hat{\beta}$.

Of all the procedures, sample enumeration is the most flexible in forecasting how policies differentially impact various segments of the population. In contrast, classification-based forecasts can be disaggregated only for the groups originally defined as distinct classes. Unfortunately the definition of classes that keep the errors of aggregation low is not necessarily the same as that which would provide information on the groups about which forecasts are needed. Explicit integration and statistical differentials do not permit easy disaggregation of population-level forecasts.

Sample enumeration also has the advantage of making no prior assumptions about the distribution of the attributes across the population. Sample enumeration, on the other hand, is difficult to use when we want forecasts that are spatially disaggregated. For example, if there are 100 traffic analysis zones, there are 100^2 or 10,000 zone pairs. If we are interested in the zone-to-zone travel demand, we would require an enormous sample to represent adequately the distribution of the population traveling from every origin to every destination.

Since the procedures differ in their computational costs, accuracy, data requirements and the ease with which they can be implemented in any particular situation, no one approach clearly dominates the others. However, most empirical applications to date have used either classification or sample enumeration. Classification has tended to be used when spatially disaggregated predictions are essential, as is often true for facility-level planning. At the other extreme sample enumeration has proved most useful when only areawide forecasts are needed. For example, for an analysis of policies such as fuel price increases, transit fare changes, or auto taxes, we often need only highly aggregated forecasts of choices such as average modal shares, trip lengths, fuel consumption, or auto ownership, perhaps disaggregated by income groups or other demographic variables. The applications of these procedures are further discussed in chapter 11, where we present two operational model systems.

The other procedures have not often been used for a variety of different reasons. Generally, the populations of interest to planners are too heterogeneous for the naive or statistical differentials procedure to provide sufficiently accurate forecasts. This is particularly true because choice sets often vary widely within the population. Explicit integration has been judged too difficult to apply in multinomial choice analysis.

6.5 Summary

This chapter has discussed the problem of using models of individual choice to obtain forecasts of the expected aggregate behavior of a population. Five qualitatively distinct approaches (some of which are special cases of others) were presented:

1. average individual,
2. classification,
3. statistical differentials,
4. explicit integration,
5. sample enumeration.

The issues that should be considered in applying each of these procedures were summarized.

The most significant conclusion in this chapter is that empirical evidence suggests that the errors due to aggregation across individuals can be made relatively small without a great deal of difficulty. Work to date has also indicated most of the approximations used in the various procedures are quite robust in the sense that only small errors result from even substantial departures from the assumed conditions. Thus as long as the problem of aggregating across individuals is approached with some care (particularly ensuring that groups within the population that have different choice sets are appropriately handled), it need not be a major source of error in the forecasting process.

7 Tests and Practical Issues in Developing Discrete Choice Models

7.1 Introduction

In the previous chapters we introduced the theory and the methods of estimating and forecasting with discrete choice models. In this chapter we consider the process of empirical model development. This process does not follow a definitive set of rules. It employs rigorous statistical methods but also requires many intuitive, model-building judgments. We emphasize in this chapter both the formal and informal tests that were found in many empirical studies to be the most useful aids in developing and evaluating discrete choice models.

The next section of this chapter is a discussion of the philosophy that underlies our model-building approach. In section 7.3 we present the mode choice example that will be used throughout most of the remainder of this chapter. This is followed by the three major sections of this chapter. Section 7.4 considers the model structure as given and investigates the specification of the utility functions. This section includes a demonstration of the use of the classical statistical hypothesis tests that were introduced in chapter 2. Section 7.5 describes tests of the basic structural assumptions of discrete choice models. We focus on the assumptions inherent in the multinomial logit model. Section 7.6 describes informal test procedures that examine the predicted choice probabilities.

7.2 The Art of Model Building

In general, it is impossible to determine the most appropriate specification of a model from data analysis. A "good fit" to the data does not necessarily mean an adequate model, and it is not unusual to find several alternative model specifications that fit the data equally well. Moreover a model can duplicate the data perfectly but give erroneous predictions.

Since we cannot rely exclusively on the "goodness-of-fit" criterion, we require additional procedures that will assist in determining the specification of a model. The most important roles in these procedures are played by formal theories and informal judgments that represent our best a priori knowledge of the phenomenon being modeled. This knowledge is reflected in a set of specific assumptions about the relationships between variables. Unfortunately we do not normally have either a comprehensive understanding of a situation or a general behavioral theory that will prescribe the specification of the exact mathematical form and variables of a model.

Furthermore, even if the correct specifications of models were known, they would be empirically infeasible. There exist practical difficulties that almost always prevent us from implementing these theoretical specifications. These difficulties stem primarily from data problems: important variables must often be omitted due to lack of data or measurement problems, and included variables are often measured with errors. It is also necessary in practical studies to use a mathematical form that is computationally feasible. Thus lack of definitive theories and practical data and computational problems imply that a priori considerations virtually never lead to a unique model being selected.

Statistical tests cannot be used as the only criteria for acceptance or rejection of a model. With classical statistical inference methods, the specification of the model is never in question; the model is virtually always assumed to be correct. The purpose of a statistical estimator or of an hypothesis test is to make inferences about the values of unknown parameters of the known mathematical functions. In other words, statistical inference cannot be conclusive as to which of a large number of alternative specifications represents the true underlying process that generated the observed data.

These observations explain why the development of a model specification is not a simple, algorithmic process with clear-cut rules. It is a mixture of applications of formal behavioral theories and statistical methods with subjective judgments of the model builder. We generally begin the estimation process with an a priori theory, or set of assumptions, that is consistent with a very large number of model specifications. Then we begin a learning process that consists of a sequence of model estimations and a variety of formal and informal tests designed to help us narrow down the range of alternative specifications. At various stages of this process we may revise some aspects of our a priori assumptions that do not agree sufficiently with the statistical findings. We may discard some assumptions and devise new ones. Finally, among the specifications that are consistent with the theory, we select the one that performs best according to "goodness-of-fit" measures and statistical significance tests.

7.3 A Mode Choice Model Example

The example of the three-alternative logit mode choice model introduced in chapter 5 will be used in most of this chapter to demonstrate some of the tests being discussed. This model predicts a worker's choice of travel mode for a trip to work. The universal set of alternatives and the determination of individual choice sets are as follows:

1. Drive alone. Available to workers from households with cars who possess driver's licenses.
2. Shared ride (car passengers and drivers with passengers). Available to all workers.
3. Transit bus. Available to workers residing and working within one-half mile distance from a transit stop.

The estimation data are a sample of 1,136 workers (who have a choice set with 2 or more alternatives, i.e., are not captive to the shared-ride mode) taken from a 1968 survey in the Washington, D.C., metropolitan area. The sample frequencies of the chosen mode are

Drive alone   57% (647)
Shared ride   27% (312)
Transit bus   16% (177)

The average values of the major explanatory variables are

1. Round trip travel time, or the sum of in-vehicle time and out-of-vehicle times (min)

Drive alone   26.7
Shared ride   36.7
Transit   56.5

2. Round trip out-of-vehicle time (min)

Drive alone   5.4
Shared ride   10.4
Transit   18.6

3. Round trip travel cost (¢)

Drive alone   88.5
Shared ride   35.4
Transit   47.1

4. One-way distance (miles)   = 8.1.
5. Household income ($/yr)   = 12,900.
6. Number of cars available to the household = 1.5.
7. Number of workers in the household   = 1.8.
8. Number of persons in the household   = 3.6.

The other explanatory variables used are two dummy variables, downtown workplace and government employee status, plus a disposable income variable equal to

max [household income ($/yr) − 800 × number of persons, 0].

The maximum likelihood estimation results of a model that will be used as the base specification for the different tests are given in table 7.1. The variables include two alternative-specific constants, three generic attributes of the travel modes, and seven alternative-specific socioeconomic and locational characteristics of the worker. The table gives the estimated values for the coefficients, their asymptotic standard errors and t ratios, and the various summary statistics defined in chapters 4 and 5. The use of these statistics will be discussed in subsequent sections. We will also use the asymptotic covariance matrix of the coefficient estimates, given in figure 7.1.

7.4   Tests of Alternative Specifications of Variables

In this section we will describe the most basic tests used in the model development process. We assume a given structure of the discrete choice model and test alternative specifications of the explanatory variables in the utility functions. The statistical tests that will be used are the asymptotic t test and the likelihood ratio tests, described in section 2.6. The tests of alternative model specifications are demonstrated by using the trinomial mode choice example of section 7.3 and include comparisons of goodness-of-fit measures and tests of nonlinear utilities.

Informal Tests of the Coefficient Estimates

The most basic test of the model estimation output is the examination of the values of the coefficient estimates. Usually we have a priori expectations with respect to the signs and relative values of coefficients. In the estimation results given in table 7.1, all the coefficient estimates have the expected signs and expected relative values. For example, $\hat{\beta}_5$, the estimate of the coefficient of travel cost, has the expected negative sign, and $\hat{\beta}_6$, the drive-alone car availability coefficient, has the expected positive sign. The relative values of $\hat{\beta}_6$ and $\hat{\beta}_7$ are also in agreement with our expectation that increasing car availability increases the probability of choosing drive

Table 7.1
Estimation results for trinomial mode choice model: base specification

Variable number	Variable name	Coefficient estimate	Asymptotic standard error	t statistic
1	Drive-alone (da) constant	-2.23	0.365	-6.1
2	Shared-ride (sr) constant	-1.37	0.278	-5.0
3	Round-trip travel time (min)	-0.0307	0.00734	-4.2
4	Round-trip out-of-vehicle time (min)/one way distance (0.01 mi)	-13.5	5.32	-2.5
5	Round-trip travel cost (¢)/household income ($/yr)	-28.7	15.7	-1.8
6	Cars/workers in the household (specific to da)	3.48	0.305	11.4
7	Cars/workers in the household (specific to sr)	1.79	0.281	6.4
8	Downtown workplace dummy (specific to da)	-0.846	0.301	-2.8
9	Downtown workplace dummy (specific to sr)	-0.446	0.259	-1.7
10	Disposable household income (specific to da)	0.0000433	0.0000215	2.0
11	Disposable household income (specific to sr)	0.0000484	0.0000205	2.4
12	Government worker dummy (specific to sr)	0.436	0.152	2.9

Summary statistics

Number of observations = 1,136

$\mathcal{L}(\mathbf{0}) = -1,207.9$

$\mathcal{L}(\mathbf{c}) = -1,037.5$

$\mathcal{L}(\hat{\boldsymbol{\beta}}) = -820.3$

$-2[\mathcal{L}(\mathbf{0}) - \mathcal{L}(\hat{\boldsymbol{\beta}})] = 775.2$

$\rho^2 = 0.321$

$\bar{\rho}^2 = 0.311$

	1	2	3	4	5	6	7	8	9	10	11	12
1	0.133											
2	0.0738	0.0771										
3	0.0^2128	0.0^3787	0.0^4539									
4	0.657	0.255	-0.0^2593	28.3								
5	-1.27	0.340	-0.0^2683	-13.6	245.0							
6	-0.0443	-0.0236	0.0^5526	0.0287	-0.224	0.0929						
7	-0.0238	-0.0279	-0.0^4245	0.111	-0.192	0.0705	0.0790					
8	-0.0248	-0.0299	-0.0^3271	-0.342	-2.53	-0.0^2853	-0.0^2825	0.0907				
9	-0.0298	-0.0306	-0.0326	-0.376	-1.16	-0.0^2641	-0.0^2737	0.0613	0.0673			
10	-0.0^3353	-0.0^2205	-0.0^8331	-0.0^5764	0.0^4959	-0.0^9961	-0.0^6929	-0.0^5146	-0.0^8857	0.0^9462		
11	-0.0^2235	-0.0^2259	-0.0^8126	-0.0^5367	-0.0^4260	-0.0^9961	-0.0^5120	-0.0^6638	-0.0^6551	0.0^9355	0.0^9422	
12	0.0^2166	-0.0^2269	0.0^2257	0.0332	-0.0176	0.0^3984	0.0^3209	-0.0^2159	-0.0^2799	-0.0^7154	-0.0^9196	0.0232
	1	2	3	4	5	6	7	8	9	10	11	12

Variable number

Variable number

Figure 7.1
Asymptotic covariance matrix of the estimates of the base specification. The entries in this matrix should be read as in the following example: $0.0^3271 = 0.000271$.

alone more than the probability of shared ride. A ratio of two coefficients appearing in the same utility function provides information about a trade-off, or a marginal rate of substitution, between the two corresponding variables. For example, the estimated value of the trade-off between the two components of travel time, out-of-vehicle and in-vehicle, is

$$1 + \frac{\hat{\beta}_4}{\hat{\beta}_3(\text{one-way distance})} = 1 + \frac{440}{(\text{one-way distance})}, \tag{7.1}$$

which for the sample average distance of 8.1 miles equals approximately 1.5 out-of-vehicle minutes per minute of in-vehicle time.

Another important trade-off is between components of travel time and cost. Since the specification given in table 7.1 distinguishes between in-vehicle and out-of-vehicle travel time, there are two relevant rates of substitution between time and cost. For in-vehicle time the implied rate of substitution is

$$\frac{\hat{\beta}_3}{\hat{\beta}_5} \times (\text{household income}). \tag{7.2}$$

For an average annual income of \$12,900, the estimate is 13.8 cents per minute of in-vehicle time, or \$8.28 (in 1968 dollars) per hour of in-vehicle time.

In the case of out-of-vehicle time the rate of substitution is given by

$$\left[\frac{\hat{\beta}_3}{\hat{\beta}_5} + \frac{\hat{\beta}_4}{\hat{\beta}_5(\text{one-way distance})} \right] \times \text{household income}. \tag{7.3}$$

Using the same average values for distance and income, we obtain an estimated rate of substitution of approximately \$12.42 per hour of out-of-vehicle time.

In addition to evaluating how well coefficients reflect our own a priori expectations, it is also desirable to compare them with analogous values from similar models calibrated for other places, times, and even other choice contexts. For example, a previous study (perhaps not even a transport-related one) may provide an estimate of the value of time that can be compared with the estimate provided by the model in question. When utilizing other sources of information, one must ascertain that the two measures are in reality comparable.

The Use of the Asymptotic t Test

The asymptotic t test is used primarily to test whether a *particular* parameter in the model differs from some known constant, often zero. It is used in the same way as the t test in linear regression, except that in the case of nonlinear models this test is valid only asymptotically—that is, it is valid only for large samples. The critical values for the test statistic are percentiles of a standardized normal distribution, which for two-tailed tests at the frequently used significance levels of 0.10 and 0.05 are ± 1.65 and ± 1.96, respectively.

For example, on the basis of the t statistics given in table 7.1 we can reject the null hypothesis that each of the parameter values is equal to zero at the 10% level of significance. Note that this hypothesis is *not* that all 12 parameters are simultaneously zero, which would require an alternate test procedure that will be described later on in this section.

As a second example we cannot reject the null hypotheses $\beta_5 = 0$ and $\beta_9 = 0$ at the 5% significance level. Note that we could have performed a one-tailed t test for the null hypothesis $\beta_5 = 0$ because according to our prior knowledge, it is appropriate to have the more specific alternate hypothesis $\beta_5 < 0$. (The alternate hypothesis $\beta_5 \neq 0$ is used in the two-tailed test.)

Using the covariance matrix information, it is also possible to calculate the statistic for an asymptotic t test of a linear relationship among parameters. For example, we can use the covariances given in figure 7.1 to calculate the estimated variance of the difference $(\hat{\beta}_8 - \hat{\beta}_9)$:

$$\text{var}(\hat{\beta}_8 - \hat{\beta}_9) = \text{var}(\hat{\beta}_8) + \text{var}(\hat{\beta}_9) - 2\,\text{cov}(\hat{\beta}_8, \hat{\beta}_9)$$
$$= 0.0907 + 0.0673 - 2 \times 0.0613 = 0.0354. \tag{7.4}$$

The test statistic for the null hypothesis $\beta_8 = \beta_9$ is then given by

$$\frac{\hat{\beta}_8 - \hat{\beta}_9}{\sqrt{\text{var}(\hat{\beta}_8 - \hat{\beta}_9)}} = \frac{-0.4}{0.188} = -2.13. \tag{7.5}$$

It is therefore possible to reject the null hypothesis that $\beta_8 = \beta_9$ at the 5% level of significance.

Similar calculations for the null hypothesis $\beta_{10} = \beta_{11}$ show that we cannot reject the equality of the two disposable income coefficients. The t statistic for this test is 0.004. Given the fact that $\hat{\beta}_{10}$ is numerically close to and statistically indistinguishable from $\hat{\beta}_{11}$, it is reasonable to reestimate the model enforcing the restriction $\beta_{10} = \beta_{11}$. (This results in a model with one less unknown parameter.) The estimation results for this specification are given in table 7.2.

Related to the use of the t statistic for hypothesis testing is its use to calculate an asymptotic confidence interval for a single parameter. The $(1 - \alpha)$ confidence interval for the kth coefficient is found by solving

$$Pr\left[-t_{\alpha/2} \leq \frac{\hat{\beta}_k - \beta_k}{\sqrt{\text{var}(\hat{\beta}_k)}} \leq t_{\alpha/2} \right] = 1 - \alpha. \qquad (7.6)$$

Rearranging terms, we obtain

$$Pr[\hat{\beta}_k - t_{\alpha/2} \cdot \sqrt{\text{var}(\hat{\beta}_k)} \leq \beta_k \leq \hat{\beta}_k + t_{\alpha/2} \cdot \sqrt{\text{var}(\hat{\beta}_k)}] = 1 - \alpha,$$

where $t_{\alpha/2}$ is the quantile of the normal distribution such that the probability is $\alpha/2$ that the t ratio will exceed $t_{\alpha/2}$. For example, the 95% interval ($t_{0.025} = 1.96$) for the travel time coefficient in the model of table 7.1 is given by

$$Pr[-0.0451 \leq \beta_3 \leq -0.0163] = 0.95. \qquad (7.7)$$

Confidence Region for Several Parameters Simultaneously

It is possible to construct confidence regions for two or more parameters jointly. However, this is computationally more difficult and is very rarely done in practice. We will demonstrate its use in the two-dimensional case. (This subsection can be skipped by readers unfamiliar with matrix operations.)

The vector of estimated coefficients $\hat{\boldsymbol{\beta}}$, found by the method of maximum likelihood, is asymptotically normally distributed with expectation $\boldsymbol{\beta}$ and covariance matrix $\boldsymbol{\Sigma}_{\boldsymbol{\beta}}$. Therefore the quadratic form

$$(\hat{\boldsymbol{\beta}} - \boldsymbol{\beta})' \boldsymbol{\Sigma}_{\boldsymbol{\beta}}^{-1} (\hat{\boldsymbol{\beta}} - \boldsymbol{\beta})$$

is asymptotically χ^2 distributed with K degrees of freedom, K being the dimension of $\boldsymbol{\beta}$ (e.g., see Theil 1971.) This is also true for any subvector of $\hat{\boldsymbol{\beta}}$ with its corresponding submatrix of $\boldsymbol{\Sigma}_{\boldsymbol{\beta}}$. The $(1 - \alpha)$ confidence region for the vector $\boldsymbol{\beta}$ is of the form

$$Pr[(\hat{\boldsymbol{\beta}} - \boldsymbol{\beta})' \boldsymbol{\Sigma}_{\boldsymbol{\beta}}^{-1} (\hat{\boldsymbol{\beta}} - \boldsymbol{\beta}) \leq \chi^2_{K,\alpha}] = 1 - \alpha, \qquad (7.8)$$

Table 7.2
Estimation results for trinomial mode choice model: equal coefficients of drive-alone and shared-ride income variables

Variable number	Variable name	Coefficient estimate	Asymptotic standard error	' statistic
1	Drive-alone (da) constant	−2.26	0.354	−6.4
2	Shared-ride (sr) constant	−1.36	0.274	−5.0
3	Round-trip travel time (min)	−0.0308	0.00734	−4.2
4	Round-trip out-of-vehicle time (min)/one-way distance (0.01 mi)	−13.6	5.32	−2.6
5	Round-trip travel cost (¢)/household income ($/yr)	−26.7	14.7	−1.8
6	Cars/workers in the household (specific to da)	3.48	0.305	11.4
7	Cars/workers in the household (specific to sr)	1.80	0.280	6.4
8	Downtown workplace dummy (specific to da)	−0.870	0.295	−3.0
9	Downtown workplace dummy (specific to sr)	−0.454	0.258	−1.8
10	Disposable household income (specific to da and sr)	0.0000464	0.0000199	2.3
11	Government worker dummy (specific to sr)	0.441	0.152	2.9

Summary statistics

Number of observations = 1,136

$\mathscr{L}(0) = -1,207.9$

$\mathscr{L}(c) = -1,037.5$

$\mathscr{L}(\hat{\beta}) = -820.4$

$-2[\mathscr{L}(0) - \mathscr{L}(\hat{\beta})] = 775.0$

$\rho^2 = 0.321$

$\bar{\rho}^2 = 0.312$

where $\chi^2_{K,\alpha}$ is the percentile of the χ^2 distribution with K degrees of freedom for the α level of significance. For a subvector of two coefficients the confidence region has the form of an ellipse:

$$Pr[a_{kk}(\hat{\beta}_k - \beta_k)^2 + a_{hh}(\hat{\beta}_h - \beta_h)^2 + 2a_{kh}(\hat{\beta}_k - \beta_k)(\hat{\beta}_h - \beta_h) \leq \chi^2_{2,\alpha}] \tag{7.9}$$
$$= 1 - \alpha,$$

where a_{kh} is the (k, h) element of $\Sigma^{-1}_{(\hat{\beta}_k,\hat{\beta}_h)}$, which is the inverse of the following covariance submatrix:

$$\Sigma_{(\hat{\beta}_k,\hat{\beta}_h)} = \begin{bmatrix} \text{var}(\hat{\beta}_k) & \text{cov}(\hat{\beta}_k, \hat{\beta}_h) \\ \text{cov}(\hat{\beta}_k, \hat{\beta}_h) & \text{var}(\hat{\beta}_h) \end{bmatrix}. \tag{7.10}$$

Consider again the example in table 7.1 and the travel time and cost coefficients. The estimated values of the coefficients and the covariance matrix are

$$\begin{bmatrix} \hat{\beta}_3 \\ \hat{\beta}_5 \end{bmatrix} = \begin{bmatrix} -0.0307 \\ -28.7 \end{bmatrix} \tag{7.11}$$

and

$$\Sigma_{(\hat{\beta}_3,\hat{\beta}_5)} = \begin{bmatrix} 0.4539 \times 10^{-3} & -0.683 \times 10^{-2} \\ -0.0683 \times 10^{-2} & 245.0 \end{bmatrix}.$$

The 95% confidence region for these two coefficients is the solution to

$$Pr[0.18600(\beta_3 + 0.0307)^2 + 0.00410(\beta_5 + 28.7)^2 \tag{7.12}$$
$$+ 1.04(\beta_3 + 0.0307)(\beta_5 + 28.7) \leq 5.99] = 0.95.$$

It has the form of the ellipse shown in figure 7.2 with center at $[-0.0307, -28.7]$. Note that almost all of the area of the confidence region is in the negative quadrant, which is in agreement with our expectation of negative travel time and cost coefficients. This may not occur if the estimates of the coefficients are highly correlated. In our example the estimated correlation between $\hat{\beta}_3$ and $\hat{\beta}_5$ is only -0.06.

The Use of the Likelihood Ratio Test

The likelihood ratio test, presented in section 2.6 is used in the same way that the F test is used in regression models for joint tests of several parameters.

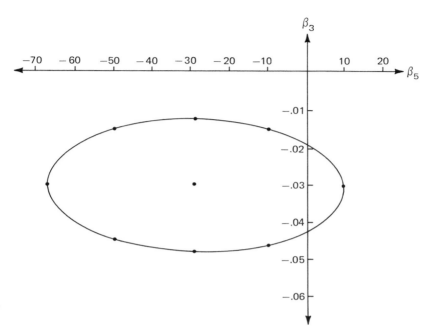

Figure 7.2
Asymptotic confidence region for travel time and cost coefficients

Under the null hypothesis that all the coefficients are zero, that is,

$$\beta_1 = \beta_2 = \ldots = \beta_K = 0, \tag{7.13}$$

the statistic

$$-2(\mathcal{L}(\mathbf{0}) - \mathcal{L}(\hat{\boldsymbol{\beta}}))$$

is χ^2 distributed with K degrees of freedom. This statistic is given as one of the summary measures in the estimation results tables. However, it is not a very useful test because almost always we can reject this null hypothesis at a very low level of significance. For example, the percentile of the χ^2 distribution with 12 degrees of freedom for a 0.005 level of significance is 28.20, and the value of the test statistic for the base specification in table 7.1 is 775.2.

It is more informative to test the null hypothesis that all the coefficients, except for the alternative-specific constants, are zero. In this case the test statistic is

$$-2(\mathscr{L}(\mathbf{c}) - \mathscr{L}(\hat{\boldsymbol{\beta}}))$$

with $K - J + 1$ degrees of freedom, where J is the number of alternatives in the universal choice set and $\mathscr{L}(\mathbf{c})$ is the log likelihood of a model with only constants. $\mathscr{L}(\mathbf{c})$ can be obtained by either estimating a model with $J - 1$ alternative-specific constants or (assuming that all observations have J alternatives) from

$$\mathscr{L}(\mathbf{c}) = \sum_{i=1}^{J} N_i \ln\left(\frac{N_i}{N}\right), \tag{7.14}$$

where N_i is the number of observations selecting alternative i and N is the total sample size. In table 7.1 the χ^2 test statistic with 10 degrees of freedom for the null hypothesis

$$\beta_3 = \beta_4 = \ldots = \beta_{12} = 0 \tag{7.15}$$

is

$$-2(-1037.5 + 820.3) = 434.4.$$

This hypothesis can also be rejected with high confidence.

The most useful applications of the likelihood ratio test are for more specific hypotheses. As described in chapter 2, the test statistic is

$$-2(\mathscr{L}(\hat{\boldsymbol{\beta}}_R) - \mathscr{L}(\hat{\boldsymbol{\beta}}_U))$$

where $\hat{\boldsymbol{\beta}}_R$ denotes the estimated coefficients of the restricted model—the model that is true under the null hypothesis—and $\hat{\boldsymbol{\beta}}_U$ denotes the coefficient estimates of the unrestricted model. This statistic is χ^2 distributed with $(K_U - K_R)$ degrees of freedom, where K_U and K_R are the numbers of estimated coefficients in the unrestricted and restricted models, respectively.

This test is used when the model under the null hypothesis is obtained by imposing two or more linear restrictions on the more general unrestricted model. The example would be the null hypothesis that two (or more) coefficients are jointly equal to zero or that three (or more) coefficients are equal to each other. For a null hypothesis with a single linear restriction this test serves the same purpose as the asymptotic t test described earlier. However, the χ^2 test is performed by comparing two estimation runs. For the hypothesis of equal disposable income coefficients in the base specification of table 7.1, we have the restricted model results given in table 7.2. The χ^2 test statistic with 1 degree of freedom is

$$-2(-820.4 + 820.3) = 0.20. \tag{7.16}$$

We cannot reject the null hypothesis even at a 0.5 level of significance ($\chi^2_{1,0.5} = 0.45$). The application of this test to more complex hypotheses in which the asymptotic t test is inapplicable will be further demonstrated in the following sections.

The Use of Goodness-of-Fit Measures

The first model estimation outputs to be examined are the signs and relative values of the coefficients estimates and the significance of individual coefficients. With the estimation of more than one specification it is also useful to compare goodness-of-fit measures. Everything else being equal, a specification with a higher maximum value of the likelihood function is considered to be better. It is more convenient to compare the value of the likelihood ratio index (rho-squared)

$$\rho^2 = 1 - \frac{\mathscr{L}(\hat{\beta})}{\mathscr{L}(0)}, \tag{7.17}$$

which is used in a fashion similar to R^2 in regression analysis. There are no general guidelines for when a ρ^2 value is sufficiently high.

For the same estimation data set the ρ^2 of a model will always increase or at least stay the same whenever new variables are added to the utility functions, a shortcoming it shares with regression statistic R^2. For this reason we also use the adjusted likelihood ratio index (rho-squared bar)

$$\bar{\rho}^2 = 1 - \frac{\mathscr{L}(\hat{\beta}) - K}{\mathscr{L}(0)}. \tag{7.18}$$

This measure is based on the idea of estimating the expectation of the sample log likelihood for the estimated parameter values over all samples with the log likelihood of the one sample we do have available. As explained in Ben-Akiva and Swait (1984b), $\mathscr{L}(\hat{\beta})$ is a biased estimate of the expectation over all samples; it is necessary to subtract K from $\mathscr{L}(\hat{\beta})$—to compensate for the fact that $\hat{\beta}$ will not be the MLE in other samples—and to remove the effect of evaluating $\mathscr{L}(\hat{\beta})$ at the estimated values rather than for the true parameters. The measure $[\mathscr{L}(\hat{\beta}) - K]$ is known as the Akaike information criterion (see Akaike 1973, Amemiya 1980, Judge et al. 1980).

This rho-squared bar is quite similar to the one proposed by Horowitz (1982, 1983a). In Horowitz's measure $\mathscr{L}(\hat{\boldsymbol{\beta}})$ is corrected only by subtracting $K/2$. The principal practical difference between the two measures is that the correction factor of K will favor more parsimonious model specifications, unless the added explanatory power of the variable is quite significant. In the following section we show how to use $\bar{\rho}^2$ for testing a certain class of hypotheses.

Table 7.3 gives the estimation results for a model of the example mode choice problem with three more parameters than in the base specification. The new coefficients (β_{12}, β_{14}, and β_{15}) cause ρ^2 to increase from 0.321 to 0.323, but $\bar{\rho}^2$ decreases by 0.001. Thus the additional variables do not appear to add sufficient explanatory power to the model to compensate for the degrees of freedom utilized by the fuller specification. It is also possible to reach the same conclusion from the t statistics (i.e., β_{12}, β_{14}, and β_{15} are *individually* not significantly different from zero at the 0.10 level) and from the likelihood ratio test for the joint hypothesis $\beta_{12} = \beta_{14} = \beta_{15} = 0$. The χ^2 test statistic for the latter test is

$$-2(-820.3 + 818.2) = 4.2, \tag{7.19}$$

which, with 3 degrees of freedom, is less than the critical value of 6.25 at the 0.10 level of significance.

Test of Generic Attributes

An important aspect of the specification of discrete choice models is the distinction between alternative-specific and generic attributes. A generic specification imposes restrictions of equality of coefficients on a more general model with alternative-specific attributes. Thus the likelihood ratio test statistic for the null hypothesis of generic attributes is

$$-2(\mathscr{L}(\hat{\boldsymbol{\beta}}_G) - \mathscr{L}(\hat{\boldsymbol{\beta}}_{AS})),$$

where G and AS denote the generic and the alternative specific models, respectively. It is χ^2 distributed with the number of degrees of freedom equal to the number of restrictions, or $(K_{AS} - K_G)$.

For the mode choice example the estimation results of a specification with alternative specific attributes is given in table 7.4. The restricted model with the generic specification is the base specification in table 7.1. The value of the test statistic with 4 degrees of freedom is

$$-2(-820.3 + 818.8) = 3.0. \tag{7.20}$$

Table 7.5
Estimation results for trinomial mode choice model: additional socioeconomic variables

Variable number	Variable name	Coefficient estimate	Asymptotic standard error	t statistic
1	Drive-alone (da) constant	−2.22	0.484	−4.6
2	Shared-ride (sr) constant	−1.78	0.384	−4.6
3	Round-trip travel time (min)	−0.0301	0.00738	−4.1
4	Round trip out-of-vehicle time (min)/one-way distance (0.01 mi)	−13.1	5.33	−2.5
5	Round-trip travel cost (¢)/household income ($/yr)	−30.1	15.8	−1.9
6	Cars/workers in the household (specific to da)	3.45	0.327	10.6
7	Cars/workers in the household (specific to sr)	1.92	0.295	6.5
8	Downtown workplace dummy (specific to da)	−0.869	0.311	−2.8
9	Downtown workplace dummy (specific to sr)	−0.443	0.268	−1.7
10	Disposable household income (specific to da)	0.0000384	0.0000228	1.7
11	Disposable household income (specific to sr)	0.0000366	0.0000219	1.7
12	Government worker dummy (specific to da)	0.0906	0.249	0.4
13	Government worker dummy (specific to sr)	0.539	0.241	2.2
14	Number of workers in the household (specific to da)	0.0350	0.147	0.2
15	Number of workers in the household (specific to sr)	0.205	0.136	1.5

Summary statistics

Number of observations = 1,136

$\mathcal{L}(0) = -1,207.9$

$\mathcal{L}(c) = -1,037.5$

$\mathcal{L}(\hat{\beta}) = -818.2$

$-2[\mathcal{L}(0) - \mathcal{L}(\hat{\beta})] = 779.4$

$\rho^2 = 0.323$

$\bar{\rho}^2 = 0.310$

Table 7.4
Estimation results for trinomial mode choice model: alternative-specific travel time and cost variables

Variable number	Variable name	Coefficient estimate	Asymptotic standard error	t statistic
1	Drive-alone (da) constant	-2.64	0.606	-4.4
2	Shared-ride (sr) constant	-2.33	0.774	-3.0
3	Round-trip travel time (min) (specific to da)	-0.0118	0.0243	-0.5
4	Round-trip travel time (min) (specific to sr)	-0.00368	0.0241	-0.2
5	Round-trip travel time (min) (specific to transit)	-0.0293	0.00964	-3.0
6	Out-of-vehicle time (min)/distance (0.01 mi) (specific to da and sr)	-5.96	7.46	-0.8
7	Out-of-vehicle time (min)/distance (0.01 mi) (specific to transit)	-16.7	6.94	-2.4
8	Travel cost (¢)/income ($/yr) (specific to da and sr)	-29.2	16.3	-1.8
9	Travel cost (¢)/income ($/yr) (specific to transit)	-8.18	35.6	-0.2
10	Cars/workers in the household (specific to da)	3.49	0.305	11.4
11	Cars/workers in the household (specific to sr)	1.80	0.282	6.4
12	Downtown workplace dummy (specific to da)	-0.938	0.319	-2.9
13	Downtown workplace dummy (specific to sr)	-0.576	0.284	-2.0
14	Disposable household income (specific to da)	0.0000353	0.0000253	1.4
15	Disposable household income (specific to sr)	0.0000393	0.0000242	1.7
16	Government worker dummy (specific to sr)	0.434	0.153	2.8

Summary statistics
Number of observations = 1,136
$\mathscr{L}(0) = -1{,}207.9$
$\mathscr{L}(c) = -1{,}037.5$
$\mathscr{L}(\hat{\beta}) = -818.8$
$-2[\mathscr{L}(0) - \mathscr{L}(\hat{\beta})] = 778.2$
$\rho^2 = 0.322$
$\bar{\rho}^2 = 0.309$

We cannot reject the null hypothesis of the generic specification even at the 0.50 significance level because $\chi^2_{4,0.5} = 3.36$.

Tests of Non-Nested Hypotheses

The classical statistical hypothesis tests that were presented in section 2.6 and demonstrated in the previous sections of this chapter can only be applied with what are called nested hypotheses. These tests are always expressed as a comparison between restricted and unrestricted models, where the restricted model forms the null hypothesis. The restrictions are placed on the values of the parameters in such a way that the model under the null hypothesis can be obtained as a special case of the unrestricted model. Thus all the models that were rejected or not rejected up to this point were always special cases of a more general model.

There are instances where we wish to compare two models, and one is not a nested hypothesis of the other. Consider, for example, the models in tables 7.3 and 7.4. The first model has one parameter less than the second model. Yet the first model cannot be obtained as a special case of the second one. The reason is that these two specifications represent two different extensions of the base model. The first model has three additional socioeconomic variables, and the second model replaces generic with alternative-specific attributes. Therefore we cannot employ the likelihood ratio test to test one of these two models as a restriction of the other.

It is possible, however, to construct a composite specification with 19 coefficients from which both the model in table 7.3 and the one in table 7.4 can be derived as two special cases. Then we can perform two likelihood ratio tests for each of the two restricted models against the composite model. This procedure is known as the Cox test of separate families of hypotheses (Cox 1961, 1962). Note that one of the possible outcomes is the acceptance of both models. Another disadvantage of this procedure is the need to estimate a model with potentially a very large number of parameters.

The adjusted likelihood ratio index $\bar{\rho}^2$ presented earlier as a goodness-of-fit measure can be used for testing non-nested hypotheses of discrete choice models. To choose between two models (called 1 and 2), Ben-Akiva and Swait (1984b) used a test developed by Horowitz (1983a) to show that, under the null hypothesis that model 1 is the true specification, the following holds asymptotically:

$$Pr(\bar{\rho}_2^2 - \bar{\rho}_1^2 > z) \leq \Phi\{-[-2z\mathscr{L}(0) + (K_2 - K_1)]^{1/2}\}, \qquad z > 0,$$

$$(7.21)$$

where

$\bar{\rho}_l^2 =$ the adjusted likelihood ratio index for model $l = 1, 2,$

$K_l =$ the number of parameters in model $l,$

$\Phi =$ the standard normal cumulative distribution function.

In other words, the probability that the adjusted likelihood ratio index of model 2 is greater by some $z > 0$ than that of model 1, given that the latter is the true model, is asymptotically bounded above by the right-hand side of equation (7.21). If we select the model with the greater $\bar{\rho}^2$, then this bounds the probability of erroneously choosing the incorrect model over the true specification. Note that when all N observations in the sample have all J alternatives, the bound becomes

$$Pr(\bar{\rho}_2^2 - \bar{\rho}_1^2 > z) \leq \Phi\{-[2Nz \ln J + (K_2 - K_1)]^{1/2}\}, \qquad z > 0. \qquad (7.22)$$

This result implies that for 250 or more observations with two or more alternatives and models having the same number of parameters, if the $\bar{\rho}^2$ of the two models differ by 0.01 or more, the model with the lower $\bar{\rho}^2$ is almost certainly incorrect.

Using this procedure, we can compare the two models of tables 7.3 and 7.4:

Model	Number of parameters	$\bar{\rho}^2$
Table 7.3	15	0.3102
Table 7.4	16	0.3089

The difference in adjusted likelihood ratios is approximately 0.0013; the probability that such a difference would be exceeded for a sample of 1,136 observations and 3 alternatives is less than 0.07, so we can be fairly sure that the model of table 7.3 is the one to merit further consideration.

Another example of the application of this test procedure is a comparison of the model in table 7.5 with any one of the previous specifications. The purpose of the model in table 7.5 is to test the importance of the socioeconomic characteristics. This model includes only the attributes of the alternatives, and the travel cost variable is not divided by income. Therefore it is not a nested hypothesis of any of the previous specifications. For a nested test against a slightly modified base specification it would have been possible to reestimate the base model with an additional travel

Table 7.5
Estimation results for trinomial mode choice model: without socioeconomic variables

Variable number	Variable name	Coefficient estimate	Asymptotic standard error	t statistic
1	Drive-alone (da) constant	0.646	0.208	3.1
2	Shared-ride (sr) constant	−0.0895	0.123	−0.7
3	Round-trip travel time (min)	−0.0389	0.00668	−5.8
4	Round-trip out-of-vehicle time (min)/one-way distance (0.01 mi)	−9.83	4.72	−2.1
5	Round-trip travel cost (¢)	−0.00725	0.00134	−5.4

Summary statistics

Number of observations = 1,136

$\mathcal{L}(\mathbf{0}) = -1,207.9$

$\mathcal{L}(\mathbf{c}) = -1,037.5$

$\mathcal{L}(\hat{\boldsymbol{\beta}}) = -966.6$

$-2[\mathcal{L}(\mathbf{0}) - \mathcal{L}(\hat{\boldsymbol{\beta}})] = 482.5$

$\rho^2 = 0.200$

$\bar{\rho}^2 = 0.196$

cost variable not divided by income. However, given the decrease in the $\bar{\rho}^2$ value from 0.311 to 0.196, we can confidently exclude a model without socioeconomic characteristics from further considerations.

Tests of Nonlinear Specifications

The models that we have considered so far are based on linear-in-parameters utility functions. As in linear regression models this assumption is made for practical reasons and is not very restrictive because it allows nonlinear specifications of variables.

Often we do not have well-founded prior knowledge about the functional forms of these nonlinear transformation of variables, and we want to test empirically a wide range of nonlinear functions of the variables. Two useful approaches that involve estimating models that are linear in the parameters are the piecewise linear approximation and the power series expansion.

With a piecewise linear approximation we test the hypothesis that a coefficient may have different values for different ranges of the corresponding variables. This approach is demonstrated for the travel time variable in the model given in table 7.6. The single travel time variable in the base specification (with a coefficient estimate of -0.0307) has been replaced with the following four variables. (For simplicity we denote the value of the round trip travel time in minutes as t.)

1. Travel time (0–20) $= \begin{cases} t & \text{if } t < 20, \\ 20 & \text{otherwise,} \end{cases}$
$\qquad\qquad\qquad\quad = \min(t, 20).$

2. Travel time (20–50) $= \begin{cases} 0 & \text{if } t < 20, \\ t - 20 & \text{if } 20 \le t < 50, \\ 30 & \text{otherwise,} \end{cases}$
$\qquad\qquad\qquad\quad = \max[0, \min(t - 20, 30)].$

3. Travel time (50–80) $= \begin{cases} 0 & \text{if } t < 50, \\ t - 50 & \text{if } 50 \le t < 80, \\ 30 & \text{otherwise,} \end{cases}$
$\qquad\qquad\qquad\quad = \max[0, \min(t - 50, 30)].$

4. Travel time (80+) $= \begin{cases} 0 & \text{if } t < 80, \\ t - 80 & \text{otherwise,} \end{cases}$
$\qquad\qquad\qquad\quad = \max(0, t - 80).$

Table 7.6
Estimation results for trinomial mode choice model: piecewise linear travel time variable

Variable number	Variable name	Coefficient estimate	Asymptotic standard error	t statistic
1	Drive-alone (da) constant	−2.31	0.391	−519
2	Shared-ride (sr) constant	−1.40	0.283	−5.0
3	Round-trip travel time (0–20 min)	−0.000209	0.00921	0
4	Round-trip travel time (20–50 min)	−0.0402	0.0124	−3.2
5	Round-trip travel time (50–80 min)	−0.00505	0.00610	−0.8
6	Round-trip travel time (80+ min)	−0.0626	0.0272	−2.3
7	Round-trip out-of-vehicle time (min)/one way distance (0.01 mi)	−17.9	5.48	−3.3
8	Round-trip travel cost (¢)/household income ($/yr)	−30.7	15.8	−1.9
9	Cars/workers in the household (specific to da)	3.52	0.305	11.6
10	Cars/workers in the household (specific to da)	1.82	0.280	6.5
11	Downtown workplace dummy (specific to da)	−0.768	0.304	−2.5
12	Downtown workplace dummy (specific to sr)	−0.346	0.263	−1.3
13	Disposable household income (specific to da)	0.0000449	0.0000217	2.1
14	Disposable household income (specific to sr)	0.0000497	0.0000207	2.4
15	Government worker dummy (specific to sr)	0.462	0.152	3.0

Summary statistics

Number of observations = 1,136

$\mathcal{L}(\mathbf{0}) = -1,207.9$

$\mathcal{L}(\mathbf{c}) = -1,037.5$

$\mathcal{L}(\hat{\boldsymbol{\beta}}) = -819.3$

$-2[\mathcal{L}(\mathbf{0}) - \mathcal{L}(\hat{\boldsymbol{\beta}})] = 777.3$

$\rho^2 = 0.322$

$\bar{\rho}^2 = 0.309$

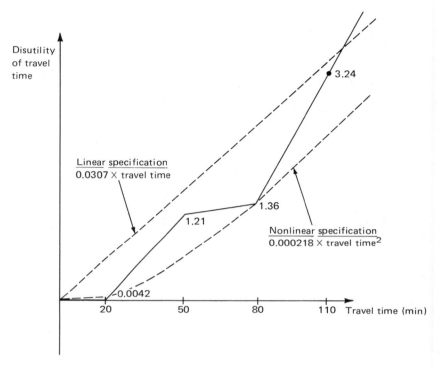

Figure 7.3
Piecewise linear approximation of the disutility of travel time

The four coefficient estimates $(\hat{\beta}_3, \hat{\beta}_4, \hat{\beta}_5, \text{and } \hat{\beta}_6)$ follow the pattern shown in figure 7.3. It is reasonable to assume that the sensitivity to changes in travel time for short trips is very small. When the trip length increases, the traveler begins to perceive differences in travel time and therefore the sensitivity in the second range (20–50) is larger and significantly different from zero. However, for yet longer trips a difference of, say, one minute, is a very small fraction of the total travel time. Thus the sensitivity per minute of travel time may decrease as shown for the third range (50–80). For very long trips (80 +) the sensitivity is again increasing. This phenomenon is consistent with the notion of a time constraint. A high disutility per minute of travel time would occur when the time constraint is binding.

The χ^2 test statistic for the null hypothesis

$$\beta_3 = \beta_4 = \beta_5 = \beta_6 \tag{7.23}$$

is obtained by comparison with the restricted model in table 7.1, yielding a χ^2 statistic of

$$-2(-820.3 + 819.3) = 2.0. \tag{7.24}$$

Since $\chi^2_{3,0.5} = 2.37$, we cannot reject the hypothesis of a linear travel time variable.

The major disadvantage of the piecewise linear approximation approach is the loss of degrees of freedom. A large number of ranges causes a large loss of degrees of freedom and potentially a very small number of observations in some of the ranges. On the other hand, significant nonlinearities may be concealed with a small number of ranges. Another minor problem with this approach is that usually the endpoints of the ranges must be decided on arbitrarily because resources are often unavailable to test different range specifications.

The second approach often used in practice is to represent a nonlinear function by a power series expansion that includes the linear specification as a special case. The travel time variable, for example, can be introduced as a parabola by including in the model the two variables of travel time and travel time squared. In principle, we can use a polynomial of a higher degree as long as we do not exhaust the available degrees of freedom. In practice, the elements of the polynomial are highly correlated, and the series must be truncated at a low degree. In the mode choice example even travel time and travel time squared are highly correlated. A model with only travel time squared is presented in table 7.7. Its goodness of fit, as measured by $\bar{\rho}^2$, is the same as that of the basic model:

Model	$\bar{\rho}^2$
Table 7.1	0.311
Table 7.7	0.311

Given this, we retain the linear specification for further consideration because of its simplicity. See also the comparison of the different functional forms of travel time in figure 7.3.

The two approaches to nonlinear utilities that we considered earlier are simple to perform because they involve estimations of models that are linear in the unknown parameters. However, it is also possible, but computationally more difficult, to test nonlinear transformations of variables

Table 7.7
Estimation results for trinomial mode choice model: squared travel time variable

Variable number	Variable name	Coefficient estimate	Asymptotic standard error	t statistic
1	Drive-alone (da) constant	−2.01	0.344	−5.8
2	Shared-ride (sr) constant	−1.30	0.272	−4.8
3	Squared round-trip travel time (min²)	−0.000218	0.0000565	−3.9
4	Round-trip out-of-vehicle time (min)/one-way distance (0.01 mi)	−17.0	5.32	−3.2
5	Round-trip travel cost (¢)/household income ($/yr)	−30.4	15.7	−1.9
6	Cars/workers in the household (specific to da)	3.47	0.304	11.40
7	Cars/workers in the household (specific to sr)	1.78	0.280	6.4
8	Downtown workplace dummy (specific to da)	−0.848	0.301	−2.8
9	Downtown workplace dummy (specific to sr)	−0.438	0.259	−1.7
10	Disposable household income (specific to da)	0.0000409	0.0000214	1.9
11	Disposable household income (specific to sr)	0.0000467	0.0000205	2.3
12	Government worker dummy (specific to sr)	0.443	0.152	2.9

Summary statistics

Number of observations = 1,136

$\mathcal{L}(0) = -1,207.9$

$\mathcal{L}(c) = -1,037.5$

$\mathcal{L}(\hat{\beta}) = -820.4$

$-2[\mathcal{L}(0) - \mathcal{L}(\hat{\beta})] = 775.0$

$\rho^2 = 0.321$

$\bar{\rho}^2 = 0.311$

that are not linear in the unknown parameters. One useful transformation for non-negative variables, proposed by Box and Cox (1964), is the following (see also the discussion of its use in regression models in Kmenta 1971):

$$\frac{x^{\lambda} - 1}{\lambda}, \qquad x \geq 0, \tag{7.25}$$

where λ is an unknown parameter. This transformation defines a family of functions that includes as special cases the linear and the logarithmic transformations. It reduces to $\ln x$ for $\lambda = 0$ and to a linear specification for $\lambda = 1$. The estimation difficulties arise from the nonlinearity with λ. A simple procedure is to estimate models for fixed values of λ and to search for the value of λ that maximize the likelihood ratio index. The use in discrete choice models of the Box-Cox transformation and its generalization to the Box-Tukey transformation,

$$\frac{(x + \alpha)^{\lambda} - 1}{\lambda}$$

with an additional unknown parameter α (interpreted as a location parameter), is discussed in Gaudry and Wills (1978) and Hensher and Johnson (1981).

Constrained Estimation

At the beginning of this section we discussed the role of prior information in the initial examination of the estimated coefficients. There are also situations where we find it useful to incorporate prior information directly in the estimation procedures. The justification for this approach is based on the assumption that the prior information is correct. By constraining parameters to what we believe to be their correct values, we improve the statistical efficiency of the model relative to the unconstrained estimates. The need for such a procedure usually arises in studies with inadequate data: either the sample is too small or one or more of the key variables have limited variability in the data. Three types of constraints are usually applied:

1. inequality constraints,
2. fixed value constraints,
3. linear constraints.

The strongest a priori information is usually about the sign of a coefficient. Thus it is possible, for example, to incorporate constraints of the form

$$\beta_k \leq 0 \qquad (7.26)$$

for the coefficients of travel time and cost. Inequality constraints require a more complex estimation procedure and raise the following practical issue: Should we use a constrained estimation procedure if unconstrained estimation produces, for example, a significantly positive coefficient when we expect a negative sign? It is possible that the wrong sign is caused by a model specification error or by erroneous data, or that the prior information is wrong. If we impose the negativity constraint in such a case, we ignore a more fundamental problem that may affect all the other estimation results. Thus an estimation procedure with inequality constraints is usually of limited practical value.

The other two types of constraints are more useful and are easier to implement computationally. Fixed value constraints are used when we have a priori information about the values of individual parameters. An example of a fixed value constraint will be provided in chapter 9.

Constraints in the form of linear relationships between parameters are also straightforward to implement computationally. They are useful in cases with prior information in the form of equality of parameters, values of trade-offs, ratios of parameters, and other linear relationships.

Consider, for example, the trade-off between travel time and cost in the mode choice model. The standard error of the travel cost coefficient is relatively large, and we may wish to impose an assumption used in many urban transportation studies that the "value of travel time" equals 40% of the wage rate. The value of time (in dollars/hour) is equal to

$$\frac{\beta_t}{\beta_c} \times \text{income}(\$/\text{yr}) \times 0.6, \qquad (7.27)$$

where β_t and β_c are the travel time and travel cost coefficients, respectively. The approximate wage rate (in $/hr) is

$$\frac{\text{income}(\$/\text{yr})}{1,850(\text{hrs/yr}) \times 1.8(\text{average number of household workers})}.$$

Constraining the ratio of the value of time divided by the wage rate to 0.4, we get

$$\frac{\beta_t}{\beta_c} = \frac{0.4}{1850 \times 1.8 \times 0.6}$$

(7.28)

$$\cong 0.0002.$$

We impose this constraint by constructing the following variable

generalized travel cost($\textcent$)/income($\$$/yr)

(7.29)

$$= [0.0002 \times \text{travel time(min)} + \text{travel cost}(\textcent)]/\text{income}(\$/\text{yr})$$

whose coefficient estimate is β_c. The estimation results for this constrained estimation is given in table 7.8. Since this model is a special case of the base specification, we can compute the value of the likelihood ratio test statistic with one degree of freedom as

$$-2(-827.4 + 820.3) = 14.2.$$

(7.30)

Since $\chi^2_{1,0.005} = 7.88$, we can reject the constrained model, or a value of time of 40% of the wage rate, from further consideration. Note that it is also possible to test this single linear restriction using an asymptotic t test and the results of the base specification. The null hypothesis is

$$\beta_t + \alpha \cdot \beta_c = 0,$$

(7.31)

where α is a known constant. The test statistic is

$$\frac{\beta_t + \alpha \cdot \beta_c}{[\text{var}(\hat{\beta}_t) + \alpha^2 \text{var}(\hat{\beta}_c) + 2 \cdot \alpha \cdot \text{cov}(\hat{\beta}_t, \hat{\beta}_c)]^{1/2}}.$$

Substituting in this expression the following values

$$\hat{\beta}_t = -0.0307,$$

$$\hat{\beta}_c = -28.7,$$

$$\alpha = -0.0002,$$

(7.32)

$$\text{var}(\hat{\beta}_t) = -0.0000539,$$

$$\text{var}(\hat{\beta}_c) = 245.0,$$

$$\text{cov}(\hat{\beta}_t, \hat{\beta}_c) = 0.00683,$$

we obtain a value of -3.06 for the test statistic. Again we can reject the null hypothesis that the value of time is 40% of the wage rate.

Table 7.8
Estimation results for trinomial mode choice model: constrained value of time

Variable number	Variable name	Coefficient estimate	Asymptotic standard error	t statistic
1	Drive-alone (da) constant	−1.67	0.311	−5.4
2	Shared-ride (sr) constant	−1.16	0.268	−4.3
3	Round-trip out-of-vehicle time (min)/one-way distance (0.01 mi)	−15.8	5.36	−3.0
4	Round-trip generalized travel cost (¢)/income ($/yr)	−39.0	12.0	−3.2
5	Cars/workers in the household (specific to da)	3.54	0.302	11.7
6	Cars/workers in the household (specific to sr)	1.84	0.276	6.7
7	Downtown workplace dummy (specific to da)	−0.965	0.284	−3.4
8	Downtown workplace dummy (specific to sr)	−0.779	0.240	−3.2
9	Disposable household income (specific to da)	0.0000449	0.0000210	2.1
10	Disposable household income (specific to sr)	0.0000583	0.0000205	2.9
11	Government worker dummy (specific to sr)	0.450	0.152	3.0

Summary statistics

Number of observations = 1,136

$\mathcal{L}(0) = -1{,}207.9$

$\mathcal{L}(c) = -1{,}037.5$

$\mathcal{L}(\beta) = -827.4$

$-2[\mathcal{L}(0) - \mathcal{L}(\beta)] = 760.9$

$\rho^2 = 0.315$

$\bar{\rho}^2 = 0.306$

7.5 Tests of the Model Structure

Up to this point the overall structure of the model was taken as given, and we explored statistical tests and informal procedures to develop acceptable specifications of the utility functions. In this section we consider the basic assumptions of the model structure itself.

In discrete choice models those assumptions are on either distributional properties of random utilities or the properties of choice probabilities. For example, the computational advantages of the multinomial logit model can be realized if we accept the property of the independence from irrelevant alternatives. The logit model also assumes that there are no random taste variations—that is, that the differences in tastes among individuals are captured by the socioeconomic variables in the model specification. We know a priori that these basic assumptions of the logit model can only be considered as reasonable approximations of more complex relationships. We are interested in finding out if significant violations occur and, if so, how to remedy the problems to obtain an acceptable model.

The direct approach to detect violations is a comparison of estimation results with a generalized model that relaxes the basic assumptions that we want to test. The practical difficulty of implementing this approach arises from the prohibitive computational costs of estimating a less restrictive model structure. The multinomial probit model with unrestricted covariance matrix and random taste variations, discussed in section 5.7, is the most general form available. However, it can be reasonably estimated only for a small number of alternatives and parameters, eliminating its use in most practical situations. Thus we will concentrate on tests that do not require estimation of probit or generalized extreme value models. The tests that will be described can be performed with a logit estimation program. Moreover, when a serious violation is detected, we will attempt to find improvements to the specification of the model that will give more satisfactory results and so will avoid the need to use a more complex model structure.

Tests of the IIA Assumption

McFadden, Tye, and Train (1977) investigated a wide range of computationally feasible tests to detect violations of the IIA assumption. (This assumption is discussed in sections 3.7 and 5.3.) We will describe here the most useful of their tests which proved to be the most powerful. The test involves comparisons of logit models estimated with subsets of alternatives from the universal choice set. If the IIA assumption (i.e., the logit model structure) holds for the full choice set, then the logit model also applies to a choice from any subset of alternatives.

The linear-in-parameters logit model for the full choice set is

$$P(i|C_n) = \frac{e^{\beta'x_{in}}}{\sum_{j \in C_n} e^{\beta'x_{jn}}}, \qquad (7.33)$$

and for a restricted choice set $\tilde{C}_n \subseteq C_n$ we obtain the following logit model

$$P(i|\tilde{C}_n) = \frac{e^{\beta'x_{in}}}{\sum_{j \in \tilde{C}_n} e^{\beta'x_{jn}}}, \qquad i \in \tilde{C}_n \subseteq C_n. \qquad (7.34)$$

With the absence of certain alternatives from $\tilde{C}_n$, it is in general possible to identify only a subvector of β. *This subvector does not include the alternative-specific parameters of alternatives not included in the restricted choice set* $\tilde{C}_n$. The estimation data used for the model with a restricted set of alternatives are a subset of the full data set, *omitting observations with chosen alternatives not in the restricted choice set.*

Thus, if the logit model is correctly specified, we can obtain consistent coefficient estimates of the same subvector of parameters from a logit model estimated with a full choice set and from a logit model estimated with a restricted choice set. Denote the estimated coefficients from the restricted set of alternatives as $\hat{\beta}_{\tilde{C}}$ and the estimated values for the same subvector of coefficients from a model with a full choice set as $\hat{\beta}_C$. Denote analogously the covariance matrices as $\Sigma_{\beta_{\tilde{C}}}$ and Σ_{β_C}, where the latter matrix is the appropriate submatrix from the estimation with a full choice set. Hausman and McFadden (1984) developed a test for the null hypothesis that $\beta_C = \beta_{\tilde{C}}$. The following test statistic

$$(\hat{\beta}_{\tilde{C}} - \hat{\beta}_C)'(\Sigma_{\beta_{\tilde{C}}} - \Sigma_{\beta_C})^{-1}(\hat{\beta}_{\tilde{C}} - \hat{\beta}_C)$$

is asymptotically χ^2 distributed with $\tilde{K}$ degrees of freedom, where $\tilde{K}$ is the number of elements in the subvector of coefficients that is identifiable from the restricted choice set model (i.e., the dimension of $\beta_{\tilde{C}}$).

Another test—an approximate likelihood ratio test—was used earlier by McFadden, Tye, and Train (1977). The approximate likelihood ratio test statistic with $\tilde{K}$ degrees of freedom is

$$-2[\mathcal{L}_{\tilde{C}}(\hat{\beta}_C) - \mathcal{L}_{\tilde{C}}(\hat{\beta}_{\tilde{C}})].$$

where the two log likelihood values are calculated on the estimation sample for the restricted choice set model. This statistic is not a proper likelihood ratio test because $\hat{\beta}_C$ is not a vector of constants. Small and Hsiao (1982) point out that the assumption that $\hat{\beta}_C$ is not stochastic is identical to assuming that $\hat{\beta}_C$ and $\hat{\beta}_{\tilde{C}}$ are uncorrelated, which is unlikely to hold. This assumption results in the approximate likelihood ratio test being asymptotically biased toward *not* rejecting the null hypothesis of IIA model structure.

Small and Hsiao propose the following correction to this test statistic to remove the bias:

$$\frac{1}{1 - N_1/(\alpha N)}\{-2[\mathscr{L}_{\tilde{C}}(\hat{\beta}_C) - \mathscr{L}_{\tilde{C}}(\hat{\beta}_{\tilde{C}})]\},$$

where N is the number of observations in the unrestricted choice set estimation, N_1 is the number of observations in the restricted choice set estimation ($N_1 < N$ since those observations with chosen alternatives not in the restricted choice set are omitted), and $\alpha \geq 1$ is a scalar. Asymptotically this corrected likelihood ratio statistic actually is χ^2 distributed with $\tilde{K}$ degrees of freedom under the null hypothesis, if it can be assumed that $\Sigma_{\hat{\beta}_{\tilde{C}}}$ and $\Sigma_{\hat{\beta}_C}$ differ (asymptotically) by at most a scalar multiple, that is, $\Sigma_{\hat{\beta}_C} = \alpha^{-1} \Sigma_{\hat{\beta}_{\tilde{C}}}$. In practice, then, use of the corrected statistic should be preceded by a check of the reasonableness of this assumption; most logit estimation programs automatically output or make easily available the covariance matrix at the estimated coefficient values, so this check is straightforward to perform. (In the following example we will show that a value of $\alpha = 1$ may be used as a screening procedure.)

If in a specific instance the assumption made by this correction that a scalar difference between the covariance matrices exists is not defensible, Small and Hsiao (1982) propose an exact test for the IIA assumption. To perform the test, randomly divide the full estimation data set into two parts, denoted A and B. On sample A, using the unrestricted choice sets, estimate $\hat{\beta}_C^A$, the subvector of coefficients corresponding to the parameters that are identifiable when the restricted set of alternatives are used; next, on sample B, using the restricted choice sets, estimate $\hat{\beta}_{\tilde{C}}^B$ and the corresponding log likelihood, $\mathscr{L}_{\tilde{C}}^B(\hat{\beta}_{\tilde{C}}^B)$; finally, again on sample B, but now based on the unrestricted choice sets, obtain $\hat{\beta}_C^B$. Small and Hsiao show that if we now form the following convex combination of $\hat{\beta}_C^A$ and $\hat{\beta}_C^B$,

$$\hat{\beta}_C^{AB} = (1/\sqrt{2})\hat{\beta}_C^A + (1 - 1/\sqrt{2})\hat{\beta}_C^B, \tag{7.35}$$

and use it to evaluate the log likelihood of the sample B with the restricted choice sets, denoted as $\mathscr{L}_C^B(\hat{\beta}_C^{AB})$, then the statistic

$$-2[\mathscr{L}_C^B(\hat{\beta}_C^{AB}) - \mathscr{L}_C^B(\hat{\beta}_C^B)]$$

is asymptotically χ^2 distributed with $\tilde{K}$ degrees of freedom, $\tilde{K}$ being the common dimension of the $\hat{\beta}_C^A$, $\hat{\beta}_C^B$, $\hat{\beta}_C^B$, and $\hat{\beta}_C^{AB}$ parameter vectors. This test, though exact (asymptotically), is more computationally intensive and time-consuming. We recommend that the simpler corrected approximate likelihood ratio test be carried out first, and then only if its underlying assumption is violated, should the exact test procedure be used.

We provide an example of testing for the validity of the IIA assumption for a mode choice logit model using 369 observations from the Brazilian city of Maceio. Four modes (bus, taxi, auto passenger, and auto drive) are represented; each mode actually represents daily home-based work tours (i.e., two or four trips per day by the same mode, depending on whether or not the traveler made a trip home for the midday meal). Bus, taxi, and auto passenger are available to all observations, but auto drive is made available only to workers 18 years or older from auto-owning households.

Table 7.9a presents the estimation results for an 11 parameter model based on these data, for which the sample frequencies of the chosen mode are as follows:

Bus   237
Taxi   12
Auto passenger   28
Auto drive   92

The choice sets are then restricted by removing the taxi alternative, and a second model, shown in table 7.9b, is estimated on 357 observations (since the 12 observations that chose taxi must be removed from the estimation sample). Note that certain parameters in table 7.9a are not identifiable once the taxi alternative is removed; hence these parameters are not included in table 7.9b.

Before conducting the formal statistical test for IIA, it is useful to examine the differences in the values of coefficient estimates. A comparison of the values in table 7.9a with those of 7.9b shows that all the coefficients in common for both models are quite stable; all the coefficients of the restricted choice set model are within one standard error of those of the unrestricted choice set model. Note, however, that there is a general in-

Table 7.9a
Estimation results for Maceio home-based work tour mode choice: full choice sets

Variable number	Variable name	Coefficient estimate	Asymptotic standard error	t statistic
1	Taxi (t) constant	−1.847	0.776	−2.4
2	Auto passenger (ap) constant	−3.394	0.496	−6.8
3	Auto drive (ad) constant	−1.936	0.611	−3.2
4	Total travel time (min/day)	−0.0134	0.0073	−1.8
5	Total travel cost (Cr\$ 1977) divided by natural logarithm of household income proxy (KwH/month)	−0.2937	0.1013	−2.9
6	Household income proxy (specific to t)	0.0034	0.0032	1.1
7	Household income proxy (specific to ap)	0.0034	0.0026	1.3
8	Household income proxy (specific to ad)	0.0051	0.0024	2.1
9	Cars/workers in household (specific to t)	3.7023	0.8761	4.2
10	Cars/workers in household (specific to ap)	4.2767	0.7038	6.1
11	Cars/workers in household (specific to ad)	4.2293	0.8035	5.3

Summary statistics

Number of observations = 369

$\mathcal{L}(0) = -444.2$

$\mathcal{L}(\hat{\beta}) = -177.3$

$-2[\mathcal{L}(0) - \mathcal{L}(\hat{\beta})] = 533.8$

$\rho^2 = 0.601$

$\bar{\rho}^2 = 0.576$

Table 7.9b
Estimation results for Maceio home-based work tour mode choice: taxi alternative removed

Variable number	Variable name	Coefficient estimate	Asymptotic standard error	t statistic
1	Auto passenger (ap) constant	−3.529	0.525	−6.7
2	Auto drive (ad) constant	−2.215	0.661	−3.4
3	Total travel time (min/day)	−0.0173	0.0090	−1.9
4	Total travel cost (Cr$ 1977) divided by natural logarithm of household income proxy (KwH/month)	−0.3158	0.1748	−1.8
5	Household income proxy (specific to ap)	0.0030	0.0027	1.1
6	Household income proxy (specific to ad)	0.0047	0.0026	1.8
7	Cars/workers in household (specific to ap)	4.5331	0.7625	5.9
8	Cars/workers in household (specific to ad)	4.6311	0.8920	5.2

Summary statistics

Number of observations = 357

$\mathcal{L}(0) = -300.6$

$\mathcal{L}(\hat{\beta}) = -127.1$

$-2[\mathcal{L}(0) - \mathcal{L}(\hat{\beta})] = 346.8$

$\rho^2 = 0.577$

$\bar{\rho}^2 = 0.551$

crease in the scale of all the parameters under the restricted choice set.

In general, we search in these comparisons for "problematic" alternatives whose presence have serious effects on the coefficients' estimates. We then attempt to improve on the specification of their utility functions. We also search for scale differences, a situation where the coefficient estimates from a restricted choice set are uniformly greater in absolute value than those from the full choice set. This implies that the random utilities of the alternatives in the restricted set may be correlated.

Scale differences will be explained in detail in chapter 10. Briefly, recall from chapter 5 that the scale parameter of a logit model is inversely proportional to the standard error of the random utility component. A greater scale therefore means reduced variance of the random utilities that are compared in the restricted choice set. Thus it may imply, for example, that an explanatory variable that distinguishes the utilities of the alternatives in the restricted choice set from the excluded alternatives was omitted or, as will be shown in chapter 10, that a nested-logit model structure is appropriate.

An examination of the covariance matrices of the two models 7.9a and 7.9b for the reasonableness of the assumption of a scalar difference between the matrices shows that it does not hold in general, especially in connection with the covariance elements related to the travel time and cost parameters. In fact the ratios of individual elements of the covariance matrix of the restricted choice set model to the corresponding elements of the covariance matrix of the unrestricted choice set model (each ratio is an estimate, of sorts, of α) vary from more than 1.0 to less than 4.0 (see figures 7.4a and b). The observation that most of this variability is introduced in the travel time and cost parameters of the specification leads us to hypothesize that separating the travel time and cost parameters for the taxi mode in the unrestricted choice set specification might reduce this variability significantly.

Table 7.9c presents the estimation results for just such a specification. (See figure 7.4c for the variance-covariance matrix of the parameters.) Note that the taxi specific travel time variable is positive but not significant and that the taxi cost variable is negative and significant. A formal statistical test will not reject the hypothesis that these two parameters are jointly zero; it would seem that there has been no advantage to performing this extra estimation. However, if we now compute estimates of α using the covariance matrices of the models in 7.9b and 7.9c, we find that the

Variable number	1	2	3	4	5	6	7	8	9	10	11
1	0.602										
2	0.0664	0.0246									
3	0.0978	0.177	0.374								
4	-0.0^2161	0.0^2187	0.0^2166	0.0^4532							
5	-0.0588	-0.0^3351	-0.0^2224	0.0^3342	0.0103						
6	-0.0^2110	-0.0^3435	-0.0^3503	-0.0^5129	-0.0^5458	0.0^4101					
7	-0.0^3337	-0.0^3764	-0.0^3619	-0.0^5175	-0.0^4121	0.0^5391	0.0^5667				
8	-0.0^3373	-0.0^3591	-0.0^3827	-0.0^5230	-0.0^4158	0.0^5437	0.0^5496	0.0^5598			
9	0.0750	0.0^2694	-0.0688	-0.0^3436	-0.0206	-0.0^3906	-0.0^3270	-0.0^3257	0.767		
10	0.0756	-0.0391	-0.0921	-0.0^3236	-0.0112	-0.0^3334	-0.0^3519	-0.0^3316	0.359	0.495	
11	0.0701	-0.0287	-0.238	-0.0^3436	-0.0121	-0.0^3348	-0.0^3310	-0.0^3289	0.427	0.453	0.645

Variable number

Figure 7.4a
Asymptotic covariance matrix of parameter estimates of table 7.9a. The entries in this matrix should be read as in the following example: $0.0^3271 = 0.000271$.

Variable number	1	2	3	4	5	6	7	8
1	0.275							
2	0.211	0.437						
3	0.0^2219	0.0^2182	0.0^4801					
4	-0.0^3677	-0.0^2701	0.0^2101	0.0305				
5	-0.0^3829	-0.0^3689	-0.0^5329	-0.0^4530	0.0^5740			
6	-0.0^3669	-0.0^3913	-0.0^5423	-0.0^4652	0.0^5572	0.0^5685		
7	-0.0542	-0.118	-0.0^2104	-0.0279	-0.0^3608	-0.0^3386	0.581	
8	-0.0478	-0.295	-0.0^2130	-0.0296	-0.0^3378	-0.0^3353	0.552	0.796
	1	2	3	4	5	6	7	8

Variable number

Figure 7.4b
Asymptotic covariance matrix of parameter estimates of table 7.9b. The entries in this matrix should be read as in the following example: $0.0^3271 = 0.000271$.

variability observed before has been reduced significantly (the range goes from around 0.77 to 1.1, concentrating at the lower end).

Thus we choose to conduct the IIA test using the corrected approximate likelihood ratio statistic based on the models of tables 7.9b and 7.9c. To calculate the test statistic, we must evaluate the log likelihood of the sample under the exclusion of the taxi alternative at the parameter values of table 7.9c; this value is found to be -127.362. We use a value of 1.0 for α, and hence the corrected likelihood ratio statistic is

$$\frac{1}{1 - 357/369}[-2(-127.362 + 127.149)] \cong 13.1. \tag{7.36}$$

This value is compared to the critical chi-square value with 8 degrees of freedom (i.e., the number of parameters in table 7.9b) and 95% confidence level, which is 15.5. Hence we cannot reject the null hypothesis of a logit model structure at this level of significance; even if this level is reduced to 90%, we still cannot reject the null hypothesis.

Small and Hsiao suggest the use of $\alpha = 1$ in the calculation for the corrected likelihood ratio statistic if the covariance of the vector of characteristics of the chosen alternative for each sample member in the restricted and unrestricted choice set situations does not differ too much between the

Table 7.9c
Estimation results for Maceio home-based work tour mode choice: full choice sets with mode-specific time and cost variables

Variable number	Variable name	Coefficient estimate	Asymptotic standard error	t statistic
1	Taxi (t) constant	−2.135	0.879	−2.4
2	Auto passenger (ap) constant	−3.421	0.502	−6.8
3	Auto drive (ad) constant	−1.939	0.620	−3.1
4	Total travel time (min/day) (specific to t)	0.0106	0.0276	0.4
5	Total travel time (min/day) (specific to modes other than t)	−0.0165	0.0085	−2.0
6	Total travel cost (Cr\$ 1977) divided by natural logarithm of household income proxy (KwH/month) (specific to t)	−0.4492	0.2127	−2.1
7	Total travel cost (Cr\$ 1977) divided by natural logarithm of household income proxy (KwH/month) (specific to modes other than t)	−0.3640	0.1671	−2.2
8	Household income proxy (specific to t)	0.0022	0.0036	0.6
9	Household income proxy (specific to ap)	0.0035	0.0026	1.3
10	Household income proxy (specific to ad)	0.0052	0.0025	2.1
11	Cars/workers in household (specific to t)	3.6577	0.9080	4.0
12	Cars/workers in household (specific to ap)	4.3469	0.7260	6.0
13	Cars/workers in household (specific to ad)	4.3016	0.8257	5.2

Summary statistics
Number of observations = 369
$\mathcal{L}(0) = -444.2$
$\mathcal{L}(\hat{\beta}) = -176.8$
$-2[\mathcal{L}(0) - \mathcal{L}(\hat{\beta})] = 534.9$
$\rho^2 = 0.602$
$\bar{\rho}^2 = 0.573$

Variable number	1	2	3	4	5	6	7	8	9	10	11	12	13
1	0.772												
2	0.0613	0.252											
3	0.0816	0.183	0.384										
4	-0.0^2349	0.0^3925	0.0^3855	0.0^3761									
5	-0.0^3228	0.0^2193	0.0^2157	0.0^4291	0.0^4715								
6	-0.0518	0.0^2756	0.0^2456	-0.0^2458	0.0^3512	0.0452							
7	-0.0148	-0.0^2116	-0.0^2747	0.0^3410	0.0^3883	0.0^2975	0.0279						
8	-0.0^2103	-0.0^3406	-0.0^3491	-0.0^4415	0.0^6189	0.0^3267	-0.0^5422	0.0^4132					
9	-0.0^3403	-0.0^3779	-0.0^3631	-0.0^3260	-0.0^5246	-0.0^5885	-0.0^5351	0.0^5417	0.0^5683				
10	-0.0^3456	-0.0^3608	-0.0^3842	-0.0^3316	-0.0^3321	-0.0^4127	-0.0^4440	0.0^5466	0.0^5513	0.0^5618			
11	0.0749	0.0128	-0.0540	-0.0^2386	-0.0^3871	-0.0^2138	-0.0380	-0.0^3784	-0.0^3254	-0.0^3242	0.824		
12	0.0388	-0.0392	-0.0876	-0.0^3446	-0.0^3957	-0.0124	-0.0337	-0.0^3343	-0.0^3496	-0.0^3287	0.382	0.527	
13	0.0332	-0.0296	-0.235	-0.0^3574	-0.0^2117	-0.0137	-0.0349	-0.0^3360	-0.0^3286	-0.0^3258	0.446	0.487	0.682
	1	2	3	4	5	6	7	8	9	10	11	12	13

Variable number

Figure 7.4c
Asymptotic covariance matrix of parameter estimates of table 7.9c. The entries in this matrix should be read as in the following example:
$0.0^3271 = 0.000271$.

two choice sets. The use of $\alpha = 1$ seems justifiable as a screening procedure. This is the reason we have strived to obtain an improved model specification in the example prior to assuming $\alpha = 1$.

Test of Taste Variations

Choice theory and the discrete choice models derived from it are, by their very nature, disaggregate relationships. They describe the behavior of an individual decision maker. Yet in estimated models we assume the same model structure and the same values of the unknown parameters for all members of the population represented by the sample. Two approaches have been applied to account for the differences in the values of taste parameters among individuals. In the first approach the socioeconomic variables that describe the decision maker are included in various forms in the specification of the utility functions. The second, and more general approach, captures unobservable taste variations by using model structures with random taste variations, also known as random coefficients models. (See the discussion of the random coefficients logit and multinomial probit models in section 5.7.)

Unfortunately random taste variation models are extremely complex and prohibitively expensive computationally. Moreover, even if we can estimate a random coefficients model, it is still desirable to capture systematic taste variations in the utility specification. It may be erroneous to assume constant parameters of the distribution of the uncaptured taste differences because they may change over time with demographic shifts. Therefore we describe a procedure, called *market segmentation*, to search for systematic variations of taste parameters among population subgroups in order to include them explicitly in the specification of the variables.

To perform the taste variation test, we first classify the estimation data into socioeconomic groups. The simplest market segmentation scheme is based on ranges of the value of a single socioeconomic characteristic, such as low-, medium-, and high-income ranges. We assume the same specification across market segments and apply the estimation procedure to the first subset of data, to the second subset, and so on, and finally estimate the pooled model with the full data set.

Denote by N_g the sample size of market segment $g = 1, \ldots, G$, where G is the number of market segments and

$$\sum_{g=1}^{G} N_g = N, \tag{7.37}$$

where N is the full sample size. The null hypothesis of no taste variations across the market segments is

$$\beta^1 = \beta^2 = \cdots = \beta^G, \tag{7.38}$$

where β^g is the vector of coefficients of market segment g. The likelihood ratio test statistic is given by

$$-2\left[\mathscr{L}_N(\hat{\beta}) - \sum_{g=1}^{G} \mathscr{L}_{N_g}(\hat{\beta}^g)\right],$$

where $\mathscr{L}_N(\hat{\beta})$ is the log likelihood for the restricted model that is estimated on the pooled data set with a single vector of coefficients $\hat{\beta}$; $\mathscr{L}_{N_g}(\hat{\beta}^g)$ is the maximum likelihood of the model estimated with the gth subset of the data. This test statistic is χ^2 distributed with the degrees of freedom equal to the number of restrictions,

$$\sum_{g=1}^{G} K_g - K,$$

where K_g is the number of coefficients in the gth market segment model. K_g is equal to K except when one or more of the pooled model coefficients are not identifiable with the gth subset of the data. For example, for the model specification in table 7.1, it is not possible to identify the coefficients of the downtown workplace dummy, β_8 and β_9, from a market segment defined by a downtown workplace.

Tables 7.10, 7.11, and 7.12 present the estimation results for market segmentation tests by income, automobile ownership, and sex on the base specification in table 7.1. The results of the likelihood ratio tests against the base specification are as follows:

Model	Test statistic	Degrees of freedom	$\chi^2_{0.05}$
Table 7.10	24.2	24	36.4
Table 7.11	33.2	12	21.0
Table 7.12	45.0	12	21.0

With this evidence we cannot reject equality of coefficients across the income market segments, but we can reject the null hypothesis for the automobile ownership and the gender market segmentation schemes.

A rejection of the hypothesis of equal vectors of coefficients across market segments suggests further exploration of the importance of and the reasons for the statistically significant differences. It is useful to know if the rejection of the joint hypothesis can be attributed to individual, or subsets

Table 7.10
Estimation results for trinomial mode choice model: market segmentation by income

Variable number	Variable name	Coefficient estimate (asymptotic standard error)		
		Income (0–8,000)	Income (8,000–16,000)	Income (16,000 +)
1	Drive-alone (da) constant	−3.15 (0.788)	−1.00 (0.734)	−2.10 (1.60)
2	Shared-ride (sr) constant	−1.79 (0.543)	−0.0779 (0.648)	−1.60 (1.49)
3	Round-trip travel time (min)	−0.0241 (0.0136)	−0.0295 (0.0101)	−0.0593 (0.0233)
4	Round-trip out-of-vehicle time (min)/one-way distance (0.01 mi)	−18.3 (10.6)	−10.5 (7.38)	−5.14 (13.0)
5	Round-trip travel cost (¢)/household income ($/yr)	−46.4 (23.5)	−45.5 (32.3)	−140.0 (93.6)
6	Cars/workers in the household (specific to da)	4.28 (0.624)	2.91 (0.408)	4.63 (0.921)
7	Cars/workers in the household (specific to sr)	2.20 (0.482)	1.13 (0.388)	3.16 (0.906)
8	Downtown workplace dummy (specific to da)	0.396 (0.707)	−0.905 (0.446)	−0.815 (0.764)
9	Downtown workplace dummy (specific to sr)	0.188 (0.522)	−0.761 (0.365)	−0.388 (0.632)
10	Disposable household income (specific to da)	0.0000780 (0.000129)	0.0000392 (0.0000664)	0.000000494 (0.0000665)

11	Disposable household income (specific to sr)	0.0000360 (0.000111)	0.0000482 (0.0000656)	0.0000144 (0.0000657)
12	Government worker dummy (specific to sr)	0.717 (0.370)	0.563 (0.217)	0.112 (0.275)

Summary statistics

Number of observations by market segment

$\mathcal{L}_{N_g}(\hat{\boldsymbol{\beta}})$

272	531	333
-180.3	-412.8	-215.1

Number of observations $= 1,136$

$\mathcal{L}(\mathbf{0}) = -1,207.9$

$\mathcal{L}(\hat{\boldsymbol{\beta}}) = -808.2$

$-2[\mathcal{L}(\mathbf{0}) - \mathcal{L}(\hat{\boldsymbol{\beta}})] = 799.4$

$\rho^2 = 0.331$

$\bar{\rho}^2 = 0.301$

Table 7.11
Estimation results for trinomial mode choice model: market segmentation by automobile ownership

Variable number	Variable name	Coefficient estimate (asymptotic standard error)	
		Auto ownership 0 or 1	Auto ownership 2+
1	Drive-alone (da) constant	-2.66 (0.455)	-3.24 (1.33)
2	Shared-ride (sr) constant	-1.14 (0.298)	-2.98 (1.21)
3	Round-trip travel time (min)	-0.0280 (0.00800)	-0.0491 (0.0200)
4	Round-trip out-of-vehicle time (min)/one-way distance (0.01 mi)	-14.7 (6.28)	-14.5 (11.2)
5	Round-trip travel cost (¢)/household income ($/yr)	-35.3 (18.3)	-35.4 (35.1)
6	Cars/workers in the household (specific to da)	4.26 (0.432)	3.56 (0.925)
7	Cars/workers in the household (specific to sr)	1.40 (0.341)	2.59 (0.933)
8	Downtown workplace dummy (specific to da)	-0.605 (0.368)	-1.13 (0.606)
9	Downtown workplace dummy (specific to sr)	-0.446 (0.297)	-0.636 (0.577)
10	Disposable household income (specific to da)	0.00000760 (0.0000281)	0.000126 (0.0000506)

11	Disposable household income (specific to sr)	0.0000327 (0.0000245)	0.000130 (0.0000508)
12	Government worker dummy (specific to sr)	0.687 (0.200)	0.0630 (0.251)

Summary statistics

Number of observations by market segment	623	513
$\mathcal{L}_{N_g}(\hat{\boldsymbol{\beta}})$	-502.6	-301.1

Number of observations $= 1{,}136$

$\mathcal{L}(\mathbf{0}) = -1{,}207.9$

$\mathcal{L}(\hat{\boldsymbol{\beta}}) = -803.7$

$-2[\mathcal{L}(\mathbf{0}) - \mathcal{L}(\hat{\boldsymbol{\beta}})] = 808.4$

$\rho^2 = 0.335$

$\bar{\rho}^2 = 0.315$

Table 7.12
Estimation result for trinomial mode choice model: market segmentation by sex

Variable number	Variable name	Coefficient estimate (asymptotic standard error)	
		Male	Female
1	Drive-alone (da) constant	−1.91 (0.549)	−3.51 (0.590)
2	Shared-ride (sr) constant	−1.45 (0.437)	−1.43 (0.383)
3	Round-trip travel time (min)	−0.0357 (0.0118)	−0.0208 (0.00979)
4	Round-trip out-of-vehicle time (min)	−29.1 (10.5)	−13.2 (6.83)
5	Round-trip travel cost (¢)/household income ($/yr)	−44.4 (23.5)	−1.49 (22.5)
6	Cars/workers in the household (specific to da)	2.97 (0.411)	4.81 (0.565)
7	Cars/workers in the household (specific to sr)	1.66 (0.402)	2.10 (0.438)
8	Downtown workplace dummy (specific to da)	−1.03 (0.436)	−0.871 (0.471)
9	Downtown workplace dummy (specific to sr)	−0.812 (0.399)	−0.126 (0.358)
10	Disposable household income (specific to da)	0.0000720 (0.0000318)	0.0000356 (0.0000329)

11	Disposable household income (specific to sr)	0.0000767 (0.0000308)	0.0000333 (0.0000297)
12	Government worker dummy (specific to sr)	0.438 (0.201)	0.420 (0.241)

Summary statistics

Number of observations by market segment	723	413
$\mathscr{L}_{N_g}(\hat{\beta})$	−469.3	−328.5

Number of observations = 1,136

$\mathscr{L}(0) = -1{,}207.9$

$\mathscr{L}(\hat{\beta}) = -797.8$

$-2[\mathscr{L}(0) - \mathscr{L}(\hat{\beta})] = 820.2$

$\rho^2 = 0.340$

$\bar{\rho}^2 = 0.320$

Table 7.13
Asymptotic t tests for coefficient differences between automobile ownership level market segments

Variable number	Variable name	t statistic
1	Drive-alone (da) constant	0.41
2	Shared-ride (sr) constant	1.48
3	Round-trip travel time (min)	0.98
4	Round-trip out-of-vehicle time (min)/one way distance (0.01 mi)	−0.02
5	Round-trip travel cost (¢)/household income ($/yr)	0.003
6	Cars/workers in the household (specific to da)	0.69
7	Cars/workers in the household (specific to sr)	−1.20
8	Downtown workplace dummy (specific to da)	0.74
9	Downtown workplace dummy (specific to sr)	0.29
10	Disposable household income (specific to da)	−2.05**
11	Disposable household income (specific to sr)	−1.73*
12	Government worker dummy (specific to sr)	1.94*

Note: * significant at the 0.10 level; ** significant at the 0.05 level.

of, coefficients. This can be done by comparing individual coefficients between market segments. The statistic for the asymptotic t test of equality of individual coefficients between two market segments (arbitrarily taken to be segments 1 and 2) is

$$\frac{\hat{\beta}_k^1 - \hat{\beta}_k^2}{(\text{var}\,(\hat{\beta}_k^1) + \text{var}(\hat{\beta}_k^2))^{1/2}}.$$

The application of this test for the market segment models in tables 7.11 and 7.12 are given in tables 7.13 and 7.14, respectively. It is possible that all the t tests will be insignificant despite the fact that the joint likelihood ratio test is significant. It is also possible that the joint test will not reject the hypothesis, though a few individual coefficients are significantly different. From table 7.13 we find that the coefficients of the two alternative specific disposable income variables and of the government worker dummy (β_{10}, β_{11}, and β_{12}) are significantly different between the two automobile owner-ship segments. The differences in β_{10} and β_{11} can be interpreted as a larger antitransit bias with increasing income in households with two or more cars. The difference between the two estimates of β_{12} suggests that carpool-

Table 7.14
Asymptotic t tests for coefficient differences between male and female market segments

Variable number	Variable name	t statistic
1	Drive-alone (da) constant	1.99**
2	Shared-ride (sr) constant	−0.03
3	Round-trip travel time (min)	−0.97
4	Round-trip out-of-vehicle (min)/one way distance (0.01 mi)	−1.27
5	Round-trip travel cost (¢)/household income ($/yr)	−1.32
6	Cars/workers in the household (specific to da)	−2.63**
7	Cars/workers in the household (specific to sr)	−0.74
8	Downtown workplace dummy (specific to da)	−0.25
9	Downtown workplace dummy (specific to sr)	−1.28
10	Disposable household income (specific to da)	0.80
11	Disposable household income (specific to sr)	1.01
12	Government worker dummy (specific to sr)	0.06

Note: ** significant at the 0.05 level.

ing incentives may have no effect on the choice of mode of workers from households with two or more cars. If these differences are deemed important in the applications of the model, it is possible to reestimate the model using the full sample with each of these coefficients (β_{10}, β_{11}, and β_{12}) replaced with two coefficients specific to the two automobile ownership levels, thus increasing the degrees of freedom.

For the market segmentation by sex we find from the results in table 7.14 that it may be useful to add to the drive alone utility a female dummy variable and a cars/worker variable specific to females. These two differences imply that, everything else being the same, female workers are less likely to drive alone and are more sensitive to changes in automobile availability.

A limited market segmentation test can be applied to a subset of the coefficients. We use the likelihood ratio test for the null hypothesis of equality of subsets of coefficients across market segments. This test is performed by comparing the pooled model with an unrestricted model that is estimated with the full data set but with a longer vector of coefficients in which a subset of the original coefficients is replaced with two or more market segment specific subsets of coefficients. A typical application is the test of the equality of the coefficients of attributes (e.g., the level-of-service variables in the mode choice model) across market segments.

In the examples given we employed simple univariate market segmentation schemes. However, the tests that were presented can be applied to all types of multivariate segmentation schemes. There are numerous empirical studies of discrete choice models that employed segmentations into life-cycle and life-style groups that produced significantly different models (e.g., see Salomon and Ben-Akiva 1983). In some of these market segment models it may be impossible to incorporate the different tastes in the specifications of the utilities, so it may be better to proceed with separate market segment models.

The market segmentation likelihood ratio tests for joint hypotheses and the individual t tests are also used in tests of spatial and temporal stability, or transferability, of models (see Atherton and Ben-Akiva 1976, Ben-Akiva 1981). In a test of transferability the samples from different locations or from different points in time are treated in the same way as samples from different socioeconomic market segments. There is, however, a major difference between market segmentation and transferability tests. The first test is useful during the model development process and is concerned with the entire set of coefficients. A transferability test, on the other hand, is focused on the stability of the policy-relevant coefficients. For the mode choice example we would be interested in the stability of the travel time and cost coefficients between different locations, but we assume a priori that alternative specific constants and coefficients of socioeconomic variables may differ. Thus the unrestricted model will be the collection of models estimated for the separate data sets. In the restricted model the coefficients of interest, such as travel time and cost coefficients, will be constrained to have the same value across data sets, and all other coefficients will be allowed to vary.

Test of Heteroscedasticity

Since the scale of the utilities of the logit model is inversely proportional to the standard error of the random utility components (see section 5.2), the basic assumption of a constant scale for all the observations is the same as the assumption of homoscedastic (or equal variance) random utilities. In a market segmentation test we may detect that the vectors of coefficients are approximately equal except for differences in scale. Consider a case with two market segments and the hypothesis that

$$\frac{\beta_1^1}{\beta_1^2} = \frac{\beta_2^1}{\beta_2^2} = \cdots = \frac{\beta_K^1}{\beta_K^2}. \tag{7.39}$$

Suppose that the ratio of the two scale parameter is a *known constant*. In this case the preceding hypothesis can be expressed as K linear restrictions, and we can use the likelihood ratio test. Unfortunately the scales are almost always unknown parameters, and we do not have any prior information about their values. Thus this set of restrictions is nonlinear, and we cannot easily estimate a restricted model and perform a likelihood ratio test.

We may, however, be able to hypothesize that the scale of an observation is a function known up to a multiplicative positive constant of some socioeconomic characteristics as

$$\mu_n = \alpha \cdot h(\tilde{S}_n), \qquad n = 1, \ldots, N, \tag{7.40}$$

where α is an arbitrary positive constant that sets the scale of the utility, $h(\ )$ is a known positive function, and $\tilde{S}_n$ is a vector of socioeconomic variables. If $\tilde{S}_n$ takes only discrete values for different market segments, then for the two market segment case we can impose the following linear restrictions:

$$\frac{\beta_k^1}{\beta_k^2} = \frac{h(\tilde{S}_1)}{h(\tilde{S}_2)}, \qquad k = 1, \ldots, K. \tag{7.41}$$

We can multiply all the explanatory variables, including alternative-specific constants, dummies, and socioeconomie variables by $h(\tilde{S}_n)$, and reestimate the models with the following transformed variables:

$$x_{ink}^* = h(\tilde{S}_n) \cdot x_{ink}, \qquad i \in C_n, n = 1, \ldots, N, k = 1, \ldots, K. \tag{7.42}$$

We can then perform a test of equality of coefficients across market segments comparing the models with the transformed variables.

A simpler test would be to compare the adjusted likelihood index of the model estimated with the transformed variables with that of the original specifications. We may accept a scale function $h(\tilde{S}_n)$ that improves the goodness of fit of the model.

For the mode choice example suppose that we want to test the hypothesis that

$$\mu_n = \alpha \cdot \text{income}_n. \tag{7.43}$$

We multiply all the explanatory variables by income and reestimate the models to obtain the results given in table 7.15 (note that one variable, the

Table 7.15
Estimation results for trinomial mode choice model: all variables multiplied by income

Variable number	Variable name[a]	Coefficient estimate	Asymptotic standard error	t statistic
1	Drive-alone (da) constant	0.0^5518	0.0^4220	0.2
2	Shared-ride (sr) constant	-0.0^4159	0.0^4203	-0.8
3	Round-trip travel time (min)	-0.0^5152	0.0^6408	-3.7
4	Round-trip out-of-vehicle time (min)/one way distance (0.01 mi)	-0.0^3940	0.0^3378	-2.5
5	Round trip travel cost (¢)/household income ($/yr)	-0.0^2715	0.0^2224	-3.2
6	Cars/workers in the household (specific to da)	0.0^3157	0.0^4133	11.8
7	Cars/workers in the household (specific to sr)	0.0^4610	0.0^4145	4.2
8	Downtown workplace dummy (specific to da)	-0.0^4331	0.0^4189	-1.8
9	Downtown workplace dummy (specific to sr)	-0.0^4119	0.0^4160	-0.80
10	Disposable household income (specific to da)	-0.0^8433	0.0^9908	-4.8
11	Disposable household income (specific to sr)	-0.0^9293	0.0^9923	-0.3

Summary statistics

Number of observations = 1,136

$\mathscr{L}(\mathbf{0}) = -1,207.9$

$\mathscr{L}(\mathbf{c}) = -1,037.5$

$\mathscr{L}(\hat{\boldsymbol{\beta}}) = -919.1$

$-2[\mathscr{L}(\mathbf{0}) - \mathscr{L}(\hat{\boldsymbol{\beta}})] = 577.6$

$\rho^2 = 0.239$

$\bar{\rho}^2 = 0.230$

Note: Entry 0.0^5518, for example, should be read as 0.00000518.
a. Variables multiplied by household income ($/yr)

government worker dummy, has been omitted from this model). We note that the $\bar{\rho}^2$ statistic decreased from 0.311 to 0.230, and therefore we reject this particular heteroscedasticity hypothesis.

7.6   Prediction Tests

The tests described in the previous sections dealt with the coefficients of the utility functions. In this section we consider tests in which we examine the predicted choice probabilities.

We distinguish between two types of data that are used in prediction tests: internal and external. Internal data are derived from the same source as the estimation sample. In many cases the prediction and estimation samples are identical. With large data sets, however, it is possible to avoid an overlap between the two samples. In general, external data are not necessarily of the same type as the estimation data and may, for example, be aggregate data. We would therefore rely on one of the aggregate prediction procedures described in chapter 6. As a consequence external data are most useful for the joint test of a system of disaggregate models combined with a particular aggregation procedure. In our discussion of tests of the disaggregate models we consider only disaggregate prediction tests in which the prediction sample may or may not overlap the estimation sample; the application of disaggregate prediction tests is essentially the same as that of the sample enumeration aggregation technique described in section 6.3.

Outlier Analysis

An outlier analysis is an important prediction test that should be performed at an early stage of the model development process. We use one of the initial specifications that were estimated to calculate, for all the observations in the estimation sample, the predicted choice probability of the chosen alternative. We then check for unusually large deviations by inspecting all the observations with predicted probabilities less than some arbitrary small value. We begin this analysis at a low limit of, say, 0.01 (or even 0.001 for models with very large choice sets). If we decide to continue the search for less serious outliers we may increase this limit to 0.05, and so on. *Under no circumstances should one simply throw out of the estimation sample these observations without further analysis.* We first check these observations for data errors. We may find, for example, that the chosen alternative was simply miscoded or uncover other coding and measurement errors. If errors are not found, the observation is then classified as an outlier.

The next step, after all the uncovered errors are corrected, is to test the sensitivity of the estimation results to the presence of outliers. If one finds a high level of sensitivity, one can conclude that the outliers contain important information about the model. One could search for improvements to the model specification that will increase the predicted probability of the chosen alternative for some of the outlier observations. It will often be the case that outlier analysis will suggest specification improvements that not only result in a better fit for the outliers but also for all observations. Note that because the model is probabilistic some outliers should exist in the data and the goal is not to eliminate them entirely.

For the mode choice example of table 7.1 an outlier analysis found that none of the observations has a predicted probability for the chosen alternative that was less than 0.1.

Market Segment Prediction Tests

The likelihood ratio index is a useful measure to compare the goodness of fit of alternative specifications. It does not, however, convey direct information about the differences between predicted probabilities and sample frequencies. The purpose of market segment prediction tests is to examine the goodness of fit of a model by its ability to replicate observed shares of alternatives for a market segment.

Denote the number of observations in market segment g choosing alternative i as N_{gi}, where

$$\sum_{i \in C} N_{gi} = N_g. \tag{7.44}$$

We compare N_{gi}, or the share N_{gi}/N_g, with the prediction given by

$$\sum_{n=1}^{N_g} P_n(i) \quad \text{or} \quad \frac{1}{N_g} \sum_{n=1}^{N_g} P_n(i),$$

respectively.

Recall from section 5.5 that for the estimation sample in a logit model with a full set of alternative-specific constants, the predicted shares are equal to the observed shares, as follows:

$$\sum_{n=1}^{N} P_n(i) = N_i, \qquad i \in C, \tag{7.45}$$

where N_i is the number of observations in the estimation sample choosing alternative i. However, this condition does not apply in general to subsets of the estimation sample. It does hold for market segments that have a full set of alternative-specific market segment dummy variables. Consider, for example, the base specification of the mode choice model in table 7.1 and the subset of observations from the estimation sample consisting of workers with a downtown workplace. The predicted mode shares for this subsample will exactly match the observed shares because the model includes a full set of downtown workplace dummies (i.e., β_8 and β_9).

The output of a market segment prediction test is in the format shown in table 7.16. The cell for alternative i (or alternative group i) and market segment g compares the number of observations in the subsample for that market segment choosing alternative i, N_{gi}, with its predicted value,

$$\sum_{n=1}^{N_g} P_n(i).$$

To make these comparisons more meaningful, it is useful to compute the standard errors of the observed and predicted values. The variance of a predicted choice probability depends on the covariance matrix of the coefficient estimates and on the predicted choice probabilities (see the more detailed derivations in Horowitz 1979). It requires complex calculations and therefore is usually not performed. Horowitz (1983b) develops and shows how to use a formal statistical test to compare predicted and observed market segment choice frequencies, but again its use is not straightforward.

Using the binomial distribution, however, it is straightforward to evaluate an approximate variance of the observed values due to sampling errors as follows:

$$\text{var}(N_{gi}) \cong N_g \left(\frac{N_{gi}}{N_g} \right) \left(\frac{1 - N_{gi}}{N_g} \right) = N_{gi} \left(\frac{1 - N_{gi}}{N_g} \right), \tag{7.46}$$

or, for the observed share

$$\text{var}\left(\frac{N_{gi}}{N_g} \right) \cong \frac{1}{N_g} \left(\frac{N_{gi}}{N_g} \right) \left(\frac{1 - N_{gi}}{N_g} \right) = \frac{N_{gi}}{N_g^2} \left(\frac{1 - N_{gi}}{N_g} \right). \tag{7.47}$$

The disaggregate prediction table is examined to detect systematic trends of over and under predictions. As a simple rule of thumb we can begin the evaluation of this table by focusing on the cells in which the deviations exceed two standard errors. Significant deviations are indicative of specifi-

Table 7.16
The format of a disaggregate prediction table

Alternative or groups of alternatives	Market segment						
	1	2	$\cdots$	g	$\cdots$	G	Total
1 Predicted	$\sum_{n=1}^{N_1} P_n(1)$	$\sum_{n=1}^{N_2} P_n(1)$	$\cdots$	$\sum_{n=1}^{N_g} P_n(1)$	$\cdots$	$\sum_{n=1}^{N_G} P_n(1)$	$\sum_{n=1}^{N} P_n(1)$
Observed	N_{11}	N_{21}		N_{g1}		N_{G1}	N_1
2 Predicted	$\sum_{n=1}^{N_1} P_n(2)$	$\sum_{n=1}^{N_2} P_n(2)$	$\cdots$	$\sum_{n=1}^{N_g} P_n(2)$	$\cdots$	$\sum_{n=1}^{N_G} P_n(2)$	$\sum_{n=1}^{N} P_n(2)$
Observed	N_{12}	N_{22}		N_{g2}		N_{G2}	N_2
.	.	.		.		.	.
.	.	.		.		.	.
i Predicted	$\sum_{n=1}^{N_1} P_n(i)$	$\sum_{n=1}^{N_2} P_n(i)$	$\cdots$	$\sum_{n=1}^{N_g} P_n(i)$	$\cdots$	$\sum_{n=1}^{N_G} P_n(i)$	$\sum_{n=1}^{N} P_n(i)$
Observed	N_{1i}	N_{2i}		N_{gi}		N_{Gi}	N_i
.	.	.		.		.	.
.	.	.		.		.	.
J Predicted	$\sum_{n=1}^{N_1} P_n(J)$	$\sum_{n=1}^{N_2} P_n(J)$	$\cdots$	$\sum_{n=1}^{N_g} P_n(J)$	$\cdots$	$\sum_{n=1}^{N_G} P_n(J)$	$\sum_{n=1}^{N} P_n(J)$
Observed	N_{1J}	N_{2J}		N_{gJ}		N_{GJ}	N_J

Note: In a policy prediction table "predicted" is replaced with "predicted under the policy" and "observed" is replaced with "predicted base."

cation errors. Therefore we attempt to correct the specification of the model to eliminate these prediction errors. This is similar to the procedure that was discussed in the market segmentation test of taste variations. Note, however, that in the prediction test we can employ a larger number of market segments and the market segment subsamples can be smaller because they are not used to estimate separate models. A small subsample will be reflected in large standard errors of the observed shares, which are inversely proportional to the square root of the sample size. In many studies this prediction test has proved to be a very valuable aid in improving the specification of discrete choice models.

To demonstrate a specific prediction test, we shall utilize a logit model of the joint choice of mode and destination for home-based nonwork trips (see chapter 9 for the techniques used in estimating destination choice models and chapter 10 for further details concerning multidimensional choice models) calibrated for the Brazilian city of Maceio. The model, which has 4 travel modes (bus, taxi, auto drive, and auto passenger) and 35 destinations, was estimated with a random sample of 774 trips.

The estimated parameters are presented in table 7.17. The interpretation of parameters in a multidimensional model is no different than in the single-dimension examples we have used thus far. Just bear in mind that each alternative is now a combination of a mode and a destination. Two principal corridors, both continuations of interstate highways, feed into the central area of Maceio. One of these is the Fernandes Lima corridor; the definition of parameter 25 of table 7.17 reflects its influence.

In table 7.18 we present disaggregate prediction results for this model for two market segmentations, income and automobile ownership level, for the mode dimension only. We have calculated, as suggested earlier, approximate 95% confidence intervals for the observed cell counts as $N_{gi} \pm 2 \cdot [\text{var}(N_{gi})]^{1/2}$, where var (N_{gi}) has been approximated by the variance of a binomial random variable. Across both market segmentations all the predicted cell frequencies lie within this confidence interval, so one can conclude that this test reveals no glaring specification errors.

A comparison of observed and predicted cell frequencies in table 7.18 for the income segmentation shows that in the low-income group there is an over prediction of the taxi and auto modes, to the detriment of bus; in the middle-income segment bus and auto drive are overpredicted; finally, in the high-income category bus and auto passenger are overpredicted. Or these

Table 7.17
Estimation results for a joint mode/destination logit choice model for Maceio (from Swait et al. 1984)

Variable number	Variable name	Coefficient estimate	Asymptotic standard error	t statistic
1	Taxi (t) constant	−0.064	0.320	−0.2
2	Auto passenger (ap) w/o automobile	−3.160	0.340	−9.3
3	Auto passenger (ap) w/automobile	−0.713	0.324	−2.2
4	Auto drive (ad)	−0.250	0.313	−0.8
5	Total travel time, minutes one-way shopping trips	−0.0606	0.0119	−5.1
6	Total travel time, minutes one-way recreation trips	−0.0228	0.0084	−2.7
7	Total travel time, minutes one-way personal business and other trips	−0.0426	0.0085	−5.0
8	Travel cost (Cr\$ 1972) divided by $\log_e$ of household income proxy (KwH/month), shopping trips	−0.8124	0.1425	−5.7
9	Travel cost (Cr\$ 1977) divided by $\log_e$ of household (KwH/month), recreation trips	−1.0740	0.1678	−6.4
10	Total travel cost (Cr\$ 1977) divided by $\log_e$ of household income proxy (KwH/month), personal business and other trips	−0.5790	0.1206	−4.8
11	Household income proxy (for t, ap, ad)	0.0078	0.0014	5.6
12	Number of household members (for t, ap, ad)	−0.1489	0.0402	−3.7
13	Dummy for trips at or after 7 pm and by t, ap, ad	0.8981	0.3208	2.8
14	$\log_e$ of service and professional employment in zone of destination, if greater than 0; 0 otherwise, shopping trips	1.2600	0.0728	17.3
15	$\log_e$ of service and professional employment in zone of destination, if greater than 0; 0 otherwise, recreation trips	0.3512	0.1301	2.7

16	Log_e of service, professional, transport and communication, and public administration employment in zone of destination, if greater than 0; 0 otherwise, personal business trips	0.9835	0.3073	3.2
17	Log_e of total employment less service, professional, transport and communication, and public administration employment in zone of destination, if greater than 0; 0 otherwise, other trips	0.2340	0.0600	3.9
18	Central core area destination dummy, recreation trips	2.028	0.483	4.2
19	Central core area destination dummy, personal, business trips	1.963	0.9815	2.0
20	Central core area destination dummy, other trips (not shopping)	2.741	0.232	11.8
21	Central peripheral area w/o retail activity destination dummy	−2.247	0.350	−6.4
22	Central peripheral area w/retail activity destination dummy	1.140	0.219	5.2
23	Marketplace destination dummy	1.447	0.1663	8.7
24	Beach area destination dummy	0.450	0.180	2.5
25	Fernandes Lima corridor destination dummy	0.628	0.150	4.2

Summary statistics

Number of observations = 774

$\mathcal{L}(0) = -2,831.0$

$\mathcal{L}(\hat{\beta}) = -1,578.0$

$-2[\mathcal{L}(0) - \mathcal{L}(\hat{\beta})] = 2,506.0$

$\rho^2 = 0.443$

$\bar{\rho}^2 = 0.434$

Table 7.18
Market segment prediction tests for mode dimension of model in table 7.17

Mode		Household income			Automobile ownership level		Total
		Low	Medium	High	0	1+	
Bus	Predicted	209.6	125.9	120.4	382.1	73.8	455.9
	Observed	218	119	118	388	67	455
	2 SE range	(205, 231)	(105, 133)	(111, 135)	(371, 405)	(53, 81)	
Taxi	Predicted	21.0	29.4	55.4	74.0	31.8	105.8
	Observed	15	34	57	68	38	106
	2 SE range	(8, 23)	(23, 45)	(43, 71)	(53, 83)	(26, 50)	
Auto passenger	Predicted	12.1	22.7	64.3	19.9	79.2	99.1
	Observed	12	28	59	20	79	99
	2 SE range	(5, 19)	(18, 38)	(45, 73)	(11, 29)	(64, 94)	
Auto drive	Predicted	7.3	24.0	81.9		113.2	113.2
	Observed	5	21	88		114	114
	2 SE range	(0, 9)	(12, 30)	(72, 104)		(97, 129)	
Total	Predicted	250.0	202.0	322.0	476.0	298.0	774
	Observed	250	202	322	476	298	774

Source: Kozel and Swait (1982).
Note: Numbers in parentheses are the approximate lower and upper 95% confidence intervals for the observed cell frequencies. Discrepancies in totals by mode are due solely to round-off error during calculation of the probabilities and the accumulation process.

results can be studied by modal alternative: for example, the taxi mode is overpredicted by 40% in the low-income group, underpredicted by 14% in the middle segment, and slightly underpredicted in the high-income market. Overall, however, it seems that the fit of the model, for the mode dimension, is satisfactory for the household income segmentation.

For the automobile ownership segmentation similar observations can be made: the taxi is overpredicted in the zero level segment (which tends to be of low income), and the bus mode displays the reverse pattern. Observe that the auto modes are very well predicted, indicating that the model specification satisfactorily accounts for the effect of auto ownership on the choice of mode for shopping trips.

Policy Forecasting Tests

The purpose of developing a model is of course forecasting. We are principally interested in the use of a model for incremental forecasts of the effects of policy changes. This is usually done using the aggregate point elasticities described in section 5.3. The validity of point elasticities, however, is limited to small changes in the variables. Therefore, to test the response predicted by the model to large changes, we perform disaggregate predictions. The difference from the previous section is that in a forecasting test we first modify the values of one or more explanatory variables in accordance with the policy being tested.

The disaggregate forecasting test is an application of the sample enumeration forecasting procedure described in section 6.3. Its use during the model development process is to check the policy sensitivity of the model. We examine the forecasts and consider whether or not they are reasonable. If not, we consider the potential underlying causes of an unexpected forecast. If an unreasonable forecast can be explained by model specification or data errors, we attempt to correct them and repeat this test.

The usefulness of a forecasting test heavily depends on the availability of prior information that can be used to determine the ranges of "reasonable forecasts." The most useful information is derived from "before and after" studies which are conducted on occasions of real changes in policy or environmental factors and which collect data on the system variables before and after changes occur. An in-depth study may also collect two samples, one before and one after, which could be used to test for stability of the coefficients. An example of such forecasting tests is provided in chapter 11.

7.7 Summary

The process of model building, which involves a great amount of judgment, is nevertheless partially susceptible to rigorous statistical procedures. We have outlined a number of procedures (statistical or otherwise) that we have found most useful for model development.

Three major categories of tests are covered. First, the model structure is taken as given, and we present formal and informal specification tests for the utility functions. Second, we no longer assume the model structure is given, and we show how to test for violation of the IIA assumption of the MNL model for the presence of taste variation in the population, as well as for heteroscedasticity (unequal variances) in the utility functions. Finally, we describe tests of model predictions and outliers that can be used once a model specification seems reasonably satisfactory.

It is important to realize that the model-building process is an iterative one. The process is begun with a set of a priori assumptions by the analyst, which may be subsequently revised as the analyst learns about the choice process in the model's development. The tests and procedures we have presented here represent a practical approach to systematizing, to the extent possible, the model-building process.

8 Theory of Sampling

In travel demand analysis we collect data for a variety of reasons, and often a single data collection effort is undertaken to serve many purposes. For example, we may interview travelers to find out their chosen alternatives and their attributes. This information is used to estimate the parameters of travel demand models as well as to estimate characteristics of the population such as the mean income of transit users or the distribution of auto ownership across households. We also sample characteristics of the transportation system to make estimates of average travel volumes, costs, speeds, and so forth.

Although travel demand data must serve a multitude of purposes, only some purposes may be fully specified at the time the data collection effort is undertaken. For example, we rarely know exactly what models will be developed from a given data base or the complete list of transportation policies that will ultimately be tested with those models. Moreover, since large-scale data collection is typically quite expensive, we often must create a data base that will serve future analysts for a decade or more.

Given the uncertainty regarding the future uses of data, the problem of designing an appropriate sampling strategy is of necessity a fuzzy one. This makes sample design a process in which an analyst's judgment must play a significant role. In this chapter we present some relevant portions of sampling and sample design theory to serve as one of the bases of an informed judgment. The reader should recognize, however, that all of sampling theory is of necessity based on simplifications of reality, and the results of that theory should be rarely used as the exclusive basis for designing a data collection strategy.

So far in our discussion of travel demand analysis we have assumed that a sample of decision makers drawn at random from the population is available. In this chapter we explore how various other types of samples can be drawn and used for travel demand analysis. As we shall show, there is a rich variety of different sampling strategies that can be effectively employed. Nonrandom sampling techniques offer the potential of both dramatically reducing the costs of data collection and increasing the precision of parameter estimates. However, the use of nonrandom sampling requires careful thought about how the resulting data should be used.

We begin the presentation of sampling theory in section 8.1 by discussing some of the basic concepts of sampling and sample design. Section 8.2 then summarizes some of the sampling methods conventionally used for inferring the characteristics of a population. Inasmuch as existing texts on sampling and sample design cover this problem in detail, our discussion in section 8.2 is limited to a brief description of each relevant sampling method and a demonstration of its most important aspects. We then turn to two related problems. Section 8.3 extends the methods defined in section 8.2 to the problem of sampling for discrete choice analysis, drawing on some of the insights developed in section 8.2 to show the potential usefulness of these different sampling strategies. In section 8.4 we examine how the various sampling strategies developed in section 8.3 can be used to estimate the parameters of discrete choice models.

Finally, in section 8.5 we explore how to choose among the limitless number of possible sample designs. A summary of the chapter is given in section 8.6.

8.1   Basic Sampling Concepts

Any discussion of sampling must necessarily begin with the definition of the population being studied. In many situations this may be far more complicated than one would first think. For example, in an urban context the pool of potential travelers consists of more than just all the residents of the metropolitan area; it also includes possible visitors and individuals passing through the city. In addition we typically adopt a rather arbitrary definition of the geographical extent of the area under study, often using jurisdictional boundaries such as county or town lines.

Populations can be treated as having either a *finite or infinite* number of members. Of course no population is truly infinite. The distinction here is whether or not the population is large enough (when compared to the size of the sample we take from it) that we can treat it as infinite relative to the size of our sample. Since most of the populations we use in travel demand studies are quite large and the samples we use are small, we will focus here almost exclusively on the simpler case of infinite populations.

A second major concept is the *sampling unit*. The sampling units must be defined to be mutually exclusive and must collectively exhaust the population. In the analysis of urban passenger travel the household has often been used as the sampling unit; for freight transportation receiving or shipping firms often serve as sampling units. In some situations, however, it may be useful to treat the individual traveler or shipment as the definition of a sampling unit.

Taken collectively, an implicit or explicit list of all the sampling units constitutes the *sampling frame*. Such lists are often derived from utility records, telephone listings, motor vehicle registry lists, or private directories of firms. Very often the creation of an appropriate sampling frame may be extremely difficult. For example, in many developing countries there are no complete listings of residents or addresses, and it may be necessary actually to visit every residence in an area to establish a reliable sampling frame.

Proceeding from our definition of the sampling unit and a sampling frame, we specify the rules by which observations will be drawn. These rules define a *sampling strategy*. The most widely analyzed class of strategies are termed *probability samples*. Such strategies have the following properties (adapted from Cochran 1977):

1. We must be able to define the possible outcomes of the sampling process. (An outcome is defined as the set of observations from the population that results from the sampling process.)
2. We must assign a probability (or probability density) to each possible outcome for the given strategy.
3. We select one of the possible outcomes *at random* with the assigned probabilities of step 2.
4. We must have a well-defined estimator that uses the sample and yields a unique estimate for each possible outcome.

Sampling strategies can use either sampling *with or without replacement*. In sampling without replacement, once a sampling unit is drawn, it cannot be drawn again. In contrast, when sampling with replacement is used, a sampling unit, once drawn, is "returned" to the population and can be drawn again. This distinction is only relevant when the population is assumed to be finite because for an infinite population the distribution of characteristics within the pool of sampling units is unaffected by the removal of any finite number of them.

All of these concepts are best illustrated by a simple example. Suppose we have a well-defined population of N households and we are interested in estimating the mean household income Y. We use each household as a sampling unit. Our frame therefore consists of all households in the population, and we define the sample to consist of $N_s < N$ households drawn without replacement from the population. This would imply that there are

$$N^* = \frac{N!}{N_s!(N - N_s)!} \tag{8.1}$$

possible outcomes of the sampling process, each representing a different combination of N households taken N_s at a time.

We now define our sampling strategy to consist of drawing N_s households *at random* from the entire population so that each sampling unit has equal probability of being drawn. In this strategy, each of outcomes has equal probability $1/N^*$ of being drawn. We call this sampling method *simple random sampling*.

Finally, suppose we use the sample average as an estimator of the mean household income:

$$\hat{Y}^R = \frac{1}{N_s} \sum_{n=1}^{N_s} y_n, \tag{8.2}$$

where y_n is the income of the nth sampled household. The variance of this estimator is

$$\text{var}[\hat{Y}^R] = \frac{\sigma^2}{N_s},$$

where σ^2 denotes the variance of the distribution of y. In chapter 2 we proved that this estimator is consistent, unbiased, and efficient for the case of random sampling from an infinite population. This is also true for a finite population when the sample design used is simple random sampling. *More important, we can easily define sampling strategies for which $\hat{Y}^R$ (as defined in equation 8.2) has only some or even none of these desirable properties.*

To see this, suppose we divide our population into two subpopulations, each consisting of half of the N households. For the purposes of exposition, define the subpopulations as consisting of central city and suburban residents, and let Y_1 and Y_2 denote their respective mean incomes. Assume the groups have different mean income, that is, $Y_1 \neq Y_2$. We now redefine our sampling strategy so that for each suburban resident in the sample we draw at random two central city residents. Under this sampling strategy the sample average income can be written as

$$\hat{Y}^R = \frac{1}{N_s} \left\{ \sum_{n=1}^{N_s/3} y_n + \sum_{n=(N_s/3)+1}^{N_s} y_n \right\}, \tag{8.3}$$

where the data are assumed to be ordered such that the first $N_s/3$ observations are suburban residents. In this case

$$\mathscr{E}[\hat{Y}^R] = \frac{1}{N_s}\left(\frac{N_s}{3}Y_2 + \frac{2N_s}{3}Y_1\right) = \frac{Y_2 + 2Y_1}{3} \neq Y. \tag{8.4}$$

Thus, as long as $Y_2 \neq Y_1$, under the new sampling strategy the sample average is biased, whereas under the simple random sampling strategy it is unbiased. ($\hat{Y}^R$ is also inconsistent under the new strategy.) In this simple example it should be obvious that one way to obtain an unbiased estimator for the new sampling strategy is to "reweight" the observations to reflect the oversampling of central city residents. Thus we could use

$$\hat{Y}^S = \frac{1}{N_s}\left\{\frac{3}{2}\sum_{n=1}^{N_s/3} y_n + \frac{3}{4}\sum_{n=(N_s/3)+1}^{N_s} y_n\right\}, \tag{8.5}$$

so that

$$\begin{aligned}
\mathscr{E}[\hat{Y}^S] &= \frac{1}{N_s}\left\{\left(\frac{3}{2}\right)\frac{N_s}{3}Y_2 + \frac{3}{4}\left(\frac{2N_s}{3}\right)Y_1\right\} \\
&= \frac{Y_2}{2} + \frac{Y_1}{2} = Y.
\end{aligned} \tag{8.6}$$

(The last line of equation 8.6 holds because the two subpopulations each represent half the total population.)

This example has demonstrated that the properties of estimators are dependent on the way in which the sample is drawn. *Rather, as we explore how nonrandom sampling strategies can be used, we will have to discuss the properties of combinations of estimators and sampling strategies.*

8.2   Overview of Common Sampling Strategies

In this section we review some of the common sampling strategies used for estimating population characteristics such as population totals, means, or variances. Although most of these strategies are also useful for obtaining data to estimate the parameters of different models, we hold off a discussion of such applications to section 8.4. This review is not intended to be rigorous or complete. Readers interested in a far more comprehensive treatment of standard sampling theory are referred to Cochran (1977) or Deming (1960).

Stratified Random Sampling

In addition to simple random sampling the most widely used design is some form of *stratified random sampling*. In this approach we begin by dividing the entire sampling frame into G mutually exclusive and collectively exhaustive groups, each called a stratum. We then sample N_{sg} observations from each stratum, using simple random sampling. Here $N_s = \sum_{g=1}^{G} N_{sg}$.

Our example of a nonrandom sampling strategy in section 8.1 was in fact a form of stratified random sampling, in which $G = 2$ (the central city and suburban residents) and $N_{s1} = 2N_s/3$ and $N_{s2} = N_s/3$. Geographic stratification, however, is only one basis for partitioning the population. Other possibilities include size of firm, housing type, number of automobiles owned, age, or sex.

As for all forms of nonrandom sample design, stratification is done for a number of not necessarily mutually exclusive reasons. First, it may be useful to know the characteristics of certain subpopulations as well as those of the whole population. For example, we may want to know something about the travel behavior of handicapped individuals. Since they will represent a very small proportion of a random sample, we may intentionally "oversample" households with such individuals in order to obtain more data on their travel choices.

Second, we may find it less expensive to obtain a stratified random sample when compared to a simple random sample of equal size. This may occur because per household sampling in high density neighborhoods is cheaper than sampling in rural areas.

A third motivation for sampling nonrandomly is to increase the efficiency with which certain characteristics of the population are estimated. To see how this can be done, let us assume we are interested in estimating the mean Y of some characteristic y. Suppose we define G strata, each of which has a different unknown mean and variance denoted as Y_g and σ_g^2, respectively. Suppose we know the proportion of the population in each stratum and denote it by W_g.

Following the line of reasoning in the previous section, one unbiased estimator for the population mean can be constructed as follows. First, we estimate the within-stratum means as

$$\hat{Y}_g = \frac{1}{N_{sg}} \sum_{n=1}^{N_{sg}} y_{gn}, \qquad g = 1, \ldots, G, \tag{8.7}$$

where y_{gn} is the nth observation on y from stratum g. Then we estimate the population mean as the weighted average of the strata estimates. In other words, we define an estimator $\hat{Y}^S$ of Y as follows:

$$\hat{Y}^S = \sum_{g=1}^{G} \hat{Y}_g W_g. \tag{8.8}$$

The reader should note that $\hat{Y}^S$ as defined in equation 8.8 is not fully efficient because it weights high variance observations the same as those with low variance. We use it here primarily for expository purposes. In the case of equation 8.8,

$$\mathscr{E}[\hat{Y}^S] = Y \tag{8.9}$$

and

$$\text{var}[\hat{Y}^S] = \sum_{g=1}^{G} W_g^2 \left(\frac{\sigma_g^2}{N_{sg}} \right). \tag{8.10}$$

Since the variance of $\hat{Y}^S$ depends on values of N_{sg}, $g = 1, \ldots, G$, we can then ask, for a given total sample size N_s, what strata sample sizes minimize the variance of the estimator of the population mean? To solve this, we find $(N_{s1}, N_{s2}, \ldots, N_{sG})$ which are a solution to

$$\min \sum_{g=1}^{G} W_g^2 \left(\frac{\sigma_g^2}{N_{sg}} \right), \tag{8.11}$$

subject to the constraint

$$\sum_{g=1}^{G} N_{sg} = N_s. \tag{8.12}$$

Setting up a Lagrangian, we can rewrite this problem as

$$\min \left[\sum_{g=1}^{G} W_g^2 \left(\frac{\sigma_g^2}{N_{sg}} \right) - \lambda \left(N_s - \sum_{g=1}^{G} N_{sg} \right) \right]. \tag{8.13}$$

The first-order conditions for this problem are

$$\frac{-W_g^2 \sigma_g^2}{N_{sg}^2} + \lambda = 0, \qquad g = 1, \ldots, G, \tag{8.14}$$

and equation 8.12. This implies

$$N_{sg} = \left(\frac{W_g \sigma_g}{\sum_{g'=1}^{G} W_{g'} \sigma_{g'}} \right) \cdot N_s. \tag{8.15}$$

This result suggests that by altering the sample sizes for each of the strata, we can alter the variance of the estimated mean. Moreover there exists a stratified random sampling strategy yielding an estimator of Y with minimum variance, in which we sample each stratum proportionately to the product of its standard deviation and the fraction of the population it represents. Thus, when the strata are of equal size, we should "oversample" those that are heterogeneous, thereby reducing the variance of the estimated mean over the estimator derived from a simple random sample of equal total size.

This same analysis can be extended to solve for the stratifed sample design that minimizes the variance of the estimated mean when sampling costs vary across the strata. Suppose that the costs of any one observation taken from stratum g is c_g and that the fixed costs of undertaking any sampling are c_s. What is the best allocation of a total budget of B? In this case we solve the following problem:

$$\min \sum_{g=1}^{G} W_g^2 \left(\frac{\sigma_g^2}{N_{sg}} \right), \tag{8.16}$$

subject to the budget constraint

$$c_s + \sum_{g=1}^{G} N_{sg} c_g = B. \tag{8.17}$$

Following the same line of analysis as in equations 8.13 through 8.15, we find

$$\frac{N_{sg}}{N_s} = \frac{W_g \sigma_g / \sqrt{c_g}}{\sum_{g'=1}^{G} W_{g'} \sigma_{g'} / \sqrt{c_{g'}}} \tag{8.18}$$

and

$$N_s = (B - c_s) \left(\frac{\sum_{g=1}^{G} W_g \sigma_g / \sqrt{c_g}}{\sum_{g=1}^{G} W_g \sigma_g \sqrt{c_g}} \right). \tag{8.19}$$

Thus the optimal fraction of the sample from any stratum is proportional to the standard deviation of the characteristic being measured and the stratum size and inversely proportional to square root of the cost per sample.

We can also explore the relative efficiency of stratified and simple random sampling. For the former case we evaluate equation 8.10 at the optimal sample sizes, obtaining

$$\text{var}[\hat{Y}^S] = \frac{(\sum_{g=1}^{G} W_g \sigma_g)^2}{N_s} \tag{8.20}$$

as compared to the variance under the simple random sample given by

$$\text{var}[\hat{Y}^R] = \frac{\sigma^2}{N_s} = \frac{\sum_{g=1}^{G} \sigma_g^2 W_g}{N_s}. \tag{8.21}$$

Taking the ratio of 8.21 ad 8.20, we obtain

$$\frac{\text{var}[\hat{Y}^R]}{\text{var}[\hat{Y}^S]} = \frac{\sum_{g=1}^{G} \sigma_g^2 W_g}{(\sum_{g=1}^{G} \sigma_g W_g)^2}. \tag{8.22}$$

Note that the numerator is the mean of the variances (i.e., standard deviations squared) across all strata and that the denominator is the square of the mean across strata of the standard deviations. Thus by Jensen's inequality (Rao 1973) and the convexity of the square function we get

$$\text{var}[\hat{Y}^R] \geq \text{var}[\hat{Y}^S].$$

We note that the two sampling strategies will yield estimators with equal variance when all the strata have equal variance; otherwise, the optimal stratified sample will be better than a random one.

One can also show that using stratified random sampling with poorly chosen strata sample sizes can actually produce samples for which the estimated mean has higher variance than the estimate under simple random sampling. For example, suppose there are two strata, each representing half of the entire population with variances σ_1^2 and σ_2^2 where $\sigma_2^2 = 9\sigma_1^2$; that is, the second stratum has nine times higher variance than the first. The optimal stratified sample is to select 25% of the total sample from the first stratum and 75% from the other. By equation 8.20 this yields a variance of

$$\frac{(\sigma_1/2 + 3\sigma_1/2)^2}{N_s} = \frac{4\sigma_1^2}{N_s}. \tag{8.23}$$

By equation 8.21 a simple random sample would have variance

$$\frac{\sigma_1^2/2 + 9\sigma_1^2/2}{N_s} = \frac{5\sigma_1^2}{N_s}. \tag{8.24}$$

However, if we chose to draw $\frac{3}{4}$ of our observations from group 1 and the remainder from group 2, the variance of our estimator in equation 8.8 would be (by equation 8.10)

$$\frac{(1/2)^2\sigma_1^2}{3N_s/4} + \frac{(1/2)^29\sigma_1^2}{N_s/4} = \frac{28}{3}\frac{\sigma_1^2}{N_s}, \tag{8.25}$$

which is greater than the variance of $\hat{Y}^R$ from the simple random sample.

More detailed discussions of stratified random sampling carry this analysis still further by exploring the properties of stratified random sample designs when ratios are estimated and when different nonoptimal strata sample sizes are used. Readers interested in such topics are referred to any standard text on sample design. For our purposes we highlight only the central message of this literature. Stratification, if done appropriately, can potentially reduce sampling costs and increase the efficiency of estimators; however, if done inappropriately, it can actually make estimators worse than if simple random sampling is used.

Cluster Sampling

In our examples of sampling we have so far assumed that the sampling unit is also the basic unit of interest in the analysis. However, in many cases each sampling unit actually consists of relevant subunits. For example, if we are interested in the trips made by individuals, each household sampled is a group, *or cluster*, of individuals. A strategy that uses sampling units that have subunits of interest is called *cluster sampling*.

The most common reason for using cluster sampling is its lower cost per observation. It is, for example, generally easier to sample five individuals from the same household than five individuals from different households. Similarly, it is easier to sample all the shipments of a single firm than the same number of shipments each from a different firm.

In general, the reduced cost of sampling in clusters comes at the expense of increased variance in the estimators of population characteristics. This is because individuals within the same cluster will tend to have characteristics that are positively correlated. For example, if one shipment of a particular commodity used by a firm is large (as compared to the mean size for the entire population), then subsequent shipments of the same firm will tend to be large also.

To see why this affects the variance of the estimated mean, suppose we have two different samples of N_s observations. In the first case the observations are taken randomly from the population (i.e., by simple random sampling). If the population variance is σ^2, then the variance of the estimated mean is σ^2/N_s. Now consider the case where the N_s observations are from M equal-size clusters in which there is a correlation ρ between any two values from the same cluster. For simplicity assume N_s is a multiple of M, so that N_s/M is an integer. The variance of the mean estimated by the sample average will be $\sigma^2(1 + [M - 1]\rho)/N_s$ which, for $\rho > 0$, exceeds σ^2/N_s (Cochran 1977). Of course, if ρ is negative, the variance of using a cluster sample will actually be less than for a random one.

Cluster sampling strategies offer a greater number of options. For example, we can sample clusters and then sample subunits within clusters. This procedure is called *two-stage cluster sampling* or *subsampling* (as opposed to *one-stage cluster sampling* in which all subunits in the sampling unit are observed). The distinction between cluster and stratified sampling is somewhat subtle. In stratified sampling the groups from which random samples are taken are not themselves samples; in cluster sampling we first draw a subset of the groups. The two-stage cluster technique is widely used by the U.S. Census for special data collection efforts such as the Annual Housing Survey, where certain geographical units are first drawn as clusters, and then housing units within the selected clusters are subsampled. The clusters are termed *primary sampling units*. Obviously multistage extensions of this approach can easily be defined.

With cluster sampling we can also use different sampling strategies for choosing the clusters. For example, if firms are defined as clusters, we can select firms entirely at random, or we can select them with probability proportionate to some measure of their size. These two strategies may have very different costs and result in estimators with different variances. Moreover the estimators that are consistent and unbiased for one strategy may not be for the other.

There are also different estimators appropriate to different forms of cluster sampling. In cases where the within-cluster variance differs from cluster to cluster, it is possible to gain efficiency by appropriately correcting for the differing within-cluster variances. To complicate matters further, we must typically estimate the within-cluster variances to apply some of the the estimators of the mean. Again a wide range of methods has been developed. Readers are referred to Cochran (1977) for a full treatment of these issues.

Double Sampling

To design a sample effectively, it is often useful for an analyst to have some information about the population. For example, to design an effective stratified sample, we must generally know the relative sizes and variances of all the strata. This data may not be available from existing sources, so a reasonable course of action would be to conduct a simple random sample to estimate the strata shares and variances and then to use that information to design a second stratified sample. We call any strategy in which one sample is used to design a second a *double sample*. The concept obviously extends to more than two levels and is often termed *multistage* or *sequential sampling*.

The literature on sequential sampling falls into two broad classes. In what might be termed the *classical sample design analysis*, estimators of relevant population characteristics made from early sampling stages and used to design later stages are treated in the sample design as fixed, not random. This greatly simplifies the analysis but is obviously an approximation that may be more or less valid depending on the size of the early sample. In *Bayesian sequential sampling* we explicitly treat the population estimates from each sampling stage as random variables and solve for the next stage sample designs which are optimal based on an expected value criterion. This unfortunately complicates the analysis enormously, and analytic solutions are only available for limited classes of distributions. Readers interested in the subject are referred to deGroot (1970).

Double sampling gives the analyst an additional dimension of control in the sample design. This is particularly valuable when very little is known a priori about the population of interest. It also, however, imposes additional costs per observation because of start-up costs associated with each of the samples. In addition the analyst must be careful to ensure that structural changes (e.g., induced by an energy crisis or an economic recession) in the characteristics being measured have not occurred in the interval between the two samples or, if changes have occurred, that they are appropriately accounted for. For example, income can be adjusted by using published data on inflation or real wages. However, many structural changes may occur and be totally unknown to the analyst.

Systematic Sampling

Although, in practice, most sampling strategies are either combinations or extensions of the ones just discussed, some relatively minor variants do exist. One of these is *systematic sampling*, in which elements are drawn from the sampling frame by deterministic rather than random rules. For example, interviewers might be told to interview every tenth house on a block or to interview all employees with social security numbers ending with a one. As long as the order of observations within the sampling frame is random, there is no real difference between a systematic sample and a simple random one. The case where they do differ is when for some reason there is nonzero correlation ρ between pairs of sampling units in the same systematic sample. In such a case one can show that for the sample average as an estimator of the mean Y,

$$\text{var}[\hat{Y}] = \frac{\sigma^2}{N_s}[1 + (N_s - 1)\rho], \tag{8.25}$$

where σ^2 is the variance of an individual observation. In most cases of practical interest, ρ can be assumed to be zero. One particular exception is where samples are being drawn over time, and observations that are equal time intervals apart are likely to be correlated.

8.3   Sampling Strategies for Discrete Choice Analysis

The different sampling strategies we have discussed were originally developed for estimating simple population characteristics. The sampling problem for discrete choice analysis is conceptually no different. Instead of seeking to estimate population means or variances, we are trying to infer the vector of parameters of the choice model, $\mathbf{\theta}$, or the distribution of the characteristics of the population, $p(\mathbf{x})$. As we will explore further in this chapter, the fact that we are attempting to infer the parameters of nonlinear choice models significantly complicates the sample design problem.

We consider first the discrete choice analog of the simple random sample. This leads us to a revised interpretation of the population distribution which will be used in section 8.4 to analyze other sampling strategies. We then describe the discrete choice analogs of stratified random sampling, cluster sampling, and double sampling. Finally, other sampling methods potentially appropriate for discrete choice analysis are briefly explored.

Simple Random Sampling

In deriving maximum likelihood estimators for different discrete choice models, we have been assuming that the sample was drawn at random from the population. Now we will be somewhat more specific about what this assumption means.

Consider first the concept of the population distribution. For discrete choice analysis we must conceptualize the population distribution as defined over both the attributes $\mathbf{x}$ *and the choice* $i \in \mathbf{C}$. Thus we will write the joint distribution of i and $\mathbf{x}$ as $f(i, \mathbf{x})$.

In modeling individuals' choices, we generally divide the joint distribution into the product of a conditional and marginal distribution

$$f(i, \mathbf{x}) = P(i|\mathbf{x})p(\mathbf{x}). \tag{8.26}$$

Of course what makes this decomposition interesting and useful is that $P(i|\mathbf{x})$ is not simply a conditional probability. Rather, it is the outcome of a model that we believe describes individuals' choices as a function of unknown parameters (e.g., the logit model). To make the functional dependence clear, it will often be convenient to rewrite the choice probability as $P(i|\mathbf{x}, \boldsymbol{\theta})$. In contrast to the choice model, the other distribution, $p(\mathbf{x})$, does not typically reflect any behavioral theory.

Given this view of the population, simple random sampling for discrete choice analysis is defined as drawing $(i, \mathbf{x})$ combinations at random from the entire population. When we explore the problem of estimating $\boldsymbol{\theta}$ with different sample designs, this interpretation will provide a basis for analyzing the log likelihood of the different samples.

General Stratified Sampling

Stratified random sampling generalizes straightforwardly to discrete choice analysis. However, because the population distribution is defined along both the choice dimension and the attributes, the definition of the strata can involve both i and $\mathbf{x}$. This gives rise to a rich class of sampling strategies which Manski and McFadden (1981) term *general stratified sampling*.

Formally a general stratified sample is drawn as follows:

STEP 1:   Partition the population into G collectively exhaustive strata, each defined in terms of combinations of choices and attributes.

STEP 2:   Select sampling fractions $H_1, H_2, \ldots, H_G$ as the fractions of the sample to be drawn from the G strata. Then select the total sample size N_s.

STEP 3:   Draw $N_{sg} = H_g N_s$ observations *at random* from stratum g for all $g = 1, \ldots, G$.

Attribute (x) Chosen mode (i)	Travel time by car (min)			Household automobile ownership			Annual household income ($)	
	≤ 15	> 15 ≤ 30	> 30	0	1	2 +	≤ 15,000	> 15,000
Drive alone								
Carpooling								
Transit								

Figure 8.1
Illustration of dimensions for general stratified sampling

STEP 4: For each observation n, observe their choice (i_n) and attributes $(\mathbf{x}_n)$.

Figure 8.1 provides an illustration of the possible dimensions for general stratified sampling in the context of a three-mode choice model. Each of the rows corresponds to possible choices and each of the columns corresponds to a range of values of a variable in a hypothetical vector $\mathbf{x}$. Any single observation would be a pair consisting of i and $\mathbf{x}$.

The simplest possible stratification would be to define only one stratum consisting of the entire population, and the corresponding sample would be drawn randomly from this single stratum. This is by definition a simple random sample.

A second stratification rule might define three income groups as follows: group 1 is all $(i, \mathbf{x})$ pairs with income ≤ \$7,500; group 2 is all $(i, \mathbf{x})$ pairs with income between \$7,500 and \$15,000; group 3 is all $(i, \mathbf{x})$ pairs with income ≥ \$15,000.

Still a third possible stratification might be to define modal user groups—such as group 1, all carpool users; group 2, all drive alone users; group 3, all transit users.

Further examples can include mixtures of these—such as group 1, all transit users with income ≤ \$7,500; group 2, everyone else.

The class of stratified sampling rules, in general, and the most relevant special cases, in particular, offer an enormous range of sample design possibilities to the analyst. In considering these options, it is important to distinguish what aspects of the sampling process the analyst does and does not control. What this person *does* control is the stratification and the number of decision makers sampled, N_{sg}. What he or she *does not* control are the identities of the decision makers then drawn. These drawings are to be independent and at random.

We have already noted that simple random sampling is a special case of general stratified sampling. Two other special cases, *exogenous sampling* and *choice-based sampling*, are defined next.

Exogenous Sampling   In an exogenous sample we define the strata by segmenting only on the attributes $\mathbf{x}$ and not on the actual choices. In other words, we divide the possible attribute vectors into collectively exhaustive sets $\mathbf{X}_1, \mathbf{X}_2, \ldots, \mathbf{X}_G$, and the pair $(i, \mathbf{x})$ belongs to stratum g if and only if $\mathbf{x} \in \mathbf{X}_g$. This case corresponds to the example of income stratification given earlier, where the subsets $\mathbf{X}_g$ are the three income classes and choice of mode does not affect the stratum to which a member of the population belongs. Many of the sample designs used for travel demand analysis rely on exogenous stratification. For example, the Washington, D.C., survey used in the examples in preceding chapters defined two strata, one for the Washington, D.C., jurisdiction and the other for all suburban counties.

Choice-Based Samples   In a choice-based sample we partition the full choice set $\mathbf{C}$ into collectively exhaustive subsets $\mathbf{C}_1, \mathbf{C}_2, \ldots, \mathbf{C}_G$. The pair $(i, \mathbf{x})$ then belongs to stratum g if $i \in \mathbf{C}_g$. Pure choice-based sample is the case where each choice in $\mathbf{C}$ corresponds to a separate stratum. In this case $G = J$, the size of the choice set.

In our mode choice example, the case of stratification by modal groups corresponds to a choice-based sample. For example, on-board transit surveys and roadside interviews are both choice-based samples for modal choice analysis.

It is important stress that whether a sample is choice-based or exogenous depends on the aspect of travel demand under study. For example, stratification by residence is exogenous if we are analyzing mode choice, but choice-based if we are analyzing households' residential location decisions.

Enriched Sampling

Cosslett (1981) defines *enriched sampling* as the pooling of exogenously stratified samples with one or more choice-based samples. For example, a simple random sample might be merged with a transit on-board survey to analyze mode choice.

This type of sample design is often an attractive way to increase the number of observations choosing alternatives with low aggregate population shares. For example in the United States, even in a large random home interview survey we might find that very few people chose to bicycle to work. If we wanted to increase the number of bicycle riders in our sample we could "enrich" the random sample with a special survey of bicycle users.

Double Sampling

Double (or multistage) sampling is used in discrete choice analysis for exactly the same reasons as discussed in section 8.2. Basically, if we have some information about the population from one sample, we can often use it to design better subsequent samples.

Two possible ways of using multistage sampling have been discussed in the literature on discrete choice analysis. In the simpler case we conduct a first-stage survey to estimate the proportions of the population in every stratum (W_g) for different stratification schemes. For example, we may conduct a telephone survey to identify the fraction of the population with various socioeconomic characteristics or that use various modes. This information can then be used to design a second-stage sampling strategy that best meets specific objectives. (We will discuss the possible objectives for a sampling strategy in section 8.5.)

A second way in which multistage sampling can be used is to estimate a model on a small sample and then use the results of that model to guide the design of a second sample (see Daganzo 1980). We will discuss how a "first-stage model" can help guide later sample designs in section 8.5.

Other Sampling Strategies

Other possible sampling schemes have been proposed but not actually used in practice. Therefore this subsection can be skipped without loss of continuity in the presentation. For example, Cosslett (1981) explores how the combination of one or more of the sampling strategies described previously can be used in conjunction with a *supplemental sample*, defined as a data source in which the attributes **x** are observed but the actual choices made are not. He shows that in some circumstances the supplemental sample may help increase the efficiency of the parameter estimates.

Another possible sample design approach is a Bayesian extension of the double sampling technique developed by Daganzo (1980). At least theoretically we could design a second-stage sample accounting for the fact that our first stage estimators are random variables. It is quite likely that the resulting sample design theory would, however, be extremely complicated.

The final sample design was explored by Lerman and González (1980). It is appropriate only for situations where the choice set **C** consists of non-negative integers (see section 5.7 for examples). They define a *proportionate endogenous sample* (PES) as one in which the probability an observation is drawn is proportional to the value of *i* chosen. For example, if we survey all bus users on a randomly selected day and ask the respondents how many bus trips they took that past week, the probability of a person who took ten trips being in the sample is ten times the corresponding probability for someone making only one trip. Lerman and González derive a simple and tractable estimator for the Poisson regression model using a proportionate endogenous sample.

8.4 Estimating Choice Models under Alternative Sampling Strategies

Having defined the major sampling options available, we now turn to the problem of estimating the parameters of discrete choice models under different sampling strategies. We begin by first reformulating the maximum likelihood estimator for random sampling in a more general fashion. The estimation problem for each of the other major sample designs is then considered.

Our approach is to summarize the key theoretical results of practical relevance. Readers interested in much more detailed and technical treatments of this area are referred to Manski and Lerman (1977), Manski and McFadden (1981), and Cosslett (1981).

Estimation with Random Samples (Revisited)

In section 8.3 we defined $f(i, \mathbf{x})$ as the joint distribution of choice and attributes in the population and noted that we can make the following decomposition:

$$f(i, \mathbf{x}) = P(i|\mathbf{x}, \boldsymbol{\theta})p(\mathbf{x}).$$

Given this view, the likelihood for any random sample of N_s observations can be expressed as

$$\mathscr{L}^* = \prod_{n=1}^{N_s} \prod_{i \in C_n} f(i, \mathbf{x}_n)^{y_{in}} = \prod_{n=1}^{N_s} \prod_{i \in C_n} P(i|\mathbf{x}_n, \boldsymbol{\theta})^{y_{in}} p(\mathbf{x}_n), \tag{8.27}$$

where, as before y_{in} is a 0, 1 variable indicating the choice of observation n and $\mathbf{x}_n$ is observation n's attributes. Taking the logarithm of $\mathscr{L}^*$, we find

$$\mathscr{L} = \sum_{n=1}^{N_s} \sum_{i \in C_n} y_{in} \ln P(i|\mathbf{x}_n, \boldsymbol{\theta}) + \sum_{n=1}^{N_s} \ln p(\mathbf{x}_n). \tag{8.28}$$

Note that equation 8.28 differs from the expression for the log likelihood function in equation 5.33 in that 8.28 has a second term that we usually ignore. This is appropriate since the unknown parameter vector, $\boldsymbol{\theta}$, over which the log likelihood function is maximized, does not affect the term involving $p(\mathbf{x}_n)$. *However, this is a result of assuming a simple random sample, and it does not hold for all types of sampling.* Indeed, there are some sampling strategies in which terms involving $p(\mathbf{x}_n)$ also involve the unknown parameters. *In such cases the estimators for $\boldsymbol{\theta}$ appropriate for simple random samples may not be consistent for other sample designs.* One such case will be discussed shortly.

Estimation with General Stratified Samples

We can express the sample likelihood of a general stratified sample with nonoverlapping strata as

$$\mathscr{L}^* = \prod_{g=1}^{G} \prod_{n=1}^{N_{sg}} \prod_{i \in C_n} \left[\frac{f(i, \mathbf{x}_n) H_g}{W_g} \right]^{y_{in}}, \tag{8.29}$$

where W_g is the fraction of the population that consists of members of stratum g. (It would be notationally more proper to write $i \in C_{ng}$ and y_{ing} to denote the choice set and choice of the nth observation from group g. However, the subscript g has been omitted for the sake of notational simplicity.) To see that equation 8.29 is the sample likelihood, consider the likelihood of drawing any observation via a stratified sampling rule. This is the probability that an observation is selected from stratum g times the conditional likelihood of drawing the observed $(i, \mathbf{x})$ pair out of this stratum. The former probability is the sampling fraction H_g. By Bayes' rule the latter conditional likelihood is $f(i, \mathbf{x})/W_g$. Since observations are drawn independently, equation 8.29 follows. We note for later use that the population fraction W_g can be expressed as an integral of the joint distribution $f(i, \mathbf{x})$ over the subset of choices and attributes defining the stratum:

$$W_g = \int_{(\mathbf{C} \times \mathbf{X})_g} f(i, \mathbf{x}) d(i, \mathbf{x}), \tag{8.30}$$

where $(C \times X)_g$ denotes the appropriate subset of choices and attributes defining stratum g.

Manski and McFadden (1981) discuss the estimation of θ in a variety of situations and develop a number of estimators other than maximum likelihood. Some of these estimators require knowledge of W_g, and others do not. We restrict ourselves in this section to their most relevant results.

Note that we can write the log likelihood function as

$$\mathscr{L} = \sum_{g=1}^{G} \sum_{n=1}^{N_{sg}} \sum_{i \in C_n} y_{in} \ln P(i|\mathbf{x}_n, \theta)$$

$$+ \sum_{g=1}^{G} \sum_{n=1}^{N_{sg}} \ln p(\mathbf{x}_n) + \sum_{g=1}^{G} N_{sg} \ln H_g \qquad (8.31)$$

$$- \sum_{g=1}^{G} N_{sg} \ln W_g.$$

In this expression the first term is the same as the one maximized for random samples. The next two terms are unaffected by the parameters θ and therefore do not affect the maximum likelihood estimate $\hat{\theta}$. The key distinction therefore between the log likelihoods for simple random and general stratified sampling lies in the term involving W_g, which as defined in equation 8.30 will generally involve θ. Moreover θ appears inside an integral, potentially making maximization of equation 8.31 computationally complex.

Fortunately under certain circumstances we can show that this term simplifies or that other, less cumbersome estimators with desirable properties exist. We consider first the case of exogenous samples (i.e., samples stratified by the $\mathbf{x}$'s). In this case the last term in equation 8.31 simplifies because

$$W_g = \int_{\mathbf{x}_g} \left[\sum_{i \in C_g} P(i|\mathbf{x}, \theta) \right] p(\mathbf{x}) \, d\mathbf{x}$$

$$= \int_{\mathbf{x}_g} 1 \cdot p(\mathbf{x}) \, d\mathbf{x} = \int_{\mathbf{x}_g} p(\mathbf{x}) \, d\mathbf{x}, \qquad (8.32)$$

which does not involve the unknown parameters θ. Thus *for exogenous samples* the maximization of the first term in equation 8.31 over $\hat{\theta}$ is equivalent to the maximization of entire log likelihood function. Consequently the usual estimation procedure, which Manski and Lerman (1977) term *exogenous sample maximum likelihood* (ESML) originally based on the assumption of simple random sample, is entirely appropriate for exogenous samples.

A second case of interest occurs when the sampling fractions H_g are chosen to be equal to the population shares W_g. In this instance the last two terms in equation 8.31 cancel each other, again making the maximum likelihood estimator for simple random samples appropriate. Application of this result requires of course that the population shares in each of the strata be known a priori. Such information is often available from published sources or can be estimated from relatively inexpensive surveys.

The applicability of ESML estimation unfortunately does not extend to choice-based samples except when $H_g = W_g$. In a choice-based sample

$$W_g = \int_{\text{all } \mathbf{x}} \left[\sum_{i \in C_g} P(i|\mathbf{x}, \boldsymbol{\theta}) \right] p(\mathbf{x}) \, d\mathbf{x}, \tag{8.33}$$

and in this case the sum inside the integral is not equal to 1. A simple interpretation of the population stratum share W_g in equation 8.33 is that it is the fraction of the entire population that chooses any of the alternatives in C_g. In the simplest case where each alternative is a stratum (i.e., $G = J$), the value of the W_g's will be the fractions of the population choosing each alternative. Since W_g is an integral involving $\boldsymbol{\theta}$, it must be part of the quantity maximized in equation 8.31. Although in the general case this makes use of equation 8.31 infeasible, there is one case where it simplifies. This occurs when the following conditions exist:

1. The sample is choice based.
2. The choice model is multinomial logit.
3. The choice model has a full set of $J - 1$ alternative-specific constants.

In this case McFadden has proved that the exogenous sample maximum likelihood procedure yields consistent estimates of all parameters except the constants (see Manski and Lerman 1977 for a proof). Moreover, if each choice is a separate stratum and the population shares (W_g) are known, then the constant for each alternative can be consistently estimated by subtracting $\ln (H_g/W_g)$ from the exogenous sample estimate. Intuitively this has the effect of increasing the value of the estimated constants for alternatives that are undersampled and reducing them for alternatives that are oversampled. In subsequent work Cosslett (1981) has proved that the estimate obtained in this way are in fact the maximum likelihood estimates.

This result is of considerable practical importance because it implies that available estimation procedures for the multinomial logit model can be

Table 8.1
Example of adjustments for choice-based samples

Mode	Sample fraction (H_g)	Population fraction (W_g)	$\ln (H_g/W_g)$
Drive alone	0.25	0.50	-0.693
Shared ride	0.25	0.40	-0.470
Transit	0.50	0.10	1.609

used without modification on choice-based samples. To illustrate how the adjustments to the estimated constants are made, suppose a three-mode logit model was estimated from a choice-based sample using exogenous sample maximum likelihood estimation, with constants defined for driving alone and ridesharing. Suppose further that the estimated constants were 2 and 1, respectively. If the sample and population shares are as in table 8.1, then the true constants are estimated as follows:

Revised drive alone constant $= 2 - (-0.693) = 2.693$.
Revised shared ride constant $= 1 - (-0.470) = 1.470$.
Revised transit constant $= 0 - 1.609 = -1.609$.

The important thing to note in this example is that we treat the transit alternative as having an implicit constant of zero, and we adjust it appropriately. Equivalently we could now modify the constants to have again a zero transit constant by adding 1.609 to each, thereby preserving their differences. (Recall from section 4.1 that we can add any arbitrary constant to all the systematic utilities without affecting the choice probabilities.) This would yield the following estimates:

Revised drive alone constant $= 2.693 + 1.609 = 4.302$.
Revised shared ride constant $= 1.470 + 1.609 = 3.079$.
Revised transit constant $= -1.609 + 1.609 = 0$.

Our final comment on choice-based samples applies to all choice models, not just logit. It is motivated by the fact that though the maximum likelihood estimator for choice-based samples is somewhat intractable, there may be other functions, which when maximized, yield consistent estimates for the parameters. Manski and Lerman (1977) prove that for a choice-based sample the solution $\hat{\theta}$ to

$$\max_{\theta} \sum_{g=1}^{G} \sum_{n=1}^{N_{sg}} \sum_{i \in C_n} y_{in} \left(\frac{W_g}{H_g}\right) \ln P(i|\mathbf{x}_n, \theta) \tag{8.34}$$

is in fact a consistent estimator for θ. Because the maximization of this function is essentially equivalent to exogenous sample maximum likelihood (as defined in equation 8.28) except that each observation is weighted by W_g/H_g, it is called the *weighted exogenous sample maximum likelihood* (WESML) *function*.

The proof that the WESML estimator is consistent under very general conditions is quite complex and beyond the scope of this book. However, some simple intuitive arguments can be made to understand why it works. Suppose our sample is choice based, and we have proportionately twice as many transit users in it as actually occur in the population. The term (W_g/H_g) for such observations would be $\frac{1}{2}$, and its effect in the WESML objective function would be to weight each transit-using observation by $\frac{1}{2}$, thereby reducing each one's effect on the value of $\hat{\theta}$ which maximizes the WESML objective function. Conversely, observations for undersampled alternatives would have weights greater than one, increasing their relative importance.

Other intuitive arguments for why the WESML estimator is consistent appear in Lerman and Manski (1977). As is noted there, *the WESML estimates are not in general asymptotically efficient*. Thus their computational tractability is gained at the expense of statistical efficiency. Finally, because the WESML estimator is not fully efficient even in the asymptotic sense, its variance-covariance matrix is slightly more complicated than that of true maximum likelihood estimators. Since the estimator is not fully efficient, its variance-covariance matrix does not asymptotically attain the Cramér-Rao bound. For WESML the asymptotic variance-covariance matrix is

$$\Sigma = \frac{1}{N_s} \Omega^{-1} \Delta \Omega^{-1},$$

where

$$\Omega = \mathscr{E}\left\{ \left[\frac{\partial \ln P(i|\mathbf{x}, \theta)}{\partial \theta} \right]\left[\frac{\partial \ln P(i|\mathbf{x}, \theta)}{\partial \theta'} \right] \right\},$$

$$\Delta = \mathscr{E}\left\{ w(i)\left[\frac{\partial \ln P(i|\mathbf{x}, \theta)}{\partial \theta} \right]\left[\frac{\partial \ln P(i|\mathbf{x}, \theta)}{\partial \theta'} \right] \right\},$$

where $w(i)$ is the weight for alternative i and expectations are taken across the distribution of i and $\mathbf{x}$ in the population.

Estimation with Enriched Samples

The likelihood function for an enriched sample is not the same as for a stratified sample because the strata in an enriched sample overlap. Although it is possible to write the likelihood function for an enriched sample (see Cosslett 1981), we only summarize the special cases of immediate practical relevance.

The first case is analogous to a result cited before for choice-based samples: *the parameters of a logit model with a full set of alternative-specific constants can be efficiently estimated from an enriched sample using exogenous sample maximum likelihood.* In fact Cosslett (1981) demonstrates that the corrections to the alternative-specific constants of a logit model calibrated on a pure choice-based sample are also applicable for an enriched sample. Basically, if $\hat{d}_i$, $i = 1, \ldots, J$, is the estimated alternative-specific constant for alternative i, using the exogenous sample maximum likelihood, then consistent estimates of the true constants are given by

$$\hat{d}_i' = \hat{d}_i - \ln(H_i/W_i), \qquad i = 1, \ldots, J, \tag{8.35}$$

where H_i, W_i have been previously defined. As before, all other coefficients are consistent.

In practice, we estimate H_i as

$$\hat{H}_i = \frac{1}{N_s} \sum_{g=1}^{G} \pi_{ig} N_{sgi}, \qquad i = 1, \ldots, J.$$

where

N_s = the total sample size over all samples,

$$\pi_{ig} = \begin{cases} 1 & \text{if alternative } i \text{ is included in subsample } g = 1, \ldots, G, \\ 0 & \text{otherwise,} \end{cases}$$

N_{sgi} = the number of observations selecting alternative i in subsample $g = 1, \ldots, G$.

W_i, the population share choosing i, can be estimated from the random (or exogenous) sample. If we let subsample 1 be the random sample then

$$\hat{W}_i = \frac{N_{s1i}}{N_{s1}}, \qquad i = 1, \ldots, J,$$

where N_{s1} is the total number of observations in the random sample.

Therefore we can rewrite equation 8.35 as

$$\hat{d}_i' = \hat{d}_i - \ln\left(\frac{N_{s1}}{N_s}\right) - \ln\left(\sum_{g=1}^{G} \pi_{ig}\frac{N_{sgi}}{N_{s1i}}\right), \qquad i = 1, \ldots, J.$$

Note that the second term on the right-hand side is a constant for all alternatives. Hence we can remove it from all the utilities and leave the probabilities unaffected. Thus the final corrections are simply

$$\hat{d}_i' = \hat{d}_i - \ln\left(\sum_{g=1}^{G} \pi_{ig}\frac{N_{sgi}}{N_{s1i}}\right), \qquad i = 1, \ldots, J.$$

Now suppose that we have a random sample, covering J alternatives, which we enrich with a choice-based sample that encompasses alternatives 1 and 2. Then the constants are corrected in the following manner:

$$\hat{d}_1' = \hat{d}_1 - \ln\left(\frac{N_{s11} + N_{s21}}{N_{s11}}\right),$$

$$\hat{d}_2' = \hat{d}_2 - \ln\left(\frac{N_{s12} + N_{s22}}{N_{s12}}\right),$$

$$\hat{d}_i' = \hat{d}_i - \ln(1) = \hat{d}_i, \qquad i = 3, \ldots, J.$$

Note that there is no correction to the constants of alternatives included only in the random sample.

The second case of interest is when we have both a choice-based and an exogenous sample, each with sufficient information to estimate all the parameters of a general choice model. In this case we could combine an ESML and a WESML estimator—that is, we could construct an objective function to be maximized which consists of an exogenous sample part and a weighted exogenous sample part. This would be as follows:

$$\max_{\theta} \left[\sum_{g=1}^{G} \sum_{n=1}^{N_{sg}} \sum_{i \in C_n} y_{in} \ln P(i|\mathbf{x}_n, \theta) + \sum_{i=1}^{J} \sum_{n=1}^{N_{si}} y_{in} \frac{W_i}{H_i} \ln P(i|\mathbf{x}_n, \theta) \right], \qquad (8.36)$$

where

G = the number of strata in the exogenous sample,

N_{sg} = the size of the sample drawn from stratum g,

N_{si} = the size of the choice-based subsample drawn from choosers of alternative i,

W_i, H_i = the fractions in the population and the choice based sample, respectively, choosing alternative i.

The resulting estimate of θ is not fully efficient unless the choice-based sample has all the weights equal to one. Thus for a logit model Cosslett's procedure is to be preferred over combining WESML and ESML. Yet, equation 8.36 may be the only tractable estimator for models other than multinomial logit.

The logit-specific result has been used by Volkmar (1978), Cambridge Systematics, Inc. (1980), Hocherman et al. (1983), and Ben-Akiva et al. (1984) in actual applications to urban passenger mode choice analysis. This paucity of actual applications is probably attributable to the lack of widespread dissemination of the recent theoretical work in the area.

Estimation with Double Samples

The estimation of the parameters of a discrete choice model when more than one sampling stage is used is conceptually straightforward. For example, we discussed earlier the possibility of pooling an exogenous and a choice-based sample by combining two objective functions (ESML and WESML) and solving for the parameters that maximized their sum. This logic can easily be extended to the pooling of any number of different samples taken in different ways as long as a consistent estimator of the parameters exists for each subsample.

Another approach to combining information in different samples is to estimate different parameters from each of the subsamples and then to take a weighted average of the various estimates. For example, suppose we had some scalar quantity α to estimate, and we had any two estimates $\hat{\alpha}_1$ and $\hat{\alpha}_2$, both of which were consistent. Then given any two constants a_1 and a_2, the estimator

$$\hat{\alpha} = \frac{a_1 \hat{\alpha}_1 + a_2 \hat{\alpha}_2}{a_1 + a_2} \tag{8.37}$$

is consistent as long as $a_1 + a_2 \neq 0$. This can be verified by a straightforward application of the Slutsky theorem as follows:

$$\text{plim } \hat{\alpha} = \left(\frac{1}{a_1 + a_2} \right) (a_1 \text{ plim } \hat{\alpha}_1 + a_2 \text{ plim } \hat{\alpha}_2)$$

$$= \frac{1}{a_1 + a_2} (a_1 \alpha + a_2 \alpha) = \alpha.$$

In general, for the case of estimating a vector of parameters, let $\hat{\boldsymbol{\theta}}_1$ and $\hat{\boldsymbol{\theta}}_2$ be different estimates of $\boldsymbol{\theta}$ derived from two different samples (possibly using two different estimators). If $\hat{\boldsymbol{\theta}}_1$ and $\hat{\boldsymbol{\theta}}_2$ are both consistent, then

$$\hat{\boldsymbol{\theta}} = (\mathbf{A}_1\hat{\boldsymbol{\theta}}_1 + \mathbf{A}_2\hat{\boldsymbol{\theta}}_2)(\mathbf{A}_1 + \mathbf{A}_2)^{-1} \qquad (8.38)$$

will also be consistent, where $\mathbf{A}_1$ and $\mathbf{A}_2$ are two matrices of the same dimensionality as $\boldsymbol{\theta}$ and $\mathbf{A}_1 + \mathbf{A}_2$ is nonsingular. One natural choice of $\mathbf{A}_1$ and $\mathbf{A}_2$, originally suggested by Durbin (1953), is the inverse of the variance-covariance matrices of $\hat{\boldsymbol{\theta}}_1$ and $\hat{\boldsymbol{\theta}}_2$, respectively (see Johnston 1973, pp. 221–227). These inverses will be the information matrices for $\hat{\boldsymbol{\theta}}_1$ and $\hat{\boldsymbol{\theta}}_2$ if the estimates are asymptotically efficient. The resulting estimate $\hat{\boldsymbol{\theta}}$ will be a "weighted average" of the two original estimates, where the weights are the relative precisions of $\hat{\boldsymbol{\theta}}_1$ and $\hat{\boldsymbol{\theta}}_2$.

When $\mathbf{A}_1$ and $\mathbf{A}_2$ are defined as the inverses of the variance-covariance matrices, then the variance-covariance matrix of $\hat{\boldsymbol{\theta}}$ is given as

$$\operatorname{var}(\hat{\boldsymbol{\theta}}) = (\boldsymbol{\Sigma}_1^{-1} + \boldsymbol{\Sigma}_2^{-1})^{-1}, \qquad (8.39)$$

where $\boldsymbol{\Sigma}_1$ and $\boldsymbol{\Sigma}_2$ are the variance-covariance matrices of $\hat{\boldsymbol{\theta}}_1$ and $\hat{\boldsymbol{\theta}}_2$, respectively. To see this, note that if $\mathbf{A}_1 = \boldsymbol{\Sigma}_1^{-1}$ and $\mathbf{A}_2 = \boldsymbol{\Sigma}_2^{-1}$, then $\hat{\boldsymbol{\theta}} = (\boldsymbol{\Sigma}_1^{-1}\hat{\boldsymbol{\theta}}_1 + \boldsymbol{\Sigma}_2^{-1}\hat{\boldsymbol{\theta}}_2)(\boldsymbol{\Sigma}_1^{-1} + \boldsymbol{\Sigma}_2^{-1})^{-1}$. Then

$$
\begin{aligned}
\operatorname{var}(\hat{\boldsymbol{\theta}}) &= (\boldsymbol{\Sigma}_1^{-1} + \boldsymbol{\Sigma}_2^{-1})^{-1}\operatorname{var}(\boldsymbol{\Sigma}_1^{-1}\hat{\boldsymbol{\theta}}_1 + \boldsymbol{\Sigma}_2^{-1}\hat{\boldsymbol{\theta}}_2)(\boldsymbol{\Sigma}_1^{-1} + \boldsymbol{\Sigma}_2^{-1})^{-1} \\
&= (\boldsymbol{\Sigma}_1^{-1} + \boldsymbol{\Sigma}_2^{-1})^{-1}(\boldsymbol{\Sigma}_1^{-1}\operatorname{var}(\hat{\boldsymbol{\theta}}_1)\boldsymbol{\Sigma}_1^{-1} + \boldsymbol{\Sigma}_2^{-1}\operatorname{var}(\hat{\boldsymbol{\theta}}_2)\boldsymbol{\Sigma}_2^{-1})(\boldsymbol{\Sigma}_1^{-1} + \boldsymbol{\Sigma}_2^{-1})^{-1} \\
&= (\boldsymbol{\Sigma}_1^{-1} + \boldsymbol{\Sigma}_2^{-1})^{-1}(\boldsymbol{\Sigma}_1^{-1}\boldsymbol{\Sigma}_1\boldsymbol{\Sigma}_1^{-1} + \boldsymbol{\Sigma}_2^{-1}\boldsymbol{\Sigma}_2\boldsymbol{\Sigma}_2^{-1})(\boldsymbol{\Sigma}_1^{-1} + \boldsymbol{\Sigma}_2^{-1})^{-1} \\
&= (\boldsymbol{\Sigma}_1^{-1} + \boldsymbol{\Sigma}_2^{-1})^{-1}.
\end{aligned}
$$

The "weighted average" procedure is potentially useful when the parameters of a model are being updated with new data. In many instances the first sample may no longer be available or may be relatively expensive to use. In this case the value of $\hat{\boldsymbol{\theta}}_1$, its variance-covariance matrix, and the new sample suffice to reestimate the model. Atherton and Ben-Akiva (1976) have used this as a "Bayesian estimator" in precisely this context.

The reader should note that the "weighted average" estimator in general will not be asymptotically efficient even if $\hat{\boldsymbol{\theta}}_1$ and $\hat{\boldsymbol{\theta}}_2$ are. In contrast, if the two samples are pooled together and objective functions that yield asymptotically efficient estimates for each subsample are combined and jointly maximized, the resulting estimate will be asymptotically efficient.

Thus the "pooling" procedure is to be preferred over the "weighted averaging" approach unless data availability or computational cost considerations are judged to outweigh the pooling procedure's efficiency advantages.

8.5 Choosing a Sample Design for Discrete Choice Analysis

Given all of the sampling options developed in sections 8.3 and 8.4, a natural question is, How does an analyst select a sample design in a specific context? We divide our discussion of this question into two areas corresponding to theoretical results and practical issues.

Theoretical Results

Whether one is sampling simply to infer one or more characteristics of the population or to estimate the parameters of travel demand models, the logical question is how to choose an appropriate sample design from the myriad of possible alternatives. In the context of discrete choice analysis this turns out to be an extraordinarily complicated question without an unambiguous answer. Most of the theoretical results available are at best a basis for making informed judgments rather than providing well-defined optimal sample designs.

A natural starting point for designing a sample is to define the criteria against which various sampling strategies can be judged. In our analysis of stratified random sampling in section 8.2, we adopted the classical sampling criterion of efficiency. In other words, we have been concerned primarily with finding a sampling strategy that minimizes the variance (or generally the asymptotic variance) of some estimator subject to implicit or explicit cost constraints.

Although we will continue to use this classical criterion, the reader should recognize that it rarely represents the entire range of true objectives in a travel demand analysis. First, we often use a sample to estimate many characteristics and models, and it will generally not be the case that a single sample design is optimal for all our estimators.

Second, we are often more interested in the errors in the forecasts we intend to make rather than in the parameters themselves. Although the asymptotic variance of any forecast will be a function of the variances of the parameters, as discussed in section 6.4 the relationship may be quite complicated.

Third, there may be many situations where variance (or asymptotic variance) is a poor measure of the consequences of errors in forecasts. For example, as a measure of error, variance treats equal positive and negative errors symmetrically. There may be some situations in which positive and negative errors in forecasts have entirely different implications. One could easily imagine a situation where a prediction that is too high has disastrous consequences (perhaps leading to an ill-advised multibillion dollar capital investment decision), whereas one that is too low results in only moderate societal costs.

Another issue in using the minimum-variance criterion is that the efficiency with which the parameters can be estimated can be affected by external sources of information (i.e., data external to the sample itself). We already discussed in section 8.4 how knowledge of the W_g's in a choice-based sample can be used to obtain consistent estimates of a logit model's constants. At least in theory the values of W_g or the distribution of $\mathbf{x}$ in the population, $p(\mathbf{x})$, can be used to increase the efficiency of the parameter estimates (see Manski and McFadden 1981, Cosslett 1981, or Hsieh et al. 1983). The practical use of such information has only recently been developed, and no general computer software to implement procedures exists as yet, so we restrict our discussion to the more usual case where prior information on W_g and $p(\mathbf{x})$ is not used directly in the estimation process.

Even given the very narrow definition of the classical sample design problem, there are only a small set of relevant theoretical results. The most general result is that for all the sample designs discussed, the asymptotic variance of the estimated parameters varies inversely with the sample size. Beyond this, however, the results available tend to be more negative than positive.

One of the most important results is that the optimum sample for estimating the parameters of a discrete choice model will depend on the values of the unknown parameters. This result is in direct contrast to the results for optimal sample design in the typical linear regression model.

To elaborate on this distinction, consider first the standard regression case. For simplicity we consider as an example the simple linear model. Let

$$y_n = \alpha + \beta x_n + \xi_n, \tag{8.40}$$

where α, β, and x are scalars and ξ is an independent disturbance with mean 0, variance σ^2. The least squares estimator of β is

$$\hat{\beta} = \frac{\sum_{n=1}^{N_s} (x_n - \bar{x})(y_n - \bar{y})}{\sum_{n=1}^{N_s} (x_n - \bar{x})^2}, \tag{8.41}$$

where $\bar{x}$ and $\bar{y}$ denote the sample averages for x and y, respectively. The variance of $\hat{\beta}$ for a sample stratified on the basis of the independent variable x is given by

$$\text{var}(\hat{\beta}) = \frac{\sigma^2}{\sum_{n=1}^{N_s} (x_n - \bar{x})^2}. \tag{8.42}$$

In this case the variance of $\hat{\beta}$ is not affected by the value of the parameter β.

This property leads directly to the standard classical result that in choosing a stratification one should oversample "extreme" values of x, that is, choose an equal number of very small and very large value of x_n thereby maximizing $\sum_{n=1}^{N_s} (x_n - \bar{x})^2$.

Now consider a simple binary logit model, where

$$P(i|x_n) = \frac{1}{1 + e^{-\beta x_n}}, \tag{8.43}$$

and β and x are scalars and x_n is defined as $x_{in} - x_{jn}$.

If the sample is an exogenous one and maximum likelihood estimation is used, then by the Cramér-Rao bound the asymptotic variance of $\hat{\beta}$ is

$$\text{var}[\hat{\beta}] = \frac{-1}{\mathscr{E}[\partial^2 \mathscr{L}/\partial \beta^2]}$$

$$= \frac{1}{N_s}\left(\mathscr{E}\left[\frac{x_n^2 e^{\beta x_n}}{(1 + e^{\beta x_n})^2}\right]\right)^{-1}. \tag{8.44}$$

Now note that if we wish to minimize the asymptotic variance of $\hat{\beta}$ for a given sample size N_s, we should maximize the term inside the expected value. If we were to adopt an analog to the standard linear model, we might try to do this by making x_{in} and x_{jn} as different as possible, thus moving x_n as close to $\pm\infty$ as practical. However, as long as $\beta \neq 0$,

$$\lim_{x_n \to \pm\infty} \frac{x_n^2 e^{\beta x_n}}{(1 + e^{\beta x_n})^2} = 0, \tag{8.45}$$

which is its minimal, not maximal, value. Thus not only is the sampling rule analogous to the one for the regression model not optimal when $\beta \neq 0$, it is the worst possible rule.

Still more troubling is that for the case where $\beta = 0$, this result changes entirely:

$$\frac{x_n^2 e^{\beta x_n}}{(1 + e^{\beta x_n})^2} = \frac{x_n^2}{4}, \tag{8.46}$$

which is now maximized for large values of x_n^2. *Thus the same exogenous stratified sampling rule that is the worst one for some values of the parameters is the best one for another value.*

This result generalizes as follows: There is no single sample design for discrete choice analysis that is unambiguously optimal for all values of the parameters. Rather, whether a sample design is good or bad (in the classical sense) depends on the unknown parameter values.

Another source of insight that can assist in designing samples is the Monte Carlo simulation method. Cosslett (1981) has used Monte Carlo experiments to study the relative estimation precision association with alternative choice-based sampling designs in the context of single parameter binary choice models. If the choice set contains the two alternatives i and j, and sampling is choice based, the analyst's control variable for sample design is the sample fraction H_i. Assuming that the choice probabilities have the logit, probit, or arctan form (see section 4.2) and that $p(x)$ is unknown, Cosslett examines how the asymptotic variance of β changes as a function of W_i and one's own prior knowledge of W_i. Although Monte Carlo findings cannot be conclusive, it appears that when W_i is not known, good designs are ones that place H_i close to $\frac{1}{2}$. This conclusion is quite strong in the logit and probit models, less so in the arctan one. On the other hand, when W_i is known, it appears optimal to oversample the rare alternative, that is, to set $H_i > \frac{1}{2}$ if $W_i < \frac{1}{2}$.

Given that the optimal sample design depends on the true parameters, Daganzo (1980) has proposed using results from a first-stage sample to obtain preliminary parameter estimates and then designing with these estimates an optimal second-stage sampling strategy. This procedure treats the first-stage estimates as the true values in designing the second-stage sample. By making the assumption that $p(\mathbf{x})$ is normal and that the choice model is either logit or probit, he derives the asymptotic variance-covariance matrix of $\hat{\theta}$ for a given sample design consisting of subsamples of different sizes drawn in different ways. He then solves for the subsample sizes that minimize some summary measure of the asymptotic variance-covariance matrix, such as the sum of its diagonal elements or its largest eigenvalue. Daganzo also notes that the analysts' informed judgment about the parameters' values (perhaps based on prior modeling experience) can be used in place of the first-stage estimates.

Recent empirical work by Tarem (1983), who tests some of Daganzo's theoretical work, indicates that the composition of an exogenously stratified second-stage sample may be relatively insensitive to the accuracy of the first-stage parameters, at least for the simplified choice context he analyzes. If this result proves more general, it indicates that minimal expenditures need be allocated to obtaining first-stage estimates, which can then be used to design the optimal composition of the second-stage sample. Alternately, use of exogenous parameter estimates (e.g., another study, perhaps even from another location) may be an acceptable compromise to actually carrying out the first-stage of the sampling plan.

Practical Concerns

We have seen in section 8.4 that the existing theoretical literature on choice model estimation is very successful in offering methods for estimating the parameters of discrete choice models. The literature is, however, very weak in providing guidance on how one should select among alternative sample designs. Given this asymmetry, the available theory of sample design must be accompanied with a great deal of judgment on the analyst's part. We give four general comments about the practicality of different sample designs:

1. Before even considering the efficiency of various alternative sampling strategies, one should first ensure that the strategies can actually provide sufficient information for estimating all the parameters. For example, in a mode choice model a sample consisting entirely of transit users will generally not enable one to estimate the complete vector of parameters. In econometric terminology, for some sample design the full set of parameters may not be fully *identified*. It should be obvious that the ability to identify the parameters is a necessary requirement before precision can even become an issue.

2. To the extent that one does become concerned with the relative precision of alternative designs, the classical statistical framework assumed in the existing theoretical literature should be applied sensibly rather than dogmatically. If the analyst has prior information about the value of θ, that information should be used in selecting among designs. If he or she views the choice model as only an imperfect approximation of reality, if should be recognized that theoretical results comparing designs can themselves hold at most approximately. If the classical measure of estimation precision, that is, the asymptotic variance-covariance matrix, differs from the measure deemed most desirable, the analyst should understand that a classical ranking of designs may not be the most appropriate.

3. All the sampling strategies we have discussed require that observations be drawn at random from one or more subpopulations. Actually implementation of this process always requires careful thought and often some theoretical compromise. The reason is that in order to sample at random within a subpopulation, one must first be able to isolate this subpopulation for the purpose of sampling. As discussed earlier in section 8.1, such isolation is sometimes difficult to achieve in practice.

Two examples will serve to illustrate this point further. Let the population of interest be all people potentially making trips within a metropolitan area, and first consider a stratification based on place of residence. A home interview survey can easily isolate and sample from the subpopulation of potential trip makers who are residents of the area. It is, however, far more difficult to isolate and sample from the remaining subpopulation, namely nonresidents.

Now consider the same population, and let the stratification be based on mode used in trip making on a given day. Transit users will be relatively easy to isolate because of their physical proximity to transit vehicles and stations. Automobile users will generally be more difficult to isolate as a group. Then of course there is the subpopulation who make no trips in the given day. Nontrip-making residents may be isolated through a home interview survey on that day. How nontrip-making nonresidents can be sampled is not clear.

The foregoing examples are fairly typical of the practical difficulties that may arise in isolating subpopulations. There do exist some situations where no practical way can be found to sample from some subpopulation. The nontrip-making nonresidents in these examples may be such a case. Then the analyst may do one of two things. First, he may ignore the problematic subpopulation, that is, define the population so as to exclude it. Second, he may assume that the attribute distribution in this subpopulation is identical to that in some "similar" subpopulation which can be sampled.

4. Even when a means of isolating and sampling from a subpopulation has been found, care must still be taken to ensure that the sample is drawn at random. How this essential requirement can be satisfied in practice must be determined on a case-by-case basis, but some potential problems can at least be highlighted.

Consider, for example, the following three surveys: (1) an on-board survey of passengers on selected bus routes, (2) a roadside interview at various points in the city, and (3) a mailback survey sent to a random selection of households.

In the first survey the relevant subpopulation might be all transit riders. However, the need to choose which routes to survey makes random drawing of transit users difficult. Some routes may have a higher percentage of elderly users, and others may attract primarily workers. Furthermore, if a sample is taken on a single day, some transit users may be interviewed more than once, and such individuals are likely to have very different characteristics than the rest of the subpopulation.

The same problems arise in the second example, where the objective would presumably be to draw randomly from all auto users.

In the third example, the high rejection rate generally associated with mailback surveys makes attainment of random drawing extremely difficult. It is often unlikely that people who choose to respond to mailback questionnaires have the same attribute distribution as the whole population. These types of nonresponse errors in transportation surveys have been analyzed by Brog and Meyburg (1981). An approach to correct these response biases using data from sources external to the survey in question has been developed by Ben-Akiva et al. (1983).

8.6 Summary

Because of rising costs of data collection for travel demand analysis, it has become increasingly important to explore the full range of possible sampling strategies. In this chapter we have reviewed the sample designs used conventionally for inferring the characteristics of a population and discussed how they can be extended to inferring the parameters of discrete choice models.

After defining the basic elements of a sampling strategy, we considered four conventional sampling approaches: (1) simple random sampling, (2) stratified sampling, (3) cluster sampling, including subsampling, (4) double sampling, and multistage extensions.

We demonstrated that each method requires careful thought to ensure that the sample is properly drawn. Stratification can be potentially useful in reducing the variance of estimators; if used inappropriately, it can lead to sample designs that produce worse estimators.

We then considered how these methods can be extended to discrete choice analysis. Both the choice and the attribute vector were viewed as possible bases for stratification. It was shown that the consistency of any given parameter estimation technique may depend on the sample design. The most relevant conclusions regarding sampling strategies for discrete choice analysis are as follows:

1. The estimation procedure used for simple random samples is appropriate to exogenous stratified samples or to any general stratified sample in which the fraction of each stratum in the sample equals the corresponding population share. We called this estimation method exogenous sampling maximum likelihood (ESML).

2. Choice-based samples in general require different estimation procedures than exogenous stratified samples. There are two relevant special cases of choice-based samples.

First, if the choice model is multinomial logit with a full set of alternative specific constants, then the estimation procedure appropriate for exogenous samples yields asymptotically efficient estimates for choice-based samples of all the parameters except the constants. Moreover, if the population shares using each alternative are known from other sources, then the estimated constants can easily be modified to give consistent and asymptotically efficient estimates.

Second, a computationally tractable but not fully efficient estimator for the parameters of any choice model can be found by weighting each observation and then treating the choice-based sample as though it were exogenous. The weight for each observation is the fraction of the population choosing the alternative selected by the decision maker divided by the corresponding fraction in the entire sample. This estimator is called weighted exogenous sample maximum likelihood (WESML).

3. Mixtures of exogenous and choice-based samples, called enriched samples, can be used to estimate a choice model's parameters. As with choice-based samples, the case of greatest interest is the multinomial logit model. The ESML estimates of all coefficients, except the alternative-specific constants of alternatives present in choice-based samples, are asymptotically efficient. Moreover a straightforward correction to the affected constants yields consistent estimates of the true values.

4. When consistent estimates of a choice model's parameters are derived from two different samples, any linear combination of them is also a consistent estimate. One natural set of relevant "weights" for combining two samples is the inverse of their variance-covariance matrices.

The last problem considered was how to select an appropriate sample design for discrete choice analysis. Perhaps the most notable aspect of this issue is the lack of directly useful theoretical results on which sample design decisions can be based. This is due to, at least in part, the fact that when using the classical criterion of minimizing the variance of the parameter estimates, the best sample design is dependent on the true values of the unknown parameters. This is in direct contrast to results for the standard linear regression, in which the variance of the parameter estimates is not a function of the true parameters.

A technique suggested by Daganzo (1980) is to use parameter estimates derived from first-stage samples to better design later sampling stages. This method can also be used when the analyst has some prior guess (based on prior experience or other informed judgment) about the parameter values.

Our final comments on sample design focused on practical concerns. Sample designs must reflect a range of potential uses for the data collected and should take into account the possible difficulties associated with randomly sampling different subpopulations. Moreover the practical problems of implementing different sampling strategies, such as nonresponse to various questions, data reliability, or extremely high costs, may often outweigh theoretical issues.

9 Aggregation and Sampling of Alternatives

9.1 Introduction

In travel demand applications the problem of defining the elements of an individual's choice set, even when we make the simplifying assumption of deterministic alternative availability and ignore the problem of choice set generation (see section 5.1), is most acute in models of destination and other spatial choices. In these models the actual alternatives from which a decision maker chooses are often unidentifiable, and aggregated geographical zones are used as the alternatives. The zones are usually defined on the basis of data availability and computational considerations. In other applications, such as the choice of a car type, the alternatives are usually grouped by the major characteristics of make, model, and vintage, and no distinction is made, for example, among cars of the same make, model, and vintage with different engines. In section 9.2 we present a theory that can be employed in these situations to formulate choice models with aggregated alternatives.

Another, related problem occurs when there are a large number of available alternatives, particularly in spatial choice problems. Section 9.3 presents a method of reducing the number of alternatives in the estimation of a logit model. Alternative methods of sampling alternatives and corresponding estimators for the choice model parameters are presented.

Finally, section 9.4 presents examples of destination choice models that were estimated in recent studies using these methods of aggregation of alternatives and estimation with samples of alternatives. These examples also employ choice-based sampling estimation procedures that were developed in chapter 8.

The presentation in this chapter is based on Ben-Akiva et al. (1984) who also consider more advanced choice-based survey designs. They present an approach to estimate a destination choice model using observations from a household survey, survey of drivers based on recorded license plates, and public transport on-board passenger surveys.

9.2 Aggregation of Alternatives

As mentioned before, the choice of trip destination is characterized by a very large number of alternatives. In some situations, such as shopping trips, it may be possible to identify a small set of distinct shopping centers (e.g., see Richards and Ben-Akiva 1975, Koppelman and Hauser 1978,

Morichi et al. 1984). However, for other trip purposes and in dense urbanized areas there are no natural boundaries that define alternative destinations.

Furthermore data on the attraction of alternative destinations are generally only available at some level of geographical aggregation. Thus in most applications the alternatives in a destination choice model must be based on aggregate alternatives. The relationship between the underlying elemental destinations and aggregated destination alternatives is developed in this section. A general theory of aggregation of alternatives is presented, and its implications for empirical models are drawn.

The Concept of Elemental Alternatives

Define the actual alternatives that decision makers are choosing as *elemental alternatives.* ˉAn example of an elemental alternative would be an individual store as the destination of a shopping trip or a dwelling unit in the choice of residential location. Any definition of alternative destinations or alternative residential locations for modeling can therefore be viewed as a scheme for grouping together elemental alternatives.

In some situations it may not be possible to define precisely what constitutes an elemental alternative. For a recreational trip, for example, it may not be possible to identify a unique establishment or a well-defined cluster of establishments that constitutes an elemental destination alternative. In these situations it will be assumed that an aggregate alternative is a grouping of elemental alternatives whose precise definition is unknown to the analyst, and as a consequence the number of elemental alternatives included in an aggregate alternative is also unobservable.

The elemental alternatives are by definition mutually exclusive and collectively exhaustive; the decision maker chooses one and only one elemental alternative. Denote by L the universal set of elemental alternatives. We assume for the sake of notational simplicity that all alternatives in L are available to a decision maker. Let $P_n(l)$ be the probability of decision maker n choosing elemental alternative $l \in L$. Partition the set L into nonoverlapping subsets:

$$L_i \subseteq L, \qquad i = 1, \ldots, J,$$

where J is the number of aggregate alternatives in the universal choice set C.

The choice probability of an aggregate alternative is equal to the probability that the decision maker chooses one of its elemental alternatives.

Thus the choice probability for decision maker n of alternative $i \in C$ is defined by

$$P_n(i) = \sum_{l \in \mathbf{L}_i} P_n(l), \qquad i = 1, \ldots, J. \tag{9.1}$$

Random Utilities of Aggregate Alternatives

Denote the random utility of an elemental alternative l to decision maker n by U_{ln} and assume, without loss of generality, that

$$U_{ln} = V_{ln} + \varepsilon_{ln}, \tag{9.2}$$

where V_{ln} and ε_{ln} are, respectively, the systematic and random components of the utility for elemental alternative l and decision maker n. Since the elemental alternatives are mutually exclusive, the utility of an aggregate alternative can be defined by

$$U_{in} = \max_{l \in \mathbf{L}_i} (V_{ln} + \varepsilon_{ln}), \qquad i = 1, \ldots, J. \tag{9.3}$$

The utility of an aggregate alternative can also be expressed as a sum of its expectation, denoted by V_{in}, and a random component, denoted by ε_{in}, as follows:

$$U_{in} = V_{in} + \varepsilon_{in}, \qquad i = 1, \ldots, J, \tag{9.4}$$

where

$$V_{in} = \mathscr{E}\left[\max_{l \in \mathbf{L}_i} (V_{ln} + \varepsilon_{ln}) \right].$$

Define the average of the elemental alternatives' systematic utilities by

$$\bar{V}_{in} = \frac{1}{M_i} \sum_{l \in \mathbf{L}_i} V_{ln}, \qquad i = 1, \ldots, J, \tag{9.5}$$

where M_i is the number of elemental alternatives in the set $\mathbf{L}_i$. The relationship between the systematic utility of the aggregate alternative (V_{in}) and the average utility of its elemental alternatives ($\bar{V}_{in}$) depends on the joint distribution function of the elemental alternatives' utilities.

Extreme Value Distribution of Random Utilities

If aggregate alternative i contains a large number of elemental alternatives, and if the utilities of the elemental alternatives are independently and identically distributed (IID), irrespective of the actual distribution, then the distribution of the utility of aggregate alternative i appropaches the extreme value (or Gumbel) distribution (see Johnson and Kotz 1970) previously given in expression 5.12:

$$F(U_{in}) = \exp[-e^{-\mu(U_{in} - \eta)}],$$

where

$F(\ )$ = a cumulative distribution function,

μ = a positive scale parameter,

η = the mode of the distribution. (The mean is equal to $\eta + \gamma/\mu$, where γ is Euler's constant, approximately equal to 0.577.)

The IID assumption implies that

$$V_{ln} = \bar{V}_{in}, \qquad \forall l \in \mathbf{L}_i,$$

In words, the utilities of the elemental alternatives in an aggregate alternative have equal means and the ε_{ln}, for all $l \in \mathbf{L}_i$, are IID. It can be shown using property 4 of the Gumbel distribution (see section 5.2) that

$$\eta = \bar{V}_{in} + \frac{1}{\mu} \ln M_i, \tag{9.7}$$

where the additional term $(1/\mu) \ln M_i$ is a measure of the "size" of aggregate alternative i.

The extreme value distribution is maintained under maximization, as stated in section 5.2. Hence, if the elemental utilities have unequal means but the random components are IID extreme value, that is,

$$F(\varepsilon_{ln}) = \exp[-e^{-\mu\varepsilon_{ln}}], \tag{9.8}$$

then the distribution of the aggregate utility of alternative i is also extreme value with the same scale parameter μ and

$$\eta = \frac{1}{\mu} \ln \sum_{l \in \mathbf{L}_i} e^{\mu V_{ln}}$$

$$= \bar{V}_{in} + \frac{1}{\mu} \ln \left[\frac{1}{M_i} \sum_{l \in \mathbf{L}_i} e^{\mu(V_{ln} - \bar{V}_{in})} \right] + \frac{1}{\mu} \ln M_i. \tag{9.9}$$

Note that the assumption reflected in equation 9.8 implies that the conditional choice probability of an elemental alternative $l \in \mathbf{L}_i$, given that the choice lies within $\mathbf{L}_i$, is given by the following logit model:

$$P_n(l|\mathbf{L}_i) = \frac{e^{\mu V_{ln}}}{\sum_{j \in \mathbf{L}_i} e^{\mu V_{jn}}}, \qquad l \in \mathbf{L}_i. \tag{9.10}$$

Thus the utility for a "heterogeneous" aggregate alternative i can be modeled by

$$U_{in} = \bar{V}_{in} + \frac{1}{\mu} \ln M_i + \frac{1}{\mu} \ln B_{in} + \varepsilon_{in}, \tag{9.11}$$

where

$$B_{in} = \frac{1}{M_i} \sum_{l \in \mathbf{L}_i} e^{\mu(V_{ln} - \bar{V}_{in})}$$

is a measure of the heterogeneity of elemental alternatives in aggregate alternative i. Note that this additional term in the aggregate utility in equation 9.11 has the following derivative:

$$\frac{\partial(1/\mu)\ln B_{in}}{\partial V_{ln}} = P_n(l|\mathbf{L}_i), \qquad l \in \mathbf{L}_i,$$

and is therefore particularly sensitive to the presence of elemental alternatives with high choice probabilities.

The convexity of the exponential functions and Jensen's inequality (Rao 1973) imply that

$$\frac{1}{M_i} \sum_{l \in \mathbf{L}_i} e^{\mu V_{ln}} \geq e^{\mu \bar{V}_{in}}.$$

From this inequality and the definition of B_{in}, we find that $B_{in} \geq 1$.

The correction for heterogeneity is therefore non-negative. The monotonicity of the logarithmic transformation also implies that this inequality can be expressed by

$$\frac{1}{\mu} \ln \left[\frac{1}{M_i} \sum_{l \in \mathbf{L}_i} e^{\mu V_{ln}} \right] \geq \bar{V}_{in}.$$

The equality holds in the case of an aggregate alternative consisting of homogeneous elemental alternatives.

The properties of the measure for the variability of the attributes among elemental alternatives were analyzed by Lerman (1975), McFadden (1978), and Kitamura et al. (1979). A useful insight can be gained by assuming that the number of elemental alternatives in an aggregate alternative is large and the distribution of the V_{ln}, for $l \in \mathbf{L}_i$, around $\bar{V}_{in}$ approaches a normal distribution with variance σ_{in}^2—a reasonable assumption in light of the central limit theorem. Under this premise it can be shown that the term $(1/\mu) \ln B_{in}$ approach $\mu \sigma_{in}^2 / 2$ using the property that if a random variable is normally distributed with mean $\bar{y}$ and variance σ^2 then $\exp(y)$ is lognormal distributed with mean equal to $\exp(\bar{y} + \sigma^2/2)$. The same result can also be obtained by a second-order Taylor series expansion about $V_{ln} = \bar{V}_{in}, l \in \mathbf{L}_i$.

Thus the utility term for the variability of attributes among elemental alternatives may be omitted if the aggregate alternatives are defined to have equal variances:

$$\sigma_{in}^2 = \sigma_n^2, \qquad i = 1, \ldots, J.$$

Lerman (1975) and Kitamura et al. (1979) have shown that in situations with heterogeneous aggregate alternatives the variance effect may play an important role in correcting for the aggregation of elemental alternatives. The principal implication of this observation is that it is important to aggregate elemental alternatives in such a way that the uniformity of the within alternative variance of attributes holds to the greatest extent possible. We seldom have complete descriptors of the size and variance effects and must thus rely on judgment, experience, and proxy variables to design aggregation of alternative schemes.

A Logit Model with Aggregate Alternatives

We have shown that the systematic utility of aggregate alternative i, denoted as V_{in}, can be expressed as the sum of

$\bar{V}_{in}$ = the average utility of the elemental alternatives in aggregate alternative i,

$(1/\mu) \ln M_i$ = the measure of the size of the alternative i,

$(1/\mu) \ln B_{in}$ = the measure of the variability of the utilities of the elemental alternatives in aggregate alternative i.

This aggregate utility can be used in a logit choice model as follows:

$$
\begin{aligned}
P_n(i) &= \frac{e^{\mu * V_{in}}}{\sum_{j=1}^{J} e^{\mu * V_{jn}}} \\
&= \frac{e^{\mu * \bar{V}_{in} + \mu' \ln M_i + \mu' \ln B_{in}}}{\sum_{j=1}^{J} e^{\mu * \bar{V}_{jn} + \mu' \ln M_j + \mu' \ln B_{jn}}}, \qquad i = 1, \ldots, J, \quad (9.12)
\end{aligned}
$$

where μ^* is a positive scale parameter and $\mu' = \mu^*/\mu$. (This model assumes that $\varepsilon_{in}, i = 1, \ldots, J$, are IID Gumbel.)

Note that the V_{in}'s were derived from a logit model of the conditional choice among elemental alternatives in an aggregate alternative, given by equation 9.10. Therefore the logit model in 9.12 actually has the nested logit form that is presented in chapter 10. The ratio of the scale parameters of the two logit models, or of the ε_{ln} and ε_{in} Gumbel distributions, is μ'. Recall from section 5.2, that the square of the scale parameter of a logit model is proportional to the inverse of the variance of the random utilities, and since the variance cannot decrease with aggregation, the following must hold:

$$0 \le \mu' \le 1.$$

The correlation between elemental utilities of different aggregate alternatives is assumed to be zero. For elemental utilities within the same aggregate alternative the correlation coefficient is equal to $(1 - \mu'^2)$ (see chapter 10). Ideally, if the average utilities are well specified, it may be possible to impose the restriction $\mu' = 1$. In this case the parameters of the choice model are not dependent on the definitions of the aggregate alternatives. This means that a model estimated for one set of aggregate alternatives can also be applied for other aggregation schemes (given of course that the size and variance measures are adjusted appropriately).

Modeling Choice among Aggregate Alternatives with Unknown Size

The average utility $\overline{V}_{in}$ is a function of the average attributes of the elemental alternatives in aggregate alternative i for individual n. The term $\ln B_{in}$ can also be treated as an attribute of an aggregate alternative. Thus with known sizes of the aggregate alternatives the logit model utility for a linear-in-parameters specification becomes

$$\mu^* V_{in} = \sum_{k=1}^{K'} \beta_k x_{ink} + \mu' \ln M_i, \qquad i = 1, \ldots, J, \tag{9.13}$$

where

β_k = the coefficient of the kth attribute,

x_{ink} = the value of the kth attribute for alternative i and decision maker n,

K' = the number of unknown coefficients of the attribute variables.

This utility is linear in the unknown parameter ($\beta_k, k = 1, \ldots, K'$, and μ'); it can be estimated with a standard linear logit estimation procedure, which can also be used to estimate the model under the equality restriction $\mu' = 1$.

As discussed earlier, in empirical applications the "size" of an aggregate alternative is often unobservable. However, it is possible to hypothesize a relationship between the size of an alternative and a set of observable "size variables." For example, in destination choice the "size variables" include attraction measures such as population, employment, and area. For consistency among different levels of aggregation, the relationship between multiple-size variables and the size of an aggregate alternative must be linear as follows:

$$M_i = \sum_{k=K'+1}^{K} \beta_k x_{ink}, \qquad i = 1, \ldots, J, \tag{9.14a}$$

where

$$(K - K') = \text{the number of size variables,}$$

$x_{ink}, k = K' + 1, \ldots, K = $ the values of the size variables for aggregate alternative i and decision maker n.

To guarantee that M_i is always positive, the size variables must be non-negative,

$$x_{ink} \geq 0, \qquad k = K' + 1, \ldots, K, i = 1, \ldots, J,$$

and their coefficients must also be non-negative,

$$\beta_k \geq 0, \qquad k = K' + 1, \ldots, K,$$

with at least one nonzero coefficient. Moreover not all the size variable coefficients can be identified, and it is necessary to impose a scaling restriction, such as $\beta_K = 1$. Obviously this restriction can only be applied to a nonzero coefficient. To facilitate the estimation process it is possible to define $\beta_k = e^{\tilde{\beta}_k}, k = K' + 1, \ldots, K$, and to estimate the values of $\tilde{\beta}_k$ that are not bounded. The estimation results presented in section 9.4 are therefore based on the following form for the size measure:

$$M_i = \sum_{k=K'+1}^{K} x_{ink} e^{\tilde{\beta}_k}, \qquad i = 1, \ldots, J, \tag{9.14b}$$

where $\tilde{\beta}_K$ is normalized to equal zero. This transformation is only appropriate for positive β_k coefficients because a zero value implies that $\tilde{\beta}_k \rightarrow -\infty$ and an iterative estimation procedure will not converge.

The case of a single-size variable is equivalent to one in which the size of each alternative is known. The size variable simply replaces the size measure, and there are no additional coefficients to estimate. If size variables are not available the model must include a full set of $(J - 1)$ alternative-specific constants to capture the size effect. In this situation the estimated alternative-specific constants become confounded with the omitted size attribute.

The general case with two or more size variables yields a logit model that is nonlinear in the parameters $\beta_k, k = K' + 1, \ldots, K - 1$. This can be seen by substituting equation 9.14 into 9.13 and placing the resulting expression in equation 9.12. This model requires a special logit estimation procedure, such as the one developed by Daly (1982).

9.3   Estimation of Choice Models with a Sample of Alternatives

Using heterogeneous aggregate alternatives may introduce measurement errors in the explanatory variables, such as travel time in a destination choice model, and thereby reduce the accuracy of the choice model. On the other hand, reducing the level of aggregation and using a large number of alternatives may cause the data preparation and the computational burden to be prohibitively expensive. The solution to this latter problem is found by utilizing the independence from irrelevant alternatives property of the logit model which permits consistent estimation with only a subset of the alternatives (including the chosen and a sample of nonchosen alternatives).

Estimation of a disaggregate choice model may include two types of sampling:

1. Sampling of observations, the subject of chapter 8.
2. Sampling of alternatives for every observation.

This section is concerned with alternative methods of sampling alternatives and their corresponding model estimation procedures.

Conditional Log Likelihood Function for Sampling of Alternatives

Denote by N the number of observations in the estimation sample and by $\tilde{J}_n(\tilde{J}_n \leq J_n)$ the number of alternatives assigned to observation $n, n = 1, \ldots,$ N. (Note that in general J_n, the number of alternatives in individual n's choice set, C_n, is less or equal to J, the number of alternatives in the universal choice set, C.) Clearly with a subset of the alternatives it would only be possible to maximize a conditional likelihood function rather than the true likelihood. An observation of a chosen alternative for decision maker n is assumed to be a random draw from a multinomial distribution whose probabilities are given by a parametric choice model, $P_n(i)$, $i = 1$, ..., J. A procedure for sampling of alternatives assigns to observation n a subset of the alternatives, denoted by D_n, with $\tilde{J}_n$ elements. It is obvious that for estimation purposes D_n must include the chosen alternative. Denote by $\pi_n(D|i)$ the conditional probability of constructing for observation n the set D, given that the chosen alternative is i. (These are such that $\pi_n(D|j) = 0$ for $j \notin D$.) The joint probability of drawing a chosen alternative i and a subset of alternatives D is

$$\pi_n(i, D) = \pi_n(D|i) \cdot P_n(i), \qquad i = 1, \ldots, J. \tag{9.15}$$

By Bayes' theorem, the conditional probability of alternative i being chosen given a sample of alternatives D is

$$\pi_n(i|D) = \frac{\pi_n(D|i) P_n(i)}{\sum_{j \in D} \pi_n(D|j) P_n(j)}, \qquad i = 1, \ldots, J. \tag{9.16}$$

The conditional probability $\pi_n(i|D)$ exists if

$$\pi_n(D|j) > 0, \qquad \forall j \in D.$$

This *positive conditioning property* was established by McFadden (1978) as a condition for a consistent estimator for the logit model with samples of alternatives. Substitute the logit choice probabilities given in equation 9.12 in the expression for the conditional probability 9.16 to obtain

$$\pi_n(i|D) = \frac{\exp[\mu^* V_{in} + \ln \pi_n(D|i)]}{\sum_{j \in D} \exp[\mu^* V_{jn} + \ln \pi_n(D|j)]}, \qquad i \in D. \tag{9.17}$$

McFadden (1978) uses 9.17 to prove that maximization of the conditional log likelihoodhood function

$$\sum_{n=1}^{N} \ln \pi_n(i|D) \tag{9.18}$$

yields, under normal regularity conditions, consistent estimates of the unknown parameters. *Note that the logit model 9.17 includes an additive alternative-specific correction for the bias introduced by the sampling of alternatives.* The coefficient of this correction variable is constrained to 1.

Sampling of alternatives is an easily applied technique for reducing the computational burden involved in estimating a choice model with a large number of alternatives. The main issue yet to be resolved is how to obtain the most effective sample of alternatives.

The computational burden of estimating a logit model is approximately linear in both the number of observations and in the number of alternatives. If sufficient observations are available, it would seem that, particularly for models with many socioeconomic characteristics, more information is obtained from the sample by using many observations with relatively few alternatives per observation, rather than few observations with a large sample of alternatives for each observation.

Two principal types of sampling strategies have been applied to alternative sampling: random sampling with uniform selection probabilities and sampling with unequal selection probabilities (designed to reflect differential level of importance of alternatives).

Simple Random Sampling of Alternatives

The simplest approach to sample design is to draw a *simple random sample* of alternatives and to add the chosen alternative if it is not otherwise included. Thus, if for each observation J' alternatives are randomly drawn without replacement from the population of J alternatives ($J' \leq J$), then the probability that the outcome is the subset $\mathbf{D}$ is

$$\pi_n(\mathbf{D}|i) = \binom{J}{J'}^{-1}, \qquad i \in \mathbf{D}, \tag{9.19}$$

where $\binom{J}{J'}$ denotes the number of combinations of J items taken J' at a time and is equal to $J!/(J - J')!J'!$. The size of the sampled choice set for observation n, denoted by $\tilde{J}_n$, is equal to J' if the observed choice is sampled; otherwise, it is equal to $J' + 1$. This sample design was used in earlier studies of destination choice, see Netherlands Ministry of Transport (1977).

To prevent the possibility of samples with different choice set sizes, it is possible to draw randomly (without replacement) J' alternatives from all the available alternatives, except for the chosen alternative. In this case the set $\mathbf{D}$ always has $J' + 1$ elements and

$$\pi_n(\mathbf{D}|i) = \binom{J-1}{J'}^{-1}, \qquad i \in \mathbf{D}. \tag{9.20}$$

This method was used to estimate a destination choice model by Silman (1980).

The two simple random sampling strategies are characterized by the *uniform conditioning property*:

$$\pi_n(\mathbf{D}|i) = \pi_n(\mathbf{D}|j), \qquad \forall i, j \in \mathbf{D}.$$

This property implies that the correction terms for alternative sampling bias in the logit model,

$$\ln \pi_n(\mathbf{D}|i). \qquad i \in \mathbf{D},$$

are equal and therefore cancel out in the choice probabilities (see equation 9.17), and a standard logit model with a choice set given by $\mathbf{D}$ yields consistent estimates.

Importance Sampling of Alternatives

It would seem that a simple random sample is not necessarily an efficient scheme because, for any given decision maker with a large choice set, the vast majority of the alternatives may have very small choice probabilities. It may be more efficient to design a sample of alternatives in which the alternatives most likely to be chosen by the decision maker have a higher probability of being selected. The basic idea of importance sampling is borrowed from Monte Carlo integration, where it is optimal to use sample selection probabilities that are proportional to the quantity being observed (see Hammersley and Handscomb 1965). For example, consider the problem of estimating a sum of choice probabilities over a subset with J_0 alternatives:

$$\sum_{i=1}^{J_0} P_n(i).$$

It is efficient to select a sample from the J_0 alternatives with selection probabilities q_{in} such that the ratios

$$\frac{P_n(i)}{q_{in}}, \qquad i = 1, \ldots, J_0,$$

vary as little as possible.

Thus an importance alternative sampling strategy is based on preliminary estimates of the choice probabilities. These estimates can be provided a priori by some simple model form. For example, in destination choice models two factors are usually considered, distance and size, which may be combined in a "gravity"-type function

$$\tilde{M}_i e^{-\alpha d_{in}}, \qquad i = 1, \ldots, J, \tag{9.21}$$

where $\tilde{M}_i$ is an approximate measure of size of destination zone i, d_{in} is a measure of distance between the origin of traveler n and destinations in zone i, and α is a scalar parameter that represents the sensitivity to distance. This approach was developed for predictions with a sample of destinations by Ben-Akiva and Watanatada (1981), who have shown that a reasonable value of α for a uniform spatial distribution of elemental destination alternatives is $2/\bar{d}$, where $\bar{d}$ is the average trip length. For $\alpha = 0$ the selection probability of a zone is proportional to its size; in other words, the elemental destination alternatives have equal selection probabilities.

The importance alternative sampling method has optimal properties for application of a model to *predict* choice probabilities but is only an intuitively reasonable sampling strategy for model estimation. We conclude this section with importance sampling strategies that have been applied in recent studies.

Independent Importance Sampling   Perform $J - 1$ independent draws, one for each element in the set of all alternatives *excluding* the chosen alternative, selecting alternative j with probability q_{jn}, and then adding the chosen alternative to the estimation choice set. The resulting sample of alternatives is characterized by the following probability distribution:

$$\pi_n(\mathbf{D}|i) = \prod_{\substack{j \in \mathbf{D} \\ j \neq i}} q_{in} \prod_{j \notin \mathbf{D}} (1 - q_{jn}), \qquad i \in \mathbf{D},$$

which can also be expressed as

$$\pi_n(\mathbf{D}|i) = \frac{1}{q_{in}} Q_n^1(\mathbf{D}), \qquad i \in \mathbf{D}, \tag{9.22}$$

where

$$Q_n^1(\mathbf{D}) = \prod_{j \in \mathbf{D}} q_{jn} \prod_{j \notin \mathbf{D}} (1 - q_{jn})$$

is the unconditional selection probability and is independent of the chosen alternative. In this method of sampling the size of the choice set is unknown and may range from 1 to J. This potential inconvenience in data management of a highly variable alternative sample size is reduced by the following sampling procedure.

Importance Sampling with Replacement   Draw a sample of size J' from the set of all J alternatives, selecting alternative j with probability q_{jn} at each draw. Delete duplicate alternatives and add the chosen alternative, if it was not sampled, to obtain the set $\mathbf{D}$ with selection probability

$$\pi_n(\mathbf{D}|i) = K_\mathbf{D} \prod_{\substack{j \in \mathbf{D} \\ j \neq i}} q_{jn} \left(\sum_{j \in \mathbf{D}} q_{jn} \right)^{J'+1-\tilde{J}}, \qquad i \in \mathbf{D},$$

where $\tilde{J}$ is the size of the set $\mathbf{D}$ and $K_\mathbf{D}$ is a proportionality constant. Note that $(J' + 1 - \tilde{J})$ is the number of duplicate alternatives. The conditional selection probability of the set $\mathbf{D}$ can also be expressed by

$$\pi_n(\mathbf{D}|i) = \frac{1}{q_{in}} Q_n^2(\mathbf{D}), \qquad i \in \mathbf{D}, \tag{9.23}$$

where

$$Q_n^2(\mathbf{D}) = K_\mathbf{D} \prod_{j \in \mathbf{D}} q_{jn} \left(\sum_{j \in \mathbf{D}} q_{jn} \right)^{J'+1-\tilde{J}}$$

is again independent of the chosen alternative. In this strategy the size of the set is bounded by

$$1 \leq \tilde{J} \leq J' + 1,$$

where the lower limit is realized when all J' draws yield the chosen alternative. Thus this importance sampling technique is advantageous over the previous method because it substantially reduces the variability of $\tilde{J}$.

Stratified Importance Sampling   The technique of stratified importance sampling avoids the need to specify a selection probability q_{jn} for every alternative $j = 1, \ldots, J$. The set of J alternatives is stratified into R disjoint subsets such that

$$\sum_{r=1}^{R} J_{rn} = J,$$

where J_{rn} is the number of alternatives in stratum r for decision maker n.

The composition of the strata for a destination choice model may differ, for example, by the origin location, hence the subscript n. The importance sampling criterion is realized by assigning different selection probabilities in different strata, while maintaining uniform selection probabilities within strata. Let $\tilde{J}_{rn}$ be the assigned sample size for stratum $r = 1, \ldots, R$, and denote by $r(i)$ the stratum of alternative i. Draw a simple random sample (without replacement) of size $\tilde{J}_{rn}$ from every stratum except that from the stratum of the chosen alternative i, draw only a sample of $(\tilde{J}_{r(i)n} - 1)$ alternatives. Then add the chosen alternative. Note that the size of the resulting set $\mathbf{D}$ can be fixed at a predetermined value such that

$$\tilde{J} = \sum_{r=1}^{R} \tilde{J}_{rn},$$

and the size of $\mathbf{D}$ is *uniform across all observations. The probability of selecting a set of alternatives* $\mathbf{D}$ is

$$\pi_n(\mathbf{D}|i) = \binom{J_{r(i)n} - 1}{\tilde{J}_{r(i)n} - 1}^{-1} \prod_{\substack{r=1 \\ r \neq r(i)}}^{R} \binom{J_{rn}}{\tilde{J}_{rn}}^{-1}, \qquad i \in \mathbf{D}.$$

It can also be expressed as

$$\pi_n(\mathbf{D}|i) = \frac{J_{r(i)n}}{\tilde{J}_{r(i)n}} Q_n^3(\mathbf{D}), \qquad i \in \mathbf{D}, \tag{9.24}$$

where

$$Q_n^3(\mathbf{D}) = \prod_{r=1}^{R} \binom{J_{rn}}{\tilde{J}_{rn}}^{-1}.$$

The main advantages of this method are its fixed sample size

$$\tilde{J} = J' + 1,$$

where J' is the total number of random draws. The selection probabilities, given by

$$q_{in} = \frac{\tilde{J}_{r(i)n}}{J_{r(i)n}}, \qquad i = 1, \ldots, J,$$

are easier to quantify than in the previous methods. This method was employed in estimating the destination choice model in Paris, as described in section 9.4.

Applications of Importance Sampling   In estimation, the importance sampling techniques described here require the calibration of a logit model of the form

$$\pi_n(i|\mathbf{D}) = \frac{e^{\mu^*V_{in}-\ln q_{in}}}{\sum_{j \in \mathbf{D}} e^{\mu^*V_{jn}-\ln q_{jn}}}, \qquad i \in \mathbf{D}. \tag{9.25}$$

The correction term for sampling of alternatives reduces to $-\ln q_{jn}, j \in \mathbf{D}$, by canceling out the unconditional probabilities of selecting a set $\mathbf{D}$.

In model applications for predictions, if a sample of alternatives is constructed with selection probabilities $q_{jn}, j = 1, \ldots, J$, the term

$$\sum_{j \in \mathbf{D}} \frac{1}{q_{jn}} e^{\mu^*V_{jn}}$$

is a natural estimator of the denominator of the logit model as in equation 9.25. One can view the term $1/q_{jn}$ as the expansion factor for alternative j. In general, let $h(\mathbf{x}_{in})$ denote a function of the vector of variables $\mathbf{x}_{in}$ describing the attributes of alternative i to individual n. The expected value of $h(\mathbf{x}_{in})$ over the entire choice set can be estimated for a logit model from a sample of alternatives by

$$\sum_{i \in \mathbf{D}} \frac{w_n(i)}{\mathscr{E}[w_n(i)]} h(\mathbf{x}_{in}) \hat{P}_n(i|\mathbf{x}_{in}),$$

where

$$\hat{P}_n(i|\mathbf{x}_{in}) = \frac{e^{\mu^*V_{in}}}{\sum_{j \in \mathbf{D}} \{w_n(j)/\mathscr{E}[w_n(j)]\} e^{\mu^*V_{jn}}},$$

$w_n(i) = $ the number of times alternative i is drawn in the process of generating the sample $\mathbf{D}$ for individual n,

$\mathscr{E}[w_n(i)] = $ the expected number of times that alternative i will be drawn in generating the sample $\mathbf{D}$ for individual n (e.g., for J' independent random draws, with replacement and with selection probabilities $q_{jn}, j = 1, \ldots, J$, it is equal to $J'q_{in}$).

The properties of this estimator were analyzed by Watanatada and Ben-Akiva (1977, 1979), who noted that it produces an unbiased numerator and an unbiased denominator, though the ratio is consistent but not unbiased.

If the sample used for estimation is also used for predictions, it is necessary to take into account the fact that the chosen alternative was always included in the sample of alternatives and the possibility that duplicates were omitted. The expansion factor is $w(i)/q_{in}$ for a nonchosen alternative, and for a chosen alternative which is always added to the sample the expansion factor is

$$\frac{w_n(i) + 1}{q_{in} + W_i/\sum_{j \in D} w_n(j)},$$

where W_i is the share of the population that selects alternative i.

9.4 Estimation Results for Three Destination Choice Models

The theory of aggregation of alternatives and the estimation methods with samples of alternatives presented in the previous sections are demonstrated by the following estimation results of destination choice models from two recent studies.

Models of Nonwork Travel for the Paris Region

As part of a larger study, the Régie Autonome des Transports Parisien estimated the models of joint choice of travel mode and destination for personal business and shopping trips, presented in tables 9.1 and 9.2 (CSE 1984).

The Île-de-France study area was divided into 595 zones constituting the alternative destinations. Of these zones 269 are in Paris, and 326 are in the suburbs. The travel modes are: walk, W, moped (or two-wheel vehicles), $2W$, Auto, A, and public transport, T. Thus the choice set in this model can include up to 595×4 alternatives. The sampling of destinations was conducted using the stratified importance sampling procedure described in section 9.3. For every origin zone the 595 destinations were divided into four nonoverlapping strata:

1. The origin zone.
2. The ten zones closest to the origin zone (but not including it).
3. The remaining zones in the city of Paris.
4. The remaining zones outside the city of Paris.

The sample consisted of the single zone in stratum 1 and two zones selected from each of the other three strata, giving a total sample choice set size of

Table 9.1
Estimation results for a joint mode and destination choice model for personal
business trips in Paris

Variable number	Variable name	Coefficient estimate	t statistic
1	Walk (W) constant	2.63	9.9
2	Two wheels ($2W$) constant	−0.43	1.0
3	Auto (A) constant	0.19	0.5
4	Travel time (W)	−0.16	15.3
5	Travel time ($2W$)	−0.16	8.6
6	In-vehicle travel time (≤ 10 min) (A)	−0.145	3.8
7	In-vehicle travel time (> 10 min) (A)	−0.053	5.2
8	Park-seek time (A)	−0.35	3.4
9	In-vehicle travel time (transit T)	−0.046	6.0
10	Out-of-vehicle travel time (T)	−0.073	6.8
11	Travel cost/income (≤ 0.06) (A)	−31.1	4.0
12	Travel cost/income (> 0.06) (A)	−8.42	1.8
13	Parking cost/income (A)	−21.9	2.6
14	Travel cost/income (T)	32.7	3.2
15	(Travel cost)^2/income (T)	−34.7	3.6
16	Number of cars (A)	0.85	4.5
17	Head of household dummy (A)	1.04	4.7
18	Male dummy ($2W$)	1.00	2.6
19	City of Paris constant	3.61	17.6
20	Suburb constant	2.97	12.4
21	Residential district constant	0.41	3.2
	Size measure (see equation 9.14b)		
22	Number of banks, post offices, and medical doctors	−1.72	5.1
23	Number of offices of local government and personal services	−4.83	2.3
24	Number of hospitals and clinics	—	—
25	Coefficient of the natural logarithm of the size measure (μ')	0.85	10.9

Summary statistics
Number of observations = 906
$\mathscr{L}(0) = -2{,}633$
$\mathscr{L}(\hat{\beta}) = -1{,}510$
$\rho^2 = 0.427$
$\bar{\rho}^2 = 0.417$

Source: CSE (1984).

Table 9.2
Estimation results for a joint mode and destination choice model for shopping trips in Paris

Variable number	Variable description	Coefficient estimate	t statistic
1	Walk (W) constant	2.16	7.0
2	Two wheels ($2W$) constant	0.29	0.8
3	Auto (A) constant	−0.44	0.9
4	Travel time (W)	−0.20	16.5
5	Travel time ($2W$)	−0.36	9.8
6	In-vehicle travel time (≤ 10 min) (A)	−0.28	9.8
7	In-vehicle travel time (> 10 min) (A)	−0.15	10.9
8	Park-seek time (A)	−0.58	4.8
9	In-vehicle travel time (T)	−0.084	8.7
10	Out-of-vehicle travel time (T)	−0.13	9.7
11	Travel cost/income/distance (A)	−24.4	1.2
12	Parking cost/income (A)	−15.2	1.5
13	Travel cost/income/distance (T)	−11.7	2.8
14	Number of autos (A)	1.07	5.4
15	Employed dummy (A)	1.12	5.6
16	Age ≤ 18 dummy (W)	0.74	2.2
17	Male dummy ($2W$)	1.46	4.6
18	City of Paris constant	3.86	16.6
19	Suburb constant	3.14	11.6
20	Residential district constant	0.86	6.8
21	Central business district and transit (T) constant	0.60	3.6
	Size measure (see equation 9.14b)		
22	Number of department stores and hypermarkets	6.48	15.1
23	Number of supermarkets	4.37	7.1
24	Number of other stores	—	—
25	Coefficient of the natural logarithm of the size measure (μ')	0.59	8.6

Summary statistics
Number of observations = 1,020
$\mathscr{L}(0) = -2{,}956$
$\mathscr{L}(\hat{\beta}) = -1{,}396$
$\rho^2 = 0.528$
$\bar{\rho}^2 = 0.519$

Source: CSE (1984).

seven for each trip. This sampling strategy results in high probabilities of selection for zones near the zone of residence and low probabilities for all other zones.

In a 1976 survey some 10,000 households in the Île-de-France region reported all the trips made during a single day and provided information on household and trip-maker characteristics. The estimation samples were constructed by subsampling from this survey. Because of the large proportion of walk and car trips for nonwork purposes, it was decided to use different subsampling rates by mode to increase the proportion of public transport and two-wheel trips in the estimation data set. This is a simple application of choice-based sampling, which with a logit model requires alternative-specific correction factors that were presented in section 8.4.

The level-of-service attributes were calculated from road and transit networks. The available measures of size of alternative destinations included the usual area, population, and employment variables and an unusually detailed data set providing the number of establishments and their employment for a very detailed breakdown of activity types.

The estimated models include a large number of travel time and travel cost variables with statistically significant coefficients. The scale parameter value is significantly different from one in the shopping model, but a constrained estimation of this model with $\mu' = 1$ did not have an important effect on the values of the other model coefficients. It was found that the size variables representing the number of establishments perform better than the employment variables. It is interesting to examine the size measure for the shopping model in table 9.2, which is

$$M_i = \exp(6.48) \cdot [\text{number of department stores and hypermarkets}]_i$$

$$+ \exp(4.37) \cdot [\text{number of supermarkets}]_i$$

$$+ 1 \cdot [\text{number of other stores}]_i.$$

This means, for example, that a supermarket attracts an estimated 79 ($= \exp(4.37)$) more trips than a small shop at the same location.

Model of Work Trips for Maceio

As a part of a study of urban transportation policies and planning methods in Brazil, the model shown in table 9.3 was estimated for the city of Maceio, located in the economically depressed northeastern Brazil (see Kozel and Swait 1982). The model predicts the choice of a daily home-based work

Table 9.3
Estimation results for a joint mode, frequency, and destination choice model for work trips in Maceio

Variable number	Variable description	Coefficient estimate	t statistic
1	One round-trip, taxi (T) constant	−3.15	4.9
2	One round-trip, auto passenger (AP) constant	−3.83	7.9
3	One round-trip, auto driver (AD) constant	−2.09	4.2
4	Two round-trips, bus (B) constant	0.71	5.9
5	Two round-trips, taxi (T) constant	−0.85	1.4
6	Two round-trips, auto passenger (AP) constant	−2.01	4.8
7	Two round-trips, auto driver (AD) constant	0.15	0.3
8	Total travel time	−0.008	5.8
9	Total travel cost/natural logarithm of electricity consumption	−0.170	4.8
10	Household electricity consumption (T)	0.008	3.7
11	Household electricity consumption (AP)	0.010	5.6
12	Household electricity consumption (AD)	0.009	5.2
13	Number of household members (T)	−0.111	1.6
14	Number of household members (AP)	−0.163	2.8
15	Number of household members (AD)	−0.186	3.1
16	Number of vehicles/number of workers (T)	1.78	3.4
17	Number of vehicles/number of workers (AP)	3.16	8.8
18	Number of vehicles/number of workers (AD)	3.01	7.3
19	Two round trips and CBD constant	1.01	6.5
20	Size measure: natural logarithm of total number of jobs, CBD	0.99	14.6
21	Size measure: natural logarithm of total number of jobs, non-CBD	1.14	12.4

Summary statistics
Number of observations = 1,016
$\mathscr{L}(0) = -3{,}641$
$\mathscr{L}(\hat{\beta}) = -2{,}071$
$\rho^2 = 0.431$
$\bar{\rho}^2 = 0.425$

Source: Swait et al (1984).

tour, characterized by a travel mode, a workplace (or destination), and a frequency of one or two round trips (when returning home for the midday meals). A significant number of workers return home for lunch, thus creating two peak periods between 11:00 and 13:00 hours.

The travel modes include bus B, taxi, T, auto passenger, AP, and auto driver, AD. The auto driver mode was only available to workers from car-owning households who are 19 years or older. If the round-trip travel time by a travel mode between home and a destination is greater than two hours, the option to return home for lunch was eliminated. The Maceio urbanized area was divided into 35 traffic zones. The origin zone was omitted, and a simple random sample of one-third of the remaining zones, minus the chosen, was drawn.

The estimation data set of 1,016 motorized daily work trips was randomly subsampled from a 1977 travel survey of a sample of about 3,200 households in Maceio. Neither household nor individual income data were gathered in this survey; instead, the household electricity consumption was collected as a proxy. This measure was found to be highly correlated with household income in studies in other Brazilian cities similar to Maceio.

Separate bus and highway networks and information on bus and taxi fares were used to generate estimates of travel times and travel costs. Employment data was available to represent the sizes of alternative zones as work places.

The possibility of committing important specification errors are many with a complex joint choice model of employment location, travel mode to work, and frequency of a midday round trip for lunch at home. Accordingly several tests of parameter stability across choice dimensions were performed by estimating conditional choice models of one or two choice dimensions holding the remaining dimension(s) constant, for example, choice of mode and frequency given destination (see section 7.5 which deals with tests of model structure). These tests evidenced a high degree of parameter stability, which supports the adopted joint choice structure. In addition a market segmentation test did not reject the hypothesis of equal model parameters for professional and nonprofessional occupation types. These results are due in large part to the inclusion in the model specification of a large set of coefficients of socioeconomic characteristics.

It is encouraging to note that the single-size variables have coefficients near one for CBD and non-CBD destinations, indicating the appropriateness of the zonal aggregation scheme and the model specification.

9.5 Summary

This chapter has explored some of the technical issues that arise when the elements of the choice set are aggregates of elemental alternatives or when the choice set is so large that it becomes essential or advantageous to sample from it in the estimation or forecasting process. Some practical results were presented for the multinomial logit model.

In some choice situations the analyst either does not know what the true elements in the choice set are or does not have data on those true elements. For example, in the case of shopping trip destination it is usually impossible to infer whether the true destination is a store, a shopping center, or some other grouping of stores. In addition unless very detailed travel data are available, the analyst usually has data on geographical areas (i.e., zones) rather than individual, distinct sites to which people travel. In these cases it was demonstrated that a useful model could be created by first aggregating the elemental alternatives into a smaller number of alternatives and estimating an appropriately corrected model on the aggregated choice set elements. The correction for the logit model was to use the average utility over all alternatives with an additional term equal to the logarithm of the number of elemental alternatives that makes up the aggregate. In instances where the number of elements in the aggregated alternative is unknown, it was shown that a linear function of observable "size" attributes could be used instead.

The second case is the one where the choice set size is extremely large. In this situation the logical strategy is to sample from the large choice set for the purposes of model estimation. It was shown that as long as the way in which the sampling of alternatives is done satisfies some specific conditions, a simple estimator for multinomial choice model parameters can be constructed. A variety of sampling strategies, including simple random sampling and variations of stratified random sampling, meet these conditions and produce computationally tractable estimators.

Three examples of choice models involving destination and mode choice that relied on these results were also presented.

10 Models of Multidimensional Choice and the Nested Logit Model

In most of our examples of discrete choice situations the choice set has been relatively simple, consisting usually of various modes or destinations. There are many situations, however, where the members of the set of feasible alternatives are *combinations* of underlying choice dimensions. For example, we may be interested in modeling shopping trips, and each alternative might be defined by both the destination of the trip and the mode used to reach that destination.

In this chapter we explore the problems of using discrete choice analysis, and particularly multinomial logit, in cases where the choice set is multidimensional. We begin in section 10.1 by first defining a multidimensional choice set. In section 10.2 we discuss how the multinomial logit model, developed in chapter 5, can be used as a joint choice model when the choice set is multidimensional. We then consider an appropriate generalization of the logit model, termed *nested logit*, in section 10.3. In section 10.4 we turn to the problem of estimating the parameters of the nested logit model and show that there exist estimators that are computationally much simpler than the complete maximum likelihood estimator. Section 10.5 briefly discusses the applicability of multinomial probit to multidimensional choice situations.

One of the interesting features of the models derived in this chapter is that they provide a scalar, summary measure of what we choose to call *accessibility*, which serves to connect models in a multidimensional choice context. The properties of this measure are discussed in section 10.6.

In section 10.7 we return to the nested logit model and show how it can be derived as a special case of the generalized extreme value (GEV) model that was introduced in chapter 5.

Section 10.8 describes an empirical example of a nested logit model. This example, adapted from Ben-Akiva (1973), is a model of mode and destination choice for shopping trips estimated on a small sample taken from Washington, D.C., in 1968. Section 10.9 is a summary of the chapter.

10.1 Multidimensional Choice Sets

Let us begin by considering any two choice sets C_1 and C_2 with J_1 and J_2 elements, respectively. Any set $C_1 \times C_2$ (where $\times$ denotes the Cartesian product) will contain $J_1 \cdot J_2$ elements and will also be a choice set. Now define C_n^* as the set of all elements of the Cartesian product that are infeasible for individual n. In this notation

$$\mathbf{C}_n = \mathbf{C}_1 \times \mathbf{C}_2 - \mathbf{C}_n^* \qquad (10.1)$$

defines a *multidimensional choice set* for individual n.

This definition is best illustrated by means of an example. Suppose we define

$$\mathbf{M} = \{m_1, m_2, \ldots, m_{J_M}\}$$

$$= \{\text{all possible modes for shopping}\},$$

$$\mathbf{D} = \{d_1, d_2, \ldots, d_{J_D}\} = \{\text{all possible shopping destinations}\}.$$

In this case

$$\mathbf{M} \times \mathbf{D} = \{(m_1, d_1), (m_1, d_2), \ldots, (m_1, d_{J_D}), (m_2, d_1), \ldots, (m_2, d_{J_D}), \ldots,$$

$$(m_{J_M}, d_1), \ldots, (m_{J_M}, d_{J_D})\}$$

will be all potential mode and destination combinations. A subset of these combinations is infeasible for person n. For example, transit may be a possible mode and a certain suburban shopping mall may be a possible destination, but that particular mall may not have transit service; thus the element of $\mathbf{M} \times \mathbf{D}$ defined by that mode and destination combination would be infeasible for all n. In a different case a person may not know transit service exists to a particular destination, and thus for him or her the combination of using transit to that destination may be infeasible.

It should be obvious that the concept of a multidimensional choice set extends to any level of dimensionality. For example, we could have frequency of travel, time of day, mode, destination, and route as distinct dimensions of choice, and we could define a multidimensional choice set in which each element was a combination of choices on each of the dimensions.

The first question that naturally arises when a choice set is multidimensional is whether it matters at all. If we examine the derivation of the different multinomial choice models discussed in chapter 5, there is no obvious restriction on how the choice set can be defined. There are, however, two related reasons why multidimensional choice situations are in some sense different. *Both of these differences arise because some of the elements in a multidimensional choice set are logically related by virtue of the fact that they share a common element along one or more dimensions.* For example, in the case where the choice set was defined as the set of feasible mode and destination combinations, some of the elements in the combined choice set share a common mode and others share a common destination. This logical linkage between elements of the multidimensional choice set makes a special analysis of multidimensional choice situations useful because it implies that (1) some of the *observed* attributes of elements in the choice set may be equal across subsets of alternatives, and (2) some of the *unobserved* attributes of elements in the choice set may be equal across subsets of alternatives. These two aspects of multidimensional choice situations have some important modeling consequences. We consider the consequence of only the first aspect in the next section, holding the consequences of the second one for section 10.3.

In most of our examples we will use mode and destination choice; extensions to other cases with more dimensions are generally straightforward and will only be discussed when they raise significant modeling issues. The reader should also be aware that the various results in the remainder of this chapter apply not only to multidimensional choice situations but also to any choice problem where the elements of the choice set shares observed and/or unobserved attributes. We will provide a specific example of such cases in section 10.3.

10.2 Multidimensional Choice Sets with Shared Observed Attributes: Joint Logit

Suppose we have a multidimensional set $\mathbf{C}_n$ whose elements are defined as mode and destination combinations. Let us define U_{dm} as the total utility of the element of $\mathbf{C}_n$ consisting of mode m and destination d. (In the following presentation we omit the subscript n denoting the individual in writing many of the utility functions and variables for the sake of notational clarity. It should be clear where this subscript is implicit.) Now suppose some elements $\mathbf{C}_n$ share common observed elements as a consequence of their sharing the same mode or destination. By extension of the partition of the total utility into systematic and random components, we can write

$$U_{dm} = \tilde{V}_d + \tilde{V}_m + \tilde{V}_{dm} + \varepsilon_{dm}, \qquad \forall (d, m) \in \mathbf{C}_n, \tag{10.2}$$

where

$\tilde{V}_d = $ the systematic component of utility common to all elements of $\mathbf{C}_n$ using destination d,

$\tilde{V}_m$ = the systematic component of utility common to all elements of C_n using mode m,

$\tilde{V}_{dm}$ = the remaining systematic component of utility specific to the combination (d, m),

ε_{dm} = the random utility component.

As an example, consider a linear-in-parameters systematic utility function for a shopping mode and destination choice model. Suppose this model had the following variables in it for alternative $i \in C_n$:

x_{i1} = the out-of-vehicle time to mode/destination combination i,

x_{i2} = the-in-vehicle time to mode/destination combination i,

x_{i3} = the-out-of-pocket cost for mode/destination combination i divided by household income,

x_{i4} = the wholesale and retail employment at the destination included in alternative i

x_{i5} = a CBD constant defined as

$$= \begin{cases} 1 & \text{if alternative } i \text{ contains the central business district as its destination,} \\ 0 & \text{otherwise,} \end{cases}$$

x_{i6} = an auto mode constant defined as

$$= \begin{cases} 1 & \text{if alternative } i \text{ contains the auto mode,} \\ 0 & \text{otherwise,} \end{cases}$$

x_{i7} = an auto-specific income variable defined as

$$= \begin{cases} \text{household income} & \text{if alternative } i \text{ contains the auto mode,} \\ 0 & \text{otherwise.} \end{cases}$$

In this example, the first three variables would be part of $\tilde{V}_{dm}$ because they vary across both the mode and destination which constitute any multidimensional alternative i. Thus in this example

$$\tilde{V}_{dm} = \beta_1 x_{i1} + \beta_2 x_{i2} + \beta_3 x_{i3}. \tag{10.3}$$

The variables x_{i4} and x_{i5} would be part of $\tilde{V}_d$ because their values do not vary across elements of $\mathbf{C}_n$ using d; any mode and destination combinations having the same destination would have the same values of x_{i4} and x_{i5}. Thus

$$\tilde{V}_d = \beta_4 x_{i4} + \beta_5 x_{i5}. \tag{10.4}$$

Finally, x_{i6} and x_{i7} vary only across modes. Thus

$$\tilde{V}_m = \beta_6 x_{i6} + \beta_7 x_{i7}. \tag{10.5}$$

Given such partitioning of the systematic utility, we now turn our attention to the random component, ε_{dm}. The distribution of the ε_{dm}'s across the alternatives and across the population will define the choice probabilities. We can use the multinomial logit model for the joint choice of destination and mode if these disturbances are independent and identically Gumbel distributed (with the scale parameter μ normalized to 1) as follows:

$$P_n(d, m) = \frac{e^{\tilde{V}_m + \tilde{V}_d + \tilde{V}_{dm}}}{\sum_{(m', d') \in \mathbf{C}_n} e^{\tilde{V}_{m'} + \tilde{V}_{d'} + \tilde{V}_{d'm'}}}. \tag{10.6}$$

Equation 10.6 is called the *joint logit model*.

In a similar way to this derivation all of the results on probit and other multinomial choice models extend directly to the multidimensional case. What makes the multidimensional choice problem interesting is that the natural partitioning of the systematic component of utility allows us to derive various conditional and marginal probabilities quite easily. For example, we might rewrite the joint probability of destination d and mode m being selected as

$$P_n(d, m) = P_n(d|m) P_n(m) \tag{10.7}$$

or as

$$P_n(d, m) = P_n(m|d) P_n(d). \tag{10.8}$$

We can also define what we will term conditional and marginal choice sets. We will denote $\mathbf{D}_n$ and $\mathbf{M}_n$ as the marginal destination and mode choice sets; thus $\mathbf{M}_n$ is the set of all modes that correspond to the mode portion of at least one element in the multidimensional choice set $\mathbf{C}_n$. Similarly $\mathbf{D}_n$ is the set of all destinations that appear in at least one element in $\mathbf{C}_n$. We will denote the conditional destination choice set as $\mathbf{D}_{nm}$, defined as the subset of destinations in $\mathbf{D}_n$ that are feasible for person n if he or she used mode m. $\mathbf{M}_{nd}$ will be the conditional mode choice set, defined as the subset of modes in $\mathbf{M}_n$ which are feasible for person n going to destination d.

Using this notation, we now derive the marginal and conditional choice probabilities. For the joint logit model these conditional and marginal probabilities have some extremely simple forms.

Marginal Choice Probabilities

In a multidimensional choice situation we are often interested in the marginal choice probabilities for the elements of the different choice dimensions. In our example where the choice set consists of mode and destination pairs, we might wish to forecast the marginal probability that transit is chosen or the marginal probability that a shopping trip is taken to the central business district.

The marginal probability can be derived in two distinct ways. First, one can simply compute all the joint probabilities and then sum along the appropriate choice dimension. Thus in our mode and destination choice example the marginal probabilities are

$$P_n(d) = \sum_{m \in \mathbf{M}_{nd}} P_n(d, m), \tag{10.9}$$

$$P_n(m) = \sum_{d \in \mathbf{D}_{nm}} P_n(d, m). \tag{10.10}$$

In this case of a joint logit model this implies

$$\begin{aligned}
P_n(d) &= \sum_{m \in \mathbf{M}_{nd}} \frac{e^{\tilde{V}_m + \tilde{V}_d + \tilde{V}_{dm}}}{\sum_{(m', d') \in C_n} e^{\tilde{V}_{m'} + \tilde{V}_{d'} + \tilde{V}_{d'm'}}} \\
&= \frac{e^{\tilde{V}_d} \sum_{m \in \mathbf{M}_{nd}} e^{\tilde{V}_m + \tilde{V}_{dm}}}{\sum_{d' \in \mathbf{D}_n} e^{\tilde{V}_{d'}} \sum_{m' \in \mathbf{M}_{nd}} e^{\tilde{V}_{d'm'} + \tilde{V}_{m'}}}.
\end{aligned} \tag{10.11}$$

If we define V_d' as follows:

$$V_d' = \ln \sum_{m \in \mathbf{M}_{nd}} e^{\tilde{V}_m + \tilde{V}_{dm}}, \tag{10.12}$$

then we can rewrite equation 10.11 as

$$P_n(d) = \frac{e^{\tilde{V}_d + V_d'}}{\sum_{d' \in \mathbf{D}_n} e^{\tilde{V}_{d'} + V_{d'}'}}. \tag{10.13}$$

Thus for a joint logit model the marginal destination choice probability can be expressed as a logit model with an additional term V_d' added to the utility function. By a straightforward extension of the preceding logic, if we define

$$V_m' = \ln \sum_{d \in \mathbf{D}_{nm}} e^{\tilde{V}_d + \tilde{V}_{dm}} \tag{10.14}$$

and derive the following marginal mode choice probability, we obtain

$$P_n(m) = \frac{e^{\tilde{V}_m + V_m'}}{\sum_{m' \in \mathbf{M}_n} e^{\tilde{V}_{m'} + V_{m'}'}}. \tag{10.15}$$

The terms V_m' and V_d' have a number of interpretations. One of the most interesting interpretations is gained by deriving the marginal choice probabilities in quite a different way. Consider again the marginal destination choice probability. The destination d will be selected by an individual if and only if one element of the original multidimensional choice set that contains d has the greatest utility. We can use this to rewrite the choice probability as

$$P_n(d) = Pr\left[\max_{m \in \mathbf{M}_{nd}} U_{dm} \geq \max_{m \in \mathbf{M}_{nd'}} U_{d'm}, \forall d' \in \mathbf{D}_n, d' \neq d \right]. \tag{10.16}$$

The term $\max_{m \in \mathbf{M}_{nd}} U_{dm}$ is the utility of the best alternative in $\mathbf{C}_n$ that contains destination d. Thus equation 10.16 states that destination d will be chosen if the best multidimensional alternative containing d is better (in the sense of having greater total utility) than the best alternative not containing d. The systematic component of the maximum utility of a subset of alternatives (or the expected maximum utility of a subset of alternatives) has been termed a measure of "inclusive value" (McFadden 1978) or accessibility (Ben-Akiva and Lerman 1979). Each term is an attempt to describe the utility of the best alternative in a subset of choices as a summary of the "value" of that subset to an individual. We return to this interpretation in section 10.6.

In the case of a joint logit model

$$\max_{m \in \mathbf{M}_{nd}} (U_{dm}) = \max_{m \in \mathbf{M}_{nd}} (\tilde{V}_d + \tilde{V}_m + \tilde{V}_{dm} + \varepsilon_{dm})$$

$$= \tilde{V}_d + \max_{m \in \mathbf{M}_{nd}} (\tilde{V}_m + \tilde{V}_{dm} + \varepsilon_{dm}). \tag{10.17}$$

Since the ε_{dm} terms are by assumption independent and identically Gumbel distributed, the maximum of the terms in parentheses in equation 10.17 is also Gumbel distributed, with parameter

$$\eta = \frac{1}{\mu} \ln \sum_{m \in \mathbf{M}_{nd}} e^{(\tilde{V}_m + \tilde{V}_{dm})\mu} \tag{10.18a}$$

(See section 5.1, property 7). Since we have chosen the scale of the disturbances so that $\mu = 1$, equation 10.18a reduces to

$$\eta = \ln \sum_{m \in \mathbf{M}_{nd}} e^{\tilde{V}_m + \tilde{V}_{dm}} = V_d'. \tag{10.18b}$$

We can therefore rewrite equation 10.16 as

$$P_n(d) = Pr(\tilde{V}_d + V_d' + \varepsilon_d^* \geq \tilde{V}_{d'} + V_{d'}' + \varepsilon_{d'}^*, \forall d' \in \mathbf{D}_n, d' \neq d), \tag{10.19}$$

where the disturbance terms (ε_d^*) are independent and identically Gumbel distributed, satisfying the assumptions of the multinomial logit model. This leads directly to equation 10.13 for the marginal destination choice probability. By analogy

$$P_n(m) = Pr(\tilde{V}_m + V_m' + \varepsilon_m^* \geq \tilde{V}_{m'} + V_{m'}' + \varepsilon_{m'}^*, \forall m' \in \mathbf{M}_n, m' \neq m), \tag{10.20}$$

and leads directly to equation 10.15.

This derivation implies that V_m' and V_d' have natural interpretations. For a joint logit model they represent the systematic components of the maximum utilities of the alternatives in $\mathbf{C}_n$ which involve m and d, respectively.

Conditional Choice Probabilities

As was the case for the marginal choice probabilities, we can derive the conditional choice models by manipulating either the choice probabilities directly or the basic random utility statements. We begin with the former of these approaches.

By definition

$$P_n(d|m) = \frac{P_n(d, m)}{P_n(m)} \tag{10.21}$$

and

$$P_n(m|d) = \frac{P_n(d, m)}{P_n(d)}. \tag{10.22}$$

In the case of a joint logit model the probability that person n goes to destination d *conditional on using a particular mode m* is given by

$$P_n(d|m) = \frac{e^{\tilde{V}_m + \tilde{V}_d + \tilde{V}_{dm}} / \sum_{(d',m') \in \mathbf{C}_n} e^{\tilde{V}_{m'} + \tilde{V}_{d'} + \tilde{V}_{d'm'}}}{e^{\tilde{V}_m + V'_m} / \sum_{m' \in \mathbf{M}_n} e^{\tilde{V}_{m'} + V'_{m'}}}$$

$$= \left(\frac{e^{\tilde{V}_m} e^{\tilde{V}_d + \tilde{V}_{dm}}}{\sum_{m' \in \mathbf{M}_n} e^{\tilde{V}_{m'}} \sum_{d' \in \mathbf{D}_{nm'}} e^{\tilde{V}_{d'} + \tilde{V}_{d'm'}}} \right) \left(\frac{\sum_{m' \in \mathbf{M}_n} e^{\tilde{V}_{m'} + V'_{m'}}}{e^{\tilde{V}_m} e^{V'_m}} \right). \tag{10.23}$$

Since by definition,

$$V'_{m'} = \ln \sum_{d' \in \mathbf{D}_{nm'}} e^{\tilde{V}_{d'} + \tilde{V}_{d'm'}}, \tag{10.24}$$

equation 10.23 simplifies (after canceling terms) to

$$P_n(d|m) = \frac{e^{\tilde{V}_d + \tilde{V}_{dm}}}{e^{V'_m}} = \frac{e^{\tilde{V}_d + \tilde{V}_{dm}}}{\sum_{d' \in \mathbf{D}_{nm}} e^{\tilde{V}_{d'} + \tilde{V}_{d'm}}}. \tag{10.25}$$

Thus *for the joint logit model the conditional choice probabilities are also given by a logit model, where the component of the systematic utility attributable entirely to the conditioning choice is omitted and the choice set is restricted to the subset of the alternatives that are feasible given the conditioning choice.*

The simplicity of this result belies its practical significance. The fact that for the joint logit model the conditional choice probabilities have the same form as their underlying joint model form is the implicit basis for a great many travel demand analyses. For example, every mode choice model is in fact a model of conditional choice, where the conditioning includes the choice of destination (or in the case of work trips, the choice of workplace), residence, and time of day. Moreover, since many mode choice models contain independent variables involving auto ownership, they are implicitly conditonal on that household choice as well. Indeed, one can even view the fact that a person makes a work trip at all as the outcome of a labor force participation decision.

This same result can be derived by considering the basic random utility statement defining the choice probabilities. In the general case

$$P_n(d|m) = Pr(U_{dm} \geq U_{d'm}, \forall d' \in \mathbf{D}_{nm}, d' \neq d | \text{mode } m \text{ chosen}). \tag{10.26}$$

In this expression the conditioning event that mode m is chosen can be expressed as the condition that

$$\max_{d \in \mathbf{D}_{nm}} (U_{dm}) \geq \max_{d \in \mathbf{D}_{nm'}} (U_{dm'}), \forall m' \in \mathbf{M}_n, m' \neq m. \tag{10.27}$$

Note first that we can rewrite equation 10.26 as follows

$Pr(U_{dm} \geq U_{d'm}, \forall d' \in \mathbf{D}_{nm}, d' \neq d | m \text{ chosen})$

$$= Pr(\tilde{V}_d + \tilde{V}_m + \tilde{V}_{dm} + \varepsilon_{dm} \geq \tilde{V}_{d'} + \tilde{V}_m + \tilde{V}_{d'm} + \varepsilon_{d'm}, \forall d' \in \mathbf{D}_{nm},$$
$$d' \neq d | m \text{ chosen}) \tag{10.28}$$

$$= Pr(\tilde{V}_d + \tilde{V}_{dm} + \varepsilon_{dm} \geq \tilde{V}_{d'} + \tilde{V}_{d'm} + \varepsilon_{d'm}, \forall d' \in \mathbf{D}_{nm}, d' \neq d | m \text{ chosen}).$$

As equation 10.28 illustrates, regardless of the distribution of the disturbances the conditional destination choice probabilities are unaffected by the portion of systematic utility dependent only on mode. However, the distribution of the disturbances in the joint choice model will in general affect the *form* of the conditional choice probabilities, since the conditioning on the choice of mode is defined by an event (given in equation 10.27) that involves the disturbance terms. Put another way, there is no guarantee that the distributions of the disturbance ε_{dm} will be the same conditional on mode m being chosen as they are unconditionally. One can show, for example, that even if the original unconditional disturbances are independent and identically normally distributed, their distribution *conditional on mode m being chosen* is not normally distributed. Thus it is a particular property of the IID Gumbel distribution assumption that, for the joint logit model, makes the conditional choice probability a logit form.

10.3 Multidimensional Choice Models with Shared Unobserved Attributes: Nested Logit

We now turn our attention to the more general case where the multidimensional structure of the choice set leads to the elements in $\mathbf{C}_n$ sharing unobserved as well as observed attributes. Using the mode and destination choice example, we can express this effect on the total utility of a multidimensional choice as follows:

$$U_{dm} = \tilde{V}_m + \tilde{V}_d + \tilde{V}_{dm} + \tilde{\varepsilon}_m + \tilde{\varepsilon}_d + \tilde{\varepsilon}_{dm}. \tag{10.29}$$

In this expression, $\tilde{\varepsilon}_m$ and $\tilde{\varepsilon}_d$ are defined as the unobserved components of the total utility attributable to the mode and destination, respectively; they vary only across modes (in the case of $\tilde{\varepsilon}_m$) or destinations (in the case of $\tilde{\varepsilon}_d$). The term $\tilde{\varepsilon}_{dm}$ is the remaining unobserved component of the total utility.

The consequence of allowing for terms such as $\tilde{\varepsilon}_d$ and $\tilde{\varepsilon}_m$ is quite significant. Consider any two elements in $\mathbf{C}_n$ sharing a common destination. The covariance of their utilities, assuming that each component of the disturbance is independent of all the other components, is given by the following equation:

$$\text{cov}\,(U_{dm}, U_{dm'}) = \text{cov}\,(\tilde{\varepsilon}_m + \tilde{\varepsilon}_d + \tilde{\varepsilon}_{dm}, \tilde{\varepsilon}_{m'} + \tilde{\varepsilon}_d + \tilde{\varepsilon}_{dm'})$$
$$= \mathscr{E}(\tilde{\varepsilon}_d^2) = \text{var}\,(\tilde{\varepsilon}_d). \tag{10.30}$$

(The contributions of terms other than $\tilde{\varepsilon}_d$ to the covariance are all zero, since all the disturbance components were assumed to be independent.) Similarly we can show that under this assumption

$$\text{cov}\,(U_{dm}, U_{d'm}) = \text{var}\,(\tilde{\varepsilon}_m). \tag{10.31}$$

Equations 10.30 *and* 10.31 *imply that when there are shared unobserved components associated with different choice dimensions, the utilities of the elements of the corresponding multidimensional choice set cannot be independent.* Thus one of the key assumptions underlying the joint logit model discussed in section 10.2 is violated. If we believe that the magnitudes of $\tilde{\varepsilon}_d$, or $\tilde{\varepsilon}_m$ are large compared to $\tilde{\varepsilon}_{dm}$, we may be forced to use significantly more complicated choice model forms. Two general approaches have been developed to cope with this problem.

The first approach is called the *nested logit model*. It requires that either $\tilde{\varepsilon}_d$ or $\tilde{\varepsilon}_m$ is small enough in magnitude so that it can reasonably be ignored. This model was first derived as a generalization of the joint logit model by Ben-Akiva (1973) and subsequently formalized in different ways based on utility maximization by Daly and Zachary (1979), Williams (1977), Ben-Akiva and Lerman (1979), and by McFadden (1978) who showed that it is a special case of the generalized extreme value (GEV) model described in section 5.7.

The second approach, using the multinomial probit model, is theoretically more appealing but computationally burdensome. This is described in section 10.5.

Assumptions of the Nested Logit Model

Let us suppose that in a particular choice situation we assume that either $\tilde{\varepsilon}_d$ or $\tilde{\varepsilon}_m$ has zero variance. Under this assumption we can derive a variant of the multinomial logit model that preserves most of its desirable properties. To do this, we consider first the case where the shared unobserved component of utility attributable to the destination is negligible, namely that $\text{var}\,(\tilde{\varepsilon}_d) = 0$. Thus we assume

$$U_{dm} = \tilde{V}_d + \tilde{V}_m + \tilde{V}_{dm} + \tilde{\varepsilon}_m + \tilde{\varepsilon}_{dm}. \tag{10.32}$$

For reasons that will be made clear shortly, we further assume the following:

1. $\tilde{\varepsilon}_m$ and $\tilde{\varepsilon}_{dm}$ are independent for all $d \in \mathbf{D}_n$ and $m \in \mathbf{M}_n$.
2. The terms $\tilde{\varepsilon}_{dm}$ are independent and identically Gumbel distributed with scale parameter μ^d.
3. $\tilde{\varepsilon}_m$ is distributed so that $\max_{d \in \mathbf{D}_{nm}} U_{dm}$ is Gumbel distributed with scale parameter μ^m.

The first of the assumptions is no different from our assumption of independence made earlier in the chapter. The second assumption is identical to that made in deriving the multinomial logit model; it was originally justified because the logistic distribution is a reasonable approximation to a normal distribution. The justification for the third assumption will become clear in the following subsection. It will also be shown that only the ratio of the two scale parameters μ^m/μ^d can be identified from the data. Thus it is possible to normalize one of them to equal one. The choice of $\mu^m = 1$ "sets the scale" of the utility measure so that the total disturbances for the nested logit model are comparable to those for the joint logit. As in the case of the multinomial logit model this assumption has no real effect on the results, so a normalization of $\mu^d = 1$ will result in the same model.

What the preceding assumptions effectively imply is that the total disturbance is divided into two independent components, the sum of which has the same variance as the disturbance in the joint logit model. As shown in equation 10.31, by having alternatives that use the same mode share an unobserved component of utility, we produce a covariance between the utilities of subsets of alternatives with a common mode.

Marginal Choice Probabilities for Nested Logit

With these assumptions we can now derive the nested logit model. We begin by first solving for the marginal probability that mode m is chosen. Our development exactly parallels the one in section 10.2. We note that

$$P_n(m) = Pr\left(\max_{d \in \mathbf{D}_{nm}} U_{dm} \geq \max_{d \in \mathbf{D}_{nm'}} U_{dm'}, \forall m' \in \mathbf{M}_n, m' \neq m \right)$$

$$= Pr\left(\tilde{V}_m + \tilde{\varepsilon}_m + \max_{d \in \mathbf{D}_{nm}} [\tilde{V}_d + \tilde{V}_{dm} + \tilde{\varepsilon}_{dm}] \right. \tag{10.33}$$

$$\left. \geq \tilde{V}_{m'} + \tilde{\varepsilon}_{m'} + \max_{d \in \mathbf{D}_{nm'}} [\tilde{V}_d + \tilde{V}_{dm'} + \tilde{\varepsilon}_{dm'}], \forall m' \in \mathbf{M}_n, m' \neq m \right)$$

Since $\tilde{\varepsilon}_{dm}$ is by assumption Gumbel distributed with parameter μ^d, the term

$$\max_{d \in \mathbf{D}_{nm}} [\tilde{V}_d + \tilde{V}_{dm} + \tilde{\varepsilon}_{dm}] \tag{10.34}$$

is also Gumbel distributed, but with parameters

$$\eta = \frac{1}{\mu^d} \ln \sum_{d \in \mathbf{D}_{nm}} e^{(\tilde{V}_d + \tilde{V}_{dm})\mu^d}, \tag{10.35}$$

and $\mu = \mu^d$. (The value of η is found by recalling that the maximum of independent, Gumbel-distributed variates is Gumbel distributed with the parameters given in section 5.4, property 7.)

Thus we can rewrite equation 10.33 as

$$\begin{aligned} P_n(m) = Pr\,(\tilde{V}_m + V'_m + \tilde{\varepsilon}_m + \varepsilon'_m \geq \tilde{V}_{m'} + V'_{m'} + \tilde{\varepsilon}_{m'} \\ + \varepsilon'_{m'}, \forall m' \in \mathbf{M}_n, m' \neq m), \end{aligned} \tag{10.36}$$

where V'_m is the same as that defined by equation 10.14 except that the systematic utilities are rescaled by μ^d as follows:

$$V'_m = \frac{1}{\mu^d} \ln \sum_{d \in \mathbf{D}_{nm}} e^{(\tilde{V}_d + \tilde{V}_{dm})\mu^d}. \tag{10.37}$$

The log of the denominator of the conditional choice probability with a scale μ^d now has a coefficient equal to $1/\mu^d$. The new disturbance term ε'_m is defined by

$$\varepsilon'_m = \max_{d \in \mathbf{D}_{nm}} (\tilde{V}_d + \tilde{V}_{dm} + \tilde{\varepsilon}_{dm}) - V'_m$$

and is Gumbel distributed with scale parameter equal to μ^d. The combined disturbance $\tilde{\varepsilon}_m + \varepsilon'_m$ is by assumption IID Gumbel with a scale parameter μ^m for all $m \in \mathbf{M}_n$, and therefore

$$P_n(m) = \frac{e^{(\tilde{V}_m + V'_m)\mu^m}}{\sum_{m' \in \mathbf{M}_n} e^{(\tilde{V}_{m'} + V'_{m'})\mu^m}}. \tag{10.38}$$

Equation 10.38 with $\mu_m = 1$ is the same as equation 10.15 for the marginal mode choice probability of a joint logit model. The difference between equations 10.14 and 10.37 is that the term V'_m in the utility of 10.38 is the log of the denominator of the conditional probability multiplied by a parameter $1/\mu^d$, reflecting the fact that the disturbance component $\tilde{\varepsilon}_{dm}$ has a scale parameter $\mu^d \neq 1$. Note that since the scale of $\tilde{\varepsilon}_m + \varepsilon'_m$ is μ^m, the following inequality must be satisfied:

$$\frac{\mu^m}{\mu^d} \le 1. \tag{10.39}$$

Recall that the variance of a Gumbel variate is *inversely* proportional to the square of its scale parameter, and therefore

$$\frac{\mu^m}{\mu^d} = \left[\frac{\text{var}(\tilde{\varepsilon}_{dm})}{\text{var}(\tilde{\varepsilon}_m + \varepsilon'_m)} \right]^{1/2}$$

$$= \left[\frac{\text{var}(\tilde{\varepsilon}_{dm})}{\text{var}(\tilde{\varepsilon}_m) + \text{var}(\tilde{\varepsilon}_{dm})} \right]^{1/2},$$

where by construction we have $\text{var}(\varepsilon'_m) = \text{var}(\tilde{\varepsilon}_{dm})$, and we assume that $\text{cov}(\tilde{\varepsilon}_m, \tilde{\varepsilon}_{dm}) = 0$. Moreover $\mu^m/\mu^d = 1$ only if the variance of $\tilde{\varepsilon}_m$ is zero; that is, as long as $\tilde{\varepsilon}_m$ is not trivial, μ^m/μ^d, the coefficient of the log of the denominator of the conditional probability in the marginal mode choice model of the nested logit model will be between 0 and 1. Also when $\mu^m = \mu^d = 1$, equations 10.38 and 10.37 reduce to the marginal choice probability of the joint model in equations 10.15 and 10.14, where we have normalized the scale to equal 1.

The ratio of the scale parameters μ^m/μ^d also has a very natural interpretation in terms of the correlation between any two total utilities for alternatives sharing a common mode. Since

$$\frac{\mu^m}{\mu^d} = \left[\frac{\text{var}(\tilde{\varepsilon}_{dm})}{\text{var}(\tilde{\varepsilon}_{dm}) + \text{var}(\tilde{\varepsilon}_m)} \right]^{1/2}$$

$$= \left[1 - \frac{\text{var}(\tilde{\varepsilon}_m)}{\text{var}(\tilde{\varepsilon}_m) + \text{var}(\tilde{\varepsilon}_{dm})} \right]^{1/2}$$

$$= \left[1 - \frac{\text{cov}(U_{dm}, U_{d'm})}{[\text{var}(U_{dm}) \, \text{var}(U_{d'm})]^{1/2}} \right]^{1/2} \tag{10.40}$$

$$= \sqrt{1 - \text{corr}(U_{dm}, U_{d'm})}.$$

Thus the value of $1 - (\mu^m/\mu^d)^2$ *is equal to the correlation of the total utilities for any pair of alternatives in* $\mathbf{C}_n$ *that share a common mode.* (The same result can also be obtained for a nonzero covariance between $\tilde{\varepsilon}_m$ and $\tilde{\varepsilon}_{m'd}$ for $m = m'$.)

The reader can show that if we had instead assumed that the variance of

$\tilde{\varepsilon}_m$ (rather than the variance of $\tilde{\varepsilon}_d$) was zero and that all the preceding assumptions applied, then

$$P_n(d) = \frac{e^{(\bar{V}_d + V_d')\mu^d}}{\sum_{d' \in \mathbf{D}_n} e^{(\bar{V}_{d'} + V_{d'}')\mu^d}},$$ (10.41a)

where V_d' is defined by

$$V_d' = \frac{1}{\mu^m} \ln \sum_{m \in \mathbf{M}_{nd}} e^{(\bar{V}_m + \bar{V}_{dm})\mu^m}$$ (10.41b)

and

$$\frac{\mu^d}{\mu^m} = \sqrt{1 - \operatorname{corr}(U_{dm}, U_{dm'})}.$$ (10.42)

The reader should note that the value of μ^d/μ^m or μ^m/μ^d will be unknown and will have to be estimated along with the unknown parameters of the model. We return to this issue in section 10.4.

Conditional Choice Probabilities for Nested Logit

From the preceding results we can derive the conditional choice probabilities. Assuming again that $\operatorname{var}(\tilde{\varepsilon}_d) = 0$ and $\operatorname{var}(\tilde{\varepsilon}_m) > 0$, we derive the probability that destination d is selected conditional on mode m being chosen. Following the line of reasoning used in section 10.2 for deriving the conditional probability of a joint logit model, we obtain

$$\begin{aligned} P_n(d|m) &= Pr[U_{dm} \geq U_{d'm}, \forall d' \in \mathbf{D}_{nm}, d' \neq d|m \text{ chosen}] \\ &= Pr[\tilde{V}_{dm} + \tilde{V}_d + \tilde{\varepsilon}_{dm} \geq \tilde{V}_{d'm} + \tilde{V}_{d'} + \tilde{\varepsilon}_{d'm}, \forall d' \in \mathbf{D}_{nm}, \\ &\qquad d' \neq d|m \text{ chosen}]. \end{aligned}$$ (10.43)

The components of the total utility attributable to $\tilde{V}_m$ and $\tilde{\varepsilon}_m$ can be omitted because they are constant across all the alternatives in $\mathbf{D}_{nm}$. Since the disturbances $\tilde{\varepsilon}_{dm}$ satisfy the assumptions of the multinomial logit model,

$$P_n(d|m) = \frac{e^{(\bar{V}_{dm} + \bar{V}_d)\mu^d}}{\sum_{d' \in \mathbf{D}_{nm}} e^{(\bar{V}_{d'm} + \bar{V}_{d'})\mu^d}}.$$ (10.44)

Thus the conditional choice probability for a nested logit is a simple logit model, where the attributes that vary only across the modes are omitted and the choice set is defined as all destinations in $\mathbf{D}_{nm}$, and the utilities are scaled by a factor of μ^d. If we normalize $\mu^d = 1$, we obtain the same conditional probability as in the joint logit model in equation 10.25.

By a comparable line of reasoning, if $\mathrm{var}(\tilde{\varepsilon}_m) = 0$ and $\mathrm{var}(\tilde{\varepsilon}_d) > 0$, then

$$P_n(m|d) = \frac{e^{(\bar{V}_{dm}+\bar{V}_m)\mu^m}}{\sum_{m' \in \mathbf{M}_{nd}} e^{(\bar{V}_{dm'}+\bar{V}_{m'})\mu^m}}. \tag{10.45}$$

Extension of Nested Logit to Higher Dimensions

We have shown that when we define $\mathbf{C}_n$ as a two-dimensional choice set and represent the utility of each element of $\mathbf{C}_n$ as having unobserved components specific to each dimension, that the assumptions underlying the joint logit model are no longer appropriate. We have also shown that if the unobserved component of utility corresponding to one of the dimensions is negligible, a set of reasonable assumptions leads to the nested logit model. The same general approach can be extended to the case where there are more than two choice dimensions that constitute the multidimensional choice set. Suppose we have L choice dimensions, and define $\mathbf{C}_n$ as the choice set for a person n along the lth dimension. We define

$$\mathbf{C}_n = \mathbf{C}_1 \times \mathbf{C}_2 \times \cdots \times \mathbf{C}_L - \mathbf{C}_n^* \tag{10.16}$$

as the multidimensional choice set. We express the total utility of any alternative $i \in \mathbf{C}_n$ as the sum of its observed and unobserved components, each further divided into components defined by the dimensions of choice over which it varies. Thus, if we add a third dimension of choice of route to our mode and destination example, we would have $L = 3$. We label the route choice set as $\mathbf{R}_n$, and denote any element of $\mathbf{R}_n$ by r.

Using this notation, we can express the utility of an alternative in $\mathbf{C}_n$ as

$$U_{dmr} = \bar{V}_d + \bar{V}_m + \bar{V}_r + \bar{V}_{dm} + \bar{V}_{mr} + \bar{V}_{dr} + \bar{V}_{dmr}$$
$$+ \tilde{\varepsilon}_d + \tilde{\varepsilon}_m + \tilde{\varepsilon}_r + \tilde{\varepsilon}_{dm} + \tilde{\varepsilon}_{mr} + \tilde{\varepsilon}_{dr} + \tilde{\varepsilon}_{dmr}. \tag{10.47}$$

For the nested logit model to be used, we must assume that the dimensions can be ordered so as to satisfy the following conditions:

1. All components of the total disturbance involve level l, but *not all* the higher levels have zero variance.
2. All disturbance terms are mutually independent.
3. The sum of the disturbance terms at level l and those at the next lower level are identically Gumbel distributed.

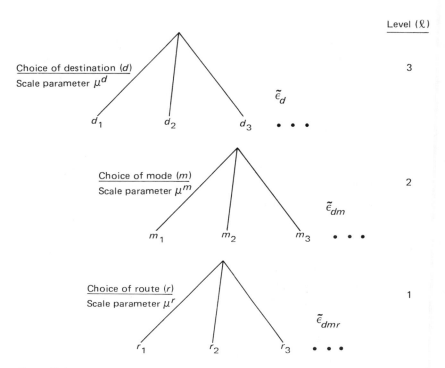

Figure 10.1
Depiction of the nested logit model for three levels

Thus in our three-level example suppose we order our dimensions as R, M, and D. For $l = 1$, condition 1 implies that var$(\tilde{\varepsilon}_r) = $ var$(\tilde{\varepsilon}_{mr}) = $ var$(\tilde{\varepsilon}_{dr}) = 0$; for $l = 2$, this same condition implies var$(\tilde{\varepsilon}_m) = 0$. Thus the random utility is assumed to be equal to $\tilde{\varepsilon}_d + \tilde{\varepsilon}_{dm} + \tilde{\varepsilon}_{dmr}$.

Condition 3 implies that $\tilde{\varepsilon}_{dmr}$ is Gumbel distributed. (Since it is the first level, it has no disturbance terms involving lower levels.) It also implies that $(\tilde{\varepsilon}_{dm} + \tilde{\varepsilon}_{dmr})$ is Gumbel distributed as is $(\tilde{\varepsilon}_d + \tilde{\varepsilon}_{dm} + \tilde{\varepsilon}_{dmr})$.

If these three conditions cannot be met for any ordering, then the assumption of the nested logit model will be violated. One way of visualizing what condition 1 implies is to describe the ordering of the choice dimension as a decision tree with the lowest level $(l = 1)$ at the bottom and the highest level $(l = L)$ at the top. This type of diagram is presented in figure 10.1 for the case $L = 3$. On each branch of the tree the relevant disturbance term of the total utility is displayed.

For the foregoing example the scale of $\tilde{\varepsilon}_{dmr}$ is denoted by μ^r, the scale of $(\tilde{\varepsilon}_{dmr} + \tilde{\varepsilon}_{dm})$ by μ^m, and the scale of $(\tilde{\varepsilon}_{dmr} + \tilde{\varepsilon}_{dm} + \tilde{\varepsilon}_d)$ by μ^d. We may choose to normalize the *total* disturbance, $\tilde{\varepsilon}_d + \tilde{\varepsilon}_{dm} + \tilde{\varepsilon}_{dmr}$, so that it has scale parameter $\mu^d = 1$. Another convenient normalization is $\mu^r = 1$.

Under the preceding assumptions we can express the nested logit choice probability as a product of marginal and conditional choice probabilities, each of which is a logit model. For the example given, the nested choice model is

$$P_n(dmr) = P_n(r|dm) P_n(m|d) P_n(d), \tag{10.48}$$

where

$$P_n(r|dm) = \frac{e^{(\bar{V}_r + \bar{V}_{mr} + \bar{V}_{dr} + \bar{V}_{dmr})\mu^r}}{\sum_{r' \in \mathbf{R}_{ndm}} e^{(\bar{V}_{r'} + \bar{V}_{mr'} + \bar{V}_{dr'} + \bar{V}_{dmr'})\mu^r}}, \tag{10.49}$$

$$P_n(m|d) = \frac{e^{(\bar{V}_m + \bar{V}_{dm} + V'_{dm})\mu^m}}{\sum_{m' \in \mathbf{M}_{nd}} e^{(\bar{V}_{m'} + \bar{V}_{dm'} + V'_{dm'})\mu^m}}, \tag{10.50}$$

$$P_n(d) = \frac{e^{(\bar{V}_d + V'_d)\mu^d}}{\sum_{d' \in \mathbf{D}_n} e^{(\bar{V}_{d'} + V'_{d'})\mu^d}}, \tag{10.51}$$

and where we define

$$V'_{dm} = \frac{1}{\mu^r} \ln \sum_{r \in \mathbf{R}_{ndm}} e^{(\bar{V}_r + \bar{V}_{mr} + \bar{V}_{dr} + \bar{V}_{dmr})\mu^r}, \tag{10.52}$$

$$V'_d = \frac{1}{\mu^m} \ln \sum_{m \in \mathbf{M}_{nd}} e^{(\bar{V}_m + \bar{V}_{dm} + V'_{dm})\mu^m}. \tag{10.53}$$

The remaining notation is a direct extension of that used earlier. For example, $\mathbf{R}_{ndm}$ is the set of all feasible routes for traveler n conditional on mode m and destination d being selected. The ratios μ^m/μ^r and μ^d/μ^m both must be positive and be less than or equal to 1 and therefore must satisfy the condition

$$\mu^d \le \mu^m \le \mu^r.$$

In other words, the variance of the random utilities is the smallest at the lowest level of the tree, and it cannot decrease as we move from a low to a higher level. For the case

$$\mu^d = \mu^m = \mu^r$$

we obtain a joint logit model.

Other Applications of Nested Logit

Although we have derived the nested logit model in the context of multidimensional choice, it is potentially applicable to a much wider range of problems. Basically it can be used to model any situation where subsets of the feasible alternatives share unobserved components of utility. For example, suppose a mode choice set has five elements defined as follows:

1. drive alone,
2. shared ride,
3. walk,
4. rail transit with walk access,
5. rail transit with bus access.

The two alternatives using rail transit might reasonably be viewed as sharing some unobserved utility related to the comfort, ride quality, safety, and other attributes of rail systems that we often omit from the systematic component of the utility function. In these situations we might use a nested logit model in which the lower level is a binary choice between alternatives 4 and 5, conditional on using rail transit, and the higher level is a marginal choice between driving alone, sharing a ride, walking, and rail transit. The decision tree representation of this model structure is shown in figure 10.2.

It is important to stress that the joint logit form is a special case of nested logit. It is therefore possible to estimate a nested logit model and test the null hypothesis that the ratio of scale parameters equals one for some or all levels. (See section 10.8 for an example of this type of test.) If we can reject this null hypothesis, then we can either continue to use the nested logit form or search for ways to measure the attributes that we believe are in the shared disturbance component and incorporate some or all of them into the specification of the systematic utility. This latter strategy (if feasible) will reduce the correlation between the utilities and will tend to make the joint form a better approximation of the choice process.

Another approach would be to estimate a joint logit model and employ the tests of the IIA propety that were presented in chapter 7. If in the preceding example we find that the logit model assumption cannot be accepted whenever alternatives 4 and 5 are included in the choice set, then we can proceed either to improve the specification of the systematic utilities of these two alternatives or to estimate a nested logit model with the structure depicted in figure 10.2.

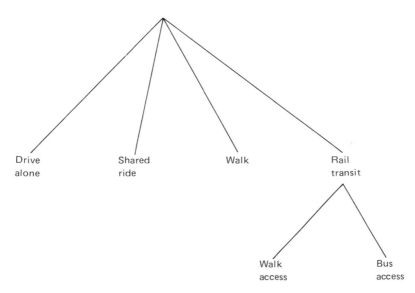

Figure 10.2
Depiction of the nested logit model for mode choice

10.4   Estimating the Nested Logit Model

The nested logit model, which was summarized for three levels in equations
10.49 through 10.53, presents what at first may appear to be a computationally difficult estimation problem. Of course, if all the μ's equal one,
the choice probabilities are given simply by the joint logit model, and the
procedures described in chapter 5 apply directly. However, in all other
cases the nested logit model is not equivalent to a simple logit model, and
new estimation problems must be addressed.

We will restrict our attention to linear in the parameters utility functions,
and we will consider first the two-level case. We define the following:

$$\tilde{V}_m = \boldsymbol{\beta}'_m \mathbf{x}_m.$$

$$\tilde{V}_d = \boldsymbol{\beta}'_d \mathbf{x}_d, \tag{10.54}$$

$$\tilde{V}_{dm} = \boldsymbol{\beta}'_{dm} \mathbf{x}_{dm},$$

where $\mathbf{x}_m$, $\mathbf{x}_d$, and $\mathbf{x}_{dm}$ correspond to attributes of destinations, modes, and
combinations of modes and destinations, respectively, and $\boldsymbol{\beta}_m$, $\boldsymbol{\beta}_d$, and $\boldsymbol{\beta}_{dm}$
are vectors of corresponding parameters.

In our example of a joint choice model given in section 10.2, this notation would imply that

$$\mathbf{x}_{dm} = \{x_{i1}, x_{i2}, x_{i3}\}',$$

$$\mathbf{x}_d = \{x_{i4}, x_{i5}\}',$$

$$\mathbf{x}_m = \{x_{i6}, x_{i7}\}'.$$

Given this notation, the most direct method to estimate a nested logit model would be to construct the likelihood function and then maximize it. If we use the case where elements of the choice set with the same mode share unobserved attributes (i.e., $\text{var}(\tilde{\varepsilon}_m) > 0$ and $\text{var}(\tilde{\varepsilon}_d) = 0$), then the likelihood function is

$$\mathcal{L}^* = \prod_{n=1}^{N} \prod_{(d,m) \in \mathbf{C}_n} [P_n(d,m)]^{y_{dmn}}$$

$$= \prod_{n=1}^{N} \prod_{(d,m) \in \mathbf{C}_n} [P_n(d|m) P_n(m)]^{y_{dmn}}, \tag{10.55}$$

where

$$y_{dmn} = \begin{cases} 1 & \text{if observation } n \text{ choose alternative } (d,m) \in \mathbf{C}_n, \\ 0 & \text{otherwise.} \end{cases}$$

Although this approach yields consistent and asymptotically efficient estimates of the parameters, it is computationally burdensome. For this reason an alternative procedure, termed *sequential estimation*, is often employed. It exploits the ease with which the nested logit model partitions into a product of distinct multinomial logit models. The log likelihood of the model for the choice of destination and mode can be expressed as

$$\mathcal{L} = \sum_{n=1}^{N} \sum_{(d,m) \in \mathbf{C}_n} y_{dmn} \ln [P_n(d|m) P_n(m)]$$

$$= \sum_{n=1}^{N} \sum_{(d,m) \in \mathbf{C}_n} y_{dmn} \ln P_n(d|m) + \sum_{n=1}^{N} \sum_{(d,m) \in \mathbf{C}_n} y_{dmn} \ln P_n(m) \tag{10.56}$$

$$= \sum_{n=1}^{N} \sum_{d \in \mathbf{D}_{nm*}} y_{dn} \ln P_n(d|m*) + \sum_{n=1}^{N} \sum_{m \in \mathbf{M}_n} y_{mn} \ln P_n(m),$$

where

$$y_{dn} = \begin{cases} 1 & \text{if observation } n \text{ choose destination } d \in \mathbf{D}_{nm*}, \\ 0 & \text{otherwise,} \end{cases}$$

$$y_{mn} = \begin{cases} 1 & \text{if observation } n \text{ choose mode } m \in \mathbf{M}_n, \\ 0 & \text{otherwise,} \end{cases}$$

and m^* denotes the chosen mode. Thus the log likelihood can be separated into two parts that correspond to the log likelihoods of the two probabilities, a conditional and a marginal log likelihood. A difficulty arises from the fact that some of the unknown parameters appear in both parts. In the preceding example $\boldsymbol{\beta}_{dm}$ and $\boldsymbol{\beta}_d$ appear in the model of $P_n(d|m)$ and are also included in the model of $P_n(m)$ through the expected maximum utility expression that we denoted by V_m'.

For the two-level model given here, the sequential estimation procedure consists of the following steps:

STEP 1:   Estimate the parameters $\mu^d \boldsymbol{\beta}_d$ and $\mu^d \boldsymbol{\beta}_{dm}$ by applying maximum likelihood estimation to the *conditional choice model*, $P_n(d|m)$. Note that when the systematic component of the utility function is linear in parameters, it is impossible to identify the effects of the coefficients $\boldsymbol{\beta}_d$ and $\boldsymbol{\beta}_{dm}$ from that of μ^d. A convenient normalization would be to set $\mu^d = 1$. Thus this stage yields estimates for $\boldsymbol{\beta}_d$ and $\boldsymbol{\beta}_{dm}$, and we will denote these estimates as $\hat{\boldsymbol{\beta}}_d$ and $\hat{\boldsymbol{\beta}}_{dm}$, respectively.

STEP 2:   Using $\hat{\boldsymbol{\beta}}_d$ and $\hat{\boldsymbol{\beta}}_{dm}$ from step 1, compute

$$\hat{V}_m' = \ln \sum_{d \in \mathbf{D}_{nm}} e^{(\hat{\boldsymbol{\beta}}_d' \mathbf{x}_d + \hat{\boldsymbol{\beta}}_{dm}' \mathbf{x}_{dm})}, \qquad \text{for all } m \in \mathbf{M}_n. \tag{10.57}$$

STEP 3:   Using $\hat{V}_m'$ *as a separate independent variable, estimate (via maximum likelihood) the parameters* $\mu^m \boldsymbol{\beta}_m$ and μ^m in the marginal choice model, $P_n(m)$. Denote these estimates $\widehat{\mu^m \boldsymbol{\beta}_m}$ and $\hat{\mu}^m$, respectively. Note that $\hat{\mu}^m$ is actually an estimate of the ratio μ^m/μ^d, since we arbitrarily normalized $\mu^d = 1$.

Then to apply the sequential estimator to the nested logit form where $\text{var}(\tilde{\varepsilon}_m) = 0$ (instead of $\text{var}(\tilde{\varepsilon}_d)$), we would estimate the parameters of $P_n(m|d)$ first, apply the normalization $\mu^m = 1$, use the resulting estimates $\hat{\boldsymbol{\beta}}_{dm}$ and $\hat{\boldsymbol{\beta}}_m$ to compute $\hat{V}_d'$, and estimate $\mu^d \boldsymbol{\beta}_d$ and μ^d from the marginal destination choice model, $P_n(d)$.

The key to this three-step procedure is the use of estimated value $\hat{V}_m'$ in place of the true value. In a sense what this does is to replace the true likelihood function with another, similar one which partitions into two distinct terms, a conditional and a marginal likelihood, as in equation

10.56, where a variable in the marginal is replaced by its estimate from the conditional likelihood. The estimates provided by this procedure are consistent, but they are not asymptotically efficient. Moreover Amemiya (1978) shows that when this procedure is applied using standard multinomial logit estimation programs, the variance-covariance matrices of the estimates printed for the marginal probabilities of higher-level models are incorrect and too small (in the matrix sense). Thus all of the reported standard errors from these programs will be too small. Amemiya also provides a formula for the correct asymptotic variance-covariance matrix for the sequential estimator in the special case where $\mu^m = 1$. McFadden (1981) has generalized this result for $\mu^m \neq 1$. In the more usual situation where $\mu^m \neq 1$, researchers often report the erroneous standard errors, recognizing that they are somewhat too small.

Using estimates from steps 1 and 3 we may wish to estimate values that are functions of estimated coefficients such as $\hat{\beta}_m / \hat{\mu}^m$ or $\hat{\beta}_d \cdot \hat{\mu}^m$. Assuming the steps 1 and 3 estimators are consistent, the consistency of these estimates are guaranteed by the Slutsky theorem. Using Cramér's approximation, the asymptotic variance of the product of two estimates, $\hat{\theta}_1$ and $\hat{\theta}_2$, can be shown to be given by

$$\mathrm{var}\,(\hat{\theta}_1 \cdot \hat{\theta}_2) = \hat{\theta}_2^2\,\bar{\mathrm{var}}(\hat{\theta}_1) + \hat{\theta}_1^2\,\mathrm{var}\,(\hat{\theta}_2) + 2\hat{\theta}_1\hat{\theta}_2\,\mathrm{cov}\,(\hat{\theta}_1, \hat{\theta}_2),$$

and the asymptotic variance of $1/\hat{\theta}_1$ is approximated by

$$\mathrm{var}\left(\frac{1}{\bar{\theta}}\right) = \frac{\mathrm{var}\,(\hat{\theta})}{4}$$

as long as θ is restricted to be not equal to zero.

To extend the sequential estimation procedure to an L-level nested choice model, we begin by estimating the conditional choice model at level $l = 1$ and then proceed "upward" through the decision tree using the log of the denominator from the $(l - 1)$th stage in the estimation of the lth stage parameters. Of course at each stage our estimate of the log of the denominator depends on all the prior stage estimates, possibly introducing significant amounts of variance. There is speculation (supported by some simulation evidence) that this compounding of error is a serious problem when one goes beyond three stages, though this obviously depends on the precision of the "lower" stage estimates.

Another estimation procedure for the nested logit model utilizes the sequential estimator as a starting point and draws on the following result used by Berndt et al. (1974):

Given any initial consistent estimator, the estimator found by taking one Newton-Raphson step toward the maximum of the log likelihood function is consistent and asymptotically efficient.

To apply this general result in this particular case, the first derivatives of the logarithm of equation 10.55 are linearized around the initial sequential estimates, and a single iteration of the Newton-Raphson step is performed. The resulting solution is asymptotically equivalent to the maximum likelihood estimates. An obvious choice of initial consistent estimates are those derived from the sequential estimation procedure. Small and Brownstone (1982) and Berkovec and Rust (1982) have applied this result.

10.5 Multidimensional Choice Models with Shared Unobserved Attributes: Multinomial Probit

Although the nested logit model has the advantage of retaining the desirable computational and other properties of the multinomial logit model, it has the disadvantage of requiring that some of the components of the total disturbance have zero variance. A natural alternative approach is to use the multinomial probit model, assuming that each component of the total disturbance is normally distributed.

As discussed in section 5.7, multinomial probit allows for any arbitrary variance-covariance structure of the disturbance terms. As a practical matter, however, multidimensional choice sets are generally large, and the number of elements in a completely arbitrary variance-covariance matrix for a large choice set will make probit estimation infeasible. For a choice set of size J there are $J(J + 1)/2$ distinct elements in the variance-covariance matrix, of which $(J + 1)$ are not identified. For $J = 20$, this implies 189 separate parameters to be estimated in addition to those associated with the V's.

Miller and Lerman (1978) argue that the natural structure of a multidimensional choice situation provides a basis for a reasonable specification of the probit variance-covariance matrix. In this section we briefly explore this special case.

Consider again the case of two choice dimensions. Recalling that

$$U_{dm} = \tilde{V}_d + \tilde{V}_m + \tilde{V}_{dm} + \tilde{\varepsilon}_d + \tilde{\varepsilon}_m + \tilde{\varepsilon}_{dm}, \tag{10.58}$$

we now assume that

$$\tilde{\varepsilon}_d \sim N(0, \sigma_d^2),$$

$$\tilde{\varepsilon}_m \sim N(0, \sigma_m^2), \qquad\qquad (10.59)$$

$$\tilde{\varepsilon}_{dm} \sim N(0, \sigma_{dm}^2),$$

and that the terms $\tilde{\varepsilon}_d$, $\tilde{\varepsilon}_m$, and $\tilde{\varepsilon}_{dm}$ are mutually independent. (Independence is not essential, but it is assumed here to simplify the presentation and retain consistency with our earlier discussion.)

Given these assumptions, we can derive the variance-covariance matrix of the total utilities for the complete multidimensional choice set. The elements of this matrix are

$$\text{var}(U_{dm}) = \sigma_d^2 + \sigma_m^2 + \sigma_{dm}^2, \qquad\qquad (10.60)$$

$$\text{cov}(U_{dm}, U_{d'm'}) = \begin{cases} \sigma_d^2 & \text{if } d = d' \text{ and } m \neq m', \\ \sigma_m^2 & \text{if } m = m' \text{ and } d \neq d', \\ 0 & \text{if } m \neq m' \text{ and } d \neq d'. \end{cases} \qquad (10.61)$$

In an actual implementation not all of the parameters σ_d^2, σ_m^2, and σ_{dm}^2 will be identified. In the simplest case where we assume that the variance of disturbance components $\tilde{\varepsilon}_d$, $\tilde{\varepsilon}_m$, and $\tilde{\varepsilon}_{dm}$ are constant across all d and m, only two of the three parameters of the variance-covariance matrix are identified; the third parameter sets the scale of the utilities. We could, however, allow the variances of the disturbance components to differ over various destinations and modes, yielding $J_D J_M + J_D + J_M$ unknown parameters. One of these parameters is not identified.

To our knowledge, work by Miller and Lerman (1981) on retail firm location and size (measured by floorspace) is the only study that uses multinomial probit for a multidimensional choice problem. Their results suggest the practicality of the approach for limited size choice sets. (Their model contained 14 alternatives per observation and relied on an approximation for the evaluation of the choice probabilities developed by Clark 1961.)

10.6 Measure of Accessibility

One of the key terms derived in section 10.2 was the systematic component of the maximum utility, denoted for the logit model by V'. We called this a *measure of accessibility* and noted that for the multinomial logit model it had a relatively tractable form. In particular, if $\mathbf{C}_n$ is a choice set, for multinomial logit

$$V'_n = \frac{1}{\mu} \ln \sum_{i \in \mathbf{C}_n} e^{\mu V_{in}}. \tag{10.62}$$

More generally we will define $\mathscr{E}[\max_{i \in \mathbf{C}_n} U_{in}]$ as our measure of accessibility, assuming that the utility scale is established such that $\mathscr{E}(\varepsilon) = 0$.

The reason we term expression 10.62 a measure of accessibility is that it is a scalar summary of the expected "worth" of a set of travel alternatives. In a more general context the systematic component of the maximum utility of all alternatives in a choice set is a measure of the individual's expected utility associated with a choice situation. This measure is individual specific, reflecting the differences in how various individuals evaluate their alternatives.

The value of this measure is not well defined unless some benchmark level of utility is established. For example, we have shown that the logit choice probabilities are unaffected by the addition of a constant to the utility of each alternative; the measure of accessibility, however, would be shifted upward by that constant. To be used properly, we must avoid comparing these measures using different models, and be careful to define the specification of the model we are using before interpreting accessibility measures.

Two properties that a scalar summary of accessibility would ideally have are as follows:

1. *Monotonicity with respect to choice set size.* This property implies that any addition to a person's choice set leaves the individual no worse off than before the addition, namely

$$\mathscr{E}\left[\max_{i \in \mathbf{C}_n} U_{in}\right] \leq \mathscr{E}\left[\max_{i \in \mathbf{C}'_n} U_{in}\right], \tag{10.63}$$

where $\mathbf{C}_n$ is a subset of $\mathbf{C}'_n$.

2. *Monotonicity with respect to the systematic utilities.* This property implies that the measure of accessibility does not decrease if the systematic utility of any of the alternatives in $\mathbf{C}_n$ increases. Mathematically this can be expressed as

$$\frac{\partial}{\partial V_{jn}} \mathscr{E}\left[\max_{i \in \mathbf{C}_n} U_{in}\right] \geq 0, \qquad \text{for all } j \in \mathbf{C}_n. \tag{10.64}$$

The first property holds for all choice models in which the expected value in equation 10.63 exists for both $\mathbf{C}_n$ and $\mathbf{C}'_n$. (See Ben-Akiva and Lerman 1977 and Williams 1977 for proofs of this proposition.) However, the second property does *not* hold for all choice models. Consider, for example, a binary probit model in which the variance of the total utility depends on the value of the measured component. Specifically assume that

$$U_{in} = V_{in} + \psi_{in} V_{in},$$
$$U_{jn} = V_{jn} + \psi_{jn} V_{jn}, \tag{10.65}$$

and (ψ_{in}, ψ_{jn}) are jointly normally distributed with mean zero, variances σ_i^2 and σ_j^2, respectively, and correlation ρ_{ij}. Under these assumptions Clark (1961) has shown that

$$\mathscr{E}[\max(U_{in}, U_{jn})] = V_{in}\Phi\left(\frac{V_{in} - V_{jn}}{a}\right) + V_{jn}\Phi\left(\frac{V_{jn} - V_{in}}{a}\right) + a\phi\left(\frac{V_{in} - V_{jn}}{a}\right), \tag{10.66}$$

where

$$\bar{a}^2 = V_{in}^2\sigma_i^2 + V_{jn}^2\sigma_j^2 - 2\sigma_i\sigma_j\rho_{ij}V_{in}V_{jn}. \tag{10.67}$$

Since $\Phi(-x) = 1 - \Phi(x)$, the right-hand side of equation 10.66 simplifies to

$$V_{jn} + (V_{in} - V_{jn})\Phi\left(\frac{V_{in} - V_{jn}}{a}\right) + a\phi\left(\frac{V_{in} - V_{jn}}{a}\right). \tag{10.68}$$

Now consider the derivative of equation 10.68 with respect to V_{in}. After some manipulation it can be shown that

$$\frac{\partial \mathscr{E}[\max(U_{in}, U_{jn})]}{\partial V_{in}} = \Phi\left(\frac{V_{in} - V_{jn}}{a}\right) + \frac{\partial a}{\partial V_{in}}\phi\left(\frac{V_{in} - V_{jn}}{a}\right). \tag{10.69}$$

Since $\Phi(x)$ and $\phi(x)$ are by definition always positive, equation 10.69 is negative when

$$\frac{\partial a}{\partial V_{in}} < \frac{\Phi[(V_{in} - V_{jn})/a]}{\phi[(V_{in} - V_{jn})/a]}, \tag{10.70}$$

where

$$\frac{\partial a}{V_{in}} = \frac{1}{a}(V_{in}\sigma_i^2 - \sigma_i\sigma_j\rho_{ij}V_{jn}). \tag{10.71}$$

It is quite possible for the condition in equation 10.70 to be met. As a numerical example, if

$$\sigma_i^2 = \sigma_j^2 = 1, \quad \rho = 0, \quad V_{in} = -1, \quad V_{jn} = 1, \tag{10.72}$$

then $\partial a/\partial V_{in} = -1/\sqrt{2} \cong -0.7171$. The expression $\tag{10.73}$

$$\frac{\Phi[(V_{in} - V_{jn})/a]}{\phi[(V_{in} - V_{jn})/a]} = \frac{\Phi(-2/\sqrt{2})}{\phi(-2/\sqrt{2})} \cong -0.5320. \tag{10.74}$$

Thus in this case the derivative of the accessibility measure with respect to V_{in} is less than zero. In intuitive terms, this inconsistency arises because the normal density is defined for both positive and negative arguments. The extreme negative tail for the distribution of ψ can make the derivative of $\mathscr{E}[\max(U_{in}, U_{jn})]$ with respect to V_{in} negative.

Harris and Tanner (1974) note that if one is willing to place a restriction on the distribution of the utilities, the derivative of the accessibility measure takes a particularly interesting form. Their restriction is what they term *translational invariance*, which can be interpreted as implying that a shift in the systematic component of the utility just translates the joint distribution of the utilities without altering its basic functional form. For example, the Gumbel distribution and the normal distribution *with a fixed variance-covariance* matrix is translationally invariant, whereas the preceding case of a normal distribution in which the variance depends on V_{in} and V_{jn} is not translationally invariant.

For the case of a translationally invariant distribution of the disturbances, one can show that

$$\frac{\partial \mathscr{E}[\max_{i \in C_n} U_{in}]}{\partial V_{jn}} = P_n(j), \qquad \forall j \in C_n. \tag{10.75}$$

In words, equation 10.75 states that the derivative of the accessibility measure with respect to the systematic component of the utility of any alternative is equal to that alternative's choice probability.

An obvious consequence of the foregoing result is that if the distribution of the utilities is translationally invariant, then

$$\sum_{j \in C_n} \frac{\partial \mathscr{E}[\max_{i \in C_n} U_{in}]}{\partial V_{jn}} = 1. \tag{10.76}$$

That is, if we increase the utility of every alternative by some amount ΔV, then the value of the accessibility measure increases by that same amount.

Another consequence of the result in equation 10.75 is that derivatives of any two choice probabilities with respect to the systematic utilities of the other alternatives are equal:

$$\frac{\partial P_n(j)}{\partial V_{in}} = \frac{\partial^2 \mathcal{E}[\max_{i \in C_n} U_{in}]}{\partial V_{in} \partial V_{jn}} = \frac{\partial P_n(i)}{\partial V_{jn}}. \tag{10.77}$$

Thus, as noted by Williams (1977), we can calculate a measure of consumer surplus. The choice model is viewed as an individual's demand curve for an alternative. The difference in an individual's consumer surplus between two situations corresponding to attribute vectors $\mathbf{x}_n^1$ and $\mathbf{x}_n^2$ or vectors of systematic utilities $\mathbf{V}_n^1$ and $\mathbf{V}_n^2$ is

$$\sum_{i \in C_n} \int_{\mathbf{V}_n^1}^{\mathbf{V}_n^2} P(i|\mathbf{V}) d\mathbf{V}, \tag{10.78}$$

where the choice probability is denoted as conditional on the vector of systematic utilities in order to make the dependency explicit. For the logit model it can be shown that the result of 10.78 is

$$\frac{1}{\mu} \ln \sum_{i \in C_n^2} e^{\mu V_{in}^2} - \frac{1}{\mu} \ln \sum_{i \in C_n^1} e^{\mu V_{in}^1}, \tag{10.79}$$

which is the difference among expected maximum utilities in the two situations (see equation 10.62). Note that this measure is expressed in utility terms that could be transformed into monetary units in various ways, such as by dividing this measure by a coefficient of travel cost. See, for example Small (1983) and Khajavi (1981) who used this consumer surplus interpretation to evaluate alternative urban road pricing and traffic management schemes.

10.7　Derivation of the Nested Logit Model from the Generalized Extreme Value Model

In this section we derive the generalized extreme value (GEV) model that was first introduced in chapter 5 and show how the nested logit model can be derived as a special case. (This section, however, can be skipped without loss of continuity.) The GEV model is

$$P_n(i) = \frac{e^{V_i} G_i(e^{V_1}, \ldots, e^{V_J})}{\mu G(e^{V_1}, \ldots, e^{V_J})},$$ (10.80)

where

$G(\ )$ = a non-negative, homogeneous of degree $\mu > 0$ function defined for non-negative arguments, $G(\ ) \to +\infty$ when any of the arguments goes to $+\infty$ and the jth partial derivative with respect to j distinct arguments is non-negative for odd j and nonpositive for even j,

$G_i(\ ) = \partial G(\ )/\partial(e^{V_i})$ is the derivative of $G(\ )$ with respect to its ith argument.

The GEV model was derived by McFadden (1978) directly from the concept of random utilities. The general expression for a random utility choice model that was presented in chapter 5 is

$$P_n(i) = \int_{\varepsilon = -\infty}^{+\infty} F_i(V_i - V_1 + \varepsilon, \ldots, V_i - V_J + \varepsilon) d\varepsilon,$$ (10.81)

where

$F(\ )$ = a cumulative distribution function of the disturbances $(\varepsilon_1, \ldots, \varepsilon_J)$,

$F_i(\ ) = \partial F(\ )/\partial \varepsilon_i$ is the joint cumulative distribution functions for all $\varepsilon_j, j \neq i$, and a density for ε_i.

The GEV model is obtained from the following cumulative distribution function:

$$F(\ ) = \exp[-G(e^{-\varepsilon_1}, \ldots, e^{-\varepsilon_J})].$$ (10.82)

To derive the GEV choice probability from the random utility model, we use equation 10.82 in equation 10.81 to obtain

$$P_n(i) = \int_{\varepsilon = -\infty}^{+\infty} e^{-\varepsilon} G_i(e^{-\varepsilon - V_i + V_1}, \ldots, e^{-\varepsilon - V_i + V_J})$$

$$\cdot \exp[-G(e^{-\varepsilon - V_i + V_1}, \ldots, e^{-\varepsilon - V_i + V_J})] d\varepsilon.$$ (10.83)

To solve this integral, we rely on the homogeneity of degree μ of $G(\ )$ and the homogeneity of degree $\mu - 1$ of $G_i(\ )$ to obtain the model in 10.80.

McFadden (1978) has shown that the properties of the function $G(\ )$ listed here imply that 10.82 is a proper cumulative distribution function. The marginal distribution of the μ homogeneous GEV distribution (10.82) is given by

$$F(\varepsilon_i) = \lim_{\substack{\varepsilon_j \to \infty \\ \forall j \neq i}} F(\varepsilon_1, \ldots, \varepsilon_J)$$

$$= \lim_{\substack{\varepsilon_j \to \infty \\ \forall j \neq i}} \exp[-e^{-\mu\varepsilon_i} G(e^{-\varepsilon_1+\varepsilon_i}, \ldots, e^{-\varepsilon_J+\varepsilon_i})]$$

$$= \exp(-e^{-\mu\varepsilon_i} \cdot G(0, \ldots, \overset{i\text{th place}}{1}, \ldots, 0)]$$

Note that $G(0, \ldots, 1, \ldots, 0)$ is a constant specific to alternative i. Define $\eta_i = (1/\mu) \ln G(0, \ldots, 1, \ldots, 0)$ and substitute in the preceding expression to obtain

$$F(\varepsilon_i) = \exp[-e^{-\mu(\varepsilon_i + \eta_i)}]$$

which is the univariate extreme value or the Gumbel distribution with scale parameter μ and location parameter η_i. The location parameters are usually assumed to be zero because a nonzero η_i is incorporated in the systematic utility V_i as an alternative-specific constant. Thus $\eta_i = 0$ implies that for all i

$$G(0, \ldots, 1, \ldots, 0) = 1. \tag{10.85}$$

Note that in this case Euler's theorem (see section 5.7) implies that for all i

$$G_i(0, \ldots, 1, \ldots, 0) = \mu. \tag{10.86}$$

The homogeneity of degree μ of $G(\ )$ and the homogeneity of degree $(\mu - 1)$ of $G_i(\ )$ imply that the GEV model (10.80) can be rewritten as

$$P_n(i) = \frac{1}{\mu} \frac{G_i(e^{V_1-V_i}, \ldots, 1, \ldots, e^{V_J-V_i})}{G(e^{V_1-V_i}, \ldots, 1, \ldots, e^{V_J-V_i})}. \tag{10.87}$$

Thus, as in the logit model, only the $(J-1)$ differences of systematic utilities could be identified. The conditions in (10.85) and (10.86) may be used to show that as the utility differences $V_j - V_i$ for all $j \neq i$ approach $-\infty$, the choice probability $P_n(i)$ approaches 1.

The GEV model (10.80) can also be expressed by

$$P_n(i) = \frac{\partial[(1/\mu)\ln G(e^{V_1},\ldots,e^{V_J})]}{\partial V_i}. \tag{10.88}$$

By comparisons with equation 10.75 (see also McFadden 1981), we observe that the expected maximum utility for the GEV model is

$$V' = \frac{1}{\mu}\ln G(e^{V_1},\ldots,e^{V_J}). \tag{10.89}$$

We will derive the nested logit model in two ways. Consider first the following $G(\ )$ function with a single-scale parameter μ:

$$G(e^{V_1},\ldots,e^{V_J}) = \sum_{m=1}^{M}\left(\sum_{i\in \mathbf{D}_m} e^{V_i}\right)^{\mu}, \tag{10.90}$$

where the choice set $(1,\ldots,J)$ is partitioned into M nonoverlapping subsets $\mathbf{D}_m$, $m = 1,\ldots,M$. The conditions on the derivative of $G(\ )$ given for equation 10.80 are as follows. The first derivative must be non-negative,

$$\frac{\partial G(\ )}{\partial e^{V_i}} = \mu\left(\sum_{j\in \mathbf{D}_m} e^{V_j}\right)^{\mu-1}, \qquad \text{for } i\in \mathbf{D}_m;$$

thus $\mu \geq 0$. The second derivative with respect to two distinct elements must be nonpositive,

$$\frac{\partial^2 G(\ )}{\partial e^{V_j}\partial e^{V_i}} = \begin{cases} \mu(\mu-1)(\sum_{j\in \mathbf{D}_m} e^{V_j})^{\mu-2} & \text{for } i \text{ and } j\in \mathbf{D}_m, \\ 0 & \text{for } i\in \mathbf{D}_m \text{ and } j\notin \mathbf{D}_m; \end{cases}$$

thus $\mu \leq 1$. These two conditions specify the range

$$0 \leq \mu \leq 1,$$

which satisfies also the conditions for the signs of higher-order derivatives. Use the $G(\ )$ function of equation 10.90 in the GEV model to obtain

$$\begin{aligned} P_n(i) &= \frac{e^{V_i}\mu(\sum_{i\in \mathbf{D}_m} e^{V_i})^{\mu-1}}{\mu\cdot\sum_{m=1}^{M}(\sum_{i\in \mathbf{D}_m} e^{V_i})^{\mu}} \\ &= \frac{e^{V_i}}{\sum_{i\in \mathbf{D}_m} e^{V_i}}\cdot\frac{(\sum_{i\in \mathbf{D}_m} e^{V_i})^{\mu}}{\sum_{m=1}^{M}(\sum_{i\in \mathbf{D}_m} e^{V_i})^{\mu}} \\ &= P_n(i|m)\cdot P_n(m). \end{aligned} \tag{10.91}$$

Define

$$V'_m = \ln \sum_{i \in \mathbf{D}_m} e^{V_i} \tag{10.92}$$

and substitute in 10.91 to get

$$P_n(m) = \frac{e^{\mu V'_m}}{\sum_{m'} e^{\mu V'_{m'}}} \tag{10.93}$$

and

$$P_n(i|m) = \frac{e^{V_i}}{e^{V'_m}}. \tag{10.94}$$

This is the formulation of the nested logit model considered in the previous sections with the scale of the lower-level model normalized to 1.

Further insight into the properties of the nested logit model can be obtained by deriving this two-level model with two scale parameters. We consider the following μ^m homogeneous $G(\ )$ function

$$G(\ ) = \sum_{m=1}^{M} \left(\sum_{i \in \mathbf{D}_m} e^{\mu^d V_i} \right)^{\mu^m/\mu^d}. \tag{10.95}$$

The conditions on the switching of signs of the derivatives are always satisfied if

$$\mu^d \geq \mu^m \geq 0.$$

Substitute the $G(\ )$ function in equation 10.95 in the GEV model to obtain the following nested logit model:

$$P_n(i) = \frac{e^{V_i}(\mu^m/\mu^d)\left(\sum_{i \in \mathbf{D}_m} e^{\mu^d V_i}\right)^{\mu^m/\mu^d - 1} \cdot \mu^d e^{V_i(\mu^d - 1)}}{\mu^m \sum_{m=1}^{M} \left(\sum_{i \in \mathbf{D}_m} e^{\mu^d V_i}\right)^{\mu^m/\mu^d}}$$

$$P_n(i) = \frac{e^{\mu^d V_i}}{\sum_{i \in \mathbf{D}_m} e^{\mu^d V_i}} \cdot \frac{\left(\sum_{i \in \mathbf{D}_m} e^{\mu^d V_i}\right)^{\mu^m/\mu^d}}{\sum_{m=1}^{M} \left(\sum_{i \in \mathbf{D}_m} e^{\mu^d V_i}\right)^{\mu^m/\mu^d}}. \tag{10.96}$$

Once again using the definition

$$V'_m = \frac{1}{\mu^d} \ln \sum_{i \in \mathbf{D}_m} e^{\mu^d V_i}, \tag{10.97}$$

we can express 10.96 as

$$P_n(i) = \frac{e^{\mu^d V_i}}{e^{\mu^d V'_m}} \cdot \frac{e^{\mu^m V'_m}}{\sum_{m'=1}^{M} e^{\mu^m V'_{m'}}}. \tag{10.98}$$

Since it is not possible to identify both μ^d and μ^m, we can denote the log of the denominator of the conditional probability by v'_m ($= \mu^d V'_m$) and $\mu^d V_i$ as v_i and rewrite 10.98 as follows:

$$P_n(i) = \frac{e^{v_i}}{e^{v'_m}} \cdot \frac{e^{(\mu^m/\mu^d)v'_m}}{\sum_{m'=1}^{M} e^{(\mu^m/\mu^d)v'_{m'}}}. \tag{10.99}$$

Therefore the higher-level scale parameter is the ratio μ^m/μ^d, with

$$0 < \frac{\mu^m}{\mu^d} \le 1.$$

Thus in the sequential estimator of the nested logit model, the coefficient of the log of the denominator variable that is created from a lower-level model is a ratio of the two scale parameters.

As we did in sections 4.2 and 5.2, we proceed now to investigate the properties of the nested logit model when the scale parameters approach their limiting values.

CASE 1 ($\mu^d \to +\infty$): The limit of the lower level probability $P_n(i|m)$, which is a standard multinomial logit model, was derived in section 5.2. It is equal to 1 if V_i is the largest systematic utility for $i \in \mathbf{D}_m$.

To obtain this limit for the marginal probability, we first consider the limit of V'_m as follows:

$$\lim_{\mu^d \to \infty} \frac{1}{\mu^d} \ln \sum_{j \in \mathbf{D}_m} e^{\mu^d V_j} = \lim_{\mu^d \to \infty} \frac{1}{\mu^d} \ln \left[e^{\mu^d V_i}\left(1 + \sum_{\substack{j \in \mathbf{D}_m \\ j \ne i}} e^{\mu^d(V_j - V_i)} \right) \right]$$

$$= V_i + \lim_{\mu^d \to \infty} \frac{1}{\mu^d} \ln \left(1 + \sum_{\substack{j \in \mathbf{D}_m \\ j \ne i}} e^{\mu^d(V_j - V_i)} \right)$$

$$= \begin{cases} V_i & \text{if } V_j - V_i < 0, \text{ for all } j \in \mathbf{D}_m, j \ne i, \\ > V_i & \text{otherwise.} \end{cases}$$

Therefore, by choosing the largest systematic utility, it is possible to write

$$\lim_{\mu^d \to \infty} V'_m = \max_{i \in \mathbf{D}_m} V_i.$$

Thus, as the variance of the random utility for the lower level of the model vanishes, the expected maximum utility approaches the value of the greatest systematic utility. In this limiting case the *lower-level* model is a *deterministic choice model*. The upper-level model from (10.98) can be written as

$$P_n(m) = \frac{\exp[\mu^m \max_{i \in \mathbf{D}_m}(V_i)]}{\sum_{m'=1}^{M} \exp[\mu^m \max_{i \in \mathbf{D}_{m'}}(V_i)]}$$

CASE 2 ($\mu^m \to 0$): The upper-level model predicts equally likely alternatives (i.e., constant shares) and the lower-level model is unchanged.

CASE 3 ($\mu^d = \mu^m = \mu$): We obtain the joint logit model

$$P_n(i) = \frac{e^{\mu V_i}}{\sum_{m=1}^{M} \sum_{j \in \mathbf{D}_m} e^{\mu V_j}}.$$

10.8   An Example of a Multidimensional Choice Model

We illustrate the application of the theory developed in this chapter by reporting some of the results of estimating the parameters of the shopping trip mode and destination choice model used as an example in section 10.2. These results are adapted from Ben-Akiva (1973). We begin by summarizing the joint estimation results for the joint logit form and then describe the comparable results for two nested logit models estimated by the different estimation procedures.

The data used were a subsample of 123 trips taken from the 1968 Washington, D.C., Home Interview Survey. All the observed travelers began their trip at home and returned there after shopping. The destination of the trip was defined as one of the 1,065 traffic analysis zones used in Washington. Each sampled trip had between 2 and 16 alternatives in the choice set.

Table 10.1 is a summary of the independent variables used in the models along with a notation for the "type of variable," defining whether the particular variable belongs to the vectors $\mathbf{x}_d$, $\mathbf{x}_m$, or $\mathbf{x}_{dm}$.

The three different model forms are depicted graphically and summarized in table 10.2. For convenience we have distinguished between the two nested logit forms by labeling them *A* and *B*. For the sake of simplicity in the graphical representation, we have assumed that each individual has two modes and J_D destinations and that all $2 \cdot J_D$ combinations are feasible. In actuality, however, the choice set varies across individuals, as indicated in the mathematical representation in table 10.2.

Table 10.1
Definition of variables in shopping mode and destination choice model

Variable number	Variable name	Type of variable	Definition
1	Out-of-vehicle time	x_{dm}	out-of-vehicle travel time (min.)
2	In-vehicle time	x_{dm}	in-vehicle travel time (min.)
3	Cost/log income	x_{dm}	travel cost (¢) divided by the natural log of household annual income* (in 1,000 $) plus one.
4	Log employment	x_d	natural log of wholesale and retail employment at destination zone
5	CBD constant	x_d	$\begin{cases} 1 \text{ if destination is in CBD} \\ 0 \text{ otherwise} \end{cases}$
6	Auto constant	x_m	$\begin{cases} 1 \text{ if mode is auto} \\ 0 \text{ otherwise} \end{cases}$

Note: The income variable used in this study was collected and coded using the following categories:

Code value	Income range (1968 $/year)
1	0–$3,000
2	$3,000–$4,000
3	$4,000–$6,000
4	$6,000–$8,000
5	$8,000–$10,000
6	$10,000–$12,000
7	$12,000–$15,000
8	$15,000–$20,000
9	$20,000–$25,000
10	≥ $25,000

Joint Logit Model

Table 10.3 presents the parameter estimates for the joint choice model. The signs and the relative magnitudes of the coefficients are as expected, with the estimated marginal effect of out-of-vehicle time greater than of in-vehicle time by about a factor of five. The estimated standard errors for the in-vehicle travel time and for the CBD destination constant are relatively high as compared to the coefficient estimates. However, this is not surprising inasmuch as the total sample was quite small.

Nested Logit Result

Form *A* Using Sequential Estimator   The estimation results for the nested logit model corresponding to form *A* are presented in table 10.4. In terms of

Table 10.2
Alternative choice model structures for example

Model structure	Mathematical form

Joint logit

$$(d_1, m_1)(d_1, m_2)(d_2, m_1)\ldots(d_{J_D}, m_2)$$

$$P_n(d, m) = \frac{e^{\beta'_d \mathbf{x}_d + \beta'_m \mathbf{x}_m + \beta'_{dm} \mathbf{x}_{dm}}}{\sum_{d' \in \mathbf{D}_n} \sum_{m' \in \mathbf{M}_{nd}} e^{\beta'_d \mathbf{x}_{d'} + \beta'_m \mathbf{x}_{m'} + \beta'_{dm} \mathbf{x}_{d'm'}}}$$

Nested form A

$$P_n(d, m) = \left(\frac{e^{(\beta'_d \mathbf{x}_d + V'_d)\mu^d}}{\sum_{d' \in \mathbf{D}_n} e^{(\beta'_d \mathbf{x}_{d'} + V'_{d'})\mu^d}} \right) \left(\frac{e^{\beta'_m \mathbf{x}_m + \beta'_{dm} \mathbf{x}_{dm}}}{\sum_{m' \in \mathbf{M}_{nd}} e^{\beta'_m \mathbf{x}_{m'} + \beta'_{dm} \mathbf{x}_{dm'}}} \right),$$

$$\text{where } V'_d = \ln \sum_{m \in \mathbf{M}_{nd}} e^{\beta'_m \mathbf{x}_m + \beta'_{dm} \mathbf{x}_{dm}}$$

Nested form B

$$P_n(d, m) = \left(\frac{e^{(\beta'_m \mathbf{x}_m + V'_m)\mu^m}}{\sum_{m' \in \mathbf{M}_n} e^{(\beta'_m \mathbf{x}_{m'} + V'_{m'})\mu^m}} \right) \left(\frac{e^{\beta'_d \mathbf{x}_d + \beta'_{dm} \mathbf{x}_{dm}}}{\sum_{d' \in \mathbf{D}_{nm}} e^{\beta'_d \mathbf{x}_{d'} + \beta'_{dm} \mathbf{x}_{d'm}}} \right),$$

$$\text{where } V'_m = \ln \sum_{d \in \mathbf{D}_{nm}} e^{\beta'_d \mathbf{x}_d + \beta'_{dm} \mathbf{x}_{dm}}$$

Table 10.3
Maximum likelihood estimation results for joint logit model

Variable number	Variable name	Coefficient estimate	Asymptotic standard error	t statistic
1	Out-of-vehicle time	-0.0619	0.0195	-3.17
2	In-vehicle time	-0.0122	0.0117	-1.04
3	Cost/log income	-0.0469	0.0110	-4.27
4	Log employment	0.515	0.167	3.09
5	CBD constant	0.628	0.480	1.31
6	Auto constant	-0.742	0.541	-1.37

Summary statistics
Number of observations $= 123$
Number of cases $= 1,253$
$\mathscr{L}(0) = -277.7$
$\mathscr{L}(\hat{\beta}) = -204.4$
$-2[\mathscr{L}(0) - \mathscr{L}(\hat{\beta})] = 146.5$
$\rho^2 = 0.264$
$\bar{\rho}^2 = 0.242$

the derivation in section 10.3, this form corresponds to the case where var $(\tilde{\varepsilon}_d) > 0$ and var $(\tilde{\varepsilon}_m) = 0$. In words, this is where the utilities of multidimensional alternatives sharing a common destination are assumed correlated, but the utilities for alternatives sharing a common mode are not.

The model was estimated using the sequential estimation technique described in section 10.4, and the reported standard errors for the second stage are not corrected. Note that two sets of summary statistics are listed, one for each stage of the estimation. For example, the "number of observations" for the first stage in table 10.4 corresponds to the count of observations used in estimating the conditional mode choice model, namely mode choice conditional on the destination decision. Similarly the first set of log likelihood values in table 10.4 are for the conditional mode choice model. Only 114 of the original 123 observations are used in the destination choice model because 9 observations have only a single destination available.

We have denoted the values of the log likelihood functions for each of the two stages somewhat differently in table 10.4. In particular, the arguments to $\mathscr{L}$ reflect the part of the total log likelihood and the parameters over

Table 10.4
Sequential estimation results for nested logit model form A: $[P(d) \cdot P(m|d)]$

Variable number	Variable name	Coefficient estimate	Asymptotic standard error	t statistic
1	Out-of vehicle time	−0.0390	0.0233	−1.67
2	In-vehicle time	−0.0252	0.0300	−0.84
3	Cost/log income	−0.0890	0.0279	−3.19
4	Log employment	0.435	0.169[a]	2.58[a]
5	CBD constant	0.615	0.443[a]	1.39[a]
6	Auto constant	−0.320	0.730	−0.44
7	Scale parameter (μ^d)	0.446	0.102[a]	4.36[a]

First-stage summary
(conditional mode choice)
Number of observations = 123
Number of cases = 123
$\mathcal{L}(0) = -85.3$
$\mathcal{L}(\hat{\beta}_m, \hat{\beta}_{dm}) = -21.6$
$-2[\mathcal{L}(0) - \mathcal{L}(\hat{\beta}_m, \hat{\beta}_{dm})] = 127.4$
$\rho^2 = 0.747$
$\bar{\rho}^2 = 0.700\ (K = 4)$

Second-stage summary
(marginal destination choice)
Number of observations = 114
Number of cases = 565
$\mathcal{L}(0) = -192.4$
$\tilde{\mathcal{L}}(\hat{\beta}_d, \hat{\mu}^d) = -181.3$
$-2[\mathcal{L}(0) - \tilde{\mathcal{L}}(\hat{\beta}_d, \hat{\mu}^d)] = 22.3$
$\rho^2 = 0.058$
$\bar{\rho}^2 = 0.042(K = 3)$

Combined model summary
$\mathcal{L}(0) = -277.7$
$\mathcal{L}(\hat{\beta}, \hat{\mu}) = -202.9$
$\rho^2 = 0.269$
$\bar{\rho}^2 = 0.244$

a. Not corrected for two-stage estimation.

which it was maximized. For example, for the first stage (the conditional mode choice model) the log likelihood is denoted as $\mathscr{L}(\hat{\beta}_m, \hat{\beta}_{dm})$ since the value of $\hat{\beta}_d$ does not enter into the first-stage estimation. The second-stage log likelihood is denoted by $\tilde{\mathscr{L}}(\hat{\beta}_d, \hat{\mu}^d)$. The tilde on $\mathscr{L}$ denotes the fact that it is not true log likelihood but rather is conditional on the first-stage estimates. The likelihood ratio statistic is also affected because for the first stage it is χ^2 distributed with degrees of freedom equal to the number of estimated parameters; in this case there are five parameters in the first stage. In the second stage the likelihood ratio statistic is conditional on the first-stage estimates.

The values of the total likelihood function at zero and at the estimated values are also given and are used to calculate a likelihood ratio index for the combined model. We note that $\bar{\rho}^2$ has increased from 0.242 for the joint logit model with six parameters to 0.244 for this nested logit model with seven parameters.

One of the notable features in table 10.4 is that the estimated value of μ^d is significantly different from one at the 95% level of confidence. (Recall that $\mu^d = 1$ corresponds to a joint logit model.) This test is somewhat biased toward rejection of the null hypothesis that $\mu^d = 1$ by the fact that the reported standard error for μ^d is too small. Thus, though not conclusive, it is indicated that we may be able to reject the null hypothesis that $\mu^d = 1$ corresponding to the joint logit model.

Form B Using Sequential Estimator   The alternative case to the one reported in table 10.4 is where we assume that var$(\tilde{\varepsilon}_m) > 0$ and var$(\tilde{\varepsilon}_d) = 0$. In words, this is the case where the utilities of alternatives sharing a common mode are correlated, but the utilities for alternatives sharing a common destination are not. The results of the two-stage estimation for this nested logit form are presented in table 10.5. Again the standard errors for the second-stage estimates have not been corrected.

In this nested logit model form the estimated coefficient for μ^m is greater than one, a contradiction to the underlying theory of the nested logit model. Using the reported standard error for $\hat{\mu}^m$, this difference between the estimated value and one is statistically significant at the 90% confidence level, suggesting that the fact that the $\hat{\mu}^d > 1$ in the alternative sequence of form A may not be attributable to sampling error. Note also that the model of form A has the largest value of ρ^2 and $\bar{\rho}^2$ of all three models.

Table 10.5
Sequential estimation results for nested logit model form B: $[P(m) \cdot P(d|m)]$

Variable number	Variable name	Coefficient estimate	Asymptotic standard error	t statistic
1	Out-of-vehicle time	-0.0566	0.0376	-1.50
2	In-vehicle time	-0.0253	0.0140	-1.81
3	Cost/log income	-0.0300	0.0127	-2.36
4	Log employment	0.419	0.171	2.46
5	CBD constant	0.606	0.471	1.29
6	Auto constant	-1.55	0.566^a	-2.75^a
7	Scale parameter (μ^m)	1.53	0.300^a	5.08^a

First-stage summary
(conditional destination choice)
Number of observations $= 114$
Number of cases $= 565$
$\mathscr{L}(\mathbf{0}) = -192.4$
$\mathscr{L}(\hat{\boldsymbol{\beta}}_d, \hat{\boldsymbol{\beta}}_{dm}) = -177.8$
$-2[\mathscr{L}(\mathbf{0}) - \mathscr{L}(\hat{\boldsymbol{\beta}}_d, \hat{\boldsymbol{\beta}}_{dm})] = 29.3$
$\rho^2 = 0.076$
$\bar{\rho}^2 = 0.050 \ (K = 5)$

Second-stage summary
(marginal mode choice)
Number of observations $= 123$
Number of cases $= 123$
$\mathscr{L}(\mathbf{0}) = -85.3$
$\mathscr{L}(\hat{\boldsymbol{\beta}}_m, \hat{\mu}^m) = -26.3$
$-2[\mathscr{L}(\mathbf{0}) - \mathscr{L}(\hat{\boldsymbol{\beta}}_m, \hat{\mu}^m)] = 117.8$
$\rho^2 = 0.691$
$\bar{\rho}^2 = 0.668 (K = 2)$

Combined model summary
$\mathscr{L}(\mathbf{0}) = -277.7$
$\mathscr{L}(\hat{\boldsymbol{\beta}}, \hat{\mu}) = -204.1$
$\rho^2 = 0.265$
$\bar{\rho}^2 = 0.240$

a. Not corrected for two-stage estimation.

Table 10.6
Maximum likelihood estimation results for nested logit model form A:
$[P(d) \cdot P(m|d)]$

Variable number	Variable name	Coefficient estimate	Asymptotic standard error	t statistic
1	Out-of-vehicle time	−0.0429	0.0128	−3.35
2	In-vehicle time	−0.0348	0.0346	−1.03
3	Cost/log income	−0.0850	0.0265	−3.20
4	Log employment	0.429	0.189	2.27
5	CBD constant	0.609	0.447	1.36
6	Auto constant	−0.603	0.866	−0.70
7	Scale parameter (μ^d)	0.433	0.177	2.45

Summary statistics
Number of observations = 123
Number of cases = 1,253
$\mathscr{L}(0) = -277.7$
$\mathscr{L}(\hat{\beta}, \hat{\mu}^d) = -202.7$
$\mathscr{L}(\hat{\beta}_m, \hat{\beta}_{dm}) = -21.7$
$\mathscr{L}(\hat{\beta}_d, \hat{\mu}^d) = -181.0$
$-2[\mathscr{L}(0) - \mathscr{\hat{L}}(\hat{\beta}, \hat{\mu}^d)] = 150.0$
$\rho^2 = 0.270$
$\bar{\rho}^2 = 0.245$

Maximum Likelihood Estimation Results

The estimation results presented thus far were obtained from a standard multinomial logit estimator. These estimates are consistent but not efficient. For this rather simple example with a small number of unknown parameters and a small sample size it is relatively simple to obtain the maximum likelihood estimates that are also asymptotically efficient. The results for the two nested logit models are presented in tables 10.6 and 10.7. The two additional scale parameters are both statistically significantly different from one (which is the restriction implied by the joint logit model). The maximum likelihood estimator of the nested logit model form B has the largest value of $\bar{\rho}^2$. In terms of the test of non-nested hypotheses using the $\bar{\rho}^2$ (see section 7.4), we can conclude that the probability that model B's $\bar{\rho}^2$ exceeds model A's $\bar{\rho}^2$ by more than 0.006, given that model A is the

Table 10.7
Maximum likelihood estimation results for nested logit model form B:
$[P(m) \cdot P(d|m)]$

Variable number	Variable name	Coefficient estimate	Asymptotic standard error	t statistic
1	Out-of-vehicle time	−0.0136	0.00680	−0.200
2	In-vehicle time	−0.0136	0.00965	−1.41
3	Cost/log income	−0.0381	0.0101	−3.77
4	Log employment	0.429	0.184	2.34
5	CBD constant	0.489	0.481	1.02
6	Auto constant	−0.969	0.978	−0.99
7	Scale parameter (μ^m)	2.89	0.967	2.99

Summary statistics
Number of observations = 123
Number of cases = 1,253
$\mathscr{L}(\mathbf{0}) = -277.7$
$\mathscr{L}(\hat{\boldsymbol{\beta}}, \hat{\mu}^m) = -201.1$
$\mathscr{L}(\hat{\boldsymbol{\beta}}_d, \hat{\boldsymbol{\beta}}_{dm}) = -178.6$
$\mathscr{L}(\hat{\boldsymbol{\beta}}_m, \hat{\mu}^m) = -22.5$
$-2[\mathscr{L}(\mathbf{0}) - \mathscr{L}(\hat{\boldsymbol{\beta}}, \hat{\mu}^m)] = 153.2$
$\rho^2 = 0.276$
$\bar{\rho}^2 = 0.251$

Table 10.8
Comparison of elasticities from the maximum likelihood estimates of the joint logit and the two nested logit models

Mode shares elasticities with respect to:	Joint logit		Nested logit: $[P(m) \cdot P(d|m)]$		Nested logit: $[P(d) \cdot P(m|d)]$	
	Bus	Auto	Bus	Auto	Bus	Auto
Bus out-of-vehicle time	−0.76	0.16	−0.39	0.08	−0.46	0.09
Bus in-vehicle time	−0.15	0.03	−0.34	0.07	−0.32	0.06
Bus travel cost	−0.63	0.13	−0.82	0.17	−0.80	0.16
Auto out-of-vehicle time	0.29	−0.06	0.12	−0.02	0.15	−0.03
Auto in-vehicle time	0.08	−0.02	0.18	−0.04	0.18	−0.04
Auto travel cost	0.50	−0.10	0.66	−0.14	0.69	−0.14

Table 10.9
Corrected standard errors for the sequential estimators

	Uncorrected standard error	Corrected standard error
Estimated Coefficients in P(d), table 10.3		
4 Log employment	0.169	0.216
5 CBD constant	0.443	0.464
7 Scale parameter (μ^d)	0.102	0.241
Estimated Coefficients in P(m), table 10.4		
6 Auto constant	0.566	0.623
7 Scale parameter (μ^m)	0.300	0.915

correct model, is less than 3%. However, model B is unsatisfactory on theoretical grounds because it has an estimated value of μ^m that is greater than one and not in agreement with the requirement that it be less than one. The maximum likelihood estimates of the nested logit model form A are very similar to those obtained from the sequential estimator.

The importance of the model structure can also be evaluated using the estimated aggregate elasticities presented in table 10.8 for the models in tables 10.3, 10.6, and 10.7. These elasticities were calculated using the sample enumeration methods, changing one variable at a time by $+10\%$ and applying the model to predict new joint probabilities of mode and destination choice. The overall pattern indicates a greater degree of similarity of elasticities between the two nested logit models relative to the joint logit model.

Corrected Upper-Level Standard Errors and One-Step Newton-Raphson Estimates

The standard errors of the coefficients' estimates in an upper-level model, which are calculated by the sequential estimator, are biased downward. The magnitude of this bias for our example is demonstrated by the corrected standard errors given in table 10.9 for the upper-level models of the two nested logit model forms. As the sample size increases, the magnitude of the required correction will diminish.

As discussed earlier, an asymptotically efficient estimator can be constructed by using only the first Newton-Raphson step toward the maximum likelihood estimator from the initial consistent estimates found by the

Table 10.10
One-step Newton-Raphson estimation results for the nested logit model form A:
$[P(d) \cdot P(m|d)]$

Variable number	Variable name	Coefficient estimate	Asymptotic standard error	t statistic
1	Out-of-vehicle time	−0.0429	0.0130	−3.31
2	In-vehicle time	−0.0491	0.0391	−1.26
3	Cost/log income	−0.0880	0.0264	−3.33
4	Log employment	0.392	0.187	2.10
5	CBD constant	0.588	0.444	1.33
6	Auto constant	−0.890	0.916	−0.97
7	Scale parameter (μ^d)	0.373	0.145	2.57

Summary statistics
Number of observations = 123
Number of cases = 1,253
$\mathcal{L}(0) = -277.7$
$\mathcal{L}(\hat{\beta}, \hat{\mu}^d) = -202.9$
$\mathcal{L}(\hat{\beta}_m, \hat{\beta}_{dm}) = -22.0$
$\mathcal{L}(\hat{\beta}_d, \hat{\mu}^d) = -180.9$
$2[\mathcal{L}(0) - \mathcal{L}(\hat{\beta}, \hat{\mu}^d)] = 149.6$
$\rho^2 = 0.269$
$\bar{\rho}^2 = 0.244$

sequential estimator. The use of a one-step Newton-Raphson procedure is demonstrated for the two nested logit models. The starting values are the sequential estimators given in tables 10.4 and 10.5. The results for the one Newton-Raphson step for the combined model are given in tables 10.10 and 10.11. In one case there is a noticeable improvement in the goodness of fit and some significant shifts in the values of some estimated coefficients. Thus the additional effort of obtaining an efficient estimator may be beneficial in small samples.

Conclusions on Example

The example described in this section has shown how joint and nested logit models can be estimated. Although the empirical results are from a relatively small sample, they suggest that the chosen structure for the choice probabilities may be important. Obviously this conclusion should be tempered by the realization that the differences we observe in the estimates for

Table 10.11
One-step Newton-Raphson estimation results for the nested logit model form B:
$[P(m) \cdot P(d|m)]$

Variable number	Variable name	Coefficient estimate	Asymptotic standard error	t statistic
1	Out-of-vehicle time	−0.0215	0.00923	−2.33
2	In-vehicle time	−0.0116	0.0102	−1.14
3	Cost/log income	−0.0439	0.0106	−4.12
4	Log employment	0.545	0.187	2.92
5	CBD constant	0.415	0.485	0.86
6	Auto constant	−1.70	0.905	−1.88
7	Scale parameter (μ^m)	2.36	0.794	2.97

Summary statistics
Number of observations = 123
Number of cases = 1,253
$\mathscr{L}(0) = -277.7$
$\mathscr{L}(\hat{\beta}, \hat{\mu}^m) = -202.9$
$\mathscr{L}(\hat{\beta}_d, \hat{\beta}_{dm}) = -178.8$
$\mathscr{L}(\hat{\beta}_m, \hat{\mu}^m) = -24.1$
$-2[\mathscr{L}(0) - \mathscr{L}(\hat{\beta}, \hat{\mu}^m)] = 149.6$
$\rho^2 = 0.269$
$\bar{\rho}^2 = 0.244$

different model structures may be attributable to the fact that all three forms are incorrect and that this fundamental misspecification manifests itself differently in each form. For example, we could estimate the multinomial probit form described in section 10.6, and we might find that the variances of both $\tilde{\varepsilon}_d$ and $\tilde{\varepsilon}_m$ are large (relative to that of $\tilde{\varepsilon}_{dm}$) and statistically different from zero. This would indicate that neither nested logit form is wholly appropriate.

10.9   Summary

In this chapter we have shown how multidimensional choice sets are generated and explored the problems that arise in analyzing individuals' choices when facing such choice sets. In the simplest case where the effect of the multidimensional choice set is confined to the observed attributes that comprise the systematic component of the utility, there is no real distinction between the multidimensional choice situations and the simpler cases analyzed in earlier chapters. If the assumptions of the multinomial logit model hold, we are able to derive both the conditional and marginal choice probabilities in a multinomial logit form. We referred to this case as the *joint logit model*.

In situations where the elements of the underlying choice sets that form the multidimensional choice set have separate unobserved components, the joint logit model no longer holds. In particular, the utilities of the multidimensional alternatives are no longer independent. In these situations we showed that it may be possible to use a generalization of the logit model, termed *nested logit*, as long as the correlations between utilities have a particular structure. In the example of mode and destination choice, we required a variety of assumptions to derive the nested logit model, the most crucial of which is that one of the following two assumptions hold:

1. The utilities of multidimensional alternatives sharing a common mode are correlated, but the utilities of alternatives sharing a common destination are not.
2. The utilities of multidimensional alternatives sharing a common destination are correlated, but the utilities of the alternatives sharing a common mode are not.

Maximum likelihood estimates of the nested logit model may be computationally difficult to find. However, a simpler sequential estimator for the parameters of the nested logit was derived. Though not fully efficient, this procedure can be used with existing multinomial logit estimation procedures.

Multinomial probit is an alternative model of multidimensional choice. A natural structure for the variance-covariance matrix of the disturbances was described. This structure is more general than the one implicit in nested logit, but maximum likelihood estimation of the parameters is difficult. Aside from the need to create specific computer programs for the special structure of this probit form, maximum likelihood estimation of the multinomial probit model can be computationally burdensome for large choice sets.

Finally, a case study of shopping mode and destination choice model was described. The results demonstrate how the sequential, the one step Newton-Raphson, and the maximum likelihood estimators can be used and illustrate the differences in coefficient estimates and elasticities that result from different assumptions about the distribution of the utilities.

11 Systems of Models

11.1 Introduction

This chapter describes the development of systems of models, their structure, and their use for forecasting. It begins with a general discussion of the issues involved in model system design and then presents two examples: an aggregate model system using aggregation by the classification method and a microsimulation model system using the sample enumeration aggregation method.

Before proceeding, we present an outline of the major steps involved in developing a model system and the major considerations in each step. The remainder of the chapter, both in the discussion and example sections, will address many, though not all, of these steps:

1. *Problem definition.* Policies to be analyzed, what forecasts are needed, resources available, time frame of the analysis, computational environment.

2. *Model system design.* Exogenous variables (inputs), model structure (market segments, alternatives, etc.), aggregation method, relationship to "supply side" (i.e., attributes of the alternatives as functions of aggregate demand).

3. *Inventory of existing data.* Available survey data, sources of information on attributes of the alternatives, transportation level of service attributes (by time of day, mode, destination, etc.), population, employment, and other land-use data.

4. *Survey data collection.* Sample design, questionnaire design, implementation, coding, error checking.

5. *Exploratory survey data analysis.* Cross tabulation of survey data (e.g., alternative choice frequencies by market segment), comparisons with other data sources, adequacy of data for the model that was designed (e.g., number of observations for an infrequently chosen mode), decision to collect additional data, if necessary (see step 2 or 4).

6. *Estimation data base.* Selection of the observations from the survey, preparation of the data files on attributes of alternatives (including level of service and land-use data), preparation of estimation data files from the survey observations and attributes data.

7. *Model estimation.* Selection of statistical model, estimation method, and software; updating and transfering previously estimated models (e.g., transfer a nonwork model and reestimate a work trip model).

8. *Disaggregate tests.* Disaggregate prediction tests, market segmentation tests, decision to return to step 7, if necessary.

9. *Forecast system(s) design.* Computational environment, aggregation method, forecasts of changes in the exogenous variables.

10. *Tests of the aggregate forecasting system(s).* Replicate base case data, decision to return to step 9 (or even 7), if necessary.

11. *Validation.* Test the prediction accuracy of the model using external data (that was not used to estimate the model) such as data from before and after a change in a transportation system, decision to return to step 7 or 9, if necessary.

12. *Forecasting and policy analysis.*

11.2   Issues in Model System Design

A model system is a collection of individual models with the links among them defined by the model system structure. All the practical issues that are present in the development of an individual model are magnified in the construction of a model system. In addition a forecasting model system must include an aggregation method. In some applications some form of demand/supply equilibration procedure is also required. Thus the design of a model system involves numerous practical and theoretical considerations, the most relevant of which are discussed in this section.

Policy Issues and the Domain of the Model System

The motivation for developing model systems is to analyze the effects of alternative policies, plans, and scenarios. These analysis needs determine the types of predictions, their level of detail and accuracy, and the time frame in which they are required. Consideration of the travel behavior under study should also lead, in light of the anticipated policy and environmental changes, to a decision about the domain of the model system. It specifies the phenomena that should be modeled and the major input and output variables of the model system. Variables that are likely to be significantly affected by policy should be explicitly treated. The variables are divided into two groups: endogenous variables that are determined within the model system and exogenous variables that are input to the model system.

Computational Environment

Computational cost is often a significant factor in model system design. This cost also includes nonmonetary aspects of computation, such as the turnaround time and ease of access. The rapid advances in computer technology have led to drastic cost reductions and greatly improved access. This in turn had led to the widespread use of large-scale simulation models for policy analysis. This chapter presents two examples of such computer models. It should be noted, however, that simpler models using calculators and small computers have also been developed (e.g., see Landau 1976, Manheim et al. 1980, Litinas and Ben-Akiva 1982).

Another important consideration is the choice of the software environment. For example, most of the recent urban transportation model systems were implemented in the software environment provided by the Urban Transportation Planning System (UTPS), developed and maintained by the U.S. Department of Transportation. The use of existing software is particularly important in large-scale model systems that require large data bases and in which program development costs and computational efficiencies play a major role.

Data Resources

Data collection can be the most expensive and time-consuming task in policy analysis and planning studies. Therefore model development studies very often rely on existing data sources. This may adversely affect the specifications of the models by dictating the definition of alternatives and choice sets and by limiting the selection of explanatory variables. Once a model system has been developed, the major data concern in the use of the models is the availability of input data or forecasts of the exogenous variables. The issue that must be addressed during the design of a model system is how to treat important explanatory variables for which reliable exogenous forecasts are not available at the level of detail that is required by the model system. On the one hand, omitting these variables from the model may cause serious specification errors. On the other hand, including them in the model will lead to forecasting errors.

Analytical Approaches and Model System Structure

The choice of models and techniques is influenced by theoretical, statistical, and practical considerations. The chosen analytical approach must satisfy the analysis requirements and must be feasible within the analysis resource constraints. The requirements are determined from the policy issues under consideration. The resource limitations arise from data, computational, personnel, and other constraints.

The major aspects of the analytical approach of a model system are (1) the structure of the choice models, or the choice hierarchy, (2) the aggregation method and the preparation of input data, and (3) the equilibration procedure, if included.

The *model system structure* specifies the flow of information between the different components or subsystems. The key assumption of the model system structure is in the form of a choice hierarchy. It is used to simplify a complex multidimensional choice problem by representing it as a sequence of choices. This sequence can be representative of a dynamic decision-making process or a structure of similarities or degree of substitution among alternatives.

The presentation of multidimensional choice models in chapter 10 elucidated the methods of linking together individual choice models. However, with a large number of choice models in complex model systems the total number of alternatives can be sufficiently large that a joint logit or a nested logit model becomes unreasonably complex. (These models may also be considered as unrealistic from a behavioral point of view.) Thus some simplifying assumptions must often be made on the basis of a priori reasoning.

As discussed in chapter 6, the selection of an *aggregation procedure* is influenced by input data availability, accuracy requirements, and the required level of detail of the forecasts. The two approaches that have been used most often in practical studies have been sample enumeration (also known as microsimulation) and market segmentation.

An *equilibration procedure* is required whenever the attributes of the alternatives cannot be assumed to be exogenous. In general, the values of the attributes of an alternative are dependent on the level of the aggregate demand for that alternative. For example, an increase in the number of commuters who drive to work results in greater congestion and longer travel times by car. However, some attributes are determined exogenously and may be controlled by the policies that are being analyzed, and others may have a weak dependence on aggregate demand that can be neglected. For example, the choice of auto type may be treated as exogenous in a short-range analysis. Practical implementation of complex demand model systems incorporating equilibration is a difficult task and so is seldom done. One example, however, is provided by Ben-Akiva et al. (1977).

The consideration of these issues is reflected in the following two sections that present two transportation model systems, one for regional transportation planning and the other for short-range policy analyses.

11.3   A System of Urban Travel Demand Models for Metropolitan Region Transportation Planning

This section is based on Ruiter and Ben-Akiva (1978). More detailed documentation is available in a three-volume report by Cambridge Systematics, Inc. (1978). The purpose of this section is to give an overview of the travel demand model system that was developed for the Metropolitan Transportation Commission (MTC), the metropolitan planning organization for the San Francisco area. The model system was designed to deal with all aspects of urban passenger travel, including the assignment of transit person trips and highway vehicle trips to the appropriate facilities. The output had to provide the basis for areawide transportation planning studies.

The data base for model development was taken from existing sources. At the time of this study, a 1965 travel survey was the most recent complete travel data set. In addition all necessary related data, such as highway and transit networks, level of service (e.g., access times and distances and parking costs), and land use, were available for 1965. All such data were also available with a common zoning system of 290 zones contained in 30 districts.

Model System Structure

Travel Choices Represented in the Model System   In general, a travel demand model is concerned with those household and individual decisions that result in trips being made. However, some other choices are so strongly interrelated with actual trip-making behavior that it is impossible to separate them from such decisions. For example, the choice of residential location is not in itself a trip-making decision. However, the combination of a worker's employment location choice and his or her household's location decision has as its consequence a trip choice, namely daily work trips.

For this reason the general framework from which the components of the MTC model system are derived begins with the following set of travel-related household choices:

1. employment location (for all workers),
2. residential location,
3. housing type,
4. automobile ownership,

5. mode to worker (for all workers),
6. frequency (for nonwork trips of each purpose),
7. destination (for nonwork trips of each purpose),
8. time of day (for nonwork trips of each purpose),
9. mode (for nonwork trips of each purpose),
10. route (for all trips).

In theory each decision may be dependent on the rest. For example, where one chooses to live is obviously linked to the housing type and the level of automobile ownership one selects. Similarly shopping trip destination and mode are likely to be closely linked. This perspective, if carried through completely, would produce a model of unmanageable dimensions. Fortunately there are some interrelationships among components of this set that are of a fundamentally different character than others. Some of the decisions, such as residential location choice, have high transaction costs and are consequently stable over fairly long time intervals; other choices, such as the frequency of social and recreational trips, are altered on a daily basis. Some decisions are more logically represented as being made collectively by the household, whereas others can be approximated as individual choices. Thus it is possible to formulate explicit hypotheses and to establish a structure of the total set of choices as a logical working hypothesis. This structure is termed a hierarchy of choice (Ben-Akiva 1973, Ben-Akiva et al. 1976).

Figure 11.1 illustrates the three-stage choice hierarchy represented by the MTC model system. At the highest level are urban development decisions, which are long run in nature. Employers decide where to provide jobs, and developers decide where to provide housing of various types. Next come household mobility decisions, which are made more frequently. These include where to live and work, how many household members will have jobs, how often they will each go to work, how many autos to own, and which modes will be used to make work trips. Finally, some short-run travel decisions are made almost daily: frequency, destination, and mode for nonwork trips and then time of day and route for all trips.

MTC has a separate, large-scale land-use model that predicts each of the development decisions shown in figure 11.1, plus the residential location decision. The travel demand models discussed here predict each of the remaining decisions.

Figure 11.2 shows in greater detail how the mobility and travel choice levels of this choice hierarchy are represented in the MTC model system.

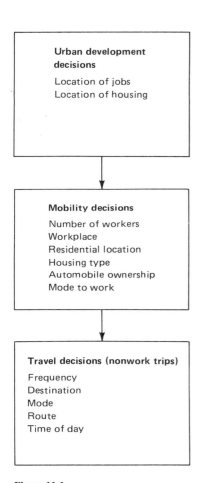

Figure 11.1
A three-stage choice hierarchy (source: Ruiter and Ben-Akiva 1978)

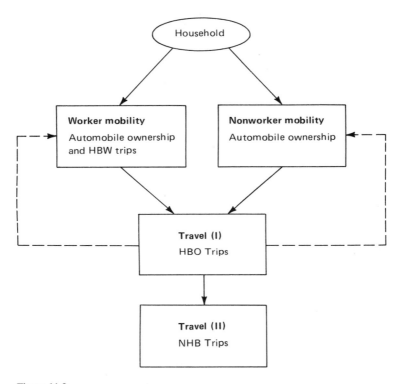

Figure 11.2
Overall structure of the MTC model system: HBW = home-based work, HBO =
home-based other, NHB = nonhome based (source: Ruiter and Ben-Akiva 1978).

The mobility decisions of households with and without workers are handled
separately, and travel decisions are divided into two groups: home-based
other travel (nonwork) and nonhome based (NHB). (A home-based trip
has either an origin or a destination at home.) The dotted lines indicate that
there is also an indirect provision for nonwork travel (HBO) to affect
mobility decisions.

The trip purposes used in the model system are (1) home-based work
trips (HBW), defined as all trips between home and work, irrespective of
direction; (2) home-based other trips (HBO), defined as home-based nonwork travel, represented by two sets of models, one for generalized shopping and personal business trips (including also medical-dental, business-
related, and serving passenger purposes), and one for social-recreational
trips (including eating, visiting, and recreation purposes); and (3) nonhome

based (NHB), defined as all trips that do not begin or end at home. These three purpose groups include all surveyed trips except school trips.

The modes considered in the models include auto and small truck drivers and passengers, as well as all bus, streetcar, railroad, and jitney trips. Trips by heavy trucks, taxi and by walkers are not represented in the models.

Although the structure shown in figure 11.2 is strongly related to the conceptual choice hierarchy shown in figure 11.1, it incorporates a number of features and approximations necessary for producing a practical regional forecasting system. These include the following points:

1. The mobility choice block for households with workers distinguishes between primary and secondary workers in a household. Each household with workers has only one primary worker, or "breadwinner". All additional workers are termed secondary.

2. The modeling system deals separately with home-based and nonhome-based trips. This simplifies the representation of trip chains (a trip from home, followed by one or more nonhome-based trips, followed finally by a trip to home).

3. There are exceptions to the sequence indicated by the solid line arrows connecting the choice blocks. These are shown by the dashed-line arrows. Each of these respresents an accessibility variable in the higher-level model (e.g., auto ownership for households without workers) that is obtained from a lower-level model (home-based other destination and mode choice). Each of these variables is based on the full set of variables of the lower-level model. These variables allow consistent representation of level-of-service effects despite the sequential structure of the model system. (A detailed presentation of these multidimensional choice models is given in chapter 10.)

4. The time-of-day decision is modeled by using historical peaking characteristics rather than a choice model based on the relationship between peak and off-peak transportation system characteristics.

5. The vehicle occupancy for nonwork travel is forecast by using historically observed rates rather than choice models.

6. The route-choice decision is modeled by using deterministic minimum path assignment techniques. (Equilibration is performed using conventional capacity restraint methods.)

Before describing the models in each of the choice blocks illustrated in figure 11.2, the nature of the linkages implied by the dashed lines in the figure will be made explicit, and the types of independent variables used in the system will be described.

Linkages between the models   The components of the MTC model system are linked in two ways. First, "low-level" models are conditional on the predicted choices of "higher-level" models, as indicated by the solid arrows in figure 11.2; second, feedback in the form of composite or accessibility variables are calculated by using lower-level models and included in higher-level models, as indicated by the dashed arrows.

The first type of linkage is determined by the assumed choice hierarchy and the resulting sequence of models. Variables resulting from higher-level choices are predetermined for lower-level choices and are attributes of the household or the individual that do not vary among alternative lower-level choices. For example, auto ownership is treated as a household characteristic in the HBO models.

The composite variables represent expectations of the outcomes of lower-level choices that could be different among alternatives of higher-level choices. For example, level-of-service by transit for shopping trips affects auto ownership. However, this variable depends on the household choice of shopping trips, a decision made only conditional on the household auto ownership. Thus the specific shopping level of service is indeterminate in the choice of auto ownership. However, composite variables representing overall shopping level of service for alternative auto ownership levels can be determined. The attributes that vary among lower-level choices are aggregated and included as composite variables in the models of higher-level choices.

It is shown in chapter 10 that if a lower-level choice is modeled by a random utility model then an appropriate composite variable defined over these choice alternatives is the expected maximum utility for this choice process. If the outcome of this choice were known, then the composite variable would be taken as the utility of the chosen alternative. For the logit model, this is equal to the natural logarithm of the denominator of the model (see section 10.3).

Variables Included   The independent variables in the MTC model system can be classified into four groups:

1. highway level of service (e.g., auto travel time and out-of-pocket cost),
2. transit level of service (e.g., fare and wait time),

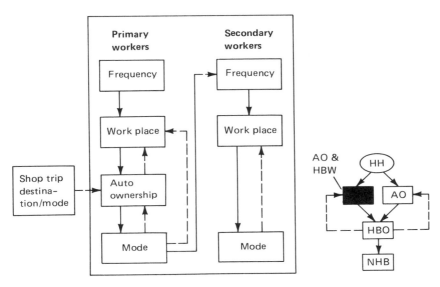

Figure 11.3
Worker mobility models (source: Ruiter and Ben-Akiva 1978)

3. land use (e.g., retail employment),
4. socioeconomic characteristics of potential travelers (e.g., annual income).

These variables affect all the travel-related choices that were described earlier. The emphasis is on full sensitivity to level of service attributes that would permit a credible forecasting of the consequences of pricing policies, auto restraint measures, and other service changes that affect not only modal choice but frequency and destination choices as well.

Component Models

Each of the four travel choice blocks shown in figure 11.2 can be discussed by presenting the component models and showing their interrelationships.

Worker Mobility Models   Figure 11.3 displays the details of the worker mobility models which include a full set of HBW models and a model of auto ownership for households with workers. Workers are differentiated into primary (one per working household, chosen on the basis of the income of the worker) and secondary (all other workers) groups. For each,

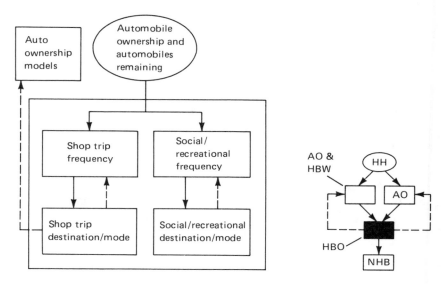

Figure 11.4
Travel models I: home-based other trips (source: Ruiter and Ben-Akiva 1978)

nested models of trip frequency, workplace choice and mode choice are provided. The trip frequency model predicts the number of HBW trips per day. The workplace choice models use accessibility terms for each destination by all modes obtained from the mode-choice models. Household auto ownership is affected by the workplace choice of the primary worker by means of an expected utility variable that measures the relative ease of traveling to this destination by auto and transit. In addition the relative ease of traveling to all shopping destinations by auto and transit is allowed to influence household auto ownership levels.

Nonworker Mobility Models   Because they make no work trips, only auto ownership is predicted for households without workers. The model uses information on the relative accessibility to shopping destinations by auto and transit, as well as household income and residential density measures to predict the probability of owning any given number of autos.

Travel Models I: Home-Based Other   As shown in figure 11.4, for each home-based other trip purpose (shopping and social/recreational) two models exist. These models predict trip frequency and the joint choice of

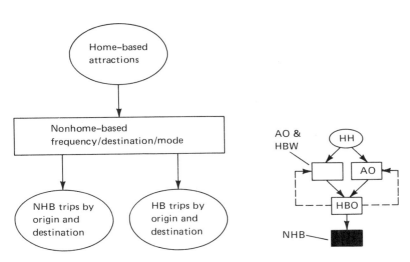

Figure 11.5
Travel models II: nonhome-based trips (source: Ruiter and Ben-Akiva 1978)

destination and mode. Trip frequency is dependent on the auto ownership, the number of cars not used for work travel by household members, and the expected utility of travel to all available destinations by either auto or transit. This structure allows the amount of nonwork travel to change as auto use for work travel varies and as the level of service in the transportation system varies.

Travel Models II: Nonhome Based   Figure 11.5 presents the structure of the NHB models. The nonhome destination of home-based trips by mode are the basis for a model of NHB trip frequency and destination choice. The frequency decision is binary; that is, either the traveler goes home (frequency 0) or he or she makes an NHB trip (frequency 1) to one of the destination alternatives in the choice set. Explicit modeling of mode choice can be omitted if the observed frequency of tours involving mode switching is negligible. In this case the mode choice for NHB trips can be assumed to be determined by the home-based trip mode choices. In other words, separate NHB models could be estimated for each mode, and the inputs to the NHB models are for a specific mode. The details of these NHB models are given in Ben-Akiva et al. (1978).

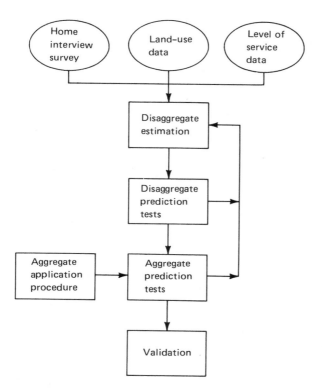

Figure 11.6
Disaggregate model development process (source: Ruiter and Ben-Akiva 1978)

Prediction Tests and Application Procedures

Disaggregate and Aggregate Prediction Tests   An aggregate forecasting system based on disaggregate models can be tested in both its aggregate and disaggregate forms. Figure 11.6 presents a schematic outline of the overall model development process, starting with estimation. Disaggregate estimation requires a·sample of observed travel decisions and socioeconomic characteristics from a home interview or other survey, land-use data to describe the attractiveness of destinations, and level-of-service data to describe travel alternatives.

As shown in figure 11.6, following model estimation, the next step in the overall model development process is a series of disaggregate prediction tests. The estimated component models can be tested one at a time, passing each observed trip in the estimation data set through the disaggregate model system to produce tables of predicted and observed choices (see section 7.6). Weakness in model specification may show up as systematic mispredictions by market segment, such as income groups, or by explanatory variable, such as travel time. The feedback loop from disaggregate prediction to disaggregate estimation in figure 11.6 represents the decision to return to the estimation step based on the failure of a given model specification. Only after each model has passed the disaggregate tests does the process proceed to aggregate prediction and validation.

In the aggregate prediction of the base-year data, it may be necessary to modify the models by changing the locations and scales of the utilities. This requirement arises from the use of average characteristics per zone to represent all households in a zone. This adjustment of the disaggregate choice model to correct for aggregation errors was described as a hybrid aggregation procedure in section 6.4. It was necessary in the MTC model system to correct the distance-related factors in the utilities of the destination choice alternatives to match observed trip length distributions. Also, in attempting to match zone-to-zone or district-to-district volumes of trips, it was necessary to add trip interchange constants (in some cases) to balance observed and predicted aggregate trip data.

If the disaggregate testing procedure in figure 11.6 is followed carefully, there should be no need to return from the aggregate tests to the disaggregate estimation because the only changes made in the models involve the adjustments of utilities described in section 6.4.

The final validation of the model requires external data sources, and preferably data from before and after a change in the transportation system that can be compared directly with the model predictions. This step has been carried out by MTC in their continuing use and updating of the model system.

Model Application Procedures   Two computerized procedures have been developed to apply the demand models. The first is oriented toward the application of an aggregate version of the model system for detailed regional network analysis in either the short- or long-range time frame. The second is oriented toward more rapid, generalized policy analysis in the short- to medium-range time frame.

1. MTC regional network analysis. The MTC regional analysis procedure includes all of the MTC travel demand models. It predicts regional travel patterns and network volumes from input of regional socioeconomic information and the level of service data for existing and proposed modes of transportation. Its structure is essentially that shown in figure 11.2. Aggregation is performed by classification or market segmentation, using average socioeconomic values for each of three income groups, initially, followed by segmentation based on auto ownership level after the prediction of auto ownership in the mobility blocks. This system provides the aggregate application procedure used for aggregate prediction tests shown in figure 11.6. The primary output is a set of eleven person-trip tables for (a) drive alone home-based work trips, (b) shared-ride home-based work trips, (c) transit home-based work trips, (d) auto home-based shopping trips, (e) transit home-based shopping trips, (f) auto home-based social/recreation trips, (g) transit home-based social/recreation trips, (h) auto nonhome-based trips, (i) transit nonhome-based trips, (j) auto home-based trips, and (k) transit home-based trips. These trip tables are used as inputs to network assignment routines to produce peak hour or 24-hour highway vehicle and transit person-trip assignments.

2. Short-range generalized policy analysis. Short-range generalized policy analysis (SRGP) is a computerized procedure that applies a subset of the MTC travel demand models for analysis. The procedure is designed to produce rapid turnaround estimates of the consequences of broadly defined transportation policy options. SRGP processing and outputs are based on the input of an updated sample of home interview survey households. The program estimates the travel behavior of the individual households subject to user-controlled facilities for expanding the results in whatever manner is appropriate to the problem. An example of the use of this sample enumeration method is given in more detail in section 11.4. Because of its orientation to short-range analysis, only the following models, which represent short-range choices within the full MTC model, are included: auto ownership for worker households, auto ownership for nonworker households, HBW mode choice, and HBO trip frequency, destination, and mode choice. As these models are applied to each household in turn, summary impacts are accumulated and reported for household income class groups or other segmentations.

11.4   A Short-Range Travel Demand Model System

This section, which is based on Ben-Akiva and Atherton (1977), presents a model system for prediction of changes in travel patterns for short-range

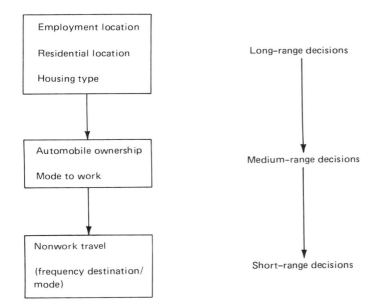

Figure 11.7
The assumed choice hierarchy for the short-range travel demand model (source: Ben-Akiva and Atherton 1977)

transport options, including carpooling incentive policies. To reflect accurately the response of travelers to alternative carpool incentives, the models represent the following direct and indirect effects on travel behavior:

1. Shifts in mode of work trips from driving alone and transit to carpooling.
2. Use of autos left at home for nonwork travel by other members of the household.
3. Changes in auto ownership levels.

The Structure of the Model System

The model system distinguishes between three different groups of travel-related decisions (figure 11.7). First are the long-range or major land-use/locational decisions. These include changes in workplace and changes in residential location and type of housing. Second are the medium-range decisions, which include automobile ownership and mode of travel to work. (The auto ownership and mode-to-work decisions are highly inter-dependent, particularly for the primary worker in a household.) The third group is composed of the short-range or nonwork travel decisions. The choices of frequency, destination, and mode for a discretionary travel purpose are considered simultaneously as a choice between various travel possibilities available to the household.

To analyze the full set of impacts resulting from the choice of a proposed transport service, it would be necessary to use demand models which explained all household locational and travel decisions. However, if one is primarily interested in the near-term response (or if the effect on long-range decisions can be assumed to be negligible), it is possible to use demand models formulated to predict household travel behavior conditional on current locational choices. Long-run mobility choices of employment location, residential location, and housing type are considered to remain fixed, and medium- and short-range decisions are predicted as conditional on these long run mobility choices.

To implement this basic framework of travel behavior for short-range policy analysis, four separate disaggregate travel demand models were integrated into a single model system:

1. A joint auto ownership/work mode choice model (for the household primary worker only).
2. A work trip mode choice model for secondary workers.
3. An auto ownership model for households without workers.
4. A joint frequency, destination, and mode choice model for nonwork trips.

The structure of the model system is depicted in figure 11.8. The data used to estimate the coefficients of the models are taken from cross-sectional household surveys. The dependent variables of the models are the reported travel choices; the independent variables are reported socioeconomic characteristics, engineering measures of travel times and costs, and survey estimates of employment, population, and land-use characteristics in the urbanized area. The explanatory variables are listed in table 11.1.

Component Models

The joint auto ownership/primary worker's mode choice model predicts the probability of the joint decision on the household's auto ownership and the primary worker's mode to work, conditional on the residence location and workplace. Explicitly, the model predicts the following:

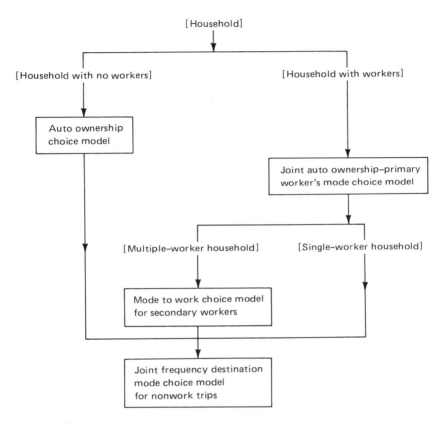

Figure 11.8
Disaggregate choice models for short-range travel demand forecasting (source: Ben-Akiva and Atherton 1977)

Table 11.1
List of explanatory variables included in the system of disaggregate travel demand models

Socioeconomic variables
Automobile ownership (can also be endogenously predicted)
Household income
License driver status
Number of licensed drivers in the household
Primary vs. secondary worker
Number of full-time workers in the household
Number of adults (and children) in the household
Type of residence
Occupation

Land-use and locational variables
Distances between origins and destinations
Workplace (CBD vs. non-CBD)
Employer size
Total employment
Retail employment
Net employment density
Retail employment density

Level-of-service variables (for drive alone, shared ride and transit in peak and off-peak periods)
In-vehicle travel time
Out-of-vehicle travel time
Total door-to-door travel time
Out-of-pocket travel cost (fare for transit; operating costs, tolls and parking costs for auto)

Source: Ben-Akiva and Atherton (1977).

$P_n(a, m_p | d_p) =$ probability that household n will own a automobiles and that the primary worker, p, will choose mode m_p to work, given the primary worker's workplace d_p;

where

$a = 0, 1,$ and 2 or more autos,

$m_p =$ drive alone, shared ride, and transit.

Five basic categories of independent variables are included in this model:

1. Transport level of service to work.
2. Auto ownership costs.
3. Housing and locational attributes.
4. Spatial opportunity variables (i.e., accessibility for nonwork travel).
5. Socioeconomic variables.

The mode-to-work choice model for secondary workers predicts the probability of the choice of mode to work for each secondary worker in a multiple-worker household, conditional on the worker's household location and workplace and the household's auto ownership:

$P_n(m_s | d_s, a) =$ probability that the secondary workers from household n will choose mode m_s to work, given the secondary worker's workplace d_s and household auto ownership a;

where

$m_s =$ drive alone, shared ride, and transit.

This formulation parallels the mode choice component of the primary worker model. Household auto ownership is one of the independent variables. It should be noted that the mode choice predictions from the models for primary and secondary workers are used in conjunction with another model that predicts the occupancy of shared ride trips, which is usually in the range of two to six persons in a car.

The auto ownership choice model for households without workers predicts the probability of auto ownership decisions for households with no workers, conditional on residential location:

$P_n(a) =$ probability that the household n will choose to own a automobiles;

where

$a = 0, 1$, and 2 or more autos.

This model includes only the auto ownership component of the joint auto ownership/mode choice model. It does not include as independent variables level-of-service attributes for work trips. It does include, however, a variable for nonwork travel accessibility.

The trips estimated by the *joint frequency, destination and mode choice model for shopping trips* are expanded to obtain estimates of all nonwork travel (i.e., home-based other trips and nonhome-based trips). The model predicts the following joint probability:

$P_n(f, d, m|a, a_r) =$ probability of household n making a trip ($f = 1$) for a specific nonwork purpose to destination d by mode m conditional on household auto ownership, a, and autos remaining after work trips, a_r (i.e., household auto ownership minus autos used by workers in the household to go to work);

where

$m =$ auto and transit.

The independent variables in this model fall into four classes:

1. Socioeconomic characteristics of the household
2. Attractiveness of destinations.
3. Mode-specific variables (e.g., auto availability).
4. Transport level of service attributes.

The variables of auto ownership and auto remaining provide the linkage of work and nonwork travel. A transport service alternative that directly affects peak hour auto travel will be predicted to have secondary effects on nonwork travel because of predicted changes in auto ownership and mode of travel to work.

Sample Enumeration Forecasting

The sample enumeration method is particularly suitable for short-range predictions. This procedure requires a sample of households from the population of interest. For short-run predictions a recent survey that may have also been used for model estimation is still representative of the actual distribution and can therefore be used for forecasting. The advantages and disadvantages of this procedure are discussed in section 6.3.

To apply the sample enumeration procedure to forecast changes in travel behavior resulting from changes in transport service, a sample of the prediction group must first be selected. This sample needs to be large enough to be representative, to an acceptable level of accuracy, of the distribution of population characteristics of interest. For the present model system, developed for Washington, D.C., a sample of 800 observations was sufficient for areawide predictions.

With a sample of households established, the superimposition of a new, alternative transport service is represented by altering the values of the independent variables of the appropriate households in the prediction group affected. Aggregate forecasts are then made by applying the disaggregate models to each household in the sample and expanding these predictions to represent the entire population.

The steps required for the forecasting process are summarized in figure 11.9. For each household the prediction process proceeds through each of the separate disaggregate models (auto ownership, work mode choice, and nonwork travel demand) as shown in figure 11.10. The required information on auto availability is sequentially passed from model to model. First, the auto ownership model is used to predict the marginal probabilities of choice of alternative auto ownership levels by a household, conditional on existing employment and residential location. These marginal probabilities are then passed to the work trip mode choice model, which is applied separately to predict the probabilities of each worker in the household choosing among available modes at each auto ownership level.

With knowledge of the mode choice probabilities at each auto ownership level, together with the probabilities of each auto ownership level, it is possible to calculate the joint probabilities for each combination of the number of autos remaining at home available for nonwork trip purposes; combinations of autos remaining and auto ownership are then used in the nonwork trip model, which is applied separately for each combination to predict the probability of a household making a trip to each available destination by each available mode. The resulting predictions of changes in household travel behavior are then transformed into changes in travel-related impacts (i.e., vehicle miles traveled, fuel consumption, modal shares).

Tests of the Disaggregate Model System

Disaggregate models, by their very level of detail, can potentially show sensitivity to a wide range of transport system characteristics and popu-

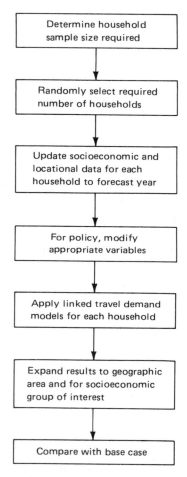

Figure 11.9
Forecasting process with sample enumeration (source: Ben-Akiva and Atherton 1977)

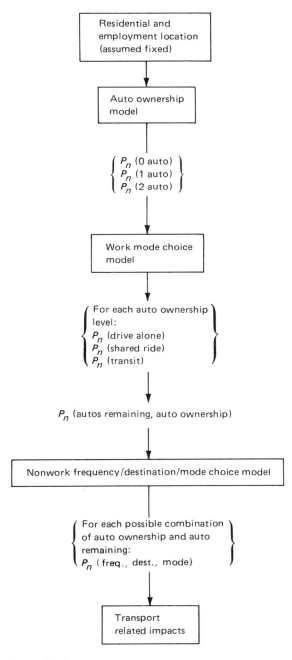

Figure 11.10
Prediction process for a household (source: Ben-Akiva and Atherton 1977)

lation attributes. As such, it is hypothesized that if such models are carefully specified and estimated, they would be geographically and temporally transferable—that is, a model estimated with data from one time/place could be applicable to another location at another point in time. If this hypothesis were to hold in practice, significant resource savings would be forthcoming. Hence the research literature in the past decade shows a significant number of references investigating various aspects of model-transferability (e.g., Watson and Westin 1975, Atherton and Ben-Akiva 1976, Ben-Akiva 1981, McCarthy 1982, Koppelman and Wilmot 1982, 1984, Koppelman and Rose 1983).

Various components of the present model system (or variations thereof) have been applied in Washington, D.C., Birmingham, Alabama, Los Angeles, and New Bedford, Massachusetts (see Atherton and Ben-Akiva 1976). Statistically equivalent coefficients for the same mode choice model specification were obtained across the four data sets but only under the condition that the systematic utility adequately account for taste variation through the inclusion of socioeconomic characteristics. In this specific instance, transferring the Washington level-of-service coefficients to the other urban areas required only updating of the alternative-specific constant to fit local aggregate shares.

A second, more significant test of a model's predictive ability is a comparison of predicted versus actual impacts observed from "before and after" a change in the transport system. As Ben-Akiva and Atherton (1977) report, the mode choice to work component of the Washington, D.C., model system was tested in two such validation studies: the Shirley Highway (in Washington itself) preferential lane project and the Santa Monica, California, carpool preferential lane project. Using the incremental logit form (see section 5.3) and aggregate level data by market segments, changes in modal shares were predicted and compared with data collected following implementation of the system changes.

Lack of resources, both monetary and temporal, usually preclude extensive model validation efforts such as the one described here. However, this should not blind us to the need for this phase of model development. Validation is an integral aspect of the model development process and is especially necessary when dealing with systems of models where unexpected effects may occur due to interactions between model components. In addition model validation can serve as a means for the end-user of the system to gain confidence in its performance and a knowledge of its limitations.

Policy Analysis Results

This model system was used to analyze the effectiveness of a number of transport policies both in promoting the use of carpooling for work trips and in reducing vehicle miles traveled (VMT). The policies that were analyzed include (1) employer-based carpool matching and promotion, (2) preferential parking measures, and (3) preferential traffic control.

The predicted impacts for each of these policies for the Washington, D.C., metropolitan area are summarized in table 11.2. For each policy the predicted percentage changes from base values are presented for work trip mode shares (drive alone, shared ride, and transit), work trip auto occupancy, vehicle miles traveled (work, nonwork, and total), and fuel consumption. Note that these percentage changes represent areawide changes resulting from a policy, regardless of what proportion of the areawide population was actually affected by that policy. For purposes of comparison, table 11.3 presents the base value for work trip modal shares and auto occupancy, vehicle miles traveled, and fuel consumption corresponding to each of the population segments defined in the more detailed presentation of results.

Employer-Based Matching and Other Methods of Promoting Carpooling

This policy represents the implementation of employer-related carpool incentive programs, such as intracompany advertising, carpool matching assistance, and advertising directed toward promotion of carpooling. Because incentives such as these cannot readily be quantified in terms of travel time and travel cost, the representation of this particular policy in the model system presents somewhat of a problem. A dummy variable was included in the work choice model to reflect the effects of carpooling promotion programs by employers that do not translate into time and cost incentives.

Since carpooling incentives such as these are feasible only for organizations with a relatively large number of employees, the most logical criterion for determining the availability of such incentives to an individual worker is employer size. For this particular policy, a lower bound of 100 employees was used to differentiate between large and small employers. Thus this dummy variable was set equal to one for those workers employed by organizations with at least 100 employees and zero otherwise.

Table 11.2
Summary of predicted areawide impacts

Transport policy	Work trip modal shares			Work trip auto occupancy	Vehicle miles traveled (miles/day)			Fuel consumption (gallons/day per household)
	Drive alone	Shared ride	Transit		Work (per worker)	Nonwork (per household)	Total (per household)	
Base values (excluding weekend travel)	0.53	0.25	0.16	1.24	11.0	15.0	26.0	2.5
Employee incentives	-1.4	4.4	-2.1	1.1	-0.62	0.17	-0.15	-0.11
Preferential parking	-2.7	8.2	-3.6	1.9	-0.74	0.24	-0.16	-0.13
Preferential parking (with pricing disincentives)	-8.6	17.7	1.4	4.8	-4.1	0.88	-1.1	-0.97
Preferential lanes	-1.7	2.9	1.1	0.9	-1.3	0.22	-0.39	-0.32

Source: Ben-Akiva and Atherton (1977).
Note: All values except base measured as percent change.

Table 11.3
Base values for the Washington, D.C., area in 1975

	Areawide	Income group			Location of residence		
		Low	Middle	High	CBD	Urban	Suburban
Percent of areawide population	100.0	23.0	42.0	35.0	28.0	36.0	36.0
Work trip mode shares							
Drive alone	0.53	0.37	0.51	0.58	0.32	0.45	0.63
Shared ride	0.25	0.24	0.22	0.27	0.19	0.26	0.24
Transit	0.16	0.29	0.19	0.10	0.30	0.24	0.06
Work trip auto occupancy	1.24	1.32	1.23	1.24	1.30	1.29	1.20
Vehicle miles traveled (miles per day)							
Work (per worker)	11.0	5.9	10.0	13.0	4.1	6.5	16.0
Nonwork							
excluding weekend travel	15.0	5.4	14.7	19.3	8.8	10.0	22.0
including weekend travel	25.0	11.0	26.0	34.0	16.0	18.0	40.0
Total							
excluding weekend travel	26.0	7.9	25.0	35.0	9.4	18.0	42.0
including weekend travel	36.0	13.0	36.0	50.0	17.0	26.0	60.0
Fuel consumption (gallons/day)							
excluding weekend travel	2.5	0.82	2.4	3.3	1.0	1.9	3.8
including weekend travel	3.5	1.4	3.5	4.7	1.7	2.7	5.5

Source: Ben-Akiva and Atherton (1977).

The results of this policy are given in table 11.4. As shown, the implementation of carpool-matching assistance and promotion programs by large employers results in a predicted 4.4% areawide increase in the number of workers in carpools.

Note that though work trip VMT is reduced by 0.62%, the increased number of autos remaining at home (and therefore available for use by other family members for other trip purposes) results in an increase of 0.17% in nonwork trip VMT, which offsets 36% of the work trip VMT savings.

The potential areawide effectiveness of this policy is muted somewhat by two conditions existing in the Washington, D.C., area:

1. Carpool incentives are available only to those workers employed by large employers, and they comprise only 68% of the work force.
2. These incentives are already available to 44%.

The result is that only 24% of the working population are affected by this policy. In other urbanized areas, where the initial level of employer-based carpool incentives is lower and/or a greater proportion of the work force is employed by large employers, the policy would be more effective in increasing carpooling and reducing VMT.

Preferential Parking Measures   Two sets of preferential parking measures are analyzed:

1. A program implemented by large employers (i.e., those with more than 100 employees) giving subsidized preferential parking locations to carpool vehicles.
2. The same employer-based program of carpool incentives coupled with areawide parking price disincentives aimed at single-occupant vehicles.

The first set of measures is represented in the model system by setting parking cost equal to zero and decreasing walk time from parking location to final destination for the shared-ride alternative and increasing walk time for the drive-alone alternative for those workers employed by large employers. The magnitude of these changes in round trip walk times is -4.27 minutes for shared ride and $+1.64$ minutes for drive alone. These values were calculated from the cumulative walk time distribution for parked vehicles during the peak period in the Washington areas, together with the percentage of all autos used for carpools. In addition to these employer-

Table 11.4
Predicted impacts for employer-based carpool incentives

Impact	Base value (areawide)[a]	Areawide	Income group Low (23%)	Middle (42%)	High (35%)	Location of residence CBD (28%)	Urban (36%)	Suburban (36%)
Work trip mode shares								
Drive alone	0.53	−1.4	−1.8	−1.1	−1.6	−1.9	−1.2	−1.5
Shared ride	0.25	4.4	5.1	4.5	4.3	5.9	4.1	4.7
Transit	0.16	−2.1	−1.8	−2.2	−2.1	−1.7	−2.1	−2.2
Work trip auto occupancy	1.24	1.1	1.6	0.7	1.0	1.2	1.0	1.0
Vehicle miles traveled (miles/day)								
Work (per worker)	11.0	−0.62	−0.42	−0.43	−0.77	−0.38	−0.31	−0.75
Nonwork (per household)	15.0	0.17	0.11	0.13	0.21	0.02	0.13	0.23
Total (per household)	26.0	−0.15	−0.01	−0.07	−0.21	−0.04	−0.09	−0.23
Fuel consumption (gallons/day per household)	2.5	−0.11	−0.01	−0.03	−0.17	−0.01	−0.05	−0.18

Source: Ben-Akiva and Atherton (1977).
Note: All values except base measured as percent change.
a. Excluding weekend travel.

based carpool parking incentives, the second set of measures included minimum parking charges for the drive-alone alternative of $2.00 in the CBD and $1.00 elsewhere in the metropolitan area (for work trips only).

The predicted results of these two parking policies are given in tables 11.5 and 11.6. In the first policy (table 11.5) the shared-ride mode share increases significantly, while the shares of both drive alone and transit decrease. In the second policy (table 11.6) an even greater increase in shared-ride usage is predicted. In this case, however, although the drive-alone share drops markedly, the transit share shows a slight increase. This occurs because the first policy consists primarily of carpool incentives, and therefore shared ride will draw from both drive alone and transit. In the second policy, however, the drive-alone disincentive dominates, and more commuters shift from drive alone to transit than from transit to share ride. As one would expect, since this second policy is primarily a pricing disincentive, workers from lower-income households are most severely affected.

Preferential Traffic Control   This policy consisted of preferential lanes for multiple-occupancy vehicles and was analyzed on an areawide basis by identifying those trips that would use facilities for which a preferential lane policy would be feasible. This approach was preferred over that of analyzing one specific facility because the relatively small sample used in forecasting results in an extremely small and statistically unreliable subsample of observed work trips on any given facility.

Once potential locations of preferential lane and ramp treatment were identified for the Washington area, differential time savings were estimated for three broad categories of work trips: (1) For trips from outside the circumferential beltway to the inner core, a differential of 16 minutes was used (8% of sample). (2) For trips from outside the beltway to inside the beltway, along the beltway, and from inside the beltway to the inner core, a differential of eight minutes was used (31% of sample). (3) For all other trips—outbound commute, circumferential within the beltway, and so forth—no time savings were assumed (61% of sample). No time savings were also assumed for nonwork trips. These travel time differentials were based on the following assumptions:

1. Average base speed of 35 mph on all facilities.
2. Average preferential lane speed of 50 mph.
3. Average nonpreferential lane facility lengths of 10 and 5 miles, respectively, for the first two categories of work trips mentioned here.

Table 11.5
Predicted impacts for employer-based preferential parking

Impact	Base value (areawide)[a]	Areawide	Income group			Location of residence		
			Low (23%)	Middle (42%)	High (35%)	CBD (28%)	Urban (36%)	Suburban (36%)
Work trip mode shares								
Drive alone	0.53	-2.7	-4.3	-2.4	-2.7	-6.4	-3.7	-1.8
Shared ride	0.25	8.2	11.7	8.5	7.1	17.4	9.9	5.4
Transit	0.16	-3.6	-4.1	-3.4	-3.5	-4.3	-3.7	-2.7
Work trip auto occupancy	1.24	1.9	3.5	1.5	1.7	4.3	2.5	1.1
Vehicle miles traveled (miles/day)								
Work (per worker)	0.11	-0.74	-0.63	-0.61	-0.85	-1.4	-0.86	-0.68
Nonwork (per household)	15.0	0.24	0.20	0.18	0.30	0.04	0.35	0.25
Total (per household)	26.0	-0.16	-0.03	-0.12	-0.21	-0.05	-0.19	-0.17
Fuel consumption (gallons/day per household)	2.5	-0.13	-0.01	-0.10	-0.18	-0.04	-0.14	-0.14

Source: Ben-Akiva and Atherton (1977).
Note: All values except base measured as percent change.
a. Excluding weekend travel.

Table 11.6
Predicted impacts for preferential parking policy with pricing disincentives

Impact	Base value (areawide)[a]	Areawide	Income group			Location of residence		
			Low (23%)	Middle (42%)	High (35%)	CBD (28%)	Urban (36%)	Suburban (36%)
Work trip mode shares								
Drive alone	0.53	−8.6	−23.2	−8.6	−6.4	−18.7	−10.5	−6.7
Shared ride	0.25	17.7	32.7	18.8	13.7	31.4	17.7	16.5
Transit	0.16	1.4	2.6	1.4	0.70	0.0	0.59	5.2
Work trip auto occupancy	1.24	4.8	14.4	4.9	4.0	11.5	6.2	4.2
Vehicle miles traveled (miles/day)								
Work (per worker)	11.0	−4.1	−12.3	−4.3	−3.1	−9.1	−5.1	−3.6
Nonwork (per household)	15.0	0.88	1.0	0.84	0.89	0.11	1.1	1.0
Total (per household)	26.0	−1.1	−2.7	−1.1	−0.88	−0.45	−1.7	−1.0
Fuel consumption (gallons/day per household)	2.5	−0.97	−2.3	−0.98	−0.73	−0.41	−1.4	−0.88

Source: Ben-Akiva and Atherton (1977).
Note: All values except base measured as percent change.
a. Excluding weekend travel.

Table 11.7
Changes in travel times resulting from preferential lane policy

Work trip category	Percent of work trips	Change in round trip travel time (in minutes)		
		Drive alone	Shared ride	Transit
a	8	+6	−10	−10
b	31	+3	−5	−5
c	61	0	0	0

Source: Ben-Akiva and Atherton (1977).

The specific changes in round trip travel times resulting from these assumptions are given in table 11.7.

The predicted impacts of this preferential lane policy are given in table 11.8. As shown, the shared-ride modal share increased 2.9%, whereas that of transit increased by only 1.1%. The reason for this difference becomes evident if one looks at the results for workers residing in suburban areas. Here, the difference is even greater, suggesting that, for those workers for whom preferential lanes are most attractive, transit availability is somewhat limited. Here again, the decrease in work trip VMT is partially offset by increased nonwork travel.

11.5 Summary

This chapter has provided an overview of the principal issues and considerations that must be addressed in the development of a disaggregate model system. The design of a model system reflects the needs of the policy analysis process as well as budgetary and computational constraints. The methodology presented balances behavioral realism and practicality.

The design of a complex model system is more an art than a science, and as such is best transmitted by example rather than abstractions. Accordingly we have presented and discussed in-depth two model systems, the MTC long-range system for the San Francisco metropolitan area and the short-range system for Washington, D.C.

The model systems described here are only two among many. Other systems are to be found in Ben-Akiva et al. (1977), Ben-Akiva et al. (1978), Daly and van Zwam (1981), Train (1984), and Swait et al. (1984), among others.

Table 11.8
Predicted impacts for preferential lanes

Impact	Base value (areawide)[a]	Areawide	Income group			Location of residence		
			Low (23%)	Middle (42%)	High (35%)	CBD (28%)	Urban (36%)	Suburban (36%)
Work trip mode shares								
Drive alone	0.53	−1.7	−0.37	−1.4	−2.1	0.0	−1.5	−1.9
Shared ride	0.25	2.9	0.27	2.5	3.7	0.0	1.6	4.6
Transit	0.16	1.1	0.24	0.91	2.1	0.0	1.1	1.9
Work trip auto occupancy	1.24	0.9	0.4	0.4	1.0	0.0	0.6	1.0
Vehicle miles traveled (miles/day)								
Work (per worker)	0.11	−1.3	−0.26	−1.1	−1.5	0.0	−1.1	−1.4
Nonwork (per household)	15.0	0.22	0.0	0.16	0.33	0.0	0.11	0.34
Total (per household)	26.0	−0.39	−0.07	−0.33	−0.49	0.0	−0.41	−0.47
Fuel consumption (gallons/day per household)	2.5	−0.32	−0.06	−0.28	−0.40	0.0	−0.34	−0.38

Source: Beb-Akiva and Atherton (1977).
Note: All values except base measured as percent change.
a. Excluding weekend travel.

12 Models of Travel Demand: Future Directions

12.1 Introduction

In the preceding chapters we have provided an in-depth treatment of the portion of travel demand analysis that is derived from discrete choice analysis and that has been put into practice. In this chapter we focus on still more recent innovations in the research area and speculate on the future directions that are likely to prove fruitful in the near term.

12.2 Components of Travel Demand Modeling Process

There are many ways in which the process of travel demand modeling can be divided. However, for the purposes of this review we divide the field into four distinct areas.

The area of *behavioral theory* which was the focus of chapter 3 encompasses four important aspects of travel demand models:

1. The attributes considered by individuals making demand choices.
2. The particular choices represented in a model, including the type of choice (mode, destination, etc.), the period over which the decision is made (day, month, year, etc.), and the nature of the set of possible choices (continuous, discrete, or mixed).
3. The decision rule (compensatory, elimination by aspects, lexicographic rules, etc.).
4. The assumptions about the information available to the decision maker, including how information is acquired and used.

However, the area we define here as behavioral theory is quite distinct from the problems of how to make that theory operational. One can imagine an entirely reasonable theory of travel behavior for which there exist no corresponding data, statistical model, or estimation technique. For example, a theory of behavior in which travel decisions at any time depend structurally on all previous travel decisions might be entirely plausible but impractical to make operational.

The second area is what we term *measurement*. This includes all aspects of data collection such as how and which attributes are measured, how travel decisions are observed, how samples are taken, and whether data are cross-sectional or longitudinal. In addition issues of whether so-called attitudinal or perceptual data are collected come under the general heading of measurement. Finally, whether the analyst measures actual choices (revealed perferences) or states preferences to hypothetical choices is part of measurement.

The third area is *model structure*. This broad category incorporates the methods through which behavioral theory and data are combined to produce a statistical model of travel demand. In the field of disaggregate travel demand analysis, the statistical model structure is usually some variant of the logit model.

The fourth area is *estimation*. Conditional on the set of measurements taken and an assumed statistical process that generated them, estimation is the technique by which unknown parameters of the model are inferred. This area has been dominated in travel demand analysis by classical statistical inference by using the methods of least squares and maximum likelihood.

In the remainder of this chapter we review some recent developments in these four areas.

12.3 Behavioral Theory

The vast majority of travel demand models have been either implicitly or explicitly derived from the hypothesis of individual utility maximization. This class of models encompasses the entire spectrum of neoclassical economic models of consumer behavior, discrete choice models, and large segments of the transportation-related research in marketing and psychology.

The reason for the widespread use of the utility maximization hypothesis is the ease with which tractable, analytic results can be derived when one assumes that decisions on multiattribute services such as transportation can be reduced to the optimization of a scalar index of worth.

Many of the objections to utility maximization as a behavioral theory can be dealt with by modifying other assumptions of the neoclassical economic model. For example, psychologists have often argued that subjects tend to rely on "satisficing" rules when they choose among many alternatives. Thus individuals select alternatives that meet certain upper and lower thresholds along their various attributes rather than combine the attributes in some compensatory fashion (e.g., a study by Golob and Richardson 1979). This type of behavior, in which a decision maker behaves as though he or she possessed fixed levels of aspiration, can be approximated by a utility-maximizing individual who faces alternatives one at a time where each alternative examined has some search cost associated with it. The resulting models, although based on the assumption of utility maximization, produce a behavior in which individuals examine alternatives until they find one with attributes leading to a utility level exceeding some fixed value. Examples of such models appear widely in the literature in statistical decision theory (e.g., de Groot 1970) and have more recently been extended in numerous works such as those by Weibull (1978) and Hall (1980).

Given the tractability of behavioral theories rooted in the assumption of utility maximization, it is not surprising that the state of the art in travel demand analysis has tended to move by extending that theory rather than by abandoning it altogether. These extensions can be viewed along the following dimensions.

Extension of Choice Sets

Travel demand models have moved steadily to encompass an ever-increasing range of potential choices. The earliest demand models that had any real underlying behavioral theory were exclusively models of modal choice (e.g., see early work by Warner 1973, Lisco 1967, Quarmby 1967, Stopher 1969, Watson 1973, Lave 1969). Since then work has been done on choice of destination, automobile ownership, time of day of travel, frequency, activity duration, automobile type, housing, residential location, and workplace. This research has lead to the development of the nested logit model presented in chapter 10 and the model systems in chapter 11.

Extension of Assumptions about Information

The simplest model of traveler behavior assumes the existence of a perfectly informed decision maker who is aware of all of the available alternatives and who knows all the attributes with certainty. Particularly when one is dealing with very large sets of feasible alternatives or travel behavior that is not routine, this assumption has been questioned. Recent work has explored the consequences of relaxing these assumptions in a number of different ways. For example, Lerman and Manski (1982) have explicitly considered how the process of information acquisition can be incorporated into discrete-choice behavior. Their work treats information as obtained from three generic types of sources:

1. Direct experience.
2. Word-of-mouth communication from other informed members of the population.
3. Media coverage transmitted through one or more mechanisms.

Other efforts have been directed toward relaxing the assumptions regarding the cost of obtaining information about alternatives. Hall (1980), for example, considers the case of an active search for housing, where the decision maker must decide whether to accept a given alternative from the set he or she knows about or to incur some actual (or psychological) expense to obtain further alternatives. The resulting models are similar to those developed by Weibull (1978) in the context of destination search.

Linking Travel Behavior to Activity Demand

Despite the consensus that transportation is a derived demand, it is only relatively recently that travel demand modelers have attempted to derive models of transportation choices from an underlying theory of the demand for activities in which individuals choose to participate. The early work by Hagerstrand (1970), Lenntorp (1976), and Chapin (1968) and more recent studies by Kostyniuk and Kitamura (1982), among others, produced a great deal of behavioral insight. Preliminary efforts at modeling time allocation by Bain (1976) and Jacobson (1979) have produced models of the duration of out-of-home activities. More recently Damm and Lerman (1981), Kitamura (1984), and Hirsh et al. (1984) have also modeled the choice of whether to participate in an activity at a given period of time during the day or the week. However, there is still no operational model that directly links choice of activities with trip making.

Interactions among Household Members

Virtually the entire body of behavioral theory deals with the choices of a single decision maker, defined as either an individual or a household. More realistically there are many household decisions that result from interactions among household members, each of whom may have different objectives. To date, there has been almost no analytic theory of intrahousehold interactions. There exists limited empirical work by Jacobson (1979) on the allocation of shopping activities between adults in the household, by Ben-Akiva and Atherton (1977) on car availability interactions, and by Ruiter and Ben-Akiva (1978) on the interaction between primary and secondary workers in a multiworker household (see chapter 11). Such interactions are probably becoming increasingly important in determining certain types of travel behavior as traditional roles in households become less and less significant determinants of the allocation of household tasks.

Choice Set Determination

The existing theory has generally been derived from the assumption that the choice set available to an individual is limited in most cases only by resource constraints (e.g., budget constraints or time constraints) or physical availability (e.g., the unavailability of an automobile). The more qualitative literature on traveler behavior suggests that there may be other constraints operating, including some that may be attributed to issues such as lack of information.

Perhaps the best examples of constraints that we do not currently represent in existing theories is what Hagestrand (1970) terms "coupling constraints." Basically these constraints arise when the decisions of two or more individuals must be coordinated for either one to make a trip. Most carpooling choices, which we represented as independent decisions of separate actors in chapter 11, are in reality constrained by the need for the members of the carpool to have matching schedules.

Most of the models we now use treat the availability of an alternative as a binary issue: either an alternative is available to an individual or it is not. A more realistic model would recognize that there are degrees of availability, which range from alternatives that are used every day to those that are simply infeasible. In the middle of this spectrum lie alternatives about which the individual has only incomplete and potentially out-of-date information.

In the context of developing countries, income limitations may often result in major constraints. Swait and Ben-Akiva (1984) have recently shown the importance of explicitly modeling the nature of the choice set generation process with data from Brazil.

Development of Intermediate Constructs

The statistical demand models in use typically treat utility as a function of a vector of observed, physically measured attributes. This approach does not explicitly represent the process by which physically measured attributes are perceived and acted on by individual decision makers. It has been proposed that individuals assess alternatives by first constructing some intermediate variables and then evaluate their alternatives based on these intermediate constructs. Most of the efforts to capture explicitly these intermediate processes in explaining traveler behavior are the result of cross-fertilization of travel demand analysis by marketing research. Examples include the use of multistage models (e.g., the Lens model first proposed by Brunswik 1952 in the marketing context) to study choice of a shopping center by Koppelman, Hauser, and Tybout (1977) and by Karash (1983).

In the Lens model physically measurable attributes are translated into actual decisions in a sequence of steps. First, physical attributes of both an alternative and a decision maker produce perceptual attributes of the alternative. These perceptions may be on a considerably smaller number of dimensions than the original attributes. The perceived attributes then induce a set of preferences for the set of alternatives. These preferences are then further modified by situational constraints that limit the actual choice made.

Obviously the Lens model is only one possible way in which intermediate constructs can be introduced into a behavioral theory. The important issue in developing such constructs is whether one can use them as a basis for an operational model. In particular, does the theory impose useful restrictions on the relationship between observable variables and the hypothesized constructs that help in developing more reasonable models?

The foregoing review suggests that even within the paradigm of the utility-maximizing individual there exists an enormous number of relevant areas for the extension of behavioral theory. The emphasis of most travel demand research has been placed on models that are operational. Thus researchers have been developing behavioral theories that are simple enough to lead to tractable, immediately operational models that can be estimated and applied to analyze transportation plans and policies. It is probably safe to argue that researchers working with such models have failed to exploit fully their potential for explaining or approximating behavior that on the surface appears contrary to the hypothesis of utility maximization.

12.4 Measurement

Measurement includes an extremely wide range of subjects of relevance in travel demand modeling. In this section we will restrict our attention to those measurement problems that relate directly to the development of mathematical models of trip making and ignore the issues that must be considered in more qualitative or exploratory travel demand analysis. This to some extent restricts the scope of the review, since many travel demand models are developed from data that were intended for other purposes.

For the purposes of exposition the work in this area will be divided into four subareas.

Attributes Collected

Data collection efforts in travel demand studies have been dominated by the use of one-day trip diaries, which are usually augmented by socioeconomic information about respondents and network-based data on the level of service provided by alternative modes. De facto this domination has resulted in an emphasis on the use of a relatively limited subset of possible attributes and has traded off large samples for high levels of reliability in the data.

Efforts to extend the range of attributes measured in travel demand analysis have been directed toward either generating data on different physically measured attributes or measuring what have loosely come to be called perceptual or attitudinal data. Examples of the former include efforts by Small (1982), Lerman et al. (1977), Abkowitz (1980), and others, to measure the reliability of modes, by either inferring the higher moments of the travel-time distribution from repeated observed trips or associating distributions of travel times on links in the network and deriving network travel-time variances. Other extensions of the types of attributes used appear in the literature on destination choice (notably for shopping trips) where typical land-use measures such as employment by type and zonal areas devoted to different uses have been enhanced by measures of the number and variety of stores, parking spaces, mean walking times to parking, and measures of physical amenities such as enclosure of malls. Examples of this type of work are that of Kern and Parcells (1981), where the Census of Retailing is used to measure a large number of attributes of different retailing centers, and the models estimated for Paris which were reported in chapter 9.

The measurement of that which is not directly, physically measurable, such as perceptions of quality or convenience, has probably received somewhat greater attention. The early research results in this area by Spear (1976) in the context of mode choice and by Kostyniuk (1975) in the context of destination choice were somewhat mixed, particularly when these measures were used along with the physically measured attributes. Although these ambiguous results could be attributable to many causes, one might speculate that the most crucial problem was lack of a clear theory about how to use this type of data appropriately. The measures used were often the result of questions in which respondents imposed their own views on what the attributes labeled comfort or convenience were measuring. What is needed is a clearer structural theory of the process by which physically measured attributes and socioeconomic characteristics interact to form these intermediate constructs and a better understanding of how the available psychometric techniques that purport to measure these constructs work. This more structural model would then provide some guidance as to how we should and should not use these types of variables and how the values of these variables can be modeled as functions of other attributes. This is an attractive area of research in the marketing field (e.g., Bagozzi 1980) and may yield some useful results for building travel demand models that rely on these nonphysical attributes. See, for example, the successful inclusion of a perceptual travel time reliability measure in a mode choice model by Prashker (1979a, 1979b).

Sample Sizes and Sampling Strategies

Advances in the analysis of sampling techniques such as stratified sampling, choice-based sampling, and various hybrid strategies have provided a much richer set of alternative sample designs. Most of this literature, however, has focused on how these different sampling strategies can be used to estimate a model and not on how one should choose a sampling method.

In chapter 8 it was shown that the optimal sampling strategy for even simple problems cannot be determined without prior knowledge of the unknown parameters of the model to be estimated. Daganzo (1980, 1982) noted this result and formulated the sample design problem as a nonlinear programming problem in which the parameters of the model were treated as known. In this model the fractions of the sample taken from each of a finite set of possible sampling strategies are the decision variables; the objective function is a measure of the efficiency of the estimated parameters such as the trace or largest eigenvalue of the variance-covariance matrix of the estimator.

Subsequent empirical experiments by Sheffi and Tarem (1983) have applied Daganzo's basic technique to sample design for logit model estimation. In their work initial parameter estimates are obtained from a small randomly drawn sample, and the resulting estimates are tested as fixed parameters and used to optimize a second-stage sample. Their results on both simulated and actual data suggest that substantial gains in efficiency are possible from use of this two-stage technique and that these gains are not particularly sensitive to the size of the first sample so long as it is greater in size than some minimal fraction of the total sample. Their work applies only to designing samples that are stratified on exogenous variables, leaving the optimal design of endogenously designed stratified samples almost entirely unresolved. A recent example of a travel survey combining exogenous and endogenous stratification is given in Ben-Akiva et al. (1984).

Preference Data

Travel demand models have historically relied on revealed preferences data. The types of alternative data on preferences that have been used include stated preferences (or rankings) of hypothetical alternatives, scaled measures of intensity of preference for either actual or hypothetical alternatives, and questions about trade-offs that individuals would be willing to make on particular attributes. Each of these types of preference data has within it a myriad of distinct options, some of which involve detailed procedures such as the allocation of a fixed number of chips by a respondent in which the number of chips given to any alternative reflects the intensity of preference (e.g., see Hauser and Shugan 1980, Karash 1983, Louviere et al. 1981).

These methods allow the analyst to extract vastly more information from each respondent, including multiple responses to different choice situations and reactions to combinations of attributes that are unobserved in revealed-preference data. These features of this type of data make it possible to model demand for new alternatives without making the strong assumptions on model structure that are required when revealed preferences for existing alternatives are used. In addition, because responses for a variety of choice situations can be elicited in collecting this type of data, it is possible to estimate demand models separately for any given individual in the sample. As demonstrated in a case study by Fischer and Nagin (1981), this greatly facilitates the diagnosis of the structure and causes of random taste variation in the population being modeled (see chapters 5 and 7). Finally, the ability to construct a very wide range of attributes in the data makes it considerably easier to determine the appropriate functional form for demand models (see Lerman and Louviere 1979 for an example).

The major deficiency of stated preference data is that people often do not actually do what they say they would do under hypothetical circumstances. Thus there may be a tendency to over commit to hypothetical new alternatives in response to questionnaires, misleading the travel demand analyst into erroneous and often overoptimistic forecasts of the demand for such innovations. Given the uncertainty that exists about how people respond to hypothetical questions, it is often argued that revealed preferences provide the best basis for modeling demand.

Although responses to hypothetical questions do indeed incorporate sources of error in the prediction of actual behavior, they provide potentially valuable information about how people will actually behave. The key to using that information is to structure an explicit theory about how stated preferences map into actual behavior. This theory would allow us to use both revealed and hypothetical preferences within the same model; the model structure would be used to control for the fact that two distinctly different types of information are represented. One conceptual basis for such a theory has already been described by Koppelman, Hauser, and Tybout (1977), who have adopted some of the work in the marketing field to the transportation context. Karash (1983) provides some further support for this hypothesis. However, there is a major unfilled gap between the conceptual theory and an operational model validated in actual practice that allows a synthesis of revealed and hypothetical preferences in a single model.

12.5   Statistical Model Structure

The recent progress in the field of model structure includes the development of new model structures and the operationalization of models that had existed in theory for some time but were considered impractical due to what appeared to be insurmountable computational difficulties. The major area of progress has been the derivation of new models by altering the assumptions about the specification of the disturbances in random utility models.

Continuous Logit

One area of significant research has been the evolution of the continuous logit model. In this work the set of alternatives is treated as continuous, and the logit model is modified so that the denominator is the integral (rather than the sum) over the entire set of feasible choices. This model was first proposed by Ben-Akiva and Watanatada (1977). It was derived by assuming that the IIA property holds with respect to subsets of continuous alternatives by McFadden (1976) and by Litinas and Ben-Akiva (1979). By assuming that the set of destinations is a continuous plane and making specific assumptions about the distribution of level of service and potential destinations over that plane, Litinas and Ben-Akiva (1979) derived closed-form expressions for vehicle-miles of travel, mean trip length, and other travel summaries.

Truncated Dependent-Variable Models

There are certain instances where the dependent variable either is restricted to a limited set of discrete outcomes or takes on some range of continuous values. The most common such instance in transportation is when activity duration is the dependent variable. Over the usual period of observation the amount of time any individual spends is either zero (i.e., he or she does not participate in the activity) or a positive, real number. The methods used to deal with such problems have been generally adapted directly from the econometrics literature initiated by Tobin (1958). Application of this method and more recent extensions to allow for simultaneous systems of truncated dependent variables appear in works by Bain (1976), Jacobson (1979), and Kitamura (1984).

Models with Mixed Continuous and Discrete Variables

There are some travel problems for which the dependent variables are both continuous and discrete. For example, one might view a commuter's work trip choice as consisting of a decision on when to depart from home to work (a continuous dependent variable) and a decision on what mode of travel to use (a discrete choice). This type of problem was first explored in a travel demand context by Westin and Gillen (1978). Their approach requires that the disturbances for both the continuous and the discrete decisions be normally distributed and that the utility of the discrete alternatives be linear in the continuous dependent variable. They derived a multistep estimation method based on work in the field of labor force participation pioneered by Heckman (1978). This method iterates between estimation of the continuous equation and the discrete equation, eventually leading to a consistent, although not fully efficient, set of parameter estimates. This was the basic approach adopted by Damm and Lerman (1981) to model the decision of workers to participate in a nonwork activity during each of five periods during the day and, if the decision is to participate, for how long.

Variants of these types of models have been developed outside the transportation field by Dubin and McFadden (1980), who use the multinomial logit model for the discrete choice and applied recently to model automobile demand by Train (1984). In other work McFadden and Winston (1981) have used full information maximum likelihood and estimated mixed continuous and discrete models of freight demand.

Time-Series Analysis

Because most of the data available to transportation analysts has been cross-sectional, the use of time-series approaches has not been emphasized in travel demand modeling. Most of the time-series methods used in travel demand analysis have been applications of well-known methods developed for the analysis of aggregate economic models, in which the dependent variable is continuous. These methods are considerably less applicable to microlevel transportation data, in which most of the observations will be sequences of discrete trip choices.

New methodological contributions in modeling time series of discrete decisions have in fact been developed by Heckman (1981) working on problems in labor economics. In the transportation literature Daganzo and Sheffi (1982) have developed a computational technique for applying probit analysis to a time series of discrete decisions. Their technique reduces the computational burden from exponential in the product of the number of time periods and alternatives to linear in the same product.

Discrete Choice Models with Probabilistic Choice Sets

Another extension to the standard discrete choice model is derived from the assumption that the analyst no longer knows the decision maker's true choice set. In this case a probabilistic model of choice set generation can be hypothesized. This model typically has unknown parameters of the utility function.

Manski (1977) has laid the theoretical foundation for this process.

Particular cases have been explored by Ben-Akiva (1977) and by Pitschke (1980). Ben-Akiva has demonstrated that the variant of the logit model proposed by Gaudry and Dagenais (1977) can be reinterpreted as a model where each individual has two possible choice sets. The decision maker is either captive to his or her chosen alternative or has the full choice set. A parameter in their model, when normalized, is the probability of captivity. Swait (1984) has conducted the most in-depth empirical work in this area as part of a study of mode choice in Brazil.

12.6   Estimation

Most of the advances in methods used by travel demand analysts to infer unknown parameters of statistical models are in fact advances in statistics and econometrics in general. Such advances, however, have had a significant impact on the state of the art in travel demand modeling. For the purposes of discussion it is useful to divide the progress made in this area into two distinct subareas.

Statistical Tests

A major area in which substantial progress has been made is the development of statistical tests that help diagnose failures of assumptions made in specific model form. This work has focused intensively on methods to test the validity of the multinomial logit model (see chapter 7).

Another distinct area of statistical tests has been investigated by Horowitz (1983). He notes that virtually all the tests developed and applied to date require that the null hypothesis be a restricted form of the alternative hypothesis. This had made it impossible to test whether different models were statistically better or worse than others unless one of them could be written as a restricted version of the others. Horowitz's results testing a number of statistics indicates that the rho-squared bar statistic is the basis for a powerful test of non-nested hypotheses (see chapter 7).

Robust Estimation

Most of the available estimation methods are based on either maximum likelihoood procedures or some variant that uses either a partial likelihood or what might, in the case of the WESML method described in chapter 8, be appropriately termed quasi-maximum likelihood. Maximum likelihood has the general advantage of being computationally tractable for many specific cases and can be shown to yield consistent and asymptotically efficient estimators for a very broad class of combinations of model form and sampling strategy. It has the distinct disadvantage, however, of requiring that the distribution of observations be known up to a finite vector of unknown parameters. Moreover there is no reason to believe that maximum likelihood methods are particularly robust with respect to either measurement errors or failures of the assumptions of the models to which they are applied. Simple numerical experiments in fact suggest that for certain types of errors, maximum likelihood can produce estimates that are extremely sensitive to just a few erroneous observations. (These cases are characterized by the miscoding of the observed choice so that a few of the alternatives chosen in the sample have very low choice probabilities when evaluated at the true parameters.)

Given the potential difficulties in using maximum-likelihood-based methods, there have been attempts to construct estimators for discrete choice models that are more robust, that is, that require less stringent assumptions yet still provide estimates with desirable statistical properties. Manski's (1975) maximum score estimator is perhaps the first example of such a technique. In this method the exact distribution of the disturbances need not be known; all that is required is that they have a set of general properties. This method results in consistent, though not fully efficient, estimates. More recently Cosslett (1983) has been exploring still more robust estimates for the case of binary discrete choice models. His only key restriction is that the choice function be monotonic in the difference in the systematic utilities of the two alternatives. As an interesting aside, the binary probit model presented as an example in section 10.6 violates this property.

12.7 Summary

As discussed in the introduction, no review can be entirely comprehensive. In this chapter we have focused on what we believe to be the most important developments in the state of the art in mathematical modeling of travel demand.

The state of the art has moved quite rapidly in certain aspects and quite slowly in others. The progress has been greatest in the fields of estimation methods and model structure. At this time the theory in these areas is quite rich. Although it is difficult to project how quickly new developments will occur, there is an often-voiced suspicion by many in this field that further revolutionary developments in discrete choice models are not particularly likely. It is more probable that we will see a period in which many of the theoretical achievements in previous years will be translated into operational tools. For example, it is likely that practical estimation codes for the use of different model structures and samples will become widely available, significantly reducing the costs of travel demand analysis.

In contrast to the rapid progress made in estimation and model structure, there has been very little shift in the state of what we have termed behavioral theory. In part this is probably due to the fact that travel behavior is extraordinarily complex and is therefore intrinsically difficult to model. However, it is also attributable to the low emphasis the profession and research funding sources have placed on this area.

The progress in measurement has been somewhat mixed. Certainly major contributions in the areas of sampling strategies and optimal sample design have been made. However, there is still a vast array of measurement methods that we do not know how to integrate effectively into the mainstream of discrete choice analysis. Given the potential benefits of being able to use data on actual and hypothetical choices within a single model structure that accounts for the underlying process by which these types of data are generated, further research in this area would appear to have extremely high potential payoff.

Bibliography

Abkowitz, M. 1980. The Impact of Service Reliability on Work Travel Behavior. Ph.D. dissertation. Department of Civil Engineering, MIT, Cambridge, Mass.

Adler, T., and M. Ben-Akiva. 1975. A Joint Frequency, Destination and Mode Choice Model for Shopping Trips. *Trans. Research Record* 569: 136–150.

Akaike, H. 1973. Information Theory and An Extension of the Maximum Likelihood Principle. In *2nd Int. Symp. on Information Theory*. B. N. Petrov and F. Csaki, eds. Akademiai Kaido, Budapest, pp. 267–281.

Albright, R., S. Lerman, and C. Manski. 1977. Report on the Development of an Estimation Program for the Multinomial Probit Model. Prepared for Federal Highway Administration, Washington, D.C.

Amemiya, T. 1975. Qualitative Response Models. *Ann. Econ. Social Measurement* 4: 363–372.

Amemiya, T. 1978. On a Two-Step Estimation of a Multivariate Logit Model. *J. Econometrics* 8: 13–21.

Amemiya, T. 1980. Selection of Regressors. *Int. Econ. Rev.* 24: 331–354.

Amemiya, T. 1981. Qualitative Response Models: A Survey. *J. Econ. Lit.* 19 (December): 1483–1536.

Atherton, T., and M. Ben-Akiva. 1976. Transferability and Updating of Disaggregate Travel Demand Models. *Trans. Research Record* 610: 12–18.

Bagozzi, R. 1980. *Causal Models in Marketing*. Wiley, New York.

Bain, J. H. 1976. Activity Choice Analysis, Time Allocation and Disaggregate Travel Demand Modelling. M.S. thesis. Department of Civil Engineering, MIT, Cambridge, Mass.

Becker, G. 1965. A Theory of the Allocation of Time. *Econ. J.* 75: 493–517.

Ben-Akiva, M. 1973. *Structure of Passenger Travel Demand Models*. Ph.D. dissertation. Department of Civil Engineering, MIT, Cambridge, Mass.

Ben-Akiva, M. 1974. Note on the Specification of a Logit Model with Utility Functions that Include Attributes of Competing Alternatives. Working paper. Department of Civil Engineering, MIT, Cambridge, Mass.

Ben-Akiva, M. 1977. Choice Models with Simple Choice Set Generation Processes. Working paper. Department of Civil Engineering, MIT, Cambridge, Mass.

Ben-Akiva, M. 1981. Issues in Transferring and Updating Travel-Behavior Models. In *New Horizons in Travel Behavior Research*. P. Stopher et al., eds. Lexington Books, Lexington, Mass.

Ben-Akiva, M., T. Adler, J. Jacobson, and M. Manheim. 1977. Experiments to Clarify Priorities in Urban Travel Forecasting Research and Development. Final Report. Center for Transportation Studies, CTS Report 77–24. MIT, Cambridge, Mass.

Ben-Akiva, M., and T. Atherton. 1977. Methodology for Short-Range Travel Demand Predictions. *J. Trans. Econ. Policy* 11: 224–261.

Ben-Akiva, M., and B. Francois. 1983. μ Homogeneous Generalized Extreme Value Model. Working paper. Department of Civil Engineering, MIT, Cambridge, Mass.

Ben-Akiva, M., H. Gunn, and H. Pol. 1983. Expansion of Data from Mixed Random and Choice Based Survey Designs. Prepared for presentation at the conference on New Survey Methods in Transport, Sydney, Australia, September 12–16.

Ben-Akiva, M., H. Gunn, and L. Silman. 1984. Disaggregate Trip Distribution Models. *Proc. JSCE*.

Ben-Akiva, M., B. Kullman, L. Sherman, and A. Daly. 1978. Aggregate Forecasting with a System of Disaggregate Travel Demand Models. *Proc. PTRC Summer Annual Meeting*.

Ben-Akiva, M., and S. Lerman. 1979. Disaggregate Travel and Mobility Choice Models and Measures of Accessibility. In *Behavioral Travel Modelling*. D. Hensher and P. Stopher, eds. Croom Helm, London.

Ben-Akiva, M., S. Lerman, W. A. Jessiman, R. L. Albright, and R. E. Nestle. 1976. A Behavioral Analysis of Automobile Ownership and Modes of Travel. Vol. 1–4. Prepared for USDOT, Office of the Secretary for Policy Planning and International Affairs, and FHWA, Washington, D.C.

Ben-Akiva, M., L. Sherman, and B. Kullman. 1978. Disaggregate Model of Non-Home Based Travel. *Trans. Research Record* 673.

Ben-Akiva, M., and J. Swait. 1984a. Choice Models with Simple Probabilistic Choice Set Generation Processes. *Trans. Research B*, forthcoming.

Ben-Akiva, M., and J. Swait. 1984b. The Akaike Likelihood Ratio Index. Working paper. Department of Civil Engineering, MIT, Cambridge, Mass.

Ben-Akiva, M., and T. Watanatada. 1981. Application of a Continuous Choice Logit Model. In *Structural Analysis of Discrete Data With Econometric Applications*. C. Manski and D. McFadden, eds. MIT Press, Cambridge, Mass.

Berkovec, J., and J. Rust. 1981. A Nested Logit Model of Automobile Holdings for One-Vehicle Households. Working paper. Department of Economics, MIT, Cambridge, Mass.

Berkson, J. 1944. Applications of the Logistic Function to Bioassay. *J. Amer. Stat. Assn.* 39: 357–365.

Berkson, J. 1953. A Statistically Precise and Relatively Simple Method of Estimating the Bioassay with Quantal Response, Based on the Logistic Function. *J. Amer. Stat. Assn.* 48: 565–599.

Berndt, E. R., B. H. Hall, R. E. Hall, and J. A. Hausman. 1974. Estimation and Inference in Nonlinear Structural Models. *Ann. Econ. Social Measurement* 3: 653–665.

Bock, R. D., and L. V. Jones. 1968. *The Measurement and Prediction of Judgement and Choice*. Holden-Day, San Francisco.

Bouthelier, F. 1978. An Efficient Methodology to Estimate and Predict with Multinomial Probit Models: Applications to Transportation Problems. Ph.D. dissertation. Department of Ocean Engineering, MIT, Cambridge, Mass.

Box, G. E., and D. R. Cox. 1964. An Analysis of Transformations. *J. Roy. Stat. Soc.* B26: 211–243.

Brand, D., and M. L. Manheim, eds. 1973. Urban Travel Demand Forecasting. Special report 143. Highway Research Board, Washington, D.C.

Brog, W., and A. H. Meyburg. 1981. Consideration of Nonresponse Effects in Large-Scale Mobility Surveys. *Trans. Research Record* 807: 39–46.

Brog, W., A. H. Meyburg, and P. R. Stopher, eds. 1981. *New Horizons in Travel Behavior*. D.C. Heath, Lexington, Mass.

Brunswik, E. 1952. *The Conceptual Framework of Psychology*. University of Chicago Press. Chicago, Ill.

Bruzelius, N. 1979. *The Value of Travel Time*. Croom Helm, London.

Cambridge Systematics Europe (CSE). 1984. *Estimation and Application of Disaggregate Models of Mode and Destination Choice*. Draft report prepared for Direction des Etudes Generales, Regie Autonome des Transport Parisien, Paris.

Cambridge Systematics, Inc. 1978. *MTC Travel Model Development Project: Final Report*. Vol. 1–3. Prepared for the Metropolitan Transportation Commission, Berkeley, Calif.

Cambridge Systematics, Inc. 1976. *A Behavioral Analysis of Automobile Ownership and Modes of Travel*. Prepared for USDOT and FHWA, Washington, D.C.

Chapin, J. S. 1968. Activity Systems and Urban Structures. *J. Amer. Inst. Planners* 34: 11–18.

Charles River Associates, Inc. 1972. *A Disaggregate Behavioral Model of Urban Travel Demand*. FHWA, Washington, D.C.

Clark, C. 1961. The Greatest of a Finite Set of Random Variables. *Oper. Research* (March–April).

Cochran, M. 1977. *Sampling Technique*. 3rd ed. Wiley, New York.

Cosslett, S. 1981. Efficient Estimation of Discrete Choice Models. In *Structural Analysis of Discrete Data with Econometric Applications*, C. Manski and D. Mcfadden, eds. MIT Press, Cambridge, Mass.

Cosslett, S. 1983. Distribution-Free Maximum Likelihood Estimator of the Binary Choice Model. *Econometrica* 51: 765–782.

Cox, D. R. 1961. Tests of Separate Families of Hypotheses. In *Proc. 4th Berkeley Symp. on Math. Stat. and Probability*, Vol. 1. J. Neyman, ed., University of California Press, Berkeley, Calif., pp. 105–123.

Cox, D. R. 1962. Further Results on Tests of Separate Families of Hypotheses. *J. Roy. Stat. Soc.* B24: 406–424.

Cox, D. R. 1970. *Analysis of Binary Data*. Methuen, London.

Daganzo, C. 1979. *Multinomial Probit: The Theory and Its Applications to Demand Forecasting*. Academic Press, New York.

Daganzo, C. 1982. On the Uniqueness and Globability of Optimal Data Gathering Strategies. *Trans. Sci.* 16: 241–245.

Daganzo, C. 1980. Optimal Sampling Strategies for Statistical Models with Discrete Dependent Variables. *Trans. Sci.* 14.

Daganzo, C., and Y. Sheffi. 1982. Multinomial Probit Models with Time Series Data: Unifying State Dependence and Serial Correlation Models. *Envir. and Planning* A14: 1377–1388.

Daganzo, C., F. Bouthelier, and Y. Sheffi. 1977. Multinomial Probit and Qualitative Choice: A Computationally Efficient Algorithm. *Trans. Sci.* 11: 338–358.

Daly, A. 1982. Estimating Choice Models Containing Attraction Variables. *Trans. Research* B16: 5–15.

Daly, A. J., and H. H. P. Van Zwam. 1981. Travel Demand Models for the Zuidvleugel Study. *Proc. PTRC Summer Annual Meeting*, July.

Daly, A., and S. Zachary. 1979. Improved Multiple Choice Models. In *Identifying and Measuring the Determinants of Model Choice*. D. Hensher and Q. Dalvi, eds. Teakfield, London.

Damm, D., and S. R. Lerman, 1981. A Theory of Activity Scheduling Behavior. *Envir. and Planning*, A13: 703–818.

De Donnea, F. X. 1971. *The Determinants of Transport Mode Choice in Dutch Cities*. Rotterdam University Press, Rotterdam, The Netherlands.

De Groot, M. 1970. *Optimal Statistical Decisions*, McGraw-Hill, New York.

Deming, W. 1960. *Sample Design in Business Research*. John Wiley, New York.

Dennis, J., and R. Schnabel. 1983. *Numerical Methods for Unconstrained Optimization and Non-Linear Equations*. Prentice-Hall, Englewood Cliffs, N.J.

Domencich, T., and L. McFadden. 1975. *Urban Travel Demand—A Behavioral Analysis.* North Holland, Amsterdam.

Dubin, J. A., and D. McFadden. 1980. An Econometric Analysis of Residential Electric Appliance Holdings and Consumption. Working paper. Department of Economics, MIT, Cambridge, Mass.

Durbin, J. 1953. Some Results in Sampling Theory When the Units are Selected with Unequal Probabilities. *J. Roy. Stat. Soc.* B15: 262–269.

Dutt, J. 1967. Numerical Aspects of Multivariate Normal Probabilities in Econometric Models. *Ann. Econ. Social Measurement* 5.

Electric Power Research Institute. 1977. Methodology for Predicting the Demand for New Electricity-Using Goods. EA-593, Project 488–1. Final report. Electric Power Research Institute, Palo Alto, Calif.

Finney, D. 1971. *Probit Analysis,* 3rd ed. Cambridge University Press, Cambridge, England.

Fisher, G. W., and D. Nagin. 1981. Random vs. Fixed Coefficient Quantal Choice Models. In *Structural Analysis of Discrete Data with Econometric Applications.* C. Manski and D. McFadden, eds. MIT Press, Cambridge, Mass.

Fleet, C. R., and S. R. Robertson, 1968. Trip Generation in the Transportation Planning Process. *Highway Research Record* 240: 257–289.

Gaudry, M., and M. Wills, 1978. Estimating the Functional Form of Travel Demand Models. *Trans. Research* 12: 257–289.

Gaudry, M. J. I., and M. G. Dagenais. 1977. The Dogit Model. Centre de recherche sur les transports, University of Montreal, Canada, Publ. 82, October.

Golob, T. F., and A. J. Richardson, 1979. Non-Compensatory and Discontinuous Constructs in Travel Behavior Models. In *New Horizons in Travel Behavior Research.* P. F. Stopher, A. H. Meyburg, and W. Brog, eds. Lexington Books, Lexington, Mass.

Gronau, R. 1970. *The Value of Time in Passenger Transportation: The Demand for Air Travel.* National Bureau of Economic Research, New York.

Hagarstrand, T. 1970. What about People in Regional Science. *Papers Regional Sci. Assn.* 24: 7–21.

Hall, P. 1980. *Search Behavior in Urban Housing Markets.* Ph.D. dissertation. Department of Civil Engineering, MIT, Cambridge, Mass.

Hammersley, J., and D. Handscomb, 1965. *Monte Carlo Methods.* Methuen, London.

Harris, A., and J. Tanner, 1974. Transport Demand Models Based on Personal Characteristics. TRRL Supplementary Report 65 UC. Department of the Environment, U.K.

Hauser, J. R., and S. M. Shugan, 1980. Intensity Measures of Consumer Preference. *Oper. Research* 28 (March–April): 278–320.

Hausman, J., and D. Wise, 1978. A Conditional Probit Model for Qualitative Choice: Discrete Decisions Recognizing Interdependence and Heterogeneous Preferences. *Econometrica* 46: 403–426.

Hausman, J., and D. McFadden. 1984. Specification Tests for the Multinomial Logit Model. *Econometrica* 52: 1219–1240.

Heckman, J. J. 1978. Dummy Endogenous Variables in a Simultaneous Equation System. *Econometrica* 46.

Heckman, J. 1981. Statistical Analysis of Discrete Panel Data. In *Structural Analysis of Discrete Data with Econometric Applications.* C. Manski and D. McFadden, eds. MIT Press, Cambridge, Mass.

Hendrickson, C., and Y. Sheffi. 1978. A Disaggregate Model of Trip Generation by Elderly Individuals. 1.202 term paper. Department of Civil Engineering, MIT, Cambridge, Mass.

Hensher, D. A., and L. W. Johnson. 1981. *Applied Discrete Choice Modelling*. Croom Helm, London.

Hensher, D. A., and P. R. Stopher, eds. 1979. *Behavioral Travel Modelling*. Croom Helm, London.

Himmelblau, D. 1982. *Applied Nonlinear Programming*. McGraw-Hill, New York.

Hirsh, M., J. Prashker, and M. Ben-Akiva. 1984. Day of the Week Models of Activity Patterns. *Trans.Research Record*, forthcoming.

Hocherman, I., J. N. Prashker, and M. Ben-Akiva. 1983. Estimation and Use of Dynamic Transaction Models of Automobile Ownership. *Trans. Research Record* 944: 134–141.

Horowitz, J. 1979. Confidence Intervals for Choice Probabilities of the MNL Model. *Trans. Research Record* 728: 23–29.

Horowitz, J. 1981. Testing the Multinomial Logit Model against the Multinomial Probit Model without Estimating the Probit Parameters. *Trans. Sci.* 15: 153–163.

Horowitz, J. 1982. An Evaluation of the Usefulness of Two Standard Goodness-of-Fit Indicators for Comparing Non-Nested Random Utility Models. *Trans. Research Record* 874: 19–25.

Horowitz, J. 1982a. Statistical Comparison of Non-Nested Probabilistic Discrete Choice Models. *Trans. Sci.* 17: 319–350.

Horowitz, J. 1982b. Testing Disaggregate Travel Demand Models by Comparing Predicted and Observed Market Shares. Prepared for presentation at the 1984 Annual Meeting of the Transportation Research Board, Washington, D.C.

Horowitz, J. 1983. Statistical Comparison of Non-Nested Probabilistic Choice Models. *Trans. Sci.* 17.

Hsieh, D., C. Manski, and D. McFadden. 1983. Estimation of Response Probabilities from Augmented Retrospective Observations. Working paper. Department of Economics, MIT, Cambridge, Mass.

Hutchinson, B. G. 1974. *Principles of Urban Transport Systems Planning*. McGraw-Hill, New York.

Jacobson, J. 1979. A Model of Activity Time Allocation. Ph.D. dissertation. Department of Civil Engineering, MIT, Cambridge, Mass.

Johnson, N., and S. Kotz. 1970. *Distributions in Statistics—Continuous Univariate Distributions*. Vols. 1 and 2. Wiley, New York.

Judge, G., W. Griffiths, R. Hill, and T. C. Lee. 1980. *The Theory and Practice of Econometrics*. Wiley, New York.

Kanafani, A. K. 1983. *Transportation Demand Analysis*. McGraw-Hill, New York.

Karash, K. 1983. *An Application of The Lens Model in Measuring Retail Attractiveness and the Effects of Transportation Programs*. Ph.D. dissertation. Department of Civil Engineering, MIT, Cambridge, Mass.

Kern, C. R., and R. J. Parcells. 1981. Policies to Foster Downtown Shopping: The Response of Home-Based Shoppers. Presented at the 60th Annual Meeting, Transportation Research Board.

Khajavi, S. 1981. Optimal Peak-Load Pricing, Investment and Service Levels on Urban Streets—A Numerical Example. *Trans. Research Record* 807: 7–14.

Kitamura, R. 1984. A Model of Daily Time Allocation to Discretionary Out-of-Time Activities and Trips. *Trans. Research* B18: 255–266.

Kitamura, R, L. Kostyniuk, and K. L. Ting 1979. Aggregation in Spatial Choice Modelling. *Trans. Sci.* 13: 325–342.

Kmenta, J. 1971. *Elements of Econometrics.* Mcmillan, New York.

Koppelman, F. 1975. *Travel Prediction with Models of Individualistic Choice Behavior.* Ph.D. dissertation, Department of Civil Engineering, MIT, Cambridge, Mass.

Koppelman, F., and M. Ben-Akiva. 1977. Aggregate Forecasting with Disaggregate Travel Demand Models Using Normally Available Data. *Proc. WCTR.* Rotterdam, The Netherlands.

Koppelman, F., and J. Hauser. 1978. Destination Choice Behavior for Non-Grocery-Shopping Trips. *Trans. Research Record* 673: 157–165.

Koppelman, F. S., J. R. Hauser, and A. M. Tybout. 1977. Preliminary Analysis of Perceptions, Preferenced, Beliefs and Usage of Transportation Services for Travel to Downtown Evanston. The Transportation Center, Northwestern University, Evanston, Ill.

Koppelman, F., and G. Rose. 1983. Geographic Transfer of Travel Choice Models: Evaluation and Procedures. Paper presented at Int. Symp. on New Directions in Urban Modelling, University of Waterloo, Canada.

Koppelman, F., and C. Wilmot. 1982. Transferability Analysis of Disaggregate Choice Models. *Trans. Research Record* 895.

Koppelman, F., and C. Wilmot. 1984. The Effect of Model Specification Improvement on Transferability. Paper presented at 63th Annual Transportation Research Board Meeting, Washington, D.C.

Kostyniuk, L. P. 1975. A Behavioral Choice Model for the Urban Shopping Activity. Ph.D. dissertation, Department of Civil Engineering, State University of New York at Buffalo, Buffalo, N.Y.

Kostyniuk, L. P., and R. Kitamura. 1982. Life Cycle and Household Time-Space Paths: Empirical Investigation. *Trans. Research Record* 879: 28–37.

Kozel, V., and J. Swait. 1982. *Maceio Travel Demand Model System Calibration Results.* Vol. 2. Studies of Urban Travel Behavior and Policy Analysis in Maceio. Center for Transportation Studies, MIT, Cambridge, Mass.

Lancaster, K. 1966. A New Approach to Consumer Theory. *J. Pol. Econ.* 74: 132–157.

Landau, U. 1976. *Sketch Planning Models in Transportation Systems Analysis.* Ph.D. dissertation. Department of Civil Engineering, MIT, Cambridge, Mass.

Lave, C. A. 1969. A Behavioral Approach to Modal Split Forecasting. *Trans Research* 3: 463–480.

Layard, P., and A. Walters. 1978. *Microeconomic Theory.* McGraw-Hill, New York.

Lentorp, B. 1976. Paths in Space-Time Environments—A Time Geographic Study of Movement Possibilities of Individuals. *Lund Studies in Geography. Series B: Human Geography,* No. 44.

Lerman, S. 1975. *A Disaggregate Behavioral Model of Urban Mobility Decisions.* Ph.D. dissertation. Department of Civil Engineering, MIT, Cambridge, Mass.

Lerman S., and M. Ben-Akiva. 1975. Disaggregate Behavioral Model of Automobile Ownership. *Trans. Research Record* 569: 43–51.

Lerman, S., M Flusberg, W. Pecknold, R. Nestle, and N. Wilson. 1980. A Model System for Forecasting Patronage on Demand Responsive Transportation Systems. *Trans. Research* A14: 13–23.

Lerman, S., M. Flusberg, W. Pecknold, R. Nestle, and N. Wilson. 1977. Method for Estimating Patronage of Demand Responsive Transportation Systems. TSC Urban and Regional Research Series. Report DOT-TST-77-77. USDOT, Washington, D.C.

Lerman, S., and S. Gonzalez. 1980. Poisson Regression Analysis under Alternate Sampling Strategies. *Trans. Sci.* 14: 346–364.

Lerman, S., and J. Louviere. 1979. Using Functional Measurement to Identify the Form of Utility Functions in Travel Demand Models. *Trans. Research Record* 673: 78–86.

Lerman, S., and H. Mahmassani. 1984. The Econometrics of Search. *Envir. and Planning,* forthcoming.

Lerman, S., and C. Manski. 1979. Sample Design for Discrete Choice Analysis of Travel Behavior: The State of the Art. *Trans. Research* A13: 29–44.

Lerman, S., and C. Manski. 1982. A Model of the Effect of Information Diffusion on Travel. *Trans. Sci.* 16: 171–191.

Lisco, T. 1967. *The Value of Commuter's Travel Time: A Study in Urban Transportation.* Ph.D. dissertation. Department of Economics, University of Chicago, Chicago, Ill.

Litinas, N., and M. Ben-Akiva. 1979. Behavioral Modelling of Continuous Spatial Distributions of Trips, Residential Locations and Workplaces. Working paper. CTS RAMP-79-3, MIT, December.

Litinas, N., and M. Ben-Akiva. 1982. Simplified Transportation Policy Analysis Using Continuous Distributions. *Trans. Research* A16: 431–445.

Louviere, J. J., D. H. Henley, G. Woodworth, R. J. Meyer, I. P. Levin, J. W. Stoner, D. Curry, and D. A. Anderson. 1981. Laboratory-Simulation versus Revealed-Preference Methods for Estimating Travel Demand Models. *Trans. Research Record* 794: 42–51.

Luce, R. 1959. *Individual Choice Behavior: A Theoretical Analysis.* Wiley, New York.

Luce, R, and P. Suppes. 1965. Preference, Utility and Subjective Probability. In *Handbook of Mathematical Psychology.* Vol. 3. R. Luce, R. Bush, and E. Galanter, eds. Wiley, New York.

Manheim, M. 1979. *Fundamentals of Transportation Systems Analysis: Basic concepts.* Vol. 1. MIT Press, Cambridge, Mass.

Manheim, M., S. Gonzalas, N. Litinas, and I. Solomon. 1980. New Computational Environments: Opportunities for More Relevant Transportation Analyses. *Proc. PTRC Summer Annual Meeting.*

Manski, C. 1973. *The Analysis of Qualitative Choice.* Ph.D. dissertation. Department of Economics, MIT, Cambridge, Mass.

Manski, C. 1975. Maximum Score Estimation of the Stochastic Utility Model of Choice. *J. Econometrics* 3: 205–228.

Manski, C. 1977. The Structure of Random Utility Models. *Theory and Decision* 8: 229–254.

Manski, C. 1981. Structural Models of Discrete Data. *Sociological Methodology* 58–109.

Manski, C., and S. Lerman. 1977. The Estimation of Choice Probabilities From Choice-Based Samples. *Econometrica* 45: 1977–1988.

Manski, C., and D. McFadden. 1981. Alternative Estimators and Sample Designs for Discrete Choice Analysis. In *Structural Analysis of Discrete Data with Econometric Applications.* C. Manski and D. McFadden, eds. MIT Press, Cambridge Mass.

Marschak, J. 1960. Binary Choice Constraints on Random Utility Indicators. In *Stanford Symposium on Mathematical Methods in the Social Sciences.* K. Arrow, ed. Stanford University Press, Stanford, Calif.

McCarthy, G. M. 1969. Multiple-Regression Analysis of Household Trip Generation: A Critique. *Highway Research Record* 297: 31–43.

McCarthy, P. 1982. Further Evidence on the Temporal Stability of Disaggregate Travel Demand Models. *Trans. Research* B16: 263–278.

McFadden, D. 1974. Conditional Logit Analysis of Qualitative Choice Behavior. In *Frontiers in Econometrics*. P. Zarembka, ed. Academic Press, New York, pp. 105–142

McFadden, D. 1976. The Revealed Preferences of a Public Bureaucracy. *Bell J.* 7: 55–72.

McFadden, D. 1976. The Mathematical Theory of Demand Models. In *Behavioral Travel-Demand Models*. P. Stopher and A. Meyburg, eds. Lexington Books, Lexington, Mass.

McFadden. D. 1978. Modelling the Choice of Residential Location. In *Spatial Interaction Theory and Residential Location*. A. Karlquist et al., eds. North Holland, Amsterdam, pp. 75–96.

McFadden, D. 1981. Econometric Models of Probabilistic Choice. In *Structural Analysis of Discrete Data*. C. Manski and D. McFadden, eds. MIT Press, Cambridge, Mass. pp. 198–272.

McFadden, D. 1982. Econometric Analysis of Qualitative Response Models. Working paper. Department of Economics, MIT, Cambridge, Mass.

McFadden, D., and F. Reid. 1975. Aggregate Travel Demand Forecasting from Disaggregated Behavioral Models. *Trans. Research Record* 534: 24–37.

McFadden, D, and C. Winston. 1981. Joint Estimation of Discrete and Continuous Choices in Freight Transportation. Paper presented at the 1981 Meeting of the Econometrics Society.

McFadden, D., W. Tye, and K. Train. 1977. An Application of Diagnostic Tests for the Irrelevant Alternatives Property of the Multinomial Logit Model. *Trans. Research Record* 637: 39–46.

McGillivray, R. G. 1972. Binary Choice of Urban Transport Mode in the San Francisco Region. *Econometrica* 40: 827–848.

Meyer, M. D., and E. J. Miller. 1984. *Urban Transportation Planning: A Decision-Oriented Approach*. McGraw-Hill, New York.

Miller, E., and S. Lerman. 1979. A Model of Retail Location, Scale and Intensity. *Envir. and Planning*, A11: 172–192.

Miller, E., and S. Lerman. 1981. Disaggregate Modelling of Retail Firm's Decisions: A Case Study of Clothing Retailers. *Envir. and Planning* A13: 729–736.

Morichi, S., H. Ishida, and T. Yai. 1984. Comparisons of Various Utility Functions for Behavioral Travel Demand Models. *Proc. WCTR*. SNV, Hamburg.

Morlok, E. K. 1978. *Introduction to Transportation Engineering and Planning*. McGraw-Hill, New York.

Muth, R. 1966. Household Production and Consumer Demand Functions. *Econometrica*, 34: 699–708.

Netherlands Ministry of Transport. 1977. *SIGMO Final Reports*. Vols. 1–4. Projectbureau IVVS, The Hague.

Oi, W. Y., and P. W. Shuldiner. 1972. *An Analysis of Urban Travel Demands*. Northwestern University Press, Evanston, Ill.

Parody, T. E. 1976. An Analysis of Disaggregate Mode Choice Models in Prediction. Paper prepared for presentation at the Annual Transportation Research Board Meeting, Washington, D. C., 1977.

Pitschke, S. B. 1980. *Choice Set Formulation for Discrete Choice Models*. M.S. thesis. Department of Civil Enginering, MIT, Cambridge, Mass.

Prashker, J. A. 1979a. Mode Choice Models with Perceived Reliability Measures. *ASCE Trans. Engineering J.* (May): 251–262.

Prashker, J. A. 1979b. Scaling Perceptions of Reliability of Urban Travel Modes Using Indscal and Factor Analysis Methods. *Trans. Research* A13: 203–212.

Quarmby, D. A. 1967. Choice of Travel Mode for the Journey to Work: Some Findings. *J. Transport Econ. Planning*, 1: 273–314.

Raiffa, H., and R. Schlaifer. 1961. *Applied Statistical Decision Theory*. Harvard University Press, Cambridge, Mass.

Rao, C. R. 1973. *Linear Statistical Inference and Its Applications*. Wiley, New York.

Rassam, P. R., R. H. Ellis, and J. C. Bennett. 1971. The *n*-Dimensional Logit Model: Development and Applications. *Highway Research Record* 369: 135–147.

Reid, F. 1978. Minimizing Error in Aggregate Predictions from Disaggregate Models. *Trans. Research Record* 673: 59–65.

Richards, M., and M. Ben-Akiva. 1975. *A Disaggregate Travel Demand Model*. D. C. Heath, Lexington, Mass.

Ruiter, E., and M. Ben-Akiva. 1978. Disaggregate Travel Demand Models for the San Francisco Area: System Structure, Component Models and Application Procedures. *Trans. Research Record* 673: 121–128.

Salomon, I., and M. Ben-Akiva. 1983. The Use of the Life-Style Concept in Travel Demand Models. *Envir. and Planning* A15: 623–638.

Sheffi, Y. 1979. Estimating Choice Probabilities among Nested Alternatives. *Trans. Research* B13: 113–205.

Sheffi, Y., and C. F. Daganzo. 1978. Hypernetworks and Supply-Demand Equilibrium Obtained with Disaggregate Demand Models. *Trans. Research Record* 673: 113–121.

Sheffi, Y., and Z. Tarem. 1982. Experiments with Optimal Sampling for Multinomial Logit Models. *Trans. Research Record* 944: 141–148.

Silman, L. 1980. Disaggregate Travel Demand Models for Short-Term Forecasting. Information paper 81. Israel Institute of Transportation Planning and Research. Tel-Aviv.

Simon, H. 1957. *Models of Man*. Wiley, New York.

Slovic, P., B. Fischenstein, and L. Lichtenstein. 1977. Behavioral Decision Theory. *Ann. Rev. Psychology*.

Small, K. 1981. Ordered Logit: A Discrete Choice Model with Proximate Covariance among Alternatives. Working paper. Department of Economics, Princeton University, Princeton, NJ.

Small, K. A. 1982. The Scheduling of Consumer Activities: Work Trips. *Amer. Econ. Rev.* 72 (June): 467–479.

Small, K. 1983. The Incidence of Congestion Tolls on Urban Highways. *J. Urban Econ.* 13: 90–111.

Small, K., and D. Brownstone. 1982. Efficient Estimation of Nested Logit Models: An Application to Trip Timing. Research memorandum 296. Econometric Research Program, Princeton University, Princeton, N.J.

Small, K., and C. Hsiao. 1982. Multinomial Logit Specification Tests. Working paper. Department of Economics, Princeton University, Princeton, N.J.

Spear, B. D. 1976. A Generalized Attribute Variable for Models of Mode Choice Behavior. *Trans. Research Record* 592: 6–11.

Stopher, P. R. 1969. A Probability Model of Travel Mode Choice for the Work Journey. *Highway Research Record* 283: 57–65.

Stopher, P. R., and T. E. Lisco. 1970. Modelling Travel Demand: A Disaggregate Behavioral Approach, Issues and Applications. Proc. Trans. Research Forum.

Stopher, P. R., and A. H. Meyburg. 1975. *Urban Transportation Modelling and Planning*. D. C. Heath, Lexington, Mass.

Strotz, R. 1975. The Empirical Implications of a Utility Tree. *Econometrica*, 25: 269–280.

Svenson, O. 1979. Process Descriptions of Decision-Making. *Org. Behavior Human Performance* 23: 86–112.

Swait, J. 1984. *Probabilistic Choice Set Formation in Transportation Demand Models*. Ph.D. dissertation, Department of Civil Engineering, MIT, Cambridge, Mass.

Swait, J., and M. Ben-Akiva. 1984a. Constraints to Individual Travel Behavior in a Brazilian City. *Trans. Research Record*, forthcoming.

Swait, J., and M. Ben-Akiva. 1984b. Incorporating Random Constraints in Discrete Choice Models: An Application to Mode Choice in Sao Paulo, Brazil. *Trans. Research B.*, forthcoming.

Swait, J., V. Kozel, R. Barros, and M. Ben-Akiva. 1984. A Model System of Individual Travel Behavior for a Brazilian City. *Trans. Policy and Decision Making* 2: 451–480.

Talvitie, A. D. 1972. Comparison of Probabilistic Modal Choice Models: Estimation Methods and System Inputs. *Highway Research Record* 392: 111–120.

Talvitie, A. 1973. Aggregate Travel Demand Analysis with Disaggregate or Aggregate Travel Demand Models. *Proc. Trans. Research Forum*. 14: 583–603.

Tarem, Z. 1982. Evaluation of a Sampling Optimization Method for Discrete Choice Models. S.M. thesis. Department of Civil Engineering, MIT, Cambridge, Mass.

Theil, H. 1969. A Multinomial Extension of the Linear Logit Model. *Int. Econ. Rev.* 10: 251–259.

Theil, H. 1971. *Principles of Econometrics*. Wiley, New York.

Thurston, L. 1927. A Law of Comparative Judgement. *Psychological Rev.* 34: 273–286.

Tobin, J. 1958. Estimation of Relationships for Limited Dependent Variables. *Econometrica* 26: 24–36.

Train, K. 1978. A Validation Test of a Disaggregate Mode Choice Model. *Trans. Research* 12: 167–174.

Train, K. 1984. *Qualitative Choice Analysis: Theory, Economics, and an Application to Automobile Demand*. MIT Press, Cambridge, Mass., forthcoming.

Train, K., and M. Lohrer. 1982. *Vehicle Ownership and Usage: An Integrated System of Disaggregate Demand Models*. Prepared for the California Energy Commission.

Transportation Research Board (TRB). 1974. *Behavioral Demand Modelling and Valuation of Travel Time*. Special report 149. Washington, D.C.

Tversky, A. 1972. Elimination by Aspects: A Theory of Choice. *Psychological Rev.* 79: 281–299.

Varian, H. 1978. *Microeconomic Analysis*. Norton, New York.

Volkmar, H. 1978. *Use of Alternative Data Collection Techniques to Analyze Demand Impacts of Bus Policies in Small Urban Areas*. S.M. thesis. Department of Civil Engineering, MIT, Cambridge, Mass.

Warner, S. L. 1962. *Stochastic Choice of Mode in Urban Travel: A Study in Binary Choice.* Northwestern University Press, Evanston, Il.

Watanatada, T. 1977. *Applications of Disaggregate Choice Models to Urban Transportation Sketch Planning.* Ph.D. dissertation. MIT, Cambridge, Mass.

Watanatada, T., and Ben-Akiva. 1977. Development of an Aggregate Model of Urbanized Area Travel Behavior. Final report prepared for USDOT, Washington, D.C.

Watanatada, T., and M. Ben-Akiva. 1979. Forecasting Urban Travel Demand for Quick Policy Analysis with Disaggregate Choice Models: A Monte Carlo Simulation Approach. *Trans. Research* A13: 241–248.

Watson, P. L. 1973. The Homogeneity of Models of Transport Modal Choice: The Dimensions of Trip Length and Journey Purpose. *J. Regional Sci.*

Watson, P. L. 1974. *The Value of Time: Behavioral Models of Modal Choice.* D. C. Heath, Lexington, Mass.

Watson, P. L., and R. B. Westin. 1975. Transferability of Disaggregate Mode Choice Models. *Regional Sci. Urban Econ.* 5: 227–249.

Weibull, J. W. 1978. A Search Model for Microeconomic Analysis—With Spatial Applications. In *Spatial Interaction Theory and Planning Models.* North Holland, Amsterdam.

Westin, R. B. 1974. Predictions from Binary Choice Models. *J. Econometrics* 2: 1–16.

Westin, R. B., and D. W. Gillen. 1978. Parking Location and Transit Demand: A Case Study of Endogenous Attributes in Disaggregate Mode Choice Functions. *J. Econometrics* 8: 75–101.

White, H. 1980. Nonlinear Regression on Cross-Section Data. *Econometrica* 48: 721–746.

Wigner, M. F. 1973. Disaggregate Model Choice Models of Downtown Trips in the Chicago Region. *Highway Research Record* 446: 49–65.

Williams, H. C. W. L. 1977. On the Formation of Travel Demand Models and Economic Evaluation Measures of User Benefit. *Envir. and Planning* 9: 285–344.

Wohl, M., and B. V. Martin. 1967. *Traffic Systems Analysis for Engineers and Planners.* McGraw-Hill, New York.

Index